the **Tommy Koh** reader

Favourite Essays and Lectures

the **Tommy Koh** reader
Favourite Essays and Lectures

Tommy Koh
Ambassador-at-Large, Singapore

World Scientific

NEW JERSEY · LONDON · SINGAPORE · BEIJING · SHANGHAI · HONG KONG · TAIPEI · CHENNAI

Published by

World Scientific Publishing Co. Pte. Ltd.
5 Toh Tuck Link, Singapore 596224
USA office: 27 Warren Street, Suite 401-402, Hackensack, NJ 07601
UK office: 57 Shelton Street, Covent Garden, London WC2H 9HE

Library of Congress Cataloging-in-Publication Data
Koh, Tommy T. B. (Tommy Thong Bee), 1937–
  The Tommy Koh reader : favourite essays and lectures / by Tommy Koh Ambassador-at-Large, Singapore.
    pages cm
  Includes bibliographical references and index.
  ISBN 978-9814571074 (alk. paper) -- ISBN 978-9814571081 (pbk : alk. paper)
  1. Koh, Tommy T. B. (Tommy Thong Bee), 1937---Political and social views. 2. Ambassadors--Singapore. 3. Diplomats--Singapore. 4. College teachers--Singapore. I. Title.
  DS610.73.K66 2013
  327.59570092--dc23
                                    2013041069

British Library Cataloguing-in-Publication Data
A catalogue record for this book is available from the British Library.

Copyright © 2013 by Tommy Koh

All rights reserved.

First Edition
10 9 8 7 6 5 4 3 2

I wish to dedicate this book to the following men and women who have or had worked with me as my Personal Assistant.

Faculty of Law, National University of Singapore

Mr Young Cheng Wah
Mr Lee Cheuk Yen

Permanent Mission of Singapore to the United Nations

Ms Ng Chwee Tee
Mr Wilson Teo
Mrs Gloria Elizabeth Monteiro
Ms Soh Geok Lian

Embassy of Singapore, Washington, DC

Mr Subramony
Mrs Jenny Tan

National Arts Council

Ms Soh Guek Keow

Asia–Europe Foundation

Mrs Jenny Tan

Institute of Policy Studies

Ms Mabel Chung
Ms Cynthia Lin
Mrs Jenny Tan
Ms Cecilia Kuek

Ministry of Foreign Affairs

Ms Lily Ng
Ms Wong Fei Joo
Ms Lee Gek Kim

Foreword

It is a great pleasure and honour to write this foreword for *The Tommy Koh Reader*, a collection of essays and lectures by one of our most esteemed members in the National University of Singapore (NUS) community, Professor Tommy Koh.

Professor Koh is a well-known figure in Singapore and internationally, having served for many decades as one of our foremost diplomats, and also for his many leading contributions to the development of the arts and culture scene of Singapore. For NUS, he was one of our brightest law students at the inception of the Law Faculty, garnering first-class honours, before going on to complete post-graduate studies in Harvard and Cambridge. He served with distinction as Dean of the Law Faculty from 1971 to 1974. Education remains a powerful passion for Professor Koh, and we are grateful that he has continued his close association with his alma mater, offering his valuable insights and wisdom for new generations of students as Rector of Tembusu College.

Professor Koh has written that he would have happily served out his career as an academic and educator. But fate would have it otherwise, and in 1968, he was asked to serve as our fledging nation's Permanent Representative to the United Nations (1968–1971, 1974–1984). From that point on, he would go forward to establish an illustrious diplomatic career, serving in a succession of high offices, including Ambassador to the US (1984–1990), Special Envoy of the UN (1993), and presently, Ambassador-at-Large.

As a diplomat, he worked tirelessly in service of Singapore, from the crucial period when it had just become a newly independent nation. His writings capture the temper of those years, with its challenges and triumphs, and in particular, he illuminates, as few can, the fortitude and courage of our post-independence leadership as they worked relentlessly to carve out the political and economic space for Singapore's survival and growth.

Though he often had to roam far from the shores of our island state, his heart was always firmly rooted in the soil of Singapore. His indefatigable passion, talents and intellect were directed especially, to the fields of arts, culture and heritage preservation — topics which lie especially close to his heart. A well-known patron and supporter of the arts, he was the founding Chairman of the National Arts Council (1991 to 1996), and subsequently, Chairman of the National Heritage Board (2002 to 2011). Working through these institutions, and often through his personal initiatives, he has made immense contributions to promoting and expanding not only the range, but the quality of artistic and cultural opportunities and experiences available to all Singaporeans.

The essays, lectures, and speeches in this collection are thus drawn from a life rich in experience and learning, and are grouped into broad categories: Family, Career, Singapore, Diplomacy, the Law, Art, Culture and Heritage, and finally, Nature and the Environment. These writings reflect Professor's Koh's diverse interests and formidable intellect, and the topics he addresses range from weighty issues such as the rule of law and income disparity, to more lighthearted fare such as Singapore's unique hawker cuisine, botany and even, the naming of roads. He has not hesitated to voice disagreement with prevailing policies or orthodoxies, but always offers his dissenting opinions in good faith, and in a manner intended to encourage greater engagement and understanding. His exposition is clear, forthright and precise; but in his more personal reflections, it is easy to discern the effervescent good humour and warmhearted humanity that has made him a widely admired public figure.

Taken together, this book is much more than a collection of written works and speeches that summarises Professor Koh's career and contributions. We are offered a rare glimpse into the values and beliefs that he holds most dearly, and which have guided his actions and undertakings in his long and distinguished career. For instance, from his mother, he writes touchingly of inheriting her keen eye for aesthetics, good graces and zest for vivacious living; from his father, the importance of learning and the joy of reading, but also the need for grit and recovering from hard knocks; and from his formative school years, an acceptance and celebration of diversity and the many hues of our multi-racial society, and an equal intolerance towards ethnic and racial prejudice.

Professor Tommy Koh describes himself amongst these pages as having been "a happy warrior for peace". It is a wonderfully apt phase, as all his efforts have indeed been directed towards the singular objective of creating a better quality of life for all in a safer world. In pursuit of that objective, he has been unsparing and devoted, and the results have been both remarkable and transformative. Yet, throughout his distinguished career, he has always retained a common touch, and an abiding interest and concern for his fellow citizens, particularly those in our society who are less fortunate, or who are more vulnerable. He remains an engaged citizen, and a man of goodwill, modesty and warm generosity.

The world has changed greatly since Professor Koh started out as a young diplomat, but his life and experiences exemplify many crucial traits that have only gained in relevance: a steadfast adherence to principles; an acceptance of diversity and multi-cultural possibilities; a joyful sense of curiosity; and living a purposeful life that impacts positively on society. We would all do well if we could emulate Professor Koh's example of being a tireless advocate for mutual respect, inclusive collaboration and shared advancement.

Professor Tan Chorh Chuan
President
National University of Singapore

Contents

Foreword   vii
by Tan Chorh Chuan

1. **Family and Friends**
   A Tribute to My Mother   3
   Memories of My Father   5
   A Toast to President and Mrs Wee Kim Wee   8
   Toasts to President S. R. Nathan on His 80th and
       85th Birthdays   12
   Eulogy for S. Rajaratnam   15
   Eulogy for David Marshall   19
   Goh Keng Swee: Ten Lessons from His Life   22
   George Yeo: A Man for All Seasons   26
   In Defence of Lim Chong Yah   29
   A Tribute to Wazir Singh   33
   Wang Gungwu: Friend, Mentor and Role Model   34

2. **Milestones of Life and Career**
   What RI Taught Me   41
   A Letter from Dean Griswold   44
   A Constitution for the Oceans   50
   Commemoration of the 30th Anniversary of the Opening
       for Signature of the 1982 UNCLOS   57
   Making Peace Between Russia and the Baltics   61
   My Cambodian Story   69

The ASEF Story: The First Three Years	77
Reflections on the Institute of Policy Studies	88
Integrating the Business Community in the APEC Process: Genesis of the Pacific Business Forum	98
Building a Better World	107

3. Singapore

Lee Kuan Yew's Foreign Policy Legacy	115
Goh Chok Tong's Foreign Policy Legacy	121
The Singapore of My Dreams	137
Don't Knock Minimum Wage Yet	146
Disagreeing with Some Hard Truths	149
Demystifying the Presidential Office	152
In Praise of Older Workers	157
Opening Eyes to Guide Dogs for the Blind	160
Should Petain Road be Renamed?	163
What Singapore Can Learn from Europe	166
Reflections on Immigration	173
Are Singaporeans a Kind or Unkind People?	175
How to be Happy	181
Singapore's Foreign Policy: Unique Features	185
7 Habits of a Happy Singaporean	191

4. Diplomacy

The Situation in Grenada	197
De Tocqueville Revisited: American Politics Viewed from a Foreign Perspective	199
Why the US Will Still be No. 1 in 2039	209
Can Any Country Afford a Moral Foreign Policy?	212
Size Is Not Destiny	222
Eight Lessons on Negotiations	232
The Art of Chairing Conferences: Lessons Learnt	238
Two Financial Crises: Five Truths from Asia	245
Australia Must Respect Asean's Role	248

	In Defence of Europe	251
	China and the World	257
	Japan's Prospects and Challenges: A View from Southeast Asia	265
	China and Japan: Frenemies?	276
	My Faith in India	281
	China and India: Chini Hindi Bhai Bhai?	285
	The ICRC at 150: Reflections of an Asian Admirer	292
5.	**Law**	
	Reflections on the Negotiating Process of UNCLOS	301
	The Quest for a World Order	315
	Will There be a Clash of Cultures Between the US and East Asia?	328
	My Adventure with International Law	359
	The Negotiating Process of the ASEAN Charter	372
	Advice to Law Freshmen	390
	WTO Dispute Settlement System: Some Reflections	394
	Is There a Role for Law in a World Ruled by Power?	411
	Mapping Out Rival Claims to the South China Sea	416
	A Tribute to Lee A. Sheridan	424
	A Tribute to Punch Coomaraswamy	426
	A Heartfelt Tribute to a Remarkable Man: Chan Sek Keong	428
	A Tribute to Satya Nandan	432
6.	**Art, Culture and Heritage**	
	10 Stops Along a Singapore Historical Trail	437
	Karel van Kleef: The Man Who Loved Singapore	440
	Tributes to José Rizal and Emilio Aguinaldo	443
	Honouring Deng Xiaoping	446

The Artist, the State and the Market	448
The Joy of Collecting	453
A Tribute to Ong Kim Seng	455
A Tribute to Lee Hock Moh	457
A Tribute to Kuo Pao Kun	459
A Tribute to Tan Swie Hian	462
A Tribute to Earl Lu	464
A Tribute to Anthony Poon	468
A Tribute to Goh Choo San	472
A Tribute to Pak Neka	473
A Tribute to Iskandar Jalil	476
A Tribute to Joanna Wong	478

7. **Nature and the Environment**

The Earth Summit's Negotiating Process: Some Reflections on the Art and Science of Negotiation	483
The Trees of Singapore	494
Biodiversity and Cities	497
Green Thoughts Inspired by Stockholm and Rio	506
The Future of Water Today	513

Timeline	517
Annex I: Books Published	525
Annex II: Awards by Singapore Government and Agencies	526
Annex III: Awards by Foreign Governments and Institutions	527
Annex IV: Awards by Academic Institutions	528

FAMILY AND FRIENDS

A Tribute to My Mother

There is a joke that if you want to have good genes, you must choose your parents well. I have often wondered what are the genes that I have inherited from my mother.

My mother was a proud Shanghainese woman. She used to tell us that the intelligence of her three sons were from her and not from our father. The Shanghainese tend to look down on the Hokkiens as an inferior breed of Chinese! My mother was certainly a very intelligent woman.

My mother was an actress and dancer before she married. Her life-long love of culture and the arts was transmitted, either by nature or nurture, to her sons. I think she was very pleased when I was appointed as the founding chairman of the National Arts Council.

My mother was a woman of refined taste, with a discriminating eye for beauty, good design and aesthetics. By growing up with her and living in a home designed by her, we have inevitably picked up some of her good taste and love of beauty.

My mother was very eloquent, outspoken and charming. She was a woman ahead of her time. She never played the role of the submissive wife. Through her, I think I have learned to respect women. I think some of my outspokenness probably came from her. I also think that all her three sons inherited, to varying degrees, her gift of the gab.

My mother was a hard-headed realist who had no illusions about people or about life. I must confess that I did not inherit this gene because I have always been and remain an idealist and a dreamer. I must have inherited this from my father or paternal grandmother.

My mother was small in size, but a dynamite of a person. Her life journey brought her from Shanghai to Singapore, and from a life in the performing arts to that of a Singapore homemaker and mother of three sons. I hope that we have lived up to her expectations and have been filial sons to her and our father.

Memories of My Father

My father, Koh Han Kok, was born on the 20th of April 1911 in Penang. My grandfather was then engaged in business in Penang.

When my father was a youngster, he was sent to school in Xiamen. A few years ago, I went to visit my father's old school, the Anglo-Chinese School, on Gulangyu. It is now called No. 2 Middle School. After completing high school in Xiamen, my father went on to study at a university in Shanghai. However, tragedy struck before he could complete his tertiary education. The Great Depression hit the world and because of it, my grandfather's flourishing business was wiped out. My grandfather was so traumatised by the disaster that he never went to work again.

My father, who was then only 19, left his university, left Shanghai and returned to Singapore to pick up the pieces. As the oldest child and eldest son, he assumed the obligation to look after his parents, his brothers and sisters. The prospect of supporting such a large family, in the midst of general economic adversity, must have looked daunting to a young man of 19, who lacked a degree, who had no profession and no working experience. What he lacked by way of qualification and skill was more than compensated by his resourcefulness, industry, resilience and his willingness to take risk — the true hallmark of an entrepreneur.

He tried his hand at several business enterprises. He encountered many failures. He bounced back after each failure to take on a new challenge until he was eventually successful.

My father was a very well-rounded man. We, his three sons, have acquired many of our good habits from him. He loved to read and our home was always surrounded by magazines and books. When I was a student at the university, he opened an account for me at the City Book

Store. I could buy any book I wanted and charge it to the account. I wish more Singapore fathers would emulate my father and give their children an account in a bookstore instead of a credit card. I can truthfully say that I have acquired my love for books not from my teachers but from my father.

My father believed in the maxim, "a healthy mind in a healthy body". He taught us to swim, to play tennis, he taught my two younger brothers to play golf and encouraged us to engage in physical exercise regularly. Until his death, my father continued to play tennis three times a week and, mostly, with players young enough to be his children. I think it gave him great satisfaction to know that even at the age of 74, he could still beat me six love in tennis. As a result of my father's example and teaching, I have acquired the life-long habit of exercising every day.

Although my father never had a chance to complete his university education, perhaps because of it, he had a great thirst for learning and an unquenchable intellectual curiosity. He attended many courses offered by the University's Department of Extra-Mural Studies. He had an aptitude for languages. Apart from Chinese, English and Malay, my father also spoke Japanese, French, German and some Thai.

My father was also an indefatigable traveller. Almost every year, he would set off to explore some part of the world. He came to know many different countries, cultures and peoples. I think the experience reinforced his basic instinct that below the surface, differences of skin pigmentation, language, religion and custom, we are all members of the human family. He was very Singaporean in his freedom from racial, religious and linguistic prejudices. I think I have inherited from my father my intolerance for any form of prejudice.

I have tried to dredge my memory in order to recall an episode which has made an impact on my life and character. I remember that once, when my brothers and I were very young, my father had brought us to visit the Great World Amusement Park. On our way home, we passed a bicycle stand and saw a commotion. On investigation, my father discovered that a neighbourhood thug was trying to take away a bicycle which did not belong to him. The attendant, who was physically a smaller man, appeared frightened by the threats of the thug. Much to our fear and admiration, my father stepped in, gave the thug a beating and chased him away. What the episode has taught me is courage, the courage to stand up to bullies and to defend the weak.

My father died of a heart attack in Washington, DC on the 30th of October 1985. My father did not leave any cash or condominium to his three children. Instead, he had given me an inheritance that no amount of money can buy. *First*, he brought me up in a morally wholesome environment. He taught me right from wrong. *Second*, he had given me a very good education. *Third*, he had instilled in me a reverence for learning and the good habit of reading. *Fourth*, he taught me the virtue of tolerance and the evil of racial, religious and linguistic prejudice. *Fifth*, he had transmitted to me the courage to stand up to bullies and to fear no one. *Sixth*, he taught me the wisdom of the Latin maxim, "a healthy mind in a healthy body". *Seventh*, he taught me what the French call *joie de vivre* or joy of living. He worked hard but he also enjoyed life to the full.

A grateful son
Tommy Koh

A Toast to President and Mrs Wee Kim Wee*

Mr President and Mrs Ong, Mr Prime Minister and Mrs Goh, distinguished guests, members of the Wee family

In November 1915, Mr and Mrs Wee Choon Lay of Holland Road, had their fourth and youngest son. They named him Kim Wee. Over in Kim Seng Road, on the bank of the Singapore River, Mrs Koh Chwee Thor had just become pregnant with her first daughter. In July 1916, the daughter was born and was named Sok Hiong.

How did Wee Kim Wee meet Koh Sok Hiong? When Kim Wee was 8½, the family moved from Holland Road to Nelson Road in Kampong Bahru. Kim Wee was a very good badminton and basketball player. One of the boys who joined him in those games was Koh Kim Swan, the second brother of Koh Sok Hiong.

Wee Kim Wee was a very bright and hardworking student. He went to one of the good schools of Singapore, Raffles Institution. However, because of the family's difficult financial circumstances, Kim Wee was obliged to leave RI after completing only Standard VII. He got a job with *The Straits Times* as a clerk in the Circulation Department.

Meantime, over at the Koh family in Pasir Panjang, grandmother felt that it was time for her oldest granddaughter, Sok Hiong to marry. Sok Hiong was doing very well at Nanyang Girls' School and had no thought of marrying. She wanted to complete high school and become a teacher. Her ambition was to be a school principal. However, her grandmother

---

*Speech by Prof Tommy Koh at the 60th wedding anniversary dinner of Mr & Mrs Wee Kim Wee on 12 April 1996 at Shangri-La hotel.

told her that she was getting old and would like to see Sok Hiong married before she died. Grandmother warned that she would be unable to close her eyes upon her death if Sok Hiong were still unmarried. Being a dutiful daughter and granddaughter, Sok Hiong allowed her elders to determine her fate.

Sok Hiong had three suitors. Wee Kim Wee was one of them. He thought that he had no chance as he was the least eligible of the three. His family was not wealthy. He had completed only Standard VII at RI. He was earning only $40 a month. However, he had two allies in Sok Hiong's family. Her second brother, Kim Swan, put in a good word for him. Sok Hiong's grandmother liked him and had assessed him to be a good man. When other members of the family objected to him on account of his modest circumstances, grandmother said [I must ask PM's permission to say it in Hokkien]:

> 如果你的命是好的，嫁一個職員他可能會變成一個皇帝。
> 如果你的命是坏的，嫁一個皇帝他也可能變成一個職員。

For the benefit of those of you who do not understand Hokkien, what grandmother said was this:

> If your karma is good, the clerk you marry may one day become the emperor. If your karma is bad, the emperor you marry may one day become a clerk.

Grandmother won and it was decided that Koh Sok Hiong would marry Wee Kim Wee in 1936. Grandmother proved to be not only a good judge of character but also gifted with prescience. Forty-nine years after the marriage, in 1985, grandmother must have been beaming in heaven when the clerk whom her granddaughter had married was appointed the President of the Republic of Singapore.

Wee Kim Wee and Koh Sok Hiong have been married to each other for 60 years. In that time, they have raised one son and six daughters.

They have 13 grandchildren. They have lived through poverty and hardship. They have survived bouts of ill health. They have suffered disappointments. They have tasted the joys of success and the privileges of high office. Their marriage has survived the trials and tribulations of life and has remained strong.

What is the secret of their marital success? Let me share with you the three lessons which I have learnt.

First, they regard marriage as a life-long commitment. Their devotion to each other and to their seven children was total. They had no illusions. They knew that life is not a bed of roses. They were, however, determined to make their marriage work.

Second, when differences occurred, they appreciated the need to compromise. As Wee Kim Wee has often put it, "You win some, you lose some." According to the children, Mr Wee won more often than he lost!

Third, they have tried to keep the flame of fun and romance burning in their marriage. When they were younger, they used to go ballroom dancing every Saturday night. Let me tell you a story. This happened when Mr Wee was our Ambassador to Japan. On one occasion, Mrs Wee was coming back alone to Singapore. Mr Wee, his personal assistant, Sylvia Toh, and some members of the staff were at the front door of the residence to bid her goodbye. The car, with Mrs Wee inside, moved off slowly. It stopped suddenly and moved backwards. Mrs Wee wound down the window of her car and beckoned to Mr Wee to approach her. Thinking that she had forgotten something, he bent down to listen to her. Mrs Wee gave him a big kiss because she had forgotten to kiss him goodbye. When he walked back to his staff, Sylvia told him that he had lipstick on his face. With his characteristic, "Oh my goodness", he gave Sylvia his handkerchief so that she could wipe away the lipstick from his face.

The kindness, modesty, and humility of Mr and Mrs Wee Kim Wee are legendary. The life, career, and achievements of Mr Wee are well known. Tonight, I want therefore to speak in praise not of Mr Wee but of Mrs Wee. Women of her generation are seldom praised for their contributions to their families, to the success of their husbands' careers, and to society.

In the Wee's marriage, there was a clear-cut division of labour. His job was to work hard and provide for the family. Her jobs were to look after the family, to raise the children, and to be his sweetheart and companion. Like other fathers of his generation, Mr Wee was seldom at home. He was a workaholic and used to put in long hours at work. Each night, he would put *The Straits Times* to bed while Mrs Wee would put the children to bed. The children were brought up mainly by their mother. Mrs Wee was their teacher, cook, tailor, washerwoman, doctor, hairdresser and friend. If Mrs Wee mothered the children at home, Mr Wee nurtured his journalists and diplomats at work. There was much love at both locations.

When Mr Wee was our High Commissioner to Malaysia and Ambassador to Japan, Mrs Wee was his secret weapon. She is one of the best cooks of Singapore. Many of the meals which Mr Wee hosted in Kuala Lumpur and Tokyo were cooked by Mrs Wee. I remember an occasion when I was in Tokyo. Mr Wee hosted a lunch in my honour. Mrs Wee personally cooked 12 dishes for the lunch. My Japanese friends ate to their hearts' content and went away burping happily! I think the Ministry of Foreign Affairs owes Mrs Wee a big debt of gratitude.

Mr President and Mrs Ong, Mr Prime Minister and Mrs Goh, distinguished guests and members of the Wee family, I request you to rise and join me in a toast to Mr and Mrs Wee Kim Wee. We warmly congratulate you on your diamond wedding anniversary and wish you many more years of marital bliss.

Toasts to President S. R. Nathan on His 80th and 85th Birthdays

Mr President and Mrs Nathan
Prime Minister and Mrs Goh
Senior Minister and Mrs Lee
Chief Justice and Mrs Yong
Deputy Prime Ministers, Ministers, Judges
Distinguished guests, ladies and gentlemen

My humble role this evening is that of your toastmaster. We have many reasons for toasting our beloved President. Allow me to highlight three of them.

First, we wish to toast the President because of his distinguished record as a family man. He is a good husband to Umi; a good father to Juthika and Osith; a good father-in-law to Gay Eng; and a very good grandfather to Monisha, Kiron and Kheshin.

Second, we, your former colleagues in the civil service, wish to salute you as the first civil servant to become President. Like our former President, Dr Wee Kim Wee, you started life from a very humble beginning. When you joined the civil service, you started as an almoner in the Singapore General Hospital. It is a testimony to your ability, determination, hard work and integrity as well as to Singapore's meritocracy, that you succeeded in climbing all the way to the top of the ladder.

Third, we, on behalf of a grateful nation, wish to thank you for the extraordinary job you are doing as our President. The Senior Minister has said that you have brought dignity and grace to your office. But, you have done much more. You have been an exceptionally well informed interlocutor for our visiting dignitaries. You have made special contributions to inter-faith understanding and to our multi-culturalism. In the recent tragedy on Nicoll Highway, a courageous foreman lost his life in order to save the lives of those who worked under him. Without any publicity, you went to visit the grieving widow and her two young children. You have made efforts to ensure that she and the children will not have to undergo the hardship and suffering which afflicted your mother, your six siblings and you when your father died prematurely. Mr President, you are a tough man with a kind and loving heart.

Kipling has praised the man who "can walk with the kings and not lose the common touch". This evening, we praise even more a "king" who can walk with other kings and not lose the common touch.

Ladies and gentlemen, will you please rise and join me in a heartfelt toast to our President. We wish him good health, long life and continued success.

2 July 2004

* * *

Mr President, Mrs Nathan and members of the Nathan family
Mr Chandra Das, Chairman of the President's fan club and fellow members of the club

Five years ago, I had the great honour of proposing the toast to the President on the occasion of his 80th birthday. Chandra Das has requested me to reprise my role this evening. I consulted my wife on what I should say. She said I could use the same speech and no one will remember what I said five years ago. I told her that the President would remember because he has an elephantine memory. So, I have come up with three new reasons to toast the President on the happy occasion of his 85th birthday.

First, we toast the President because he always has a special compassion for our poor, our needy and our underprivileged. Ten years ago, President Nathan launched the President's Challenge. It has, to date, raised $70 million and benefited about 400 charitable organisations. In addition to the President's Challenge, the President has also taken a personal interest in and helped many of our less fortunate citizens. This is usually done anonymously and the beneficiaries therefore do not know who their benefactor is. President Nathan has a big heart.

Second, President Nathan has helped to define and develop the office of the presidency. He is the longest serving Elected President. By the time the President's second term ends in 2011, he will have been our longest serving President. The presidency is still an evolving institution. A recent test case was the President's consent to draw upon our past reserves for the Resilience Package. Before giving his consent, the President considered the request seriously, consulted the Council of Presidential Advisers and did what he thought was the right thing to do, in the circumstances, and for the country's interest. The President's overriding concern is to safeguard the Constitution and protect the interests of our country and our people.

Third, because of his previous experience as the Permanent Secretary of the Ministry of Foreign Affairs and our Ambassador to the United States and Malaysia, President Nathan has a flair for dealing with foreign leaders and foreign countries. He is an activist President and has visited more foreign countries than all his predecessors put together. Through these State visits, the President has strengthened our links with other countries in all parts of the world, expanded our political and economic space and opened the door to new opportunities for our business leaders. The feedback we have received from our foreign friends is full of admiration for our President. They speak of his ability, beyond engaging them in substantive issues, to put his foreign counterparts at ease and of his ability to create good chemistry and empathy with foreign leaders. These are skills which have been forged, over a life time, through the President's career as a social worker, trade unionist and diplomat. Mr President, you are Singapore's super-Ambassador.

Ladies and gentlemen, please rise and join me in a toast to our President on his 85th birthday. We wish him good health, long life and success in all his endeavours. To the President!

Thank you very much.

2 July 2009

Eulogy for S. Rajaratnam*

President, Prime Minister and members of the cabinet, the Chief Justice and members of the Judiciary, the Head of the Civil Service and members of the Civil Service

I have the honour to speak on behalf of the many men and women of the Singapore Foreign Service, both serving and retired, who had the privilege of working with and under the leadership of Mr S. Rajaratnam. In this eulogy, I wish to mention three of his most important achievements.

First, I am confident that history will acknowledge the important contributions which Mr Raja, as we all affectionately called him, made to Singapore's foreign policy and the foreign service. On the 9th of August 1965, Singapore suddenly became independent. Mr Raja became its Foreign Minister, a job he would hold for 15 years. A month later, on the 21st of September 1965, he spoke to the UN General Assembly on the occasion of Singapore's admission. In that seminal speech, he identified a number of principles of Singapore's foreign policy which continue to be the basis of our foreign policy after 40 years.

Mr Raja faced many challenges. His first challenge was to win international recognition for the newly independent country. This he accomplished in his first year. His second challenge was to create stability in Southeast Asia. ASEAN was created to achieve this objective. His third challenge was to expand Singapore's political and economic space. Mr Raja travelled the world tirelessly in pursuit of this objective. He would spend a month at the UN each autumn, in order to meet other Foreign Ministers, to understand how the UN worked, and to use the

---

*Delivered at the State funeral service for the late S. Rajaratnam, 25 February 2006.

UN as a platform to project Singapore to the world. The high profile and credibility which Singapore enjoys today at the UN can be traced back to Mr Raja's pioneering efforts.

He started to build a foreign service from scratch. In the beginning, he had to borrow individuals from both the public and private sectors to serve in the Ministry and in a few missions abroad. In 1972, a career foreign service was born. He attracted many idealistic young men and women to join this new enterprise. Mr Raja was their leader, teacher and role model. He did not demand but he earned the respect and affection of those who served under him. He never lost his temper or raised his voice with his subordinates, but he had their wholehearted support because of the brilliance of his intellect, the passion of his commitment to Singapore and by his eloquence and charm. We were a band of happy warriors for peace.

Second, I want to mention the important contributions which Mr Raja had made to our regional organisation, the Association of Southeast Asian Nations or ASEAN. Mr Raja was one of the five visionary leaders who, on 8 August 1967, had signed the Bangkok Declaration which established ASEAN. The other four were Thanat Khoman of Thailand, Adam Malik of Indonesia, Abdul Razak of Malaysia and Narciso Ramos of the Philippines. Mr Raja was deeply committed to ASEAN but he was clear-eyed about the challenge of turning ideal into reality.

Speaking after the signing ceremony, he spoke about the difficult task of "marrying nationalist thinking with regional thinking" and of the need to make "painful modifications to nationalist practices and thinking in our respective countries". Five years later, however, Mr Raja was able to note that, "the habit of cooperation has now been established and slowly expanded". ASEAN was making progress.

In 1975, the Vietnam War ended with victory to North Vietnam. Cambodia and Laos fell to the rising red tide. Vietnam made threatening noises to the non-Communist states of Southeast Asia. Faced with such threats, some of the leaders of ASEAN were in danger of losing their nerves. Mr Raja rallied them to take a united stand and to support Thailand, the frontline State.

In December 1978, Vietnam invaded and occupied Cambodia. Mr Raja succeeded in uniting the ASEAN family which decided to take the issue to the UN. The odds seemed against us at that time as Vietnam had the support of the Soviet Union, the Warsaw Pact countries, and such powerful Non-Aligned leaders as Cuba and India. Miraculously, the UN supported ASEAN against Vietnam and with increasing majorities. The success of ASEAN's diplomatic campaign gave the organisation self-confidence and credibility. ASEAN's success was due, in no small part, to Mr Raja's strength of character, his skilful diplomacy and his ability to work with his ASEAN colleagues as a team.

Third, I want to mention Mr Raja's contributions to what I would call the Singapore school of diplomacy. He was a realist but he was not a fatalist. He did not believe that small states were powerless. When faced with a situation in 1980, where Cambodia was occupied by Vietnam and Afghanistan by the Soviet Union, Mr Raja wrote:

> Do we then resign ourselves to what both the Soviets and Vietnamese insist are irreversible actions? We believe that small states are not all that helpless. Both in Kampuchea and Afghanistan, patriots are fighting to reverse the irreversible.... We in the United Nations can sustain the patriotism and courage of hard-pressed freedom fighters by not betraying them....

One characteristic of the Singapore school of diplomacy is to be realistic about the world, but not to be intimidated by more powerful states. This and other characteristics of our diplomacy such as our preference for clarity over opacity, our adherence to international law, our proactivity, can be traced back to the seeds planted by Mr Raja, Minister Mentor Lee Kuan Yew and Dr Goh Keng Swee.

Conclusion

My colleagues and I in the Singapore Foreign Service mourn the passing of our illustrious leader, Mr Raja. But, we celebrate his life and thank him for his legacy. We thank him for teaching us the virtue of courage which he demonstrated in full measure when he single-handedly stood up to the bully boys at the Non-Aligned Summit in Havana in 1979. We thank him for teaching us the virtue of magnanimity when he extended his hand of friendship to the Vietnamese Foreign Minister, Nguyen Co Thach. We thank him for teaching us to treat our subordinates, the secretaries, security officers, drivers, the domestic heip with kindness. We thank him for teaching us to love and respect our wives as he did his beloved Piroska. We thank him for teaching us to believe in the Singapore Pledge. We thank him for teaching us that it is possible to be a good man in this wicked world.

I would like to conclude by quoting a few lines from Rabindranath Tagore's poem, *Gitanjali*, which captures so well Mr Raja's legacy to us:

> Where the mind is without fear and the head is held high;
> Where knowledge is free;
> Where the world has not been broken up into fragments by narrow domestic walls;
> Where words come out from the depth of truth;
> Where tireless striving stretches its arms towards perfection;
> Where the clear stream of reason has not lost its way into the dreary desert sand of dead habit;
> Where the mind is led forward by thee into ever-widening thought and action;
> Into that heaven of freedom, my Father, let my country awake.

Thank you very much.

Eulogy for David Marshall*

David Marshall was Singapore's first Ambassador to France, where he served for 15 years. During this period, he was also accredited as Singapore's Ambassador to Spain, Portugal and Switzerland. As Ambassador, David Marshall served Singapore with distinction, dedication and honour. He brought Singapore's relations with France to a higher plane, raising Singapore's profile in France through his exceptional personality and charisma. He was so well-known in the French political scene that a former Ambassador of France to Singapore mentioned, just before the 1988 presidential election, that whichever candidate was to win the election, David Marshall would have privileged access to the new President of France. He also became widely known in the French Establishment as the "Ambassadeur à orchidée", referring to the orchid which always adorned his lapel.

When David Marshall left France in July 1993, the most prestigious French daily *Le Monde*, carried an article commenting on his departure from Paris. The personal impact that he left on France was summed up in these quotations from *Le Monde*:

> With his departure, it is one of the most flamboyant figures of the Parisian diplomatic world who leaves. Known for his frankness and his love for life, Francophile and Francophone in soul, he said "I discovered the French language like a duck finding its pond." During his stay in France, of an exceptional duration, he has been a permanent and convincing advocate of the strengthening of French presence in Southeast Asia, which is not limited to the countries of former Indochina.

David Marshall's contributions to Singapore were not solely in strengthening Franco-Singaporean relations. He was also a great asset to

---
*Delivered at the memorial service for the late David Marshall, 17 December 1995.

the Ministry of Foreign Affairs because of his exceptional historical perspective and knowledge during Singapore's road to independence.

He was ever ready to impart his knowledge and experiences in his daily dealings with his staff in Paris and the Ministry at large. His signature green ink had become a hallmark in the Ministry's archives!

David Marshall will also be remembered for his warmth and humane and generous personality. During his 15 years as Ambassador, he and his family made it a point to open their home to all Singaporeans residing in France, as well as to the frequent visitors to Paris, official or unofficial, from Ministers to exchange students. Many of us here would have experienced his hospitality more often than not in the form of a "plateau de fruits de mer" (seafood platter) or "profiteroles" with hot chocolate sauce.

David Marshall was also the ideal representative of Singapore to Paris, the European capital renowned for its culture and the arts. Aside from his many qualifications, he was truly an avid patron of the arts. His love for the visual arts has resulted in an enduring legacy to Singapore.

David Marshall was on a visit to London when he saw a bronze life-sized sculpture of a girl on a swing by British sculptor Sydney Harpley. He commissioned Harpley to create a similar sculpture, using an Asian girl in native dress as the model. This work of art became the first of three gifts to the Singapore Botanic Gardens by the same sculptor. They give much joy and pleasure to many visitors to the Botanic Gardens. Let us hope that David Marshall's dream of a graceful Singapore endowed by beautiful sculptures in public places will soon be fulfilled.

Finally David Marshall was also a man of immense courage and perseverance. In spite of his poor eyesight and bouts of illness, he still carried the Singapore flag in France with dignity and pride, never allowing these handicaps to prevent him from performing his duties to the fullest. SM, then PM, after an official visit to France in 1990, commended David Marshall for his courage and dedication as follows:

> Your enthusiasm, energy and shrewdness have made the French government take note of Singapore as more than just another country in

Southeast Asia. I sensed their regard for you from the attitude of French leaders I met, including Fabius and Raymond Barre. Your efforts have the imprint of excellence which Singapore needs to make its mark.

Your spirit is remarkable. You cannot read, you cannot see very clearly. From the back of my head, you mistook me for the Frenchman who chaired the meeting. But you have guts and gusto, and have carried on with your job.

We shall remember David Marshall for these extraordinary qualities. We will all miss him dearly.

Goh Keng Swee
Ten Lessons from His Life

Singapore was blessed with an extraordinary team of founding fathers. After Lee Kuan Yew, Goh Keng Swee had made the most important and enduring contributions to the prosperity, security and quality of life of Singapore. Dr Goh's passing is a teachable moment. I would like to deduce ten lessons from his life and achievements.

Lesson No. 1: Courage, Optimism and Can-Do Spirit

When Dr Goh became Finance Minister, he faced formidable challenges: widespread poverty, high unemployment, poor resource endowment, small domestic market and industrial strife. In 1965, when Singapore was asked to leave Malaysia, Singapore lost its hinterland. In the face of such odds, Dr Goh never despaired. He had courage, optimism and a can-do spirit. This is the first lesson.

Lesson No. 2: Most Problems Have Solutions

The second lesson he taught us is that, if we think hard enough, there are solutions to most problems. After exiting Malaysia, Dr Goh made the world our hinterland. He swam against the tide by inviting multinational corporations to invest in Singapore. He made the word "profit" a good word instead of a bad word. He created a pro-business environment which made Singapore stand out in the Third World.

Lesson No. 3: Defy Conventional Wisdom

The third lesson is that we should think for ourselves and not be a slavish follower of conventional wisdom and fashionable theories. Dr Goh was a rebel. For example, he was not afraid to deviate from Keynesian economics and the Western ideological bias against industrial policy. He would insist on thorough homework, study the experiences of others, but, in the end, adopt a solution which fits our circumstances and works.

Lesson No. 4: Build Institutions

The fourth lesson is that institutions matter. Dr Goh built many new institutions. Most of them have endured and prospered. Many charismatic leaders of the Third World have made the mistake of using their charisma, instead of institutions, to get things done. Dr Goh has left us with a rich legacy of strong institutions.

Lesson No. 5: Focus on Singapore's Prosperity and Independence

The fifth lesson is that the people in our government, both politicians and civil servants, must be focused, not on their personal agenda, but to secure the prosperity of Singapore and to protect her sovereignty and independence. In many countries, both developed and developing, people aspire for public office in order to enrich themselves. Dr Goh once said that taking up public office in Singapore is like joining a holy order.

Lesson No. 6: Respect and Help the Poor

The sixth lesson is that one of the purposes of government is to make the world a little less unfair for the poor, the disabled and the disadvantaged. Perhaps because Dr Goh started his professional life in the social welfare department and he represented Kreta Ayer, one of the poorest constituencies in Singapore, Dr Goh never looked down upon nor ignored the interests of the little people. I recently asked a Latin-American friend, what is the biggest difference between the politics of Singapore and her country. She replied that, unlike her country, Singapore's ruling elite respects and cares for our poorer citizens.

Lesson No. 7: Ideas Are Important

The seventh lesson is that Dr Goh respects scholarship, research and ideas. He founded the Institute of Southeast Asian Studies, the predecessor of the East Asia Institute of NUS, and others. He was well-read and enjoyed meeting with and picking the brains of scholars and thinkers.

Lesson No. 8: Beyond Money and Material Things

Dr Goh was a well-rounded individual. He loved music and founded the Singapore Symphony Orchestra. He created the Chinese and Japanese Gardens in Jurong. He was also the founder of the Bird Park and the Zoo. The eighth lesson is that life is more than making money and eating well. It is also about learning to enjoy music, to commune with nature and to marvel at the splendours of the bird and animal kingdoms.

Lesson No. 9: Lead a Simple and Frugal Life

Dr Goh's thrift is legendary. Even when he could well afford it, he continued to live a simple and frugal life. He shunned ostentation and consumerism. When I called on him at MAS, when he was its Chairman, he apologised for the size of his office. I do not think Dr Goh would approve of the trend in Singapore, which is for some of our wealthy citizens to flaunt their wealth and to lead self-indulgent lives.

Lesson No. 10: Never Stop Being Curious

The tenth lesson is that one should always be curious and never stop thinking of new ideas. Dr Goh's interests span an incredible spectrum. When I was serving at the UN in New York, I would receive requests from him for papers on such esoteric topics as falconry and Mormonism. Dr Goh had a child-like curiosity about the world and an unquenchable thirst for knowledge.

[Originally published in *The Straits Times*, 23 May 2010.]

George Yeo
A Man for All Seasons

One of my hopes for the 2011 General Elections was that those who won would be magnanimous and those who lost would be gracious.

Foreign Minister George Yeo was gracious in defeat. In his concession speech, he congratulated Mr Low Thia Khiang and his Workers' Party team on their victory and wished them success. Of the other defeated candidates, only Mr Desmond Choo of the People's Action Party and Ms Nicole Seah of the National Solidarity Party were just as gracious.

A man's character can be gleaned from his conduct, both in victory and in defeat. Mr Yeo is a gentleman and an honourable man, whatever the conditions.

I have had the pleasure of working under his leadership in three of his ministerial portfolios. He was our first minister of the then Ministry of Information and the Arts, or MITA. During nine years at MITA, he changed Singapore from a so-called cultural desert to a cultural oasis.

He appointed Mr Tan Chin Nam, chairman of the newly created National Library Board, and Mr Tan, together with Mr Christopher Chia, revolutionised our library system and made it one of the best in the world. Mr Yeo also appointed Mr Lim Chee Onn, chairman of the National Heritage Board, and me, chairman of the National Arts Council.

It was under his leadership that the Esplanade was built, the Asian Civilisations Museum was envisioned, the Arts Festival was made an annual event, the LaSalle College of the Arts took off, and the Government agreed, for the first time, to subsidise arts education. Today, Singaporeans enjoy a rich and varied cultural life. They should not forget the person who planted the seeds that have blossomed.

Mr Yeo brought the same energy, imagination and enthusiasm to the Ministry of Trade and Industry. He realised that because trade is Singapore's life blood, it should play a proactive leadership role in global trade forums like the World Trade Organisation (WTO). He quickly won the admiration and trust of his peers. They asked him to chair the negotiations on agriculture, one of the most contentious issues. WTO Director-General Pascal Lamy is an admirer of Mr Yeo.

In order to enlarge Singapore's economic space, Mr Yeo championed the idea of linking Singapore's economy with other economies by way of free trade agreements (FTAs) and comprehensive economic partnership (CEP) agreements. During his watch, he launched more than a dozen FTA and CEP negotiations.

He appointed me chief negotiator in our negotiations with the United States. During the journey of two years, we encountered many difficulties. Throughout, Mr Yeo remained calm, optimistic and creative. He worked relentlessly with the different stakeholders in the US to earn their support and to find acceptable solutions to the difficulties.

In the final stage of the negotiations, there was a shortlist of issues that the two chief negotiators could not resolve. Those issues were finally resolved by Mr Yeo and his American counterpart, Mr Robert Zoellick, in a marathon negotiating session that extended through the night without dinner and ended successfully at dawn. Members of the Singapore delegation were deeply impressed by the cool and masterly way in which Mr Yeo had negotiated with Mr Zoellick.

Mr Yeo has been Singapore's Foreign Minister for nearly seven years now. He inherited a ministry in good order as a result of the legacy of Mr S. Rajaratnam, Mr S. Dhanabalan, Mr Wong Kan Seng and Professor S. Jayakumar. What contributions did Mr Yeo make to that heritage? I would single out three.

First, he taught us to think strategically and to prioritise. He constantly asked his staff to ensure that our most important bilateral relationships were in excellent order. He scanned the horizon for new opportunities — such as in the Middle East and Latin America.

Second, he was the first foreign minister to use history and culture as instruments of diplomacy. He persuaded the Chinese Chamber of Commerce to restore the Sun Yat Sen Villa and to turn it into a historic site linking Singapore, China and Taiwan. He requested that the National Heritage Board restore the memorial to Subhas Chandra Bose, who is celebrated in India as a nationalist and independence fighter. It was due to the leadership of Mr Yeo, a Roman Catholic, and of former Indian president Abdul Kalam, a Muslim, that the ancient Buddhist university at Nalanda, Bihar is being reincarnated.

Third, Mr Yeo believes in the importance of friendship in diplomacy. He often invited his foreign guests to his home to have dinner with him and his family. He went out of his way to show warmth and friendship to his foreign interlocutors. When Tan Sri Syed Hamid Albar was Malaysia's foreign minister, Mr Yeo visited him in his constituency in Malaysia to pay his respects during Hari Raya.

Mr Yeo is blessed with high IQ, EQ and CQ — cultural intelligence. He is an exceptionally gifted man. Although an engineer by training and a soldier by profession, he is also a philosopher and historian. Although a devout Roman Catholic, he is a champion of inter-faith dialogue and understanding.

Mr George Yeo is ideally qualified to play a leadership role on the global stage, and I sincerely hope he will do so.

[Originally published in *The Straits Times*, 9 May 2011.]

In Defence of Lim Chong Yah

Professor Lim Chong Yah is one of Singapore's most distinguished economists. He was the Professor of Economics at the National University of Singapore (NUS), before moving on to the Nanyang Technological University (NTU) to become the first Albert Winsemius Professor of Economics.

He is currently Emeritus Professor of Economics of both NUS and NTU.

Prof Lim is both a scholar and practitioner. He was the founding chairman of the National Wages Council (NWC), a post which he held for more than 30 years. No one has contributed more to the success of this unique Singapore institution than he. In view of his credentials and track record, we should study carefully his three proposals for a more inclusive Singapore wage policy.

Prof Lim proposes:

- that the NWC should continue with the issuance of a quantitative wage increase guideline for those earning less than $1,000 to $1,500 a month, over the next two years;
- that the NWC should call for an across-the-board temporary three-year moratorium of salaries of top executives earning more than $1 million a year, both in the private and public sectors; and
- that should the wages of the lowest-paid resident workers remain stubbornly very low in two or three years' time, serious consideration be given to introducing a compulsory minimum wage scheme with, say, $1,000 a month as the start-off quantum.

Freezing Salaries at the Top

Why is Prof Lim asking for a freeze, for three years, of salaries above $1 million a year?

I think he has done so because our growing income inequality is due to the inflation of salaries at one end of the spectrum and the deflation of salaries at the other end. His objective is to raise the wages at the bottom and slow down the escalation of salaries at the top.

Is it wrong for Prof Lim to interfere with the market and to urge restraint?

I do not think it is wrong.

Having served on the board of directors of two publicly listed companies, I have observed that in recent years, we have been looking to the West for inspiration when it comes to the compensation of our chief executive officers and other key personnel in senior management.

I do not think it is wise to look, for example, to America for inspiration, because the American culture is very individual-centred, whereas our culture is more communitarian.

One consequence of the American model of capitalism is the Occupy Wall Street Movement and the increasing polarisation of American society and politics between the 1 percent and the 99 percent. We do not want to import such trends, which Americans themselves are so worried about, into Singapore.

Consider the following facts extracted from Professor Michael Sandel's book, *Justice: What Is The Right Thing to Do?* In 1980, the average CEO in America earned 42 times more than the average worker. In 2007, the average CEO earned 344 times more than the average worker.

During the period 2004 to 2005, the average CEO in top companies in the US, Europe and Japan earned US$13.3 million, US$6.6 million and US$1.5 million, respectively. Japan, like Singapore, has a communitarian culture and is a better role model for us than the US or Europe.

I would also call attention to what the Conservative British Prime Minister David Cameron said recently when he opposed the payment of extravagant salaries and bonuses in the financial industry in London.

He said that there was an incestuous element in the composition of boards. As a result, there was a certain "I scratch your back, you scratch my back" phenomenon at work.

I think that his comment is probably applicable to Singapore, where the talent pool is smaller, and the same people serve on multiple boards.

I also suspect that there is an unspoken competition among some of our leading companies to see whose chief executive officer will receive the highest salary. We would actually be more impressed if the competition is to see which company will pay its workers more.

I, therefore, sympathise with Prof Lim's proposal to slow down the escalation of the salaries at the top. I do not, however, think that his specific proposal will be accepted by the NWC.

I suspect that the NWC would focus on raising the wages at the bottom and not interfere with the wages at the top. Singaporeans, especially those at the top, should, however, reflect deeply on Prof Lim's proposal and on their responsibility to society.

Raising Wages at the Bottom

I support Prof Lim's proposal that the NWC should continue with the issuance of a quantitative wage increase guideline for our low-wage workers for the next two years.

A one-time increase of $50 will not have a significant impact on the lives of the low-wage workers. However, a $150 increase, over three years, would be more impactful.

I agree with Prof Lim that if the situation does not improve in two to three years' time, we should seriously consider introducing a minimum wage. We know from the experiences of Japan, South Korea, Taiwan and Hong Kong that the introduction of the minimum wage did not increase unemployment or frighten away foreign investors in those jurisdictions.

Hong Kong introduced the minimum wage one year ago. According to a report in this newspaper last month, the Hong Kong experience has been a positive one. There was no increase in unemployment and no decrease in foreign investment. In fact, unemployment remained low and there was an increase in the number of new businesses. The minimum wage has raised the income of over 140,000 low-wage workers.

In conclusion, I wish to thank Prof Lim for being our moral conscience. He has reminded us that our mission is to achieve growth with equity. Our ambition is to build a fair and prosperous Singapore. What we have achieved so far is a prosperous but unfair society.

Prof Lim has warned us that we have deviated from our original path and that we are dangerously close to a point when our inequality could adversely affect our cohesion and harmony.

[Originally published in *The Straits Times*, 3 November 2012.]

A Tribute to Wazir Singh

I wish to salute my old teacher, Mr Wazir Singh, and through him, all my teachers in primary and secondary schools.

I joined Raffles Institution from Outram School in 1952. Like many students in their first year at Raffles, I felt both elation and anxiety. I was proud to be a Rafflesian but nervous as to whether I was good enough for Raffles.

Mr Wazir Singh was my form master in Secondary 1. I will always be grateful to him because he had confidence in me and encouraged me to aim high.

Mr Wazir Singh was a good teacher in mathematics and a good form master. He treated everyone fairly. He had no favourites and no scapegoats.

He taught me to work hard and to enjoy learning. He also taught me the virtues of honesty and compassion.

The fact that he is a Sikh and a Punjabi and a good man is fortuitous. It helped me to overcome the virus of racial and religious prejudice. I have learnt from him to judge a person, not by the colour of his skin or his religious faith, but by the quality of his heart and mind.

Mr Wazir Singh is an example of the many good teachers I had at RI. Good parents and good teachers produce good children. Good children grow up to become good citizens. If we want Singapore to succeed and to be a morally wholesome society, we must have good teachers. This is why it is important for us to respect the teaching profession and to hold up outstanding teachers such as Wazir Singh as a role model for others to emulate.

[Originally published in *If Not for My Teacher: A nation's tribute to teachers in Singapore*, p. 13, COMPASS, Singapore. © 1999 Ministry of Education]

Wang Gungwu
Friend, Mentor and Role Model

I first met Wang Gungwu in 1957. He had just received his Ph.D. from the School of Oriental and African Studies of London University. He returned to Singapore and began his academic career as an Assistant Lecturer in the History Department of the University of Malaya, in Singapore. The University was located at the small and charming Bukit Timah Campus. The year 1957 was also the one in which, after many years of appeals to the British colonial government, the University of Malaya started a law department. I was one of the students in that pioneering class.

The total student population a the Bukit Timah Campus was small enough for us to know the students of other departments and faculties. Although the study of law was quite demanding, we still found the time to attend the classes in other departments and faculties. Through good friends studying history, such as Chu Tee Seng, I was told about a brilliant young history lecturer, Wang Gungwu. He had an extra appeal to those of us who were members of the University Socialist Club because he was the Club's founding president. We also admired his lovely young wife, Margaret.

I had studied history at Raffles Institution and found it boring. History lessons consisted of learning by heart, facts, dates and names. Wang Gungwu's lectures on history were entirely different. The facts, dates and names were not neglected, but the emphasis was on how to frame them into a coherent narrative. To challenge our young minds, he invited us to interpret that narrative from different points of view: the official versus the non-official, the winner versus the loser, the aggressor versus the victim, etc. In 1957, Wang Gungwu was a dashing young man, charismatic and eloquent.

The members of the University Socialist Club were very passionate about our quest to build a more democratic, just and equal world. We often invited the Club's former members, such as Wang Gungwu, Lim Hock Siew, Poh Soo Kai, Ong Pang Boon, James Puthucheary, and S Woodhull, to attend our meetings and debates. My recollection was that Gungwu was more focused on his intellectual pursuits than on the political activities of the time. He held progressive left-wing views, but was not an ideologue. At that time, the Socialist Club was a big tent and accommodated a diversity of views. Those I was closest to, such as Gopinath Pillai, TPB Menon, Chu Tee Seng and Tan Guan Heng, were more attracted to the moderate views of Gungwu than to the more radical views of other friends.

In 1959, we were very sad when Gungwu decided to leave Singapore and join the pioneering group which started the University of Malaya in Pantai Valley, just outside Kuala Lumpur. From across the Causeway, we followed, with admiration, the meteoric rise of Gungwu's career: Assistant Lecturer in 1957, Lecturer in 1959, Senior Lecturer in 1961 and Professor in 1963.

In 1968, we were very proud when we heard that he was appointed Professor of Far Eastern History at the Australian National University (ANU). We were overjoyed when we learnt, in 1975. that he was the first Asian to be appointed as the Director of the Research School of Pacific Studies at ANU. In 1986, Gungwu left Canberra to succeed Dr Rayson Huang as the Vice-Chancellor of the University of Hong Kong.

I had lost contact with Gungwu for almost 20 years, the period I had spent, first, in New York and, subsequently, in Washington, DC. I had, however, continued to follow his illustrious career from afar and read some of his publications, especially those on the Chinese overseas and the re-emergence of China.

We met again in 1992, in San Francisco, I was given a most unusual assignment that year by Mr Wee Cho Yaw, the then President of the

Singapore Federation of Chinese Clan Associations (SFCCA) and Mr George Yeo, the then Minister in charge of the Ministry of Information and the Arts (MITA). The assignment was to submit a plan to them for the establishment of the Chinese Heritage Centre (CMC), which would be housed in the historic library building at Singapore's Nanyang Technological University. Mr Wee's chief adviser, Ms Pang Cheng Lian, and I set off on a world tour to visit other heritage centres. The trip culminated in San Francisco, the venue of the inaugural Conference of the International Society for the Studies of the Chinese Overseas. Gungwu delivered the inaugural lecture.

Pang Cheng Lian and I consulted Gungwu on the plan to establish the CHC and secured his agreement to serve on its board. He also offered to introduce us to Ms Lynn Pan, the author of the excellent book *Sons of the Yellow Emperor*. We subsequently succeeded in persuading Ms Pan to accept our offer to be the founding Director of the CHC. Her enduring legacy is the *Encyclopedia of the Chinese Overseas*, which she ably edited.

In the period leading up to 1997, when Hong Kong would join the PRC as a Special Administrative Area, many Western pundits were pessimistic about Hong Kong's prospects, post-1997. Probably as a reaction to the Western doom and gloom prognosis, Hong Kong University organised a series of lectures about Hong Kong's future, Gungwu invited me to deliver a lecture in the series, in which I offered a relatively optimistic view from the Southeast Asian perspective. During my visit to Hong Kong University, in September 1994, I was impressed by the esteem and affection with which Gungwu and Margaret were treated by the faculty and leaders of Hong Kong.

After a hiatus of 47 years, Gungwu and Margaret returned to Singapore in 1996. Gungwu's energy seems inexhaustible and his productivity is simply awesome. Because of his leadership of the East Asian Institute (EAI), first, as Director and, subsequently, as Chairman, he has put the EAI on the world's map of leading think-tanks on modern China. Under the leadership of Gungwu, as Chairman, and Ambassador K. Kesavapany, as Director, the Institute of Southeast Asian Studies (ISEAS) has regained its pre-eminence as a world-class centre of research on Southeast Asia.

Gungwu is also the founding Chairman of the Board of Governors of the Lee Kuan Yew School of Public Policy. Gungwu has empowered the dynamic Dean of the School, Professor Kishore Mahbubani, and together, they have succeeded in elevating the School, in only a few short years, to the major league of the world's elite schools of public policy. In addition to these three chairmanships, Gungwu is a member of 11 other boards in Singapore and 17 overseas. He chairs the editorial board of two journals and serves on the board of many others. He continues to author or edit one outstanding book after another.

I have known Wang Gungwu for 53 years. He is one of the most brilliant men I have had the good fortune to befriend. He is not only knowledgeable but also wise. He has been honoured both by his academic peers and by governments. Yet he is totally unspoilt by fame and success. He has always been a modest and humble man. He is, by temperament, optimistic and positive. In all the years I have known him, I have never heard him utter an unkind word about any person, institution or country. Gungwu's father was a teacher and a Confucianist. If he and his wife were alive today, they would be very proud of their only child. I think his father would approve when I describe Wang Gungwu as a living example of a Confucianist "junzi", or scholar-gentleman. His devotion to his wife of 55 years, Margaret, is an inspiration for all of us to emulate.

[Originally published in *Wang Gungwu: Junzi: Scholar-Gentleman in Conversation with Asad-ul Iqbal Latif*, pp. xiii–xvii. © 2010 Institute of Southeast Asian Studies]

MILESTONES OF LIFE AND CAREER

What RI Taught Me

The Headmaster, Mr Eugene Wijeysingha; the Deputy Chairman of the Board of Governors, Mr Sat Pal Khattar; governors; the President of the Old Rafflesians Association, Dr Chan Peng Mun; distinguished guests and fellow Rafflesians

I would like to thank RI and the larger Rafflesian community for inviting me to be the Guest-of-Honour at this, the 170th Founder's Day Ceremony of the school. It is an honour which every Rafflesian would treasure.

I hope I have come suitably attired. In place of a suit, I decided to wear my prefect's blazer. I won't, of course, tell you whether it is the original one. Some of my friends have asked me, "Aren't you a little too old to wear your high school blazer?" I replied, "Not if you were as proud of your school as I am."

I spent five and a half very happy years, between 1952 and 1957, in RI. I shall always be grateful to the school for the excellent and rounded education I received. Today, I wish to praise RI not for its excellent academic programme or its commitment to sports but for something else; something less obvious but no less important. I want to talk about a few of the values which I learnt from the school.

First, I learnt to judge a person by his ability and the content of his character and to oppose all forms of discrimination based on race, colour and creed. How did I learn this value at RI? Through its multi-racial faculty and student body. It is hard to believe in the prejudices against the Malays when I had an excellent Malay teacher in chemistry, Mr Ismail bin Abdul Aziz; and one of the heroes of my class, the school's soccer star, is Mr Wan Hussin Zoohri. It is equally hard to believe in the negative stereotypes about Indians when you have been taught by outstanding teachers like Mr Wazir Singh, Mr V. Ambiavagar and Mr Richard Tambyah and you have close friends like Mr T. P. B. Menon. RI taught me that there are good and bad people in every race, religion and of every colour and that the qualities of a man's mind and heart have nothing to do with his race, colour or creed.

Second, RI taught me to reject every form of social snobbery. Because RI was a public school and admission was based solely on merit, most of my classmates were from working class homes. I learnt early that wealth and high social status were not synonymous with ability and good character. I hope that Singapore will always be a society in which able students from the lower rungs of our socio-economic pyramid will have opportunities to rise to the top. I hope RI will never be a school only for rich men's sons. I understand that despite its conversion to independent status and the attendant charging of higher fees, RI and its Board of Governors are doing all within its means to preserve its character as a school for all.

Third, I learnt, from my ten years in the Boy Scout movement, three important values. I learnt that it is good to be altruistic, to want to do good deeds for others, especially for those in need of help. I learnt that one must take care of those over whom one exercises authority. I also learnt that one can lead others, not by instilling fear in them, as Machiavelli taught the prince to do, but by inspiring them with one's example and through teamwork.

Fourth, I learnt neither to look up to nor to look down upon the white men. I treat them as my equal and I expect them to treat me as their equal. Our headmaster, Mr John Young, and three of my expatriate teachers, Mr T. J. Evans, Mr A. J. Lippitt and Mr W. T. Andrews, treated us in an exemplary manner. As a result, I have neither a pro- nor an anti-*orang puteh* complex. I am grateful to them.

Finally, I want to acknowledge my intellectual and moral debt to my teachers. They taught me much of what I know. They helped to mould my character through both precept and example. To Mr V. Ambiavagar, Mr Philip Liau, Mr Wazir Singh, Mr Lim Teng Law, Mr Richard Thambyah, Mr N. Vaithinathan, Mr J. T. Christie, Mr Low Kee Pow, Mr Tan Teck

Chwee, Mr Ismail bin Abdul Aziz, Mr Tharam Singh, Mr Abdul Karim bin Bagoo, Mr C. T. Arasu, Mr Koh Eng Kiat, Mr Wee Seong Kang, Capt S. C. Thong and Mr Mallal, I want to use this opportunity to say, thank you. I also want to say that, in the final analysis, what will make RI a great school is not the excellence of its physical plant but the quality of its soft infrastructure, ie, the quality of the headmaster, the teachers and the student body.

Auspicium Melioris Aevi

Note added: RI's 170th Founder's Day Ceremony was held on 7 August 1993.

A Letter from Dean Griswold

In 1961, I was in my final year studying law at the Law Faculty of the University of Malaya — the antecedent of the National University of Singapore. In our final examinations, we had both internal and external examiners. One of my external examiners was Professor Sir James (Jim) Gower of London University. After the oral examination, Sir Jim asked me for my future plans. I told him that I would like to qualify to practise law and then proceed to England to study for a post-graduate degree in law.

Sir Jim Gower

Sir Jim advised me to reconsider my plans. He said that the legal education in England was very similar to that in Singapore. He thought I would derive more value by studying at Harvard Law School than at Oxbridge. He said he would recommend me to his friend, the Dean of Harvard Law School.

A Letter from Dean Griswold

A few months later, I received a letter from the then dean of Harvard Law School, Professor Erwin Griswold, offering me admission to the LLM class, plus a Harvard Law School Fellowship and a Fulbright Fellowship. It was an offer that was too good to refuse.

Two years later, in 1963, after I had been admitted to the legal profession and had spent a year teaching at the Law School, I left Singapore for Cambridge, Massachusetts, and joined the most famous law school in America, and possibly in the world, Harvard Law School.

Harvard Law School

I spent only one academic year, 1963–1964, at Harvard Law School, but Harvard has made an indelible impact on my life and on my attitude towards legal education and towards the law. Let me explain how this has happened.

Passion of the Teachers

First, how did Harvard influence my attitude towards legal education? I learnt many things at Harvard. I was very inspired by the passion of the professors for their work. All of them seemed to be writing learned books, articles or briefs. They were in their offices day and night. Their commitment to legal education and to the law seemed total. I felt privileged to study in a community where the teachers shared a high sense of purpose and were constantly thinking, talking and breathing about the law.

Harvard Case Class

Another thing which both inspired and intimidated me was the manner in which classes were taught. In Singapore, almost all my courses were taught by lectures and tutorials. At Harvard, almost all the classes were taught by the case class. Before going to each class, we had to read and digest the assigned reading.

In class, we had to sit in our assigned seats. The teacher would come to class carrying a huge chart with our photos and names. The teaching was in the form of a Socratic dialogue between the teacher and the students. The case class was a torture for students who were unprepared, timid or inarticulate. It was exhilarating for the good students. This method of teaching is, actually, not new. Both Socrates and Confucius had used it in their teaching.

Teaching Law in "The Grand Manner"

Unlike the traditional British style of legal education, which emphasised the black letter law, at Harvard, law was taught in what Justice Oliver

Wendel Holmes had called "the grand manner". What did that mean? It meant that we were encouraged to investigate the policy behind the law. It was desirable to do this so that we would be able to interpret and apply the law to achieve its intended policy. We were also encouraged to read non-legal materials because many solutions to a society's problems needed an inter-disciplinary approach. I took courses in law and economics, law and physical planning, law and sociology, and law and philosophy. We were challenged to think whether law could and should always be an instrument of justice. We agonised over the lawyer's ethical response to a situation in which the law was being used as an instrument of injustice or oppression. We were also challenged to be creative and to think out of the box. We were told not to be limited by precedent and by what had been tried before. We were rewarded, not punished, for coming up with new ways of solving a client's legal problems, of accommodating competing legal interests and of promoting justice.

From Harvard to the UN

Second, I think I should give Harvard some credit for my long connection with the United Nations. When my academic year was coming to an end, I saw Professor Joseph Leininger, the director of International Legal Studies, to seek his advice on what I could do during the summer of 1964 before I went across the Atlantic to join Cambridge University. In an act of serendipity or divine inspiration, Professor Leininger advised me to apply for an internship at the UN. I did so and was accepted. And the rest, as they say, is history. Four years later, in 1968, I would be back at the UN as Singapore's Permanent Representative. I would spend 13 years of my life at the United Nations.

Law of the Sea

As I look back on my long career at the UN, I derive great satisfaction from four challenging assignments. The first was to chair the Third UN Conference on the Law of the Sea. The conference was convened in 1973 to write a new constitution for the world's oceans. The president of the conference, Shirley Amerasinghe of Sri Lanka, had died of a heart attack in 1980. Following an unsuccessful attempt by the Asia Group to mediate between two competing candidates, the group requested that I succeed Amerasinghe as the president of the conference. I had the daunting task of resolving all outstanding disagreements and forging consensus on the 320 articles and nine annexes of the treaty. The 1982 Convention on the Law of the Sea has survived the test of time. It has brought legal order, certainty and peace to the world's oceans and seas. It is often regarded as one of the UN's most important contributions to the rule of law in the world.

Earth Summit

The second assignment was to chair the preparatory committee for, and the main committee at, the UN Conference on Environment and Development, often referred to as the Earth Summit. The UN had convened the historic Conference on the Human Environment in Stockholm, Sweden, in 1972, That conference had brought to humankind's urgent attention, the need to protect the world's natural environment. Twenty years later, the UN decided to convene an even more ambitious conference, to reconcile environment with development. I was elected by the UN in 1990 to chair the preparatory committee. After two years of hard work, the committee was unable to agree on any of the substantive issues except for the Rio Declaration of Principles on Environment and Development. When the Summit convened in Rio de Janeiro in June 1992, I was elected to chair the main committee. It was a race against time. In the space of just over a week, we had to achieve consensus and remove the brackets around over 300 disputed texts. We worked day and night, in big groups and small groups. It was a miracle that we were eventually able to adopt all the deliverables of the Earth Summit by consensus.

Making Peace Between Russia and the Baltic States

In 1993, the then UN Secretary-General, Boutros Boutros-Ghali, appointed me as his Special Envoy to undertake a peace mission to Russia,

Estonia, Latvia and Lithuania. Following the dissolution of the Soviet Union, the three Baltic States had recovered their independence. There were, however, some Russian troops and many Russian settlers in those countries. My mandate was to persuade Russia to agree to an early withdrawal of their troops and to persuade the three Baltic States to treat the Russian settlers, especially the elderly ones, with kindness. On the completion of my mission, I submitted a report to the UN General Assembly through the Secretary-General. I am very pleased that today, Russia and her three Baltic neighbours live at peace with one another and that Estonia, Latvia and Lithuania are part of the European Union.

Helping Cambodia

Cambodia has played a big part in my life since 1965. Cambodia was one of the first countries to recognise Singapore's independence. At the request of the Singapore government, the Singapore Institute of International Affairs was requested to send a goodwill delegation to Cambodia, in response to an invitation from Prince Norodom Sihanouk. I was a member of that delegation. In 1970, I was at the UN when Sihanouk was overthrown by General Lon Nol. In 1975, I was back at the UN when the Lon Nol government was overthrown by the Khmer Rouge. In 1978, the Khmer Rouge government was, in turn, overthrown by an invading Vietnamese army. From 1979 to 1991, I was part of the ASEAN team at the UN whose objectives were (a) to liberate Cambodia from Vietnam's occupation; (b) to prevent the Khmer Rouge from usurping power following Vietnam's withdrawal; and (c) to give the Cambodian people an opportunity to choose their own government and destiny. These objectives were finally achieved in 1991 at the Paris Conference. ASEAN's persistent diplomacy has paid off. Cambodia has been given a new lease of life.

Love Affair with America

Finally, I would like to give thanks to Sir Jim Gower, Dean Erwin Griswold and Harvard for having brought me to America in 1963. That fateful journey would alter the rest of my life. I have spent over 20 happy years in America, a country which I admire and regard as my second home. In another twist of fate, I was to meet Dean Griswold again many years later when I was Singapore's Ambassador in Washington, DC and he served as President Reagan's Solicitor-General. Griswold was already in his seventies but still fit and feisty. After he retired from government service, he remained in Washington and worked in a leading law firm. I had lunch with him on several occasions. He was very happy to learn that his 1961 letter to me had had such a major impact on my life journey.

I served as Singapore's ambassador to the United States from 1984 to 1990. The highlight of my posting was the campaign to persuade the two houses of the US Congress to invite Mr Lee Kuan Yew to address a joint session of the US Congress. The happy event occurred in October 1985. More recently, I was privileged to have served as Singapore's chief negotiator in the two-year negotiations to conclude a free trade agreement between the US and Singapore. I would like to thank The Asia Foundation for having asked me twice, in 1992 and in 2004, to chair workshops on Southeast Asia and to write reports on America's role in this region. I have also had the pleasure of serving on the board of directors of the Institute for the Study of Diplomacy at Georgetown University and as a co-convenor of the Williamsburg Conference of the Asia Society.

My association with Harvard has been a happy one. Over the past 40 years, my links with Harvard have expanded beyond the Law School to include the Kennedy School, the Business School, the Yengching Institute and the Institute for International Development. One of my happiest memories was the celebration of Harvard's 350th birthday. On that occasion, I had the great pleasure of speaking on a panel at the Kennedy School on *De Tocqueville Revisited*.

Being a son of Harvard has been a great blessing.

[Originally published in *The Harvard Exprience — Crimson Essays*, eds. B.H. Koh, K.W. Lee and A.S.C. Teo. © 2006 Harvard Singapore Foundation]

A Constitution for the Oceans

On 10 December 1982, we created a new record in legal history. Never in the annals of international law had a Convention been signed by 119 countries on the very first day on which it was opened for signature. Not only was the number of signatories a remarkable fact but just as important was the fact that the Convention had been signed by States from every region of the world, from the North and from the South, from the East and from the West, by coastal States as well as landlocked and geographically disadvantaged States.

When we set out on the long and arduous journey to secure a new Convention on the Law of the Sea, covering 25 subjects and issues, there were many who told us that our goal was too ambitious and not attainable. We proved the skeptics wrong, and we succeeded in adopting a Convention covering every aspect of the uses and resources of the sea.

The question is whether we achieved our fundamental objective of producing a comprehensive constitution for the oceans which will stand the test of time. My answer is in the affirmative for the following reasons:

- The Convention will promote the maintenance of international peace and security because it will replace a plethora of conflicting claims by coastal States with universally agreed limits on the territorial sea, on the contiguous zone, on the exclusive economic zone and on the continental shelf.
- The world community's interest in the freedom of navigation will be facilitated by the important compromises on the status of the exclusive economic zone, by the régime of innocent passage through the territorial sea, by the régime of transit passage through straits

used for international navigation and by the régime of archipelagic sea-lanes passage.
- The world community's interest in the conservation and optimum utilization of the living resources of the sea will be enhanced by the conscientious implementation of the provisions in the Convention relating to the exclusive economic zone.
- The Convention contains important new rules for the protection and preservation of the marine environment from pollution.
- The Convention contains new rules on marine scientific research which strike an equitable balance between the interests of the research States and the interests of the coastal States in whose economic zones or continental shelves the research is to be carried out.
- The world community's interest in the peaceful settlement of disputes and the prevention of use of force in the settlement of disputes between States have been advanced by the mandatory system of dispute settlement in the Convention.
- The Convention has succeeded in translating the principle that the resources of the deep sea-bed constitute the common heritage of mankind into fair and workable institutions and arrangements.
- Though far from ideal, we can nevertheless find elements of international equity in the Convention, such as revenue sharing on the continental shelf beyond 200 miles, giving landlocked and geographically disadvantaged States access to the living resources of the exclusive economic zones of their neighbouring States, the relationship between coastal fishermen and distant-water fishermen, and the sharing of the benefits derived from the exploitation of the resources of the deep seabed.

I would like to highlight the major themes which I found in the statements made by delegations at Montego Bay.

First, delegations said that the Convention does not fully satisfy the interests and objectives of any State. Nevertheless, they were of the view that it represents a monumental achievement of the international community, second only to the Charter of the United Nations. The Convention is the first comprehensive treaty dealing with practically every aspect of the uses and resources of the seas and the oceans. It has successfully accommodated the competing interests of all nations.

The second theme which emerged from the statements is that the provisions of the Convention are closely interrelated and form an integral package. Thus it is not possible for a State to pick what it likes and to disregard what it does not like. It was also said that rights and obligations go hand in hand and it is not permissible to claim rights under the Convention without being willing to shoulder the corresponding obligations.

The third theme I heard was that this Convention is not a codification Convention. The argument that, except for Part XI, the Convention codifies customary law or reflects existing international practice is factually incorrect and legally insupportable. The régime of transit passage through straits used for international navigation and the régime of archipelagic sea lanes passage are two examples of the many new concepts in the Convention. Even in the case of article 76 on the continental shelf, the article contains new law in that it has expanded the concept of the continental shelf to include the continental slope and the continental rise. This concession to the broad margin States was in return for their agreement for revenue-sharing on the continental shelf beyond 200 miles. It is therefore my view that a State which is not a party to this Convention cannot invoke the benefits of article 76.

The fourth theme relates to the lawfulness of any attempt to mine the resources of the international Area of the seabed and ocean floor. Speakers from every regional and interest group expressed the view that the doctrine of the freedom of the high seas can provide no legal basis for the grant by any State of exclusive title to a specific mine site in the international Area. Many are of the view that article 137 of the Convention has become as much a part of customary international law as the freedom of navigation. Any attempt by any State to mine the resources of the deep seabed outside the Convention will earn the universal condemnation of the international community and will incur grave political and legal consequences. All speakers have addressed an earnest appeal to the

United States to reconsider its position. The United States is a country which has, throughout its history, supported the progressive development of international law and has fought for the rule of law in the relations between States. The present position of the United States Government towards this Convention is, therefore, inexplicable in the light of its history, in the light of its specific law of the sea interests and in the light of the leading role which it has played in negotiating the many compromises which have made this treaty possible.

A final theme which emerged from the statements concerns the Preparatory Commission. Now that the required number of States have signed the Convention, the Preparatory Commission for the establishment of the International SeaBed Authority and the International Tribunal for the Law of the Sea will begin its work. The Commission will have to adopt the rules and procedures for the implementation of resolution II, relating to pioneer investors. It will, *inter alia*, draft the detailed rules, regulations and procedures for the mining of the seabed. If it carries out its work in an efficient, objective and business-like manner, we will have a viable system for the mining of the deep seabed. This will induce those who are standing on the sidelines to come in and support the Convention. If, on the other hand, the Preparatory Commission does not carry out its tasks in an efficient, objective and practical manner, then all our efforts in the last 14 years will have been in vain.

In the report of the Secretary-General on the work of the United Nations (A/37/1) dated 7 September 1982, he wrote:

> We have seen, in the case of the law of the sea..., what remarkable results can be achieved in well-organized negotiations within the United Nations framework, even on the most complex of issues...

It may be helpful to identify those features of the negotiating process of this Conference which were productive, and to distil some wisdom from our experience.

I would point, *first* of all, to the importance of reaching agreements on substantive matters on which States have important interests by consensus.

The Conference was wise to resist the temptation of putting substantive proposals to the vote, because those who vote against a proposal would naturally not feel bound by it. The consensus procedure, however, requires all delegations, those in the majority as well as those in the minority, to make efforts, in good faith, to accommodate the interests of others.

Second, the Conference took the wise decision that the package deal approach did not preclude it from allocating the 25 different subjects and issues to different negotiating forums, so long as the results were brought together to form an integral whole.

Third, the group system in the Conference contributed to its work by helping delegations to identify their positions and by enabling negotiations to take place between competing interest groups. The group system should, however, be used with flexibility and not be allowed to paralyze the negotiating process with rigidity.

Fourth, the negotiations in this Conference could not have been brought to a successful conclusion if we had failed to progressively miniaturize them. It is obvious that no meaningful negotiations can take place in a forum consisting of 160 delegations.

Fifth, there is a role for the main committees, for formal negotiating groups, for informal negotiating groups and even for privately convened negotiating groups. In general, the more informal a negotiating group, the more likely are we to make progress. Some of the most intractable problems of the Conference were resolved in privately convened negotiating groups, such as the Evensen Group and the Castañeda Group.

Sixth, the Drafting Committee and its language groups played a very important role in the negotiating process. It was due to their hard work that we have one treaty in six languages and not six treaties in six languages.

Seventh, the leaders of a conference can play a significant role in determining the success or failure of a conference. In our case, we were extremely fortunate that the Collegium worked well together. The Conference could well have floundered during its many crises if the Collegium had not been united and if it had failed to provide the Conference with leadership.

Eighth, the Secretariat played an important role in the work of this Conference. The members of the Secretariat, under the able leadership of the Special Representative of the Secretary-General, not only provided the Conference with excellent services but also ably assisted the President and the Chairmen of the various committees and groups in the negotiations. I should like to take this opportunity to thank Mr Bernardo Zuleta and his loyal Deputy, Mr David Hall.

Ninth, I should also acknowledge the role played by the non-governmental organizations, such as the Neptune Group. They provided the Conference with three valuable services. They brought independent experts to meet with delegations, thus enabling us to have an independent source of information on technical issues. They assisted representatives from developing countries to narrow the technical gap between them and their counterparts from developed countries. They also provided us with opportunities to meet, away from the Conference, in a more relaxed atmosphere, to discuss some of the most difficult issues confronted by the Conference.

Although the Convention consists of a series of compromises, they form an integral whole. This is why the Convention does not provide for reservations. It is therefore not possible for States to pick what they like and disregard what they do not like. In international law, as in domestic law, rights and duties go hand in hand. It is therefore legally impermissible to claim rights under the Convention without being willing to assume the correlative duties.

Let no nation put asunder this landmark achievement of the international community.

I cannot conclude without recalling, once more, our collective debt to two men, Hamilton Shirley Amerasinghe [former President of the Conference] and Arvid Pardo [former Permanent Representative of Malta to the United Nations]. Arvid Pardo contributed two seminal ideas to our work: first, that the resources of the deep seabed constitute the common heritage of mankind, and second, that all aspects of ocean space are interrelated and should be treated as an integral whole. Shirley Amerasinghe led our efforts from 1968 until his untimely death in 1979.

In the final analysis, I believe that this Conference succeeded because it brought together a "critical mass" of colleagues who were outstanding lawyers and negotiators. We succeeded because we did not regard our counterparts in the negotiations as the enemies to be conquered. We considered the issues under dispute as the common obstacles to be overcome. We worked not only to promote our individual national interests but also in pursuit of our common dream of writing a constitution for the oceans.

We have strengthened the United Nations by proving that with political will, nations can use the Organization as a centre to harmonize their actions. We have shown that with good leadership and management, the United Nations can be an efficient forum for the negotiation of complex issues. We celebrate the victory of the rule of law and of the principle of the peaceful settlement of disputes. Finally, we celebrate human solidarity and the reality of interdependence which is symbolized by the United Nations Convention on the Law of the Sea.

[Adapted from statements by the President on 6 and 11 December 1982 at the final session of the Conference at Montego Bay. Reproduced by kind permission of the United Nations.]

Commemoration of the 30th Anniversary of the Opening for Signature of the 1982 UNCLOS*

Mr President, Mr Secretary-General, Distinguished Delegates, Ladies and Gentlemen. I wish to greet my colleagues from the Law of the Sea Conference who are here. With advancing age, they have become a highly endangered species of homo sapiens. Let us extend a warm welcome to them.

Thirty years ago, the United Nations Convention on the Law of the Sea, was adopted after a decade of patient and painstaking negotiations. On the 10th of December, 1982, the Convention was opened for signature and was signed by 119 States. The Convention today has 161 Parties who are members of the United Nations. This means that there are 32 Member States which have not yet become parties to the Convention. One of them is our host country, the United States of America. I apologise in advance to the distinguished representative of the United States in case she or he will be offended by what I am about to say. When my wife asked me recently when the US will accede to the Convention, I answered her by quoting Churchill, who once said that we can always count on the United States to do the right thing, after it has tried everything else. I hope we do not have to wait much longer as the Convention is clearly in the interests of the United States and of the other 31 States.

I wish to make three points.

---

*Speech delivered on 10 December 2012 at the 30th Anniversary Commemoration Ceremony.

First, I wish to observe that the Convention has become the constitution for the oceans and seas. It is both comprehensive and authoritative. It has established a stable maritime legal order. It has kept the peace at sea. In this way, it has made a significant contribution to the Rule of Law in the world. The only parts of the world's oceans in which maritime disputes could threaten international peace are the East China Sea and the South China Sea. I would like to use this opportunity to call upon all the claimant States to act with restraint and to resolve their disputes peacefully and strictly in accordance with international law and the United Nations Convention on the Law of the Sea. Negotiations should always be our first preference. However, if negotiations do not succeed, I would urge the parties to consider referring their disputes to conciliation, mediation, arbitration or adjudication by the International Tribunal for the Law of the Sea or the International Court of Justice. As an Asian, I know that in some Asian cultures, there is a reluctance to take a friend to court. To those clamaint states who feel this way, I would encourage them to focus on the joint development of the disputed areas.

Second, I wish to point out that the Convention represents a careful balance of the competing interests of all States, both developed and developing, coastal States and landlocked and geographically disadvantaged States, port States and seafaring States, States with artisanal fishermen and States with distant water fishermen, etc. The balance was arrived at through an open, transparent and inclusive process, in which all States had the opportunity to participate and to contribute to the compromises. The balance has worked well and stood the test of time. We should therefore be faithful in our interpretation and application of the Convention. We should avoid undermining the integrity of the Convention by taking actions of questionable legality in order to further our short-term national interests. In some cases, States have taken advantage of ambiguous language in the text of the Convention. In other cases, they are finding ambiguity where none exists. Let me cite some examples. Some States have drawn straight baselines when they are not entitled to do so. Some States have enacted domestic legislation to regulate certain activities in the Exclusive Economic Zone (EEZ) even though the Convention has not conferred such jurisdiction on the coastal States.

Other States have acted on the mistaken assumption that the EEZ is part of the High Sea, forgetting that the Convention enjoins them to have due regard to the rights and duties of the coastal State and to comply with the laws and regulations adopted by the coastal State provided, of course, that such laws and regulations are in accordance with the Convention. Some States have acted in contravention of the regime of transit passage. Some States have made maritime claims from insular features which exceed what is justified under the Convention. This is not an exhaustitive list.

Third, I wish to refer to the Secretary-General's initiative, The Oceans Compact, which he unveiled at the Yeosu International Conference, on the 12th of August 2012. The Compact has the following three objectives: (i) to protect vulnerable people and improve the health of the oceans; (ii) to protect, recover and sustain the oceans' environment and natural resources and to restore their full food production and livelihood services; and (iii) to strengthen knowledge and the management of the oceans. Let me make a few comments on the Secretary-General's initiative.

The Food and Agriculture Organization (FAO) has repeatedly called the world's attention to the crisis in the world's fisheries. The crisis has been caused by overfishing; by illegal, unreported and unregulated fishing; by the ineffectiveness of the regional fishery management organisations and by the use of destructive and unsustainable methods of fishing. Subsidies for the fishing industry should be phased out because they have led to overcapacity. The world can learn from the successful experiences of Iceland and New Zealand in the management of their fisheries. The IMO should consider requiring all commercial fishing vessels to be licensed and to carry transponders. Regional fishery management organisations should be established in all regions of the world and they should be empowered to make their decisions by consensus if possible and by majority votes if necessary. Certain highly destructive methods of fishing should be banned. The FAO's code of conduct for responsible fisheries should be strengthened.

The nexus between climate change and the oceans is not sufficiently understood. The oceans serve as the blue lungs of the planet, absorbing carbon dioxide from the atmosphere and returning oxygen to the atmosphere. The oceans also play a role in regulating the world's climate system. One impact of global warming is that our oceans are getting warmer and more acidic. This will have a devastating impact on the world's coral reefs and on marine biodiversity. The welfare of 150 million people, who live in coastal communities, will be affected if we allow the reefs to degenerate and die.

Another impact of global warming and climate change is the rise of sea levels. The problem is not theoretical but real. Low-lying countries such as Bangladesh and island countries such as the Maldives and those in the South Pacific, have already experienced the loss of land to the rising sea. The members of the Association of Small Island States (AOSIS) have made a compelling case and we should listen more attentively to them. If sea levels continue to rise, millions of people will lose their homes and become ecological refugees. I hope that our colleagues who are engaged in the ongoing climate change negotiations will address this threat expeditiously.

I also support the Secretary-General's call to strengthen knowledge and the management of the oceans. We seem to know less about the oceans than about outer space. The oceans are our last frontier. The United Nations University, under the able leadership of its new President David Malone, should ignite a new interest in research on the oceans and on oceans law and policies. The UN, under the leadership of Patricia O'Brien and Serguei Tarrsenko, should incentivise the law schools of the world to promote research in and the teaching of the law of the sea.

I shall conclude. Fifty years ago, the old maritime legal order was crumbling. There were many maritime disputes between States. Two European countries even fought a brief war over cod. In response to this situation, the United Nations convened the Third United Nations Conference on the Law of the Sea to negotiate a new legal order. The Conference held its first session in 1973. After nine years of negotiations, the Convention was adopted in 1982. Many learned men and women, of good will, from over 150 countries, participated in that historic endeavour. Many have passed away. However, their legacy of a new maritime legal order, bringing peace, order and equity, will never be forgotten.

Thank you very much.

Making Peace Between Russia and the Baltics*

Introduction

In 1992, the then UN Secretary-General, Dr Boutros Boutros-Ghali, had approved of the manner in which I had managed and chaired the Earth Summit in Rio de Janeiro. He asked me to join his cabinet in New York and to take charge of all matters relating to environment and sustainable development. I declined on the ground that I saw a conflict of interest in going from chairing the UN Conference on Environment and Development (UNCED) to taking on a position on the issues covered by the Conference, in the UN Secretariat. He told me that he did not see any conflict of interest.

A few months later, Dr Boutros-Ghali called me and requested me to accept appointment as his Special Envoy to undertake a "mission impossible". I told the Secretary-General that the chances of success were very slim but would be enhanced if I had the unanimous support of the five permanent members of the Security Council. I requested him to inform them of his intention to appoint me and to get their backing. Dr Boutros-Ghali refused to do so on the ground that the resolution adopted by the UN General Assembly had empowered him to make the

---

*This speech was prepared by Tommy Koh as Guest-of-Honour at the Singapore Mediation Centre's 10th Anniversary celebrations on 17 August 2007. Footnotes have been added by AJM Editor only to explain abbreviations.

appointment without consulting the Security Council. I respected his position but declined the appointment.

In the summer of 1993, I received another call from Dr Boutros-Ghali requesting me to accept appointment as his Special Envoy to Russia, Latvia, Lithuania and Estonia. I decided not to rebuff him for the third time but confessed to him that I had never been to the four countries. In a humourous response, he said, "That's good. You will go with an open mind and carry no baggage from the past." When my appointment was reported in *The Straits Times*, several of my wife's friends called her to express concern for my safety. They had, understandably, confused the Baltics with the Balkans!

The Historical Background

The three Baltic countries, Estonia, Latvia and Lithuania, are, like Singapore, relatively small countries. Estonia has a population of 1.3 million. Its beautiful capital is Tallinn. Its neighbours are Russia to the east, Latvia to the south and Sweden to the west. It lies opposite Finland, with which it shares commonalities of language and culture. Estonia existed as an independent country from 1918 to 1939 and since 1991. Estonia was occupied by the Soviet Union in 1940 and by Nazi Germany from 1941 to 1944 and lost its independence when Stalin incorporated it into the Soviet Union in the fall of 1944.

In 1993, there were between 5,000 and 6,000 Russian troops and about 50,000 Russian veterans and retirees in Estonia. There was also a Russian nuclear submarine training centre in Paldiski which had been closed but had to be carefully dismantled and removed.

Latvia

Latvia has a population of 2.2 million and its beautiful capital is called Riga. It is located between Estonia in the north, Russia to the east,

Lithuania to the south and Belarus to the southeast. It was an independent country from 1918 to 1939. It was occupied by Nazi Germany from 1941 to 1944 and also lost its independence when it was incorporated into the Soviet Union at the end of the Second World War.

In 1993, there were 18,000 Russian troops and about 20,000 Russian pensioners and their families in Latvia. In addition, Russia had a naval base in Liepaja, an anti-ballistic missile early warning system in Skrunda and a facility in Venspils to monitor space objects (Russian version) or to eavesdrop on communications in Northern Europe (Latvian version).

Lithuania

Lithuania has a population of 3.5 million and its historic capital is called Vilnius. It is located between Latvia to the north, the Baltic Sea to the west and Poland to the south. Russia enjoys sovereignty over a corridor passing through Lithuanian territory to the Baltic port of Kaliningrad. Lithuania was the luckiest of the three Baltic States and suffered the least harm and damage from Stalin. Estonia and Latvia had resisted Stalin's unilateral decision to incorporate them into the Soviet Union. In reprisal, Stalin sent the anti-Soviet elites of the two countries into exile in Siberia. Many perished. In Lithuania, as then President Brazauskas had explained to me, they decided not to resist Stalin. Instead, they all joined the Communist Party. As a result, there were very few Russian soldiers or settlers in Lithuania.

Break-up of the Russian Empire

The end of the Cold War and the dissolution of the Russian empire was a truly historic event. A major burden for the new Russian Government was the return of the Red Army from the various Soviet Republics which had become independent, and the need to build housing and to find jobs for the returnees. I saw for myself, at a military camp outside Moscow, the terrible conditions in which the troops and their families, which had returned from

Lithuania, were being housed. This convinced me that the withdrawal of the Russian troops had to be phased and that there should be an international effort to help Russia built decent housing for the returnees.

The UN General Resolution 47/21 of 1992

On 24 August 1991, Russia agreed to restore independence to Estonia, Latvia and Lithuania and formally recognized their independent status on 6 September 1991. The Baltic States demanded the withdrawal of Russian troops from their territories. The four governments held several rounds of talks between 1992 and 1993 on an agenda consisting of the timing of the withdrawal of the Russian troops, the welfare of the Russian populations in those countries, and questions relating to the submarine training centre in Estonia, and the three facilities in Latvia. Frustrated by the slow pace of progress, Estonia, Latvia and Lithuania submitted the question to the UN General Assembly and succeeded in persuading the Assembly to adopt a resolution (47/21) which, inter alia, urged the Secretary-General to "use his good offices". The Secretary-General appointed me to carry out his mandate.

The Office of the UN Secretary-General's Envoy

Role of UN Special Envoy

The role of the Special Envoy is similar to that of an international mediator. He is not an arbitrator or a judge. A Special Envoy can only make recommendations to the parties to a dispute. It is up to them to decide whether to accept his recommendations or not. Before embarking on my mission, I spent several months reading all the books and literature I could find on the histories and cultures of the three Baltic countries and their relations with Russia, Germany and other neighbours. When I visited Moscow, Lithuania, Latvia and Estonia, I practiced the art of deep listening. I tried my best to understand their different perspectives, their demand and their feelings and to be fair in my recommendations.

I enlisted the support of the five permanent members of the Security Council, the European Community, the CSCE[1] (now called OSCE[2]), and countries which were willing to help resolve the problem, such as, the United States, Germany and the Scandinavian countries. I tried to persuade the Russians, Estonians, Latvians and Lithuanians to show goodwill and flexibility towards each other. In Estonia and Latvia, where I encountered strong anti-Russian feelings, I urged them to forgive Stalin for the many atrocities he had committed against them and to look to the future. I gently reminded them that they were destined to live next door to Russia, which was weak then but would be strong again. At the end of my mission, I submitted a report to the Secretary-General which was, in turn, submitted to the UN General Assembly.

My Recommendations

Lithuania

I will never forget the day I arrived in Vilnius from Moscow, on 31 August 1993. I was received by the Chief of Protocol at the airport and taken to the square in front of the Parliament where I found that thousands of people had gathered to celebrate the happy day on which the last Russian combat troops had left Lithuanian territory. From the Parliament Square, I was escorted to the President's Residence where another party was being held. When I was introduced to President Brazauskas, I congratulated him and asked him for the story. He was a big and humourous man. He was formerly the head of the Lithuanian Communist Party and a good friend of Boris Yeltsin. He said that, in anticipation of my visit, he had called Yeltsin on 30 August and persuaded him to agree to withdraw the

---
[1] Council for Security and Cooperation in Europe.
[2] Organisation for Security and Cooperation in Europe.

few remaining Russian troops the next day. I was, of course, overjoyed because the problem had been solved.

Latvia

The situation in Latvia was more complicated. I made the following recommendations. *First*, on the timing for the withdrawal of Russian troops, I appealed to both sides to compromise. To the Russians, I explained that an earlier date was important to the Latvians for political and psychological reasons. To the Latvians, I pleaded for patience in order to give the Russians the time needed to build housing for the 18,000 troops and their families. *Second*, on the fate of the 20,000 Russian military pensioners and their families, I found out that 87 percent of them would like to remain in Latvia and become Latvian citizens. I recommended that those who had settled in Latvia, before 4 May 1990, the date on which Latvia had declared its independence, should be granted permanent residence. As most of the pensioners were elderly, I also recommended that their housing and medicare should not be withdrawn. *Third*, after visiting the Russian naval base in Liepaja, I was not persuaded by Russia's request to retain the base for an additional five to six years. *Fourth*, as for Skrunda and Venspils, I recommended that the two sides should negotiate agreements for Russia to lease those facilities, for an agreed period of time, so that she could replace those facilities inside Russian territory.

Estonia

Estonia was the most difficult case. This was partly due to the fact that of the three countries, Estonians suffered the most under Stalin and because of the large numbers of Russian military retirees and their families, amounting to 52,000. The then President of Estonia, Mr L. Meri, explained to me that about a third of the Estonian population, including his own family, had been deported to Siberia. The recent incident, resulting from the Estonian Government's decision to relocate the statue of a Russian soldier from the centre of the city to a less conspicuous location, is a reminder that both communities in Estonia are still haunted by the ghosts of the past. I was scolded by some members of the Estonian Parliament when I urged them to embrace the virtue of forgiveness.

I made the following recommendations concerning Estonia. *First*, on the date of the troop withdrawal, I suggested a compromise between the Estonian's deadline of end 1993 and the Russian's deadline of end 1994. *Second*, concerning the discontinued nuclear submarine training centre at Paldiski, I urged the two sides to solve the problem as a technical, not a political one. The nuclear reactors had been deactivated but the nuclear fuel rods, the nuclear waste in storage and other nuclear materials had to be taken out by rail to St. Petersburg. If necessary, I suggested to the two parties to request the help of IAEA.[3]

Third, the most contentious issue was the fate of the 52,000 Russian settlers who wished to remain in Estonia because they had no homes in Russia to go back to. I recommended that all those who had retired before Estonia regained its independence should be allowed to remain in Estonia and continue to enjoy their housing and medical benefits. In a meeting with representatives of the Russian Union of Veterans and Pensioners, I told them that they could no longer expect to enjoy special rights and privileges but should be treated with fairness and humanity. I also said that those Russians who wanted to become Estonian citizens must be loyal to Estonia, learn its language and respect its culture.

Success of the Mission

My peace mission to Russia and the Baltics was successful because I was lucky with the timing and because my efforts complemented those of several other organisations, countries and individuals. In 1993, Russia was weak and in serious economic difficulties. Yeltsin needed the help of the West and was willing to be cooperative in the Baltics. The Baltic countries had many champions apart from the UN, including the European Community, the Council for Security and Cooperation in Europe (now renamed as OSCE), the Council of Europe, the United States, Germany and the

---
[3] International Atomic Energy Agency.

Scandinavian countries. Denmark, Norway and the US had provided Russia with financial assistance to help her build housing for the returning troops and their families. I must also acknowledge my thanks to the then US Ambassador in Moscow, Tom Pickering. Ambassador Pickering arranged for me to meet one of President Yeltsin's staffers in the Kremlin, who apparently had more influence with the President than the hardliners in the Ministries of Foreign Affairs and Defence with whom I was negotiating.

Conclusion

My one experience of having served as an international mediator was a positive one. I am glad that I was able to make a small contribution to Estonia, Latvia and Lithuania and their important relations with Russia. Since 1993, the three Baltic countries have made impressive economic progress. They also feel more secure as members of the EU and NATO.

I believe that there are other Singaporeans as well as other Asians who would make good international mediators. I hope that the Singapore Mediation Centre, which has been successful in promoting mediation as a modality for settling disputes in Singapore, would consider expanding its role to include international mediation.

I am very pleased that the mediation centres of Hong Kong, Indonesia, Malaysia, Philippines and Singapore will be signing a Memorandum of Understanding to establish the Asian Mediation Association. I wish the Association success in the years ahead.

[Originally published as "International Mediation: The Experience of a UN Special Envoy", *Asian J. Mediation*, 2008, pp. 1–6.]

My Cambodian Story

My Cambodian story begins in 1965, when Singapore suddenly found itself separated from the Federation of Malaysia and became a new sovereign and independent country. The Kingdom of Cambodia, headed by Prince Norodom Sihanouk, was one of the first countries to recognise Singapore's independence. A few months later, as a gesture of goodwill, the government of Cambodia invited the government of Singapore to send a goodwill delegation to visit Cambodia. As the newly established Ministry of Foreign Affairs was still finding its feet, the Singapore government turned to a non-governmental organisation, the Singapore Institute of International Affairs (SIIA), to organise such a delegation.

Goodwill Delegation to Cambodia: 1965

The SIIA was founded by a group of like-minded friends, who were interested in international affairs, in 1961. I was one of the founding members. As the Honorary Secretary of the Institute, I had corresponded with the Royal Institute of International Affairs (Chatham House), to seek their guidance and advice. The President of the Institute was a Scottish colonial official, Mr G. G. Thomson, who was the Director of the Political Studies Centre, established by the PAP government to educate the civil servants on the political trends and developments of the region and the political agenda of the government.

A Magical Evening at Angkor Wat

Mr Thomson and I organised a delegation of about 20 members, consisting mainly of members of the Institute. We were a motley crew, consisting of both locals and expatriates. We spent a week in Cambodia, visiting Phnom Penh and Siem Reap. Phnom Penh was, at that time, a small, beautiful and peaceful city. The war in South Vietnam seemed far away and we did not understand why the senior Cambodian officials we met had expressed the fear that Cambodia might be sucked into that conflict. In Siem Reap, we were treated to an unforgettable experience. We were invited to watch a performance by the Royal Cambodian Ballet, with Princess Bopha Devi as the prima ballerina, under a full moon, at Angkor Wat. It was a magical evening. Thus began my involvement with Cambodia, with eight encounters with this beautiful but tragic country.

Lon Nol Seizes Power

My next encounter with Cambodia occurred five years later, in 1970. In that year, the Prime Minister, General Lon Nol, overthrew Prince Norodom Sihanouk and seized power. Unlike Samdech Sihanouk's stance of neutrality, Lon Nol supported the South Vietnamese and the Americans in their fight against the Viet Cong and North Vietnam. As a result, Cambodia was consumed by the Vietnam War.

Cambodia's Seat at the UN: 1970

In 1970, I was the Permanent Representative of Singapore to the United Nations. The issue at the UN was who should occupy Cambodia's seat. There were two contenders for that seat: Sihanouk's government-in-exile based in Beijing and the government of General Lon Nol. Singapore followed the British and mainstream views on recognition. Although our sympathies were with Sihanouk, we recognised the government of Lon

Nol because it complied with the criteria prescribed by international law, namely, it was in occupation of the country's territory and enjoyed the obedience of the people.

Cambodia's Seat Occupied by Khmer Rouge: 1975

My third encounter with Cambodia occurred in 1975. Following the fall of Saigon and South Vietnam, it was a matter of time before the two neighbouring States, Cambodia and Laos, would fall to the communists. Laos accepted the inevitable and the change of power took place peacefully. In the case of Cambodia, the regime of General Lon Nol fell to the forces of the Khmer Rouge, after several years of bloody civil war. Cambodia's seat at the UN was vacated by Lon Nol's representatives and occupied by representatives of the Khmer Rouge, which styled the country as "Democratic Kampuchea". The ASEAN countries were wary of the Khmer Rouge and kept their distance. Sihanouk had returned from exile as the nominal Head of State. The world knew little of what was going on inside Cambodia, although we heard unconfirmed stories of the horrors taking place inside that country.

Saving Cambodian Lives

My fourth encounter with Cambodia occurred in the late 1970s. After years of rumours about how the Khmer Rouge had turned Cambodia into a living hell, thousands of sick, desperate and starving Cambodians had fled to the Thai-Cambodian border. They had escaped their Khmer Rouge captors and trekked for days and weeks towards the border to seek refuge and succour. The UN Secretary-General, Dr Kurt Waldheim; UN agencies, led by UNHCR; the ICRC; ASEAN countries, led by Thailand; and the international community, sprang into action. Huge refugee camps were built, inside Thai territory, to look after tens of thousands of Cambodians. I visited one such camp called Khao-I-Dang, and was very impressed by what I saw.

Vietnam Invades Cambodia: 1978

My fifth encounter with Cambodia began on Christmas Day 1978. Vietnam sent its armed forces into Cambodia, to overthrow its former ally, the Khmer Rouge, and to replace it with a Vietnam-backed regime headed by Heng Samrin. The ASEAN countries were faced with a moral dilemma. On the one hand, ASEAN, like the rest of the world, was relieved that the Khmer Rouge had been ousted from power. On the other hand, ASEAN regarded the precedent set by Vietnam as a danger to its own security. ASEAN decided that the Vietnamese invasion and occupation of Cambodia was the greater of the two evils. ASEAN, therefore, requested an urgent meeting of the UN Security Council to consider the situation and to demand a withdrawal of Vietnamese forces from Cambodia. The Council voted on a draft resolution submitted by ASEAN. Although it received 11 positive votes, it was vetoed by the Soviet Union.

ASEAN's Diplomatic Objectives

As part of my sixth encounter with Cambodia, I was involved in ASEAN's Cambodian diplomacy, from December 1978 until the signing of the Paris Agreement in 1991. During this long campaign, ASEAN's objectives were as follows:

(a) Prevent the Heng Samrin regime from occupying Cambodia's seat at the UN;
(b) Isolate Vietnam diplomatically and economically in order to pressure Vietnam to come to the negotiating table;
(c) Persuade the Khmer Rouge; the Cambodian resistance movement led by Sihanouk and his son, Ranariddh; and the resistance movement led by the nationalist, Son Sann; to form a coalition government;
(d) Help the armed resistance against the Vietnamese to gain traction and prevent the Vietnamese occupation of Cambodia from becoming a *fait accompli*;

(e) Work closely with the UN Secretary-General, the UN Security Council and the Non-Aligned Movement to persuade Vietnam, and its patron, the Soviet Union, that the only solution to the Cambodian conflict was a negotiated one; and

(f) Negotiate an international agreement to bring the Cambodian conflict to a peaceful conclusion, to accept the UN as the interim administration of Cambodia, to give the people of Cambodia the right to determine their own future and to restore Cambodia's sovereignty and independence in a free and fair election.

The Paris Conferences of 1989 and 1991

In August 1989, France convened the first international conference on Cambodia, in Paris. The reason why the conference was convened by France and not by the UN was that Vietnam and the Phnom Penh regime would not attend a conference convened by the UN. We understood that Vietnam and Sihanouk had appealed to France to be the convener.

The Paris Conference was co-chaired by France and Indonesia. France invited Indonesia to be the co-chair because Indonesia had paved the way for the convening of the Paris Conference. It had done so by convening the first and second Jakarta Informal Meeting (JIM), which brought together the four Cambodian parties, Vietnam, Laos and the ASEAN countries. JIM I and JIM II had succeeded in defining the issues and narrowed the gap between the two sides.

The 1989 Paris Conference failed. It failed because France had misjudged the timing. In the summer of 1989, Vietnam was not ready to compromise. It had still hoped for victory on the battle field.

The Cold War ended in 1991 with the collapse of the USSR and, with it, the Soviet empire was dissolved. Vietnam lost its patron, the Soviet Union. In 1991, France re-convened the conference. This time, all the parties were ready to settle and to compromise. It was a very happy day for me to be present at the signing of the Paris Agreement, putting an end to a conflict which had lasted over twenty years. Thus ended my seventh encounter with Cambodia.

UNTAC

My eighth encounter with Cambodia was to help the UN Transition Authority in Cambodia (UNTAC) succeed in its mission. The UN Secretary-General had chosen Japan's most senior UN official, Yasushi Akashi, as his Special Representative and head of UNTAC. I was serving as Singapore's Ambassador to the United States at that time. The Chairman of the Sub-Committee on East Asia and the Pacific of the Committee on Foreign Affairs of the US House of Representative, Congressman Stephen Solarz, had asked for my opinion on who the UN Secretary-General should appoint to that post. I told Congressman Solarz that the UN should appoint a Japanese. Akashi was (and is) a close friend and I did everything I could to help him succeed in his difficult task. Singapore contributed a police contingent to help keep the peace. When Akashi wanted to start a UN radio in Cambodia, he asked me to help him recruit a competent Singaporean. I managed to find Ms Zhou Mei, who did a very good job. The UN radio played an important role in persuading the Cambodian people not to be afraid of the Khmer Rouge and to go and cast their ballots.

Mission Impossible

The Khmer Rouge had refused to lay down their arms and to participate in the UN-supervised elections. One day, I received a telephone call from the UN Secretary-General, Dr Boutros-Ghali. He asked me to undertake a secret mission on his behalf. The mission was to see the Khmer Rouge leader, Pol Pot, and to persuade him to participate in the elections. I told the Secretary-General that it was a mission impossible as the UN did not know where to find Pol Pot. I urged him to speak to China and Thailand, and to ask for their assistance. In the end, the Khmer Rouge boycotted the elections and tried unsuccessfully to intimidate the Cambodian people to do the same.

UNTAC: Lessons Learnt

In 1994, Dr Marcel Boisard, the Executive Director of UNITAR, and I, as Director of the Institute of Policy Studies (IPS), co-convened an international conference on UNTAC, to review its successes and failures and to seek lessons to be learnt. The conference was co-chaired by Boisard, me and Hisashi Owada, currently the President of the International Court of Justice. The conference also led to the publication of a book in 1995, edited by Nassrine Azimi of UNITAR, entitled *The United Nations Transitional Authority in Cambodia (UNTAC): Debriefing and Lessons*. The conference was the first opportunity for those involved in UNTAC to debrief their experiences. The conference also paved the way for the establishment of the Lessons Learned Unit, in the UN Department of Peacekeeping Operations.

Reflections

I wish to conclude with three reflections.

First, the Paris Agreement of 1991 represents, for the world, the victory of international law and the rule of law over military might. It was also a victory for diplomacy and negotiations. During the debate in the UN Security Council, in early 1979, the Permanent Representative of Vietnam to the UN told me that the situation in Cambodia was irreversible. He also said that the world would soon come to accept the *fait accompli*. ASEAN refused to be intimidated by the so-called reality on the ground. We persisted in our mission because we believed that our cause was just and that we would eventually succeed in helping Cambodia to recover its independence and, at the same time, to be liberated from the terror of the Khmer Rouge.

Second, the ASEAN diplomacy on Cambodia was the most important diplomatic battle which ASEAN has fought since its founding. In the beginning, the odds against us were formidable. Vietnam enjoyed the support of the Soviet bloc as well as the pro-Soviet wing of the Non-Aligned Movement, including such influential countries as India and Cuba. ASEAN diplomacy succeeded because the ASEAN team of five was united, tireless and skilful. A whole generation of ASEAN diplomats forged their skills in the decade-long campaign. Our success at the UN put ASEAN on the map as a diplomatic player of substance and significance.

Third, twenty years have passed since the signing of the Paris Agreement in October 1991. Fifty-six years have passed since my first visit to Cambodia. When I look back to the past and reflect on the present, I feel both sad and optimistic. I feel sad because I have seen so much suffering, mass killing and destruction in Cambodia. I feel optimistic because in the past twenty years, Cambodia has, like the proverbial phoenix, emerged from the ashes of war. Cambodia has made enormous progress in the last twenty years, in nation-building and in becoming a contributing member of the ASEAN family. In 2005, I led a delegation from the National Heritage Board of Singapore to visit Cambodia. Our mission was to make friends with the Cambodian officials in charge of culture and their museums and to offer Singapore's friendship and help. I wish Cambodia, a country I love, continued success in its journey to a bright future.

[Originally published in *Cambodia: Progress and Challenges since 1991*, eds. P. Sothirak, G. Wade and M. Hong, pp. 11–17. © 2012 Institute of Southeast Asian Studies]

The ASEF Story
The First Three Years

PM Goh's Vision

The historic summit in Bangkok, between the sixteen leaders of the European Union and ten leaders of East Asia, held on 1 March 1996, was the realisation of Singapore Prime Minister Goh Chok Tong's vision. In September 1994 in Singapore, and subsequently at Davos in early 1995, Prime Minister Goh made the argument that the time had come for the European Union and East Asia to forge closer ties to complement their strong ties with the United States. At the Bangkok Summit, Prime Minister Goh made an interesting observation and proposal. He observed that the new and comprehensive partnership between Asia and Europe should not be confined to government and business. It should include the civil societies of the two regions. Towards this end, he proposed the establishment of the Asia–Europe Foundation (ASEF). He offered to host the Foundation in Singapore, to provide the Foundation with its first Executive Director, and to give it an initial grant of US$1 million. PM Goh's proposal was adopted by the summit (see Annex I for the text of the relevant paragraphs in the Chairman's Statement).

The Period of Gestation

In May 1996, I was asked by my government to agree to be nominated as the first Executive Director of the Asia–Europe Foundation. Although an Americanist rather than a Europeanist by background, I accepted the challenge of building bridges between East Asia and the European Union with enthusiasm.

The first concept paper on ASEF was written by Dr Lee Tsao Yuan of the Institute of Policy Studies. After several revisions, the paper was circulated to the 26 partners of the Asia Europe Meeting process (ASEM) in July 1996. The paper appears in Annex II.

Consultations on the concept paper were held bilaterally and multilaterally from May to October 1996. In order to accelerate the process of consultations and achieve a better understanding of the thinking in Europe, I was asked to undertake a trip to the major capitals of the European Union. Accompanied by Michelle Teo-Jacob, of the Ministry of Foreign Affairs, I visited Bonn, Brussels, London and Paris from 7 to 15 October 1996. In Brussels, I was disheartened to learn from my interlocutors in the European Commission that it would normally take two years to translate a vision into reality. I responded that I was determined to translate the vision of the Bangkok Summit into reality in eleven months. Why eleven months? Because the first ASEM Foreign Ministers' Meeting would be held in Singapore on 15 February 1997. Upon my return to Singapore, I revised the concept paper and wrote an explanatory note dated 17 October 1996. These appear in Annex III.

The Dublin Principles

I attended the ASEM Senior Officials Meeting (SOM) in Dublin on 19 and 20 December 1996. When the meeting started, there was still no agreement on the legal basis on which the Asia–Europe Foundation would be established. What was the sticking point? The sticking point was whether the Foundation would be incorporated as an international organisation, under an international legal agreement, or under Singapore's domestic law. The preference of the ASEAN partners, including Singapore, was for the first option. However, this was not acceptable to the European partners, Japan and Korea because of the legal complications of ratifying an international legal agreement under their respective constitutions.

I undertook a series of consultations on the margin of the SOM on 19 December. As a result of those consultations, consensus was achieved. The ASEM SOM adopted the Dublin Principles (Annex IV) on 20 December 1996.

Impressive Show of Support

Following the adoption of the Dublin Principles, every delegation took the floor to express its support for ASEF. Some delegations, namely, France, Singapore and the United Kingdom, pledged financial support as well as the secondment of staff. Other delegations pledged financial support. The spontaneous and generous expressions of support were a good omen for ASEF's future.

The Process of Incorporation

Upon my return from Dublin, and working closely with our first Company Secretary, Mr Foo Kim Boon, our first Singapore Governor, Dr Yeo Ning Hong, and my former Special Assistant, Ms Leigh Ann Pasqual, we succeeded in incorporating ASEF under Singapore's Company Act, as a company limited by guarantee. The Ministry of Finance agreed to confer on it the status of an institute of public character (IPC), thereby exempting it from tax. The Ministry of Foreign Affairs agreed to grant ASEF the same privileges and immunities as it had granted the APEC Secretariat. The Ministry of Communications and the Ministry of Manpower also acceded to ASEF's requests for exemptions in respect of the cars purchased and domestic help employed by ASEF's non-Singaporean professional staff. The Singapore Government agreed to make available a historic colonial building, at No. 1 Nassim Hill, as the premises of the Foundation.

The Birth of ASEF

On 15 February 1997, Singapore hosted the first meeting of ASEM foreign ministers. In a special ministerial declaration (Annex V), the ministers welcomed the establishment of ASEF and renewed their commitment to ensuring its success. On that evening, a reception was held at the Foundation's premises. The plaque of the Foundation was unveiled by the Foreign Minister of Singapore, Professor S. Jayakumar, and the Foreign Minister of the Netherlands, Mr Hans van Mierlo, representing the Presidency of the European Union, in the presence of their ministerial colleagues.

First Board Meeting

The first meeting of the Board of Governors was held on 17 February 1997. The meeting elected Dr Helmut Haussmann of Germany as its first Chairman and Ambassador Koji Watanabe of Japan as Vice-Chairman.

The Board appointed me as the Foundation's Executive Director and Mr Pierre Barroux as Deputy Executive Director for a period of three years, on secondment from our respective governments. The Board empowered us to form the management of the Foundation. It also approved the budget and the programme of work.

The Board also created an Executive Committee consisting of the Chairman, Vice-Chairman, the Governor of Singapore, the Executive Director and Deputy Executive Director.

Evolution of the Board and Governance

In order to give as many governors as possible an opportunity to serve as chairman and vice-chairman, the Board decided to limit their tenure to one year. In the second year, Ambassador Koji Watanabe served as Chairman and Mr Edmond Israel of Luxembourg as Vice-Chairman. In the third year, Mr Israel served as Chairman and Ambassador Jay-Hee Oh of Korea as Vice-Chairman.

The Board decided to meet twice a year, once in Asia and once in Europe. The frequency of the Board meetings serves two useful purposes. First, it accelerates the bonding of the governors as friends and colleagues. Second, it gives the different host countries a greater sense of ownership of the Foundation. The Board has met in Singapore, Luxembourg, Bangkok, The Hague, Beijing, Copenhagen and Vienna. The management has also tried to organise projects alongside each Board meeting to give the Board more opportunities to take part in the work of the Foundation.

The third Chairman, Mr Edmond Israel, made three important contributions to the Board's governance. With the consent of the Board, he expanded the membership of the Executive Committee to include the two immediate former chairmen, and created an Audit Committee and a Nominating Committee.

ASEF's Management

Pierre Barroux and I gradually built up our management team. We urged governments of ASEM members to second personnel to the management, again to encourage their sense of ownership of the Foundation. The Director for Intellectual Exchange, Mr Duncan Jackman, was seconded by the British Government. He joined the team in August 1997. The Director for People-to-People Exchange, Mr Ulrich Niemann, was seconded by the German Government. He joined the team in August 1997. The Director for Cultural Exchange, Mr Cai Rongsheng, was seconded by the Chinese Government. He joined the team in September 1998. The Director for Public Affairs, Ms Peggy Kek, joined ASEF in June 1997. The Director for Administration and Finance, Mr Terence Tan, joined ASEF in April 1998, succeeding Ms Lee Geok Lian. Ms Leigh Ann Pasqual, the Special Assistant to the Executive Director, joined ASEF on 17 February 1997 and left on 10 December 1999. Ms Sharon Ong joined ASEF in April 1997, initially as a Special Assistant for Projects and now works as a Project Manager in Intellectual Exchange. Mr Andreas Sieren is a Project Manager in People-to-People Exchange. Ms Amelia Lim is a

Project Manager in Public Affairs. As a matter of policy and preference, the management team has always been small. It is a relatively flat organisation with no bureaucracy.

No organisation can work effectively without a good team of supporting staff. This is true of ASEF. The Executive Director and Deputy Executive Director are supported by Jenny Tan, Maggie Ramalingam, Christine Sipiere and Satwant Kaur. The Director of Intellectual Exchange is supported by Betty Ng and Geraldine Ang. The Director for People-to-People Exchange is supported by Angeline Toh and an intern, Carolyne Byrne. The Director of Cultural Exchange is supported by Wendy Lee and Marie Le Sourd. The Director of Public Affairs is supported by Tia Siew Keng and Yap Su-Yin. Finally, the Director of Administration is supported by Jenny Fong. The Foundation's two drivers are Mr S. Vetrivelu and Mr Basri bin Borhan.

ASEF's Mission

The mission of ASEF is enshrined in the Chairman's Statement at the Bangkok Summit. It is to enhance better mutual understanding between Asia and Europe. How would this be achieved? Through greater intellectual, cultural and people-to-people exchanges. In addition to those three sectors we have added public affairs. Why? Because it is not enough for the Foundation to do good work. We have to let the world know about it. Also, the mass media is another constituency that we wish to cultivate. The Foundation, therefore, has four constituencies in the two regions: intellectuals, cultural leaders, talented and outstanding young people and members of the media.

ASEF's Agenda

What is ASEF's agenda? The first agenda item is to create networks in the four sectors which did not exist earlier. Towards this end, we have brought together, for example, high schools in the two regions through the use of the Internet; university students at our summer schools; young parliamentarians; editors and journalists; scholars, think-tankers and universities; painters, musicians, playwrights, arts managers, publishers and other representatives of cultural industries; and high officials and other policy-makers. ASEF has gone a long way towards fulfilling its first agenda item of networking.

Interpreter

The second item on the agenda of ASEF is to interpret important developments taking place in one region to the people of the other region. Let me cite a few examples. When East Asia was first hit by a monetary and economic crisis in 1997, there was very little understanding in Europe of the underlying causes of the crisis. Much of the analysis and commentary in the popular press in Europe was distorted by stereotypes and generalisations. ASEF co-organised a meeting in Paris with a French think-tank, CEPII, to forge a better understanding of the crisis.

The European Monetary Union (EMU) is a monumental achievement. The birth of the "euro" has transformed Europe and it will have a major impact on the world. Unfortunately, there is very little understanding of the EMU and the euro in Asia. In order to rectify this situation, ASEF has held three EMU roadshows, in Hong Kong, Singapore and Beijing.

Convergence and Divergence

The third agenda item of ASEF is to increase the points of convergence and reduce the points of divergence between the thinkers of the two regions. Towards this end, ASEF has organised or co-organised conferences, colloquia, seminars and workshops on important and controversial topics, such as human rights and values; whether trade should be linked to core labour standards and social conditions; the question of Myanmar; good governance and good economic management; and issues relating to the proposal to launch a new round of World Trade Organization (WTO) negotiations.

Flagship Projects

It is often said that a good organisation should have one or more flagship projects. Does ASEF have any flagship projects? I would identify a few. *First*, the ongoing series of Asia–Europe Lectures. Our first three lecturers were the former president of the European Commission, Jacques Santer; the former prime minister of Thailand, Anand Panyarachun; and the current prime minister of Luxembourg, Jean-Claude Juncker.

Second, the annual Europe–Asia Forum which brings together about 50 high-level officials and business and civil society leaders. The forum is co-organised with the Herbert Quandt Stiftung of Germany, and the Institute of Policy Studies of Singapore.

Third, the annual ASEF Summer School for university students. This brings together some of the brightest students of the two regions for two weeks of living, learning and networking.

Fourth, the ASEF Young Parliamentarians' Meeting. This is a unique forum which brings together parliamentarians below the age of 40. The first two meetings, held in the Philippines and Portugal, were highly successful. It is now an annual event.

Fifth, the ASEF Editors' Roundtable. The first roundtable took place in Luxembourg in October 1997. The journalists were asked to comment on the results of a research, commissioned by ASEF, on how the print media of each region was reporting on the other. The second ASEF Editors' Roundtable will take place in Seoul at the time of ASEM III in October 2000 to look at "The Media's Impact on Public Opinion and Foreign Policy". In October 1998, the Colloquium for Journalists was held in Singapore, on the margin of the World Economic Forum's East

Asia Economic Summit, on "How Europe Can Help East Asia without Provoking a Backlash". In June 1998, ASEF brought together in Jakarta, Indonesia, a group of Asian and European journalists to preview the historic elections in Indonesia.

Sixth, ASEF has put on its website the most comprehensive inventory of ASEM activities. It is called "An ASEM Companion" and is updated regularly. "An ASEM Companion" provides summaries of meetings convened by ministers and senior officials in fields such as trade, economics and foreign affairs. It also provides links to all the official ASEM websites.

Landmark Projects

ASEF has held some landmark events, which have led to other projects. The Cultural Forum, held in Paris in February 1998, was one such event. The forum was not only attended by an impressive cast of participants, but it also resulted in seven deliverables. Another highly successful event was the conference held at INSEAD, in Fontainebleau, France, to brainstorm on the Asia–Europe Education Hub proposal. The meeting was attended by some of the best universities from the two regions. The meeting agreed to proceed to launch the education hub project. Almost 200 new scholarships were offered by the participating universities. The third example was the conference on education in a knowledge-based economy, held in Luxembourg in May 2000. This conference was conceptualised as the first of a series of conferences inspired by the overarching theme of "New Thinking for a New Millennium".

ASEF's Philosophy

From the outset, ASEF decided not to function like a traditional, grant-giving Foundation. Instead, it preferred to be proactive in setting its own agenda. It preferred to use its limited funds to seed its agenda and to be actively involved in conceptualising and implementing its projects. This decision disappointed the research community, which had hoped that ASEF would function like a traditional grant-giving foundation.

ASEF's philosophy is to be proactive and not exclusive. On the contrary, its preference is to be inclusive. Therefore, for almost all of its projects, it has looked for partners in the host country and elsewhere. As a result, ASEF has developed an extensive network of partners with which it has co-organised projects. In addition, it has been very successful in finding co-sponsors from the private sector. This is important not just financially but because we believe that, in our new world, we should encourage the government, business and civil societies to work together in a spirit of tripartitism.

Part of ASEF's philosophy is to avoid duplicating what has been done before. We will not undertake a project unless it adds value. We will not accept any proposal unless it satisfies our twin criteria of relevance and coherence. We will usually not undertake an initiative unless it has at least a deliverable. Finally, we will decline a request if we feel that it is in an area which ASEF has no comparative advantage.

Conclusion

In the first three years of ASEF's life, it has implemented 55 projects in 18 of our 25 partner-countries. We have an alumni of 3,000. As the leader of the first management team, I look back on our first three years with pride and satisfaction. We have succeeded in building many new bridges of understanding and friendship between our two civil societies. We have also strengthened many existing bridges. In a modest way, I believe that we have enhanced mutual understanding between Asia and Europe. The first team is preparing to pass the baton to the second team. We wish our successors good luck and success in this collective endeavour that is important not only to Asia and Europe but also to the rest of the world.

Note added: Annexes I–IV are not reprinted here. Refer to pp. 147–171 of *Asia and Europe*.

[Originally published in *Asia and Europe: Essays and Speeches by Tommy Koh*, edited by Yeo Lay Hwee and Asad Latif, World Scientific, 2000, pp. 137–146.]

Reflections on the Institute of Policy Studies

Introduction

I have spent nearly 20 years of my life with IPS: 11 years as Director, 11 years as a Governor and 5 years as Chairman. Looking back on the last 19 years, I have many happy memories of the work we did, of the colleagues I worked with and the publications we produced. In this essay, I would like to touch on some of the highlights of my journey with IPS.

Mandate from Patron

I still remember the lunch which Senior Minister Goh Chok Tong (as Patron of IPS) hosted for me, at the Ministry of Defence, in the summer of 1990. In addition to my job at the Ministry of Foreign Affairs, he asked me to be the Director of IPS. I asked him what was my mandate. He said he wanted IPS to be an inclusive forum in which Singaporeans with different points of view could meet and exchange ideas. He said he did not want IPS to be a mouthpiece of the government, but to generate alternative ideas and constructive proposals to fine-tune government policies. Later, he also asked me to launch an initiative to build a bridge to the business leaders.

Role of IPS in Singapore

Over the years, IPS has come to occupy a unique niche in the intellectual life of Singapore. We are close to the government but we are not part of the government. We act as a bridge between the government, the scholars, the business community, the civil society and other opinion makers in Singapore.

Launching Three Key Projects

I launched three flagship projects which have endured. The first was called "Singapore: Year In Review", which my successor, Dr Lee Tsao Yuan, rebranded as "Perspectives". It is the Singapore equivalent of a US town hall meeting. The second is the Young Singaporeans Conference. The third is the Corporate Associates Scheme.

Corporate Associates

I am pleased that the three projects have continued to thrive. The Singapore Perspectives Conference has now become an established feature of Singapore's intellectual agenda and many look forward to it when it is held in January annually. Many of our Young Singaporeans Conference alumni have become leaders in organisations in the public, private and people sectors, becoming IPS' ambassadors in their own space. The Corporate Associate Scheme, which was revamped by IPS' first Head of Public Affairs, Ms Peggy Kek, and now ably administered by Ms Chang Li Lin, continues to offer our donors regular networking and special briefing sessions. I want to thank our Corporate Associates who have nourished us intellectually and financially over the last 15 years.

Research and Publications on Singapore

IPS has made several important contributions to our understanding of Singapore and its public policies. In the area of the economy, I would highlight two contributions:

(a) The Singapore Economic Roundtable, co-organised with *The Business Times*, held twice a year; and

(b) The IPS Report on the Restructuring of the Singapore Economy, submitted to the government in 2002.

In the area of demography and family, Dr Yap Mui Teng has conducted a number of key confidential studies for the Singapore government, particularly the Ministry of Community Development, Youth and Sports (MCYS). She has contributed to the formulation of policies towards the elderly through her research and as a resource person for Inter-Ministerial Committees. MCYS has appointed IPS and her as the co-ordinator of the newly formed Family Research Network (FRN).

In 1998, Dr Lee Tsao Yuan and Mr Arun Mahizhnan co-edited an important book, *Singapore: Re-engineering Success*. It is time for IPS to revisit the subject of how Singapore should re-invent itself in order to remain competitive and successful.

In the relatively new area of the State's relations with civil society, I would mention the pioneering book, *State-Society Relations in Singapore* by Dr Gillian Koh and Professor Ooi Giok Ling, published in 2000.

In the area of urban studies, I would highlight the World Conference on Model Cities, which IPS co-organised with the Urban Redevelopment Authority in 1999, and Professor Ooi Giok Ling's two-volume publication, *Model Cities: Urban Best Practices* (2000).

From March to May 2003, Singapore was attacked by an invisible enemy, SARS (severe acute respiratory syndrome). It practically shut down the economy and terrified the population. It killed 33 people and hospitalised hundreds. When the nightmare was over, the government requested IPS to publish a book to tell the story. We agreed and commissioned a senior writer with *The Straits Times*, Ms Chua Mui Hoong, to write the book. *A Defining Moment: How Singapore Beat SARS* was published in 2004.

In 2006, IPS published an important book, edited by Dr Cherian George on journalism and the internet. This is an area in which he, Mr Arun Mahizhnan and Mr Tan Tarn How have continued to research and publish.

I wish to acknowledge three important publications by Dr Lai Ah Eng:

(a) her 2004 book, ethnic pluralism and social cohesion in Singapore;
(b) her 2006 book, co-authored with Dr Noor Aisha Abdul Rahman, on Madrasah education; and
(c) her 2008 book on religious diversity in Singapore.

Finally, I will mention the two books which Ms Chang Li Lin and I co-edited and a third book which she assisted me with. They are:

(a) *The United States-Singapore Free Trade Agreement: Highlights and Insights* (2004);
(b) *The Little Red Dot: Reflections by Singapore's Diplomats* (2005); and
(c) *The Making of the ASEAN Charter* (2009).

IPS' External Wing

Like the Singapore economy, IPS also has two wings, an internal wing focused on the study of Singapore's public policies and an external wing. The external wing has many facets. We offer a platform for visiting dignitaries, such as Japanese Prime Minister Toshiki Kaifu, South Korean President Kim Young-sam, Philippines President Gloria Macapagal-Arroyo, World Bank President James Wolfensohn, the Special Envoy of His Holiness The Pope, Cardinal Martinho, to address a knowledgeable audience. Ms Irene Lim and her dedicated team have honed the art and science of organising conferences to perfection. We have tried to be helpful in nurturing good relations between Singapore and other countries.

Singapore–Malaysia Relations

In 1992, the Singapore High Commission in Kuala Lumpur requested IPS to organise and lead a business delegation to visit Kuala Lumpur. The visit took place in the same year, and was extremely successful. The delegation was received by and hosted to lunch at Carcosa by then Prime Minister Dr Mahathir. It also called on the then Finance Minister, Anwar

Ibrahim, and other officials. The Malaysian delegation paid a return visit to Singapore in 1993 and was warmly received by then Prime Minister Goh Chok Tong, who also hosted lunch for the visitors, and had a fruitful dialogue with then Foreign Minister S. Dhanabalan. In 2002, IPS and the Malaysian think-tank, the Asian Strategy & Leadership Institute (ASLI), co-organised a business roundtable in Kuala Lumpur.

Singapore–US Relations

Following the Michael Fay incident, relations between the US and Singapore became acrimonious. In order to cool the dispute and to increase mutual understanding, IPS and a Washington-based think-tank, the Center for Strategic & International Studies (CSIS), co-organised a US-Singapore Consultative Group, co-chaired by Dr Yeo Ning Hong and Dr Harold Brown. The Group met three times in Washington, in 1995, 1996 and 1997. It ceased to meet when our bilateral relations returned to normality.

On the positive side, IPS has worked closely with two American institutions, the Asia Society and the Asia Foundation. With the Asia Society, we co-organised three very successful meetings in Singapore:

(a) A seminal conference on Asian and American perspectives on Democracy and Capitalism (1993);
(b) The Annual Asia Society's Corporate Conference (1994); and
(c) The Williamsburg Conference (2000).

We assisted the Asia Foundation on three occasions by convening and chairing regional workshops on America's role in Southeast Asia, in contributing to the writing of the reports and in launching them in Singapore.

In 2007, IPS, ISEAS (Institute of Southeast Asian Studies) and an American think-tank, the Center for New American Security (CNAS), organised a very successful ASEAN-US Symposium, to take stock of the state of USA's relations with ASEAN and to identify some initiatives which the two sides should take to bring the relationship to a higher level.

Singapore–Japan Relations

The Prime Ministers of Japan and Singapore agreed in 1994 to launch a new initiative which would help to thicken the relations between the two countries and increase the networks between them. The then Prime Minister Goh Chok Tong requested IPS to co-organise the Japan-Singapore Symposium, with a Japanese partner. The Symposium is one of the institutional links between the two countries. It has met on seven occasions: 1995, 1996, 1998, 2001, 2003, 2006 and 2009.

Singapore–Europe Relations

Following the birth of Asia-Europe Meeting (ASEM) and Asia-Europe Foundation (ASEF), two initiatives of Senior Minister Goh Chok Tong, IPS has tried to play a modest role in growing the strategically important relationship between Asia and Europe. When I was the Executive Director of ASEF, ASEF, IPS and the Herbert Quandt Foundation of Germany, co-organised the annual Europe-Asia Forum, which brought together opinion makers from the two continents for an annual dialogue.

Singapore–UN Relations

The United Nations (UN) is very important to Singapore's national interests. IPS has tried to make a contribution to Singapore's relations with the UN system. This took the form of the so-called Singapore Conference on UN Peace-Keeping and Peace-Making. This initiative occurred accidentally. Following the successful conclusion of the UN peace-keeping operation in Cambodia, UNTAC (UN Transitional

Authority in Cambodia), we found to our horror, that the UN did not have the money or the will to convene a conference of all the stakeholders in order to learn lessons from it. IPS, together with UNITAR (UN Institute for Training and Research) and Japan, decided to take the initiative to convene such a conference. The success of the first conference inspired the three partners to convene six more conferences, in 1995, 1997, 1999, 2001, 2002 and 2005 to examine the following topics:

(a) The Role and Functions of Civilian Police in United Nations Peace-Keeping Operations;
(b) Humanitarian Action and Peace-Keeping Operations;
(c) The Nexus between Peacekeeping and Peace-Building;
(d) The Reform Process of United Nations Peace Operations;
(e) The United Nations Transitional Administration in East Timor; and
(f) United Nations as Peacekeeper and Nation-Builder: Continuity and Change — What Lies Ahead?

Each conference has resulted in a book, co-edited by Ms Chang Li Lin and Dr Nassrine Azimi.

Singapore–IMO Relations

Singapore is the world's largest port State. It is also one of the world's top shipping nations and an increasingly important international maritime centre. For these reasons, Singapore participates actively in the work of the International Maritime Organization (IMO). Because I had served as the President of the Third UN Conference on the Law of the Sea, the IMO approached me and suggested that the IMO and IPS should co-organise an international conference on the Straits of Malacca and Singapore. The objective was to encourage the three straits States, namely, Indonesia, Malaysia and Singapore, the user States and other stakeholders to agree to establish a cooperative mechanism in accordance with Article 43 of the Law of the Sea Treaty. Two such conferences were held, in 1996 and 1999, but the parties were not ready to act. In September 2007, the IMO requested me to chair a meeting in Singapore which adopted an agreement to establish the cooperative mechanism. I was overjoyed and felt that the efforts of IPS had not been in vain.

Singapore-APEC Relations

Singapore is the current chair of the Asia-Pacific Economic Cooperation (APEC). We have always attached importance to APEC, because we share the vision of free trade and vision in the Pacific and because it is a forum which links the two sides of the Pacific. APEC has an active business advisory council or ABAC. Over the years, ABAC has put benign pressure on the governments to press on with the liberalisation and integration agenda.

In 1994, a senior official from the US Trade Representative's Office, Sandy Kristoff, came to visit IPS. She requested me to convene a meeting, in Singapore, of representatives from the private sector of all the APEC economies. She also requested IPS to serve as the executive secretariat of the group which was initially called the Pacific Business Forum (PBF). We agreed and organised the meetings of PBF, in 1994 and 1995, as well as assisted the group in writing their reports for submission to the APEC Leaders. Dr Lee Tsao Yuan, Mr Arun Mahizhnan and I worked very hard, for two years, to get the group off to a good start. In 1996, the PBF rebranded itself as the APEC Business Advisory Council, and the Philippines offered to take over the secretariat (supposedly for one year).

Singapore-IMF-World Bank

Singapore was given the onerous privilege of hosting the annual meetings of the International Monetary Fund (IMF) and World Bank Group (WBG) in 2006. Beginning 12 years ago, the formal meetings were complemented by a successful side event called the Programme of Seminars (PoS). The

Singapore government requested IPS to take the lead in working with IMF and WBG to organise PoS. We agreed and spent two years of our time in doing so. I wish to acknowledge my debt of gratitude to Mr Arun Mahizhnan, Dr Tan Kee Wee and Ms Rica Agnes Castaneda for their contributions.

First, we negotiated with IMF and WBG on a new paradigm of cooperation. In the past, the PoS was organised by those two institutions, with no input from the host country. We said that we would cooperate only if we were an equal intellectual partner, helping to conceptualise the programme, choosing the themes and topics and selecting the speakers. IMF and WBG agreed.

Second, we convened a meeting of all Singapore think-tanks and research institutions in order to obtain their suggestions and to involve them in the process.

Third, we convened a regional workshop and invited 50 of Asia's most respected thinkers and think-tanks and obtained very useful inputs from them on topics for discussion and the names of Asian speakers.

The 2006 PoS was three days long. It had an unprecedented number of themes and sessions and attracted a record number of participants. I was particularly proud of the fact that, for the first time in the history of the Programme, half the speakers were Asians who acquitted themselves well. I think we lived up to our tagline, "Asia in the World, the World in Asia".

The People of IPS

At the end of the day, the most important asset of IPS is its people. I will always remember, with appreciation and gratitude, the many wonderful people I have worked with at IPS. I thank my kind chairman, Mr Hsuan Owyang and the supportive members of the board. I am deeply indebted to my two able deputies, Dr Lee Tsao Yuan and Mr Arun Mahizhnan, and to all the talented members of the research team. I salute the first-class administrative team, ably led by Mr Ang Leng Huat, Ms Shirley Lim and now by Ms Irene Lim.

Conclusion

I hope that IPS has been useful to Singapore in a myriad of ways. I suspect that most people, including some members of the IPS family, are not fully aware of the many ways in which we have tried to be relevant and useful. This is my excuse for this rather long reflection.

[Originally published in *IPS: Celebrating 20 Years of Engaging Minds & Exchanging Ideas,* Institute of Policy Studies, 2008, pp. 6–11.]

Integrating the Business Community in the APEC Process

Genesis of the Pacific Business Forum*

Introduction

On a clear November day in 1993, some of the world's most powerful political leaders had a good idea to boost economic development: they decided to engage the people who are most directly involved in economic development — the business community.

Though APEC was inaugurated in 1989, it was not till 1993 that a schedule of annual meetings of the top leaders of APEC was set in place. The very first Leaders Meeting was held on the serene and beautiful Blake Island, near Seattle, in 1993, under the chairmanship of President Bill Clinton. At this meeting, the Leaders decided to ask the business community of APEC to establish a forum to "identify issues APEC should address to facilitate regional trade and investment and encourage the further development of business networks throughout the region". Thus was born the Pacific Business Forum (PBF), later renamed as the APEC Business Advisory Council or ABAC in short.

The PBF was perhaps the first ever formal and independent business forum that was to be appended to the annual summit of a major grouping of economies. In the past, though economic development was often at the top of the agenda in many international groupings, political leaders and government officials rarely engaged the business community directly and formally in their meetings. APEC Leaders made a significant

---

*Co-authored with Lee Tsao Yuan and Arun Mahizhnan.

departure from this practice and decided to integrate the business community as part of the APEC deliberative process. They personally appointed the PBF members and heard directly from them without the usual layers of intermediaries.

Establishment of PBF

The APEC Leaders' decision to establish the Pacific Business Forum was transmitted by a US emissary, Ms Sandra Kristoff, Assistant US Trade Representative, to Professor Tommy Koh who, while being an Ambassador-at-Large with the Government of Singapore, was also the head of a Singapore think tank, the Institute of Policy Studies (IPS). Sandy Kristoff requested Koh to convene the first meeting of the PBF and for IPS to act as its Secretariat. The US probably felt that it was better for a small country than for the US to act as convenor. Singapore is small, friendly and acceptable to all the APEC members. Koh accepted the US request.

In convening the first meeting of the PBF, Koh and his working group proposed a framework for this Forum — the membership, the modus operandi for the meetings and the process of making final recommendations to the Leaders. The membership of PBF was, in some ways, preordained — it would have representation from each member economy of APEC and each representative would be personally nominated by the Leaders. It was also decided that in the first instance each economy would be invited to send two representatives, one representing large business and the other from the small and medium business sector. In the end, however, three economies preferred to send only one representative, thus making the total membership 33, instead of 36, in the first PBF.

The first PBF meeting was convened in Singapore in June 1994, and the group decided to elect two co-chairs for the Forum. The co-chairs were Mr Les McCraw, representing the current chairman and Mr Bustanil Arifin of Indonesia, representing the next chairman of APEC. In future, PBF would have a troika of co-chairs, representing the current chairman, the next chairman and the immediate past chairman.

The co-chairs and the PBF Secretariat were supported by a number of staffers drawn from the co-chairs' own companies and the APEC Secretariat, thus providing both professional and expert support for the Forum's deliberations. The IPS team, led by Tommy Koh, Lee Tsao Yuan and Arun Mahizhnan, the co-chairs' staffers and the APEC Secretariat officials worked harmoniously. We made several good friends with whom we have stayed in touch over the years.

Within a span of five months, the PBF met three times in Singapore: (a) 10–15 June; (b) 5–6 August; and (c) 2–3 September, and held extensive and spirited discussions on many written and oral submissions on what the PBF should focus on. From the level of small businesses to the level of global conglomerates, from passport control for frequent business travellers to international policy on trade and investment, from individual action to regional collaboration, every critical aspect affecting the business community's performance in regional economic development was put on the table. Despite initial apprehensions of potential conflict and divergence, the PBF managed to surprise many by submitting a comprehensive and consensual report to the APEC Leaders in October 1994, in Indonesia.

First PBF Report

The report was called "A Business Blueprint for APEC: Strategies for Growth and Common Prosperity". In the report, the PBF members first reiterated their independent stand in arriving at their conclusions, which might or might not coincide with their own government's views. Second, they pointed out that despite the very diverse levels of economic development in their different economies, they all shared the same business philosophy — "of doing business better, faster and more effectively" — which led to a prompt and prudent consensus on what needs to be done. Third, they set out their own vision for an Asia Pacific region where dynamic and lasting growth will benefit all the peoples of the region and enhance the standard of living of all of them. They clearly signalled their preference for growth with equity over growth as the only objective. Finally, they offered a set of recommendations that would help fulfil that vision.

PBF Recommendations

Of all the recommendations of PBF's first blueprint for business growth, free trade and investment liberalisation were considered to be the cornerstone of their strategies and programmes. It argued that without liberating the flow of goods, services, capital and labour within the region, all else would be captive to unproductive and self-serving regulations and barriers. Therefore, it recommended an immediate standstill on such new regulations and barriers and an accelerated dismantling of old ones. It even suggested a firm deadline for the liberalisation of trade and investment throughout the APEC economies by 2010. In sum, this set of recommendations reflected the frustrations and impatience of a business community that was raring to grow beyond their national borders.

The blueprint also addressed other critical issues faced by the business community. Business facilitation was such an issue. The cumbersome variety of regulations and controls within the region, which rose from distant and different historical trends, further complicated by corruption and inefficiency, seriously inhibited businesses from crossing borders and growing fast. So the PBF made specific recommendations on simplifying and standardising customs and immigrations rules and regulations, using new technology to speed up documentation processing as well as on training relevant officials with the knowledge and skill to implement the recommendations. The report also argued for improvements in intellectual property rights, setting up of mutual recognition agreements, the easing of restrictions on technology transfers and the establishment of dispute settlement mechanisms.

Another major concern for the business community centred on human resource development policies. The disparity in development of human resources across the region and the potential for great improvements in their capacity and skill sets prompted PBF to urge the Leaders to intensify region-wide training programmes as well as skills and technology transfer across borders. The report also pointed out that business development within the region could be speeded up with conducive policies that favoured small and medium enterprises, improved access to capital and offered substantial tax incentives. Businesses also needed rapid and well coordinated infrastructure development to facilitate economic development. To this end, the reported recommended the setting up of a joint public and business sector task force on region-wide infrastructure development.

The report also stressed that the partnership between the government and the private sector should extend beyond infrastructure development into many other areas of mutual concern and benefit. In order to examine these areas of partnership as well as to dialogue with each other on a continual basis, the PBF recommended that the Leaders establish an APEC Business Advisory Forum which will report directly to them to help achieve APEC's long term objectives.

The above is not an exhaustive account either of the PBF process or the policy recommendations but only an indicative summary that would suggest the depth and breadth of the business community's concerns over regional economic development.

The first report of PBF was submitted to then APEC Chairman, President Soeharto of Indonesia, on 15 October 1994, for consideration by APEC leaders at their Bogor meeting in November that year.

PBF II

At their Bogor meeting, the Leaders adopted the goal of free and open trade and investment for all APEC economies by 2015 for developed economies and 2020 for developing economies in accordance with the recommendation of the APEC Group of Eminent Persons (EPG). The positive experience and outcome of the first round of PBF encouraged the Leaders to request PBF to continue its work. The Forum was asked to assess the progress of APEC, to provide further recommendations for increasing cooperation, and to review the interrelationships between APEC and the various subregional economic arrangements. However, subsequent to this request, an Eminent Persons Group took up the last area for further examination, leaving the PBF to focus on the first two aspects. The tone and temperament of the new brief was to move from a visioning exercise to an action mode. The second PBF did just that.

Through 1995, the PBF held three rounds of consultations among its members in order to prepare its second report to the Leaders meeting in Osaka later that year. The three meetings were held in: (a) Singapore, 26–27 May; (b) Tokyo, 14–15 July; and (c) Newport Beach, 1–2 September. The leadership of PBF now included a Japanese co-chair, Mr Minoru Morofushi, in addition to the two past co-chairs. As the first PBF report had provided a blueprint for business growth, the second report focused on specific action plans. Hence its title: "The Osaka Action Plan: Roadmap to Realising the APEC Vision".

PBF II Recommendations

The second PBF report was both shorter and sharper than the first, reflecting the concerns of both the Leaders and the business community to show some real action to overcome the "talk-shop" image APEC was acquiring after six years of existence. It made 15 specific recommendations in three broad areas: (a) a roadmap to 2020 with three components – guiding principles, agreement on timelines, and regular progress reviews; (b) 10 Osaka deliverables; and (c) two recommendations for business participation in APEC.

For reasons of brevity, the following is just a selection of those recommendations, to offer a sense of the concerns and the urgency the region's business community was feeling at that time.

In terms of guiding principles, the report cautioned that in creating an APEC-wide free trade and investment regime, there must be consistency with WTO rules. It also prudently argued for flexible consensus among member economies so that those lagging behind could catch up later. Given the overarching globalisation process, the Forum also wanted to ensure that any regional agreement left room for inclusion of others by adopting the "open regionalism" concept. Perhaps the most problematic principle to implement, yet the most urgent would be PBF's call for transparency.

As timelines are an integral part of any action plan, the PBF report argued strongly for clear and agreed timelines for member economies to follow through. It also stressed the need for intermediate milestones so improvements could be measured and good examples could be shared among members to encourage those behind their targets. Above all, PBF urged that progress must be consistently and regularly reviewed, at various levels, including the Leaders level, so that the parties involved would feel the pressure to deliver on commitments.

In terms of deliverables, the report urged the Leaders to take a tactical as well as strategic approach. It argued that in addition to the final deadlines to be met in 2020, the Leaders should begin the process of implementation immediately, in Osaka. For example, PBF wanted the Leaders to announce in Osaka its intention to strengthen the APEC Non-Binding Investment Principles by the 1996 meeting in the Philippines. It wanted visa-free business travel throughout the region by 1999 and the first phase of it to be introduced in 1996. The report also addressed similar deliverables in areas such as customs harmonisation, intellectual property rights, infrastructure development and human resource development.

In its recommendations on strengthening business community's participation in the APEC process, the most significant was, perhaps, the 'self-destruct' proposal to establish the APEC Business Advisory Council (ABAC) which would automatically lead to the demise of PBF itself. The PBF was originally set up more as an exploratory consultative mechanism, without a long term commitment to its continuation. The work of PBF over the two years had convinced the business community and those beyond in government and academia that a permanent advisory forum was needed to provide good counsel and strong support for the Leaders' various initiatives on the economic development of the region. Thus, PBF recommended that the Leaders announce the establishment of ABAC as its permanent advisory body at their Osaka meeting. The report also recommended regular and continuous involvement of business representatives in APEC's working groups to help formulate sound business policies and to help implement them effectively.

The second PBF report and recommendations were submitted to the Chairman of APEC, Prime Minister Tomiichi Maruyama of Japan, on 22 September 1995 in Tokyo, ahead of their Osaka meeting in November that year.

The PBF Experience

The notion of APEC leaders personally appointing business leaders from each of their economies to form a forum for business policy discussions and hearing directly from them without the intervention of any intermediaries was both unusual and untested when PBF was first mooted in 1993. Fortunately, for both the business community and the political leaders, the actual experience of the interactive process over the first two years turned out to be positive.

The business community of the Asia Pacific region found, for the first time in their history, a common forum for them to critically but collegially address their serious business concerns, with the authority and influence bestowed on them by their respective Leaders. They also found, again for the first time, a direct channel to communicate directly to their Leaders.

The Leaders of APEC, for their part, made an unprecedented and potentially risky decision to engage the business leadership directly but, in the end, were rewarded by a frank, robust, thoughtful and constructive feedback on how to get things right and how to make things better. It seemed worth the risk.

Though the recommendations of PBF I & II were received with genuine interest on the part of the Leaders, its two-year life span was too short a time to determine the effectiveness of those recommendations. It is the case that even among those recommendations accepted by the Leaders, most needed long term gestation and implementation to see the end results. It is also a fact that some of the short-term recommendations that were accepted were not actually implemented or effectively executed. However, some recommendations were accepted and swiftly implemented. One of them has resulted in hassle-free travel for our business people, travelling from one APEC economy to another in some but not all the member economies. At some airports, there are even designated lanes for APEC business travellers. The PBF scorecard was and had to be a work in progress. The entire region is watching that scorecard today, 15 years after its inception. In other chapters in this book, the reader will find some of those results.

Rebirth of PBF

The APEC Leaders accepted the recommendation to set up the new permanent advisor body, and PBF was re-born as ABAC at Osaka in November 1995. Koh and IPS relinquished their roles as PBF convenor and secretariat and handed over the responsibilities to Filipino colleagues, led by Mr Roberto Romulo, who set up the permanent international secretariat of ABAC in Manila. It is one of those reincarnations where good karma seems to lead to good consequences.

[Originally published in *APEC at 20: Recall, Reflect, Remake*, eds. K. Kesavapany and H. Lim, pp. 97–103. © 2009 Institute of Southeast Asian Studies]

Building a Better World*

Minister Yaacob Ibrahim, Mr Ralph Peterson, Mr Ron Advani, distinguished guests, ladies and gentlemen

I must begin by thanking CH2M Hill for giving me this prestigious award. The prize money has been given to IPS. My wife was looking at my programme for this week during the past weekend. She looked puzzled. She wanted to know who is CH2M Hill and why it is giving me this award. I hope Mr Ralph Peterson has explained to my wife's satisfaction why you are giving me this award. I also hope that Minister Yaacob's speech contains enough information on CH2M Hill, which is a great company, and the good work it has done and is doing, both in Singapore and elsewhere in the world. I wish also to thank Minister Yaacob for honouring us with his presence this evening. Under his able leadership, MEWR has ascended to a higher peak. Under his enlightened leadership, Islam continues to be practised in Singapore in a tolerant manner and as a peace-loving religion.

My wife and I have been married for nearly 39 years. My wife has always told our friends that, in reality, we have been married for only half that time. My acceptance speech this evening has a target audience of one, my wife. My purpose is to explain to her what I have been doing with my life, especially in the years that I have travelled away from home.

I am a born optimist and idealist. I suppose my life-long inspiration has been to help build a better world. What kind of a better world?

---

* Acceptance speech at CH2M Hill's "Building a Better World" Award Dinner, 15 June 2006.

First, I believe that the law can and should be used as a means to render justice and not as an instrument of oppression. I had spent many happy years teaching law at NUS, including three happy years as Dean of the Law Faculty. I believe that where righting a wrong is beyond the reach of the law, such as, in the exercise of administrative discretion, we need to complement the courts with another institution, whether an administrative tribunal or an ombudsman, which is empowered to protect the citizens from the abuse of discretionary power.

Second, I believe in the rule of law, both domestically and in the relations between States. In pursuit of this goal, I had spent over 10 years of my life in negotiating and crafting the 1982 UN Convention on the Law of the Sea. I had also spent over 10 years of my life, as a member of the ASEAN team, in campaigning for the liberation of Cambodia from the twin evils of rule by the Khmer Rouge and by a foreign country.

Third, I believe that disputes between States should be settled by peaceful means: by mediation, arbitration and adjudication. In 1993, the UN Secretary-General sent me to make peace between Russia, on the one hand, and its three Baltic neighbours, Estonia, Latvia and Lithuania, on the other. I have responded positively twice to the WTO's requests to chair dispute panels to settle trade disputes between the US and New Zealand against Canada, in one case, and, between Australia and New Zealand against the US, in the other. I am privileged to have acted and to be acting as Singapore's agent, in two disputes between Singapore and Malaysia. In the first case, the dispute over Singapore's land reclamation in the Straits of Johor was brought by Malaysia to the International Tribunal for the Law of the Sea, but eventually settled through negotiations. The dispute over Pedra Branca will be heard by the International Court of Justice sometime next year.

Fourth, I believe in the imperative of reconciling the human enterprise and the natural world. I feel very blessed to have had the opportunity to serve the UN twice in this respect. The first time was as a member of the committee preparing for the groundbreaking 1972 Stockholm Conference on the Environment. On the second occasion, I was elected to chair the committee preparing for the 1992 UN Conference on Environment and Development, aka the Earth Summit. At the Summit, I was elected to chair the main committee. It was only by a miracle that we managed to forge consensus on the deliverables of the Summit. At home, I am the patron of the Nature Society. I think Singapore is probably Asia's greenest city. Our water is potable, our air is breathable, our seas are swimmable, our sewage is collected daily, our land has not been poisoned and our parks and gardens are wonderful. We can, however, make our air quality even better. I look forward to the day when more Singaporeans would emulate the good example of Minister Yaacob by buying and operating a hybrid car, and when our buses and taxis would be powered by non-polluting fuel systems. The wisdom is that the high quality of our environment is not only good for our citizens and residents, it is also a comparative advantage in the competition for investment and global talent.

Fifth, I believe in promoting mutual understanding between peoples of different races, religions, countries, regions and civilisations. I have devoted time and energy to promoting better mutual understanding between the US, on the one hand, and Singapore and Asia on the other. I was very happy when I was appointed as Singapore's chief negotiator in negotiating a free trade agreement with the US. I have served for over 10 years as a co-convenor of the annual Williamsburg Conference which brings together opinion makers from the US and Asia. I was very grateful for the opportunity to serve as the founding Executive Director of the Asia–Europe Foundation and to help build bridges of understanding between Asia and Europe. Last year, I was very pleased to chair the inaugural Asia–Middle East Dialogue, which is off to a promising start. I have also tried to promote better mutual understanding between Singapore and China, through the China–Singapore Forum; and between Singapore and Japan, through the Japan–Singapore Symposium.

Sixth, I believe that people with disabilities are fellow human beings. They should be treated with kindness and respect. They should be given greater opportunities in education and employment. Our physical environment should have as few barriers as possible so that those who are physically disabled can get around our city with ease. More important than our physical environment is our mindset. We must free our minds from our negative stereotypes and prejudices. Only in this way could Singapore become a disabled-friendly city. I am the patron of the Rainbow Centre; of an NGO called Very Special Arts, Singapore; of Hi! Theatre, and a member of the Singapore Deaf Association.

Seventh, I believe in the value of culture and the arts. I am so happy that Singapore can no longer be described as a cultural desert. The arts are blooming in Singapore and throughout East Asia. I feel very privileged to have served as the founding Chairman of the National Arts Council and as the current Chairman of the National Heritage Board (NHB). Our collective ambition at NHB is to make our museums world class and to embed them firmly in the soil of Southeast Asia.

Eighth, I believe that scholars in our universities and research institutions as well as our think-tanks play a useful and important role in society. I hope that one day, our philosophers and writers will enjoy the status that they do in France and our think-tanks will be as influential as they are in the United States. In the meantime, my colleagues and I at IPS try our best, with limited resources, to research on the public policies of Singapore and by offering constructive alternative views. The recently held post-election forum is an example of how IPS has tried to add value by commissioning an independent survey of the attitudes of the electorate and sharing the results with the public.

Ninth, I have devoted some of my energies to building up the Chinese Heritage Centre (CHC) over the past 11 years. The CHC has become an important centre in the world for the study of the Chinese overseas. The Centre has published an encyclopedia and a journal. It also hosts an interesting exhibition called "Chinese, More or Less". The President of NTU, Professor Su Guaning, has taken over the Centre's chairmanship from me two days ago.

Tenth, I believe the moral character of a people is partly reflected in how they treat their animals. I love animals, especially dogs. When the former Executive Chairman of Wildlife Reserves Singapore, Dr Kwa Soon Bee, requested me to chair a committee on ethics and animal welfare for the Zoo, Night Safari and Bird Park, I readily agreed. I will be handing over the chairmanship of the committee to my good friend, Professor Leo Tan.

It has been a busy and fulfilling life. I am sure it has not been easy for my wife to understand why I have been so busy and have to travel so often. I hope that after listening to me tonight she will understand that all these activities have one unifying objective — to build a better world. I thank her for her love and support.

Thank you.

3

SINGAPORE

Lee Kuan Yew's Foreign Policy Legacy

For the past 25 years, Lee Kuan Yew has personified Singapore to the world. He has been the principal architect of Singapore's foreign policy. He has also been Singapore's chief diplomat to the world. He hands over to his successor a principled and pragmatic foreign policy which has enabled Singapore to survive and prosper. This article will attempt briefly to assess Lee Kuan Yew's foreign policy achievements.

Mini in Size but Not Influence

With a population of 2.6 million and a physical area of only 626 square kilometres, Singapore is one of the world's smallest states. However, Singapore enjoys a role and influence in the world quite unlike those enjoyed by other countries of similar size. This is due to two factors: the stature of Singapore's Prime Minister and the country's record of achievements.

Lee Kuan Yew's Impact on Foreign Leaders

Why is Lee Kuan Yew so greatly admired by his peers abroad? Because of his intellectual brilliance, his political experience, extraordinary powers of analysis and judgment, his eloquence, his willingness to offer candid and disinterested advice and his domestic record of success. His political longevity places him in a very special category of elder statesmen in the world. He is the longest serving Prime Minister in the Commonwealth and the longest serving Head of Government in Asia. His address to the Joint Meeting of the US Congress on 9 October 1985 was a reflection of the esteem which US leaders of both parties have for him. In the same way, the fact that he had often been asked to be the keynote speaker at the biennial meeting of Commonwealth Heads of Government is an example of the respect he commands from the Prime Ministers of the Commonwealth countries. In Asia, his views on world affairs are sought and listened to with respect by the leaders of countries ranging from China and Japan to Hong Kong and Papua New Guinea.

Fellows of Harvard and Yale

Lee Kuan Yew has won the admiration of many foreign scholars. The many meetings between him and the professors of Harvard, Yale and other universities and think-tanks in America always produced intellectual discourse of the highest order. It is quite extraordinary for the Prime Minister of a Third World country to have held fellowships at both Harvard and Yale, and to have been conferred honorary doctoral degrees by three prestigious universities in the United States and two in the United Kingdom.

Relations with Foreign Media

Lee Kuan Yew has always had a love-hate relationship with the foreign, especially American and British, press. On the one hand, he enjoys his intellectual encounters with the more able and gifted members of the Western media. On the other hand, his sensitivity to criticism, his contempt for those who had not done their homework and his resentment against any attempt by the "whites" to preach at him, have given him and Singapore a rather bad press in the West in recent years. The fundamental cause of the disagreement is the Western media's insistence that Singapore should follow the principles of Western liberal democracy and Lee Kuan Yew's belief that such principles had to be adapted to the special circumstances of Singapore. However, even his critics admire his moral and intellectual courage in being willing to face them. He appeared before the International Press Institute in Helsinki (1971), the American Society of Newspaper Editors in Washington, D.C. (1988), the Commonwealth Press Union and the Foreign Correspondents' Club in Hong Kong (1990) and earned the respect if not the agreement of those audiences. From the point of view of the Third World, Lee Kuan Yew's willingness to stand up to the Western media has helped to strengthen Singapore's credentials as a country which is independent-minded, notwithstanding its general pro-Western foreign policy.

The Defects of Our Virtues

No human is perfect. Even a great man like Lee Kuan Yew is not without foibles. Indeed, we all suffer from the defects of our virtues. Thus, Lee Kuan Yew's brilliance sometimes causes him to appear arrogant, his single-mindedness can come across as dogmatism and his candour as indiscretion. I remember that I once urged the Prime Minister to be more discreet in his remarks about other countries. I think it was after a speech he made in Singapore during which he made some disparaging remarks about the Calypso culture of the Caribbean countries. The remark had been widely reported by the Caribbean media and had caused offence to our Caribbean friends. The Prime Minister replied that he was known for his candour and should not be expected to speak like a diplomat. He said that if he had ruffled any feathers, it was the job of our diplomats to smoothen those feathers. I protested that as our Prime Minister, he was our chief diplomat to the world.

The Seven Pillars of Singapore's Foreign Policy

What foreign policy legacy is Lee Kuan Yew leaving to his successor? What is his vision of Singapore's role in the region and the world? Below are seven pillars of Singapore's foreign policy which bear the imprint of Lee Kuan Yew.

First, we have a pragmatic foreign policy based not on any ideology or doctrine, but upon the fact that our foreign policy must be constantly guided by one lodestar — the security and prosperity of Singapore.

Second, we rely, first and foremost, on ourselves. Thus, believing that the world does not owe us a living, Singapore has never sought foreign aid from the developed countries. This belief in self-reliance has also led us to develop a capacity to deter aggression. To quote Lee Kuan Yew, "In a world where the big fish eat small fish and the small fish eat shrimps, Singapore must become a poisonous shrimp."

Third, we must accept the world as it is and not as we would like it to be. This has installed in us a pragmatic and hard-headed attitude towards realities. Our realism, however, is not a fatalistic attitude. We are constantly seeking to change the *status quo* for the better.

Fourth, Singapore is committed to making ASEAN work and to maintain good relations with our five regional partners, especially our two immediate neighbours, Indonesia and Malaysia. Lee Kuan Yew's support for ASEAN and his personal rapport with President Soeharto and Prime Minister Mahathir are important assets.

Fifth, Singapore is a member of a larger, dynamic and increasingly prosperous Asia Pacific community. Singapore supported the creation of the Asia Pacific Economic Cooperation (APEC) grouping and is the location for the Secretariat of the Pacific Economic Cooperation Conference (PECC). Singapore has played and will continue to play a seminal role in the evolution of the Pacific community. Her commitment to ASEAN is not inconsistent with its support for the Pacific community.

Sixth, Singapore is a member of the world community and is a good citizen of the world. Singapore has supported the primacy of the principles of the UN Charter and the collective security system centred on the UN Security Council. As a small country, Singapore has a vested interest in ensuring respect by all states for the principles of international law governing relations among states. Singapore's free trade policy, its environmentally sensitive development policy, its strong support for the UN and GATT, and the role of her diplomats as neutral chairmen are some examples of Singapore's contributions to the world community.

Seventh, Singapore will work with other countries to ensure a stable and peaceful environment in our region. Singapore favours the continued presence of the United States in East and Southeast Asia and is against its precipitate withdrawal from the region. We favour a balance of power in Southeast Asia which produces a stable political order and are against an arms race by the regional powers, or any destabilizing changes. Singapore is not, however, against the need to re-assess existing security arrangements in the region in the light of the ending of the Cold War.

Conclusion

With the help of Goh Keng Swee, Toh Chin Chye and S. Rajaratnam in the earlier years, and S. Dhanabalan and Wong Kan Seng in more recent years, Lee Kuan Yew has masterminded Singapore's external relations. In 1965, Singapore's independence was questioned by some. Today, no one does. In 1965, Singapore's economic prospects looked dubious. Today, Singapore's economy is one of the powerhouses of the dynamic Asia Pacific region. Singapore's place in Southeast Asia is secure because of ASEAN and because of Singapore's good relations with her neighbours. Singapore is plugged into the world grid of trade, investment and technology flows and is a good economic partner of the United States, Japan and the European Community. Singapore is viewed by others as a good citizen of the world community. In sum, Singapore's relations with other countries, both within and outside the region, are excellent. This happy state of affairs is due to the collective efforts of an extraordinary crew but, especially, to its illustrious captain, Lee Kuan Yew.

[Article contributed to *Trends*, a monthly publication of the Institute of Southeast Asian Studies (ISEAS) distributed with *The Business Times*, 15 November 1990.]

Goh Chok Tong's Foreign Policy Legacy

Fourteen years ago, Goh Chok Tong succeeded Lee Kuan Yew as the second Prime Minister of Singapore. At the time of that transition, I had tried to sum up Lee Kuan Yew's foreign policy legacy. I wrote that, "Singapore's relations with other countries, both within and outside the region, are excellent. This happy state of affairs is due to the collective efforts of an extraordinary crew but, especially, to its illustrious captain, Lee Kuan Yew."

Lee Kuan Yew's Legacy

I also wrote that Lee Kuan Yew was the architect of Singapore's successful foreign policy which was founded on the following seven principles:

- promoting the security and prosperity of Singapore is our lodestar
- be self-reliant
- accept the world as it is and not as we would like it to be
- make ASEAN work and Southeast Asia peaceful and prosperous
- work for a stable political/security order in the Asia-Pacific
- support the evolution of an Asia-Pacific community
- be a good citizen of the world

PM Goh's Foreign Policy Achievements

What is Goh Chok Tong's foreign policy legacy? What are the most important foreign policy achievements of the Goh Chok Tong administration? Did he develop a flair for diplomacy?

Goh Chok Tong has made many contributions to Singapore's foreign policy. He has consolidated Lee Kuan Yew's legacy and expanded upon it.

1. Singapore in Southeast Asia

Indonesia

Goh Chok Tong worked hard to build upon Lee Kuan Yew's strong personal relationship with President Soeharto. During the more than 30 years when Indonesia was ruled by Soeharto, power was concentrated in Merdeka Palace and all important decisions were made by Soeharto. Goh Chok Tong therefore had to develop a good rapport with Soeharto and to earn his trust and confidence. This he succeeded in doing. This made it possible for the two countries to broaden as well as deepen their bilateral cooperation. For example, the development of Batam and Bintan; the extensive cooperation between our defence forces, including the building of the firing range in Sumatra; the expansion of air links between the two countries; and Singapore's participation in the development of the tourist industry in Bali, all took place during this period.

A Friend in Need

There is a saying that a friend in need is a friend indeed. Goh Chok Tong proved that he is a friend of Indonesia during the 1997 financial crisis. Between the critical months of October 1997 and January 1998, PM Goh visited Soeharto three times to convey personally the support of Singapore for Indonesia. Singapore, together with Japan and Australia, tried to be helpful to Indonesia during the crisis by interceding with the IMF. In response to Soeharto's request, PM Goh offered Indonesia a loan of US$5 billion, to be used after the loans from IMF and the World Bank were exhausted. Following Singapore's lead, Brunei pledged US$1.2 billion and Malaysia US$1 billion. In the post crisis period, PM Goh has encouraged Singapore's private sector to invest in Indonesia in order to re-start the economy. In the period 1997 to 2003, Singapore companies have invested a total of US$7.7 billion in Indonesia.

Malaysia

Relations between Singapore and Malaysia, during the past 14 years, were like a roller coaster, sometimes up and sometimes down. Much of the dynamics of this erratic pattern was attributable to the mercurial personality of the former Prime Minister of Malaysia, Dr Mahathir bin Mohamad. Although Dr Mahathir received his medical education in Singapore and has many friends here, he appears to have a love-hate attitude towards Singapore.

Although PM Goh and PM Mahathir met each other many times during the past 14 years, the two men never developed a close friendship. PM Goh tried very hard to keep the relationship on an even keel and to insulate the logic of cooperation from the acid of bilateral politics. In spite of the frequent eruptions of anti-Singapore episodes, there were some significant achievements. The economies of Johor and Singapore are increasingly integrated. Malaysia has displaced the US and Japan to become Singapore's No. 1 trading partner since 2000. Singapore has become Malaysia's largest foreign investor and largest source of tourists. The change of Prime Minister in Malaysia, at the end October 2003, has brought about a brightening in the bilateral relationship. The mood has become more positive, the tone more collegial and the anti-Singapore rhetoric has largely ceased. The two governments should therefore seize this window of opportunity to resolve the old outstanding issues and to grow a new win-win agenda.

Brunei

PM Goh is a true believer in ASEAN. He worked very hard to strengthen ASEAN as an organisation and Singapore's bilateral relations with each of the member States. With Brunei, PM Goh initiated the Brunei-Singapore Exchange Visits. He has encouraged Singapore's ministers to make frequent visits to Brunei and to prevent the special relationship between these two countries from being devalued by complacency.

Thailand

With Thailand, PM Goh developed a close relationship with several of Thailand's Prime Ministers. For example, PM Goh worked closely with PM Anand Panyarachun in launching the ASEAN Free Trade Agreement (AFTA) in 1992 and with PM Banharn Silpa-Archa in launching the Asia Europe Meeting (ASEM) in 1996. Singapore also worked closely with Thailand to launch the ASEAN Regional Forum in 1994, in Thailand, with PM Chuan Leekpai serving as convenor and host.

During the past seven years, PM Goh and PM Thaksin have launched several initiatives to deepen the relationship between the two countries. In 1997, they initiated the Singapore-Thailand Enhanced Partnership (STEP) which was intended to serve as a platform for a long-term strategic partnership between the two countries. In 2002, they launched a complementary initiative, the Singapore-Thailand Enhanced Economic Relationship (STEER) to focus on four sectors of cooperation: economic relations, defence relations, civil service exchanges and people-to-people exchanges. The two Prime Ministers have also started a tradition of meeting each other, in each other's country, together with a few of their ministerial colleagues, in order to brainstorm on bilateral issues and on other issues of mutual interest. Perhaps taking a cue from their political leaders, the two private sectors have responded positively. In the period, 1997 to 2003, Singapore's companies have made a total investment of

US$16 billion in Thailand. Trade and tourism between the two countries are booming.

Vietnam

PM Goh has a close relationship with the leaders of Vietnam. His advice on Vietnam's efforts to restructure its economy, to liberalise its trade policy and improve its governance, has been sought and received with appreciation in Hanoi. The Singapore-Vietnam Industrial Park is a success. Singapore has become Vietnam's largest foreign investor with a cumulative FDI of US$7.37 billion. The Vietnam-Singapore Technical Training Centre in Hanoi, is very well utilised and is an excellent example of the practical way in which Singapore seeks to share its expertise with its ASEAN partners.

Cambodia, Laos and Myanmar

PM Goh has also tried to be helpful to Cambodia, Laos, and Myanmar. At the fourth Informal ASEAN Summit in Singapore in 2000, he launched the Initiative for ASEAN Integration or IAI. The purpose of IAI is to help the four new member countries, Cambodia, Laos, Myanmar and Vietnam, catch up with the older members and integrate smoothly into ASEAN. Under this initiative, Singapore has set up training centres in each of the four countries. To date, the centres have trained over 3,000 officials in such fields as English language, trade, tourism, negotiation skills, IT, WTO accession, etc. In the case of Cambodia, PM Goh played a role in persuading Prime Minister Hun Sen to allow for direct flights to Siem Reap in order to grow the tourist industry around the Angkor Wat. In a quiet and non-confrontational way, PM Goh has advised the leaders of Myanmar to open up their economy, to seek reconciliation with the opposition and to make more rapid progress in the political evolution of the country. Singapore's private sector, especially the small and medium enterprises, have invested in all three countries. Singapore is Cambodia's No. 6 investor, Myanmar's No. 1 investor and Laos' No. 12 investor.

2. Strengthening ASEAN

PM Goh has made many important contributions to strengthening ASEAN. He is, however, very modest and often prefer not to take the credit for his ideas. What are his most important contributions?

First, PM Goh was the proponent of the ASEAN Free Trade Agreement (AFTA). He decided, however, that Singapore should not champion the proposal because of its free port status. He persuaded the then Prime Minister of Thailand, Anand Panyarachun, to champion the proposal. AFTA is one of ASEAN's most important achievements.

Second, when the Cold War ended, PM Goh decided that in the new circumstances it was feasible and desirable for the Asia-Pacific to have a security forum. Again, he decided not to take the credit for his initiative but to persuade Thailand to host the inaugural meeting of the ASEAN Regional Forum or ARF. The ARF has endured and is growing in effectiveness. It continues to be driven by ASEAN.

Third, ASEAN's leaders used to meet about once every five years, at a summit meeting. PM Goh thought that it was desirable for them to meet annually. In 1995, his proposal was accepted and, since 1996, ASEAN's leaders have met at an annual summit. The more frequent interaction among the leaders has helped to enhance mutual trust and confidence among them and to move the group forward more rapidly on its agenda.

Fourth, PM Goh was increasingly worried by the growing competition which major Asian countries such as China and India were posing to ASEAN. He came to the conclusion that the best way for ASEAN to respond is to integrate more broadly and deeply so that ASEAN could compete as a single economy of 500 million people. At the ASEAN Summit in 2002, PM Goh proposed that ASEAN should move beyond

AFTA and become an economic community, a single market and production base, with the free flow of goods, services and skilled labour and the freer flow of capital, by 2020. The proposal was adopted by the Summit in 2003 and incorporated in the Bali Concord II.

Fifth, PM Goh thought that ASEAN would benefit if it were linked to the dynamic economies of China, Japan, Korea and India. In 1996, he proposed that ASEAN should hold a summit with China, Japan or Korea, as a group, as well as summits with each of them individually. Since 1997, the leaders of ASEAN and those of China, Japan and Korea have been meeting at an annual summit called ASEAN+3. In 2000, he proposed holding an ASEAN+India Summit. Such a summit was held in 2002 and has also become an annual event. The journey to integrate Southeast Asia, Northeast Asia and India has begun. If successful, this will eventually produce the world's largest regional economy. As European integration has shown, it will also contribute to peace in Asia.

3. Linking ASEAN with Northeast Asia

The connection between Southeast Asia and Northeast Asia is not immediately obvious. In the past 50 years, we have become accustomed to referring to Southeast Asia and Northeast Asia as if they were distinct geographic regions. The truth is that the two sub-regions are closely linked to each other through history, culture and economics, and geography. In the period before Southeast Asia came under the domination of European powers, China had extensive links with the sub-region. During the Second World War, Southeast Asia was conquered and ruled by Japan. The economic connectivity between the two sub-regions was dramatically illustrated during the 1997 financial crisis when the Thai baht was attacked by the currency market. One of the dominoes which fell after the baht was the Korean won. In the aftermath of that crisis, the intellectuals of the two sub-regions realised that their destinies were intertwined. This has given a new impetus to East Asian regionalism.

Japan

PM Goh made several important contributions to Singapore's relations with Japan. He had to overcome two major obstacles. *First*, he had to deal with Japan's hierarchical worldview. In that worldview, Singapore, being a small country, occupies a relatively low position on the Japanese totem pole. PM Goh had to convince Japan that Singapore is a small country which punches above its height, and that it can be a useful partner for Japan's engagement with Southeast Asia. *Second*, PM Goh had to convince Japan that Singapore, despite its ethnic composition, is not a proxy of China.

It was because of PM Goh's successful diplomacy that Japan agreed, in 2000, to negotiate its first free trade agreement with Singapore, styled the Japan-Singapore Economic Agreement for a New Age Partnership (JSEPA), the agreement was signed by PM Goh and PM Koizumi in January 2002 and came into force in November of the same year. It has also inspired Malaysia, Thailand and the Philippines to seek similar agreements with Japan. Japan and ASEAN are negotiating a closer economic partnership.

China

On 3 October 1990, China and Singapore established formal diplomatic relations with each other. During the past 14 years, relations between the two countries have grown from strength to strength. The recent hiccup over DPM Lee's visit to Taiwan should not obscure the fact that relations between China and Singapore are extensive and substantial. Singapore is China's no. 1 trading partner and foreign investor in Southeast Asia. Singapore is a good friend of China. It will never work against China's core interests.

What contributions has PM Goh made to Singapore's relations with China? *First*, PM Goh proposed to President Hu Jintao the establishment of the Joint Council for Bilateral Cooperation which has become a reality.

The Council is co-chaired by Deputy Prime Ministers. It provides a strategic platform for the leaders of the two countries to oversee bilateral relations.

Second, PM Goh proposed to PM Wen Jiabao the establishment of a China Centre in Singapore. The China Centre will embrace a commercial centre, a cultural and media centre and a centre for Chinese medicine.

Third, PM Goh is also responsible for the establishment of the Singapore China Foundation, the Singapore-Shandong Business Council and the Singapore-Sichuan Trade and Investment Committee.

Fourth, PM Goh succeeded in persuading China to launch a free trade agreement with Singapore. Negotiations are due to start in November. China and ASEAN are already negotiating a free trade agreement to be completed within 10 years.

Korea

The Republic of Korea is sandwiched between two giants, China and Japan. This should not, however, obscure its intrinsic significance. The Republic of Korea has the world's 11th largest economy and several world class companies and brand names, such as, Samsung, LG, Hyundai, etc. The Korean people are intelligent, well educated, disciplined, diligent and creative. It is a country with a bright future. PM Goh cultivated former President Kim Dae-jung and current President, Roh Moo-hyun, and convinced them to launch a free trade agreement with Singapore. The negotiations are expected to be completed before the end of 2004. The Korea-Singapore FTA will serve as a template for the Korea-ASEAN FTA. In the meantime, trade, investment and cultural exchange between the two countries are flourishing.

4. Linking ASEAN with India

The two giants of Asia are China and India. The two countries' engagement with Southeast Asia are equally ancient. Until the arrival of Islam and the West, Southeast Asia was deeply influenced by the Indian civilisation. This heritage, however, dissipated with time. It was not until the early 1990s that Prime Minister Narasimha Rao announced a new "look east" policy. In the past decade, India has sought to re-establish its historic ties with Southeast Asia. India needed a champion in ASEAN to make this possible. PM Goh is India's champion. It was therefore very gratifying for India to have awarded him the Nehru Prize in July 2004.

What are PM Goh's most important contributions to India's engagement with ASEAN and Singapore? *First*, PM Goh persuaded ASEAN to upgrade India's status to a full dialogue partner, to admit India to the ARF and to hold a summit with India. *Second*, PM Goh acceded to PM Narasimha Rao's request for Singapore to build a Technology Park in Bangalore. *Third*, PM Goh persuaded PM Vajpayee to agree to negotiate a free trade agreement with Singapore. The Comprehensive Economic Cooperation Agreement or CECA will be concluded before the end of this year. This will serve as a paving stone to an ASEAN-India FTA.

For a long time, Singapore's focus was concentrated on India to the exclusion of other countries in South Asia. In July 2004, PM Goh rectified this by making a historic visit to Pakistan, Bangladesh and Sri Lanka. Singapore has agreed to negotiate free trade agreements with Pakistan and Sri Lanka. In launching these initiatives, Singapore is acting as a path finder in forging closer economic relations between Southeast Asia and South Asia. It would be good if, in the future, AFTA and the South Asia Free Trade Agreement could be linked to each other.

5. Linking ASEAN with Australia and New Zealand

Australia and New Zealand aspire to be accepted by East Asia as part of the family. Singapore would welcome them. The issue is not ethnicity but interest. Do East Asia and Australia and New Zealand share a convergence of interests? Singapore would argue that they do and point to such areas as security, trade, investment, tourism, education, where there is extensive cooperation. It should also be noted that Australia and New Zealand have made positive contributions to ARF and APEC.

New Zealand was the first country with which Singapore concluded a free trade agreement. Since the agreement came into force in 2001, there has been a significant increase in trade and investment between the two countries. They have recently agreed to extend their cooperation into such new areas as the media and creative industry. New Zealand has established its first technology centre overseas in Singapore. New Zealand, Singapore and Chile are negotiating a trilateral free trade agreement.

Singapore has also concluded a free trade agreement with Australia. In addition, the two countries have a Joint Ministerial Council, consisting of the ministries of defence, trade and foreign affairs. The engagement between Singapore and Australia are deep and broad.

The ASEAN Economic Ministers have recently agreed to negotiate with Australia and New Zealand, in order to establish a link between AFTA and the Australia-New Zealand FTA called closer economic partnership or CER. This link will help to convince ASEAN that it should welcome Australia and New Zealand into the East Asian family.

6. Inter-Regional Cooperation and Understanding

Asia and Europe

It is often said that we live in a unipolar world, with the US as the sole superpower. Economically, the world is not unipolar but multipolar. Indeed, the new EU of 25 members, has a combined GDP which is greater than that of the US. In addition to its economic power, the EU also wields considerable political, diplomatic, intellectual and cultural power. The EU is therefore important to Asia and the world.

In 1994, PM Goh had an idea. After examining the relations among the United States, Europe and East Asia, he came to the conclusion that there was a missing link in this triangle. Relations between the US and Europe were old and substantial. There were many institutions which link the two sides of the Atlantic. In the case of relations between the US and East Asia, the ties were younger but substantial. Institutions such as APEC link the two sides of the Pacific. PM Goh saw a missing link between Europe and East Asia. This led him to propose in 1995, that a forum be established consisting of the 15 member countries of the EU and the member countries of ASEAN, China, Japan and Korea. In March 1996, the inaugural summit of the Asia Europe Meeting (ASEM) was held in Bangkok. Since then, ASEM has met once every two years, alternating between Asia and Europe.

Another one of PM Goh's ideas which has borne fruit is the Asia-Europe Foundation. Based in Singapore, the Foundation was conceptualised to promote social, cultural, intellectual and people-to-people exchanges between Asia and Europe. Begun in 1997, the Foundation has organised over 200 projects, involving over 5,000 people from the two countries and civilisations.

PM Goh has worked very hard to forge closer and more substantial ties between Singapore and the different countries of Europe, large and small. He has visited 16 of the 25 EU countries. He is on good personal terms with many of the leaders of Europe, including both the incoming and outgoing Presidents of the European Commission.

America

Relations between Singapore and the US have occupied two peaks. The first peak was in 1985, when the then PM, Lee Kuan Yew, was invited to address a joint meeting of the US Congress. With the end of the Cold War, the relationship began to drift. Things got worse after the Michael Fay affair. PM Goh never wrote the relationship off. With the help of the former US Ambassador to Singapore, Steven Green, he began to turn the relationship around and to cultivate President Clinton. Common interests in APEC and the WTO helped to re-invigorate the relationship.

By a stroke of good timing and luck, PM Goh managed to persuade President Clinton, in November 2000, two months before the end of his term, to launch negotiation for a free trade agreement. The terrorist attack on the US in September 2001 created a new threat perception in Washington, DC and offered new opportunities for Singapore and the

US to work together. With the signing of the US-Singapore FTA, by President Bush and PM Goh, in Washington in May 2003, it would be fair to say that the bilateral relationship has scaled a new peak, higher than that in 1985. The two countries are currently negotiating a Framework Agreement for the Promotion of a Strategic Cooperation Partnership in Defence and Security. On the business side, the Singapore-US Business Council, chaired by Deputy Prime Minister, Dr Tony Tan, serves the useful purpose of enabling the Singapore Government to engage a selected group of US business leaders at a very senior level.

Singapore is not a treaty ally of the United States. However, the relationship between Washington and Singapore is substantial, multi-dimensional and reliable. PM Goh has made a major contribution to the excellent relations which exist today between Washington and Singapore.

Asia and Latin-America

On a visit to Chile, in 1998, PM Goh launched another new initiative. He wanted to connect East Asia and Latin-America, two regions of the developing world which showed promise. The Forum for East Asia-Latin America Cooperation or FEALAC, consists of 15 countries from East Asia, including Australia and New Zealand, and 17 countries from Latin America. The Forum provides a platform for political leaders, government officials, business leaders and scholars to meet and congregate in many areas, such as, culture, economics, education, science and technology. The relationship between these two regions is starting from a relatively low base. It will, therefore, take some time to overcome the knowledge gap, to raise the comfort level and to identify areas of converging interests.

Middle East and Africa

Singapore is a member of the UN and the Commonwealth. Through these and other forums, PM Goh has befriended several African leaders.

Singapore helped Botswana to build a very successful productivity centre. The President of Nigeria, Olusegun Obasanjo, is a friend and admirer of PM Goh and of Singapore. PM Goh has made several suggestions to South Africa to deepen the engagement between the two countries.

Following the 9/11 attack on America and other terrorist acts in other parts of the world, there has been a backlash against Islam and the Arabs, in the West. PM Goh decided to launch a diplomatic initiative to build links between Singapore and moderate Islamic and Arab countries. Thus, Singapore has concluded its first FTA with an Arab country, Jordan, and has agreed to negotiate FTAs with Bahrain, Qatar, Egypt, Iran, Kuwait and South Africa. PM Goh has visited Oman, UAE, Egypt, Jordan, Bahrain and Iran. He has proposed establishing a Dialogue between Asia and the Middle East whose inaugural meeting will be held in 2005.

7. Singapore and the World

United Nations

It was during PM Goh's term that Singapore was successfully elected, for the first time, to the United Nations Security Council (UNSC). During the two-year term, from 2000 to 2002, PM Goh was actively engaged and helped Singapore to resolve several tricky issues that the Council had to deal with. He also co-launched a "Global Initiative on Sustainable Development" together with the then Chancellor Helmut Kohl (Germany), former President Fernando Cardoso (Brazil), and then Deputy President Thabo Mbeki (South Africa) on the occasion of the 5th Anniversary of the UN Conference on Environment and Development (UNCED). Following this initiative, Singapore organised the World Conference on Model Cities, bringing together the urban best practices of the world. Singapore has also enhanced its role in peacekeeping activities and humanitarian relief under PM Goh's leadership. In the area of peacekeeping missions,

Singapore has sent military and police detachments to various UN peacekeeping missions, including Iraq. At the UN's Millennium Summit, in 2000, PM Goh chaired one of the Roundtables for Heads of State and Government.

In the area of humanitarian relief, the Singapore International Foundation (SIF) has sent over 500 Singaporeans to serve in Bhutan, Botswana, Cambodia, China, Ghana, Indonesia, Laos, Malaysia, Myanmar, Nepal, Philippines, Sri Lanka, Timor Leste and Vietnam since 1991. SIF has also sent seven medical/technical relief teams, comprising 11 mission teams to the following six countries, Afghanistan, Cambodia, India, Mongolia, Sri Lanka and Vietnam. The relief missions have brought assistance to 19,000 disaster victims. Singapore has also been supportive of capacity-building and development through its Technical Cooperation Programme (TCP). The TCP has brought thousands of officials from developing countries for training in Singapore in the areas of Singapore's competence and expertise.

Singapore hosted the WTO's first Ministerial Conference in 1996 and has been serving on the Governing Council of the International Maritime Organisation (IMO) and the International Civil Aviation Organisation (ICAO).

8. Goh Chok Tong's Diplomacy

The Prime Minister is a country's chief diplomat to the world. Has Goh Chok Tong been a successful diplomat for Singapore? I accompanied him on one of his trips to Europe. After a meeting with a European leader, PM Goh asked me whether it was unusual for the European leader to tell him that he liked PM. It was unusual. PM Goh has been as successful abroad, as he has been at home, and for the same reasons. He is intelligent and knowledgeable without being arrogant or dogmatic. He is shrewd but not cynical. He is sincere but not naive. He is an original thinker and a fountain of ideas. He is warm and personal and has a gift for winning friends.

Conclusion

Goh Chok Tong leaves us with a rich legacy of foreign policy achievements. *First*, he has consolidated Singapore's position in Southeast Asia. He has launched several initiatives to make ASEAN more integrated and more competitive. *Second*, he has expanded Singapore's political and economic space. He is the architect of our FTA policy. Our free trade agreements have enabled Singapore to transcend the limitations of its small size by linking up with other economies. *Third*, he has made a major contribution to inter-regional cooperation and understanding, viz, between ASEAN and Northeast Asia, between ASEAN and India, between Asia and Europe, between Asia and Latin-America and between Asia and the Middle East. He has kept Singapore safe and at peace with the world. He has earned the goodwill and respect of many foreign leaders for himself and for his country. He has shown that the leader of a small country can make a significant contribution to the building of a more peaceful and prosperous world.

[Originally published in *Impressions of the Goh Chok Tong Years in Singapore*, eds. B. Welsh, J. Chin, A. Mahizhnan and T.H. Tan, Institute of Policy Studies and NUS Press, 2009, pp. 119–127.]

The Singapore of My Dreams

This essay will complement another essay by Terence Chong. He will comment on the important events and developments which took place in Singapore in 2008. One of the editors, Daljit Singh, has requested me to focus my essay on my "hopes and expectations". I have decided to write my essay on the Singapore of my dreams. My dreams have obviously changed over the years. I will begin with my school boy's dreams.

A School Boy's Dreams

I grew up in colonial Singapore. After the Second World War, my parents sent me to a Chinese primary school. After a few years, because of my unsatisfactory progress, my parents decided to switch me to the English stream. I spent a bridging year in a Catholic school and then joined the Outram School, which was then a government primary school. I completed my secondary education at Raffles Institution (RI).

What were my school boy's dreams for Singapore?

First, I dreamt that one day Singapore would be independent and we would be able to rule ourselves. I was greatly influenced by the anti-colonial struggles and nationalist movements then taking place in Asia and Africa. I remember debating the merit and demerit of colonialism with one of my expatriate teachers in RI.

Second, I dreamt that one day Singapore would be without slums and all Singaporeans would have access to good housing, clean water and modern sanitation. I had relatives living in Bukit Ho Swee[1] and they lacked all three. I used to accompany my mother and aunt to visit them. I am very glad that this dream of mine has come true.

Third, I dreamt that all families would earn enough income to enable them to live decently. After the war, there were a lot of poor people in Singapore. Today, the situation is vastly different. If we use the internationally accepted criteria of US$1 per day or US$2 per day, there are no poor people in Singapore. However, the reality is that for the bottom thirty percent of our population, life is very tough. We should do more to help our poor and disadvantaged families without undermining our work ethic and our culture of self-reliance.

Fourth, I dreamt that one day we would live in a society in which the law would be just and people did not fear either the gangsters or the police. In those days the rule of law was weak and the people lived in fear of both the gangsters and the colonial police. I was angered by the sight of the police going around arresting the hawkers. I wrote an article for my school magazine, *The Rafflesian*, protesting against such arrests and pleading that the government should create places for the hawkers to ply their trade. I suffered my first experience of censorship by the British Director of Education and was told that my article could not be published. Today, the rule of law in Singapore is strong, with good law and order, an honest and competent police force, and an independent and non-corrupt judiciary.

A Young Man's Dreams

I was one of the lucky students who, in 1957, was admitted to study law at the University of Malaya, in Singapore. I graduated in 1961 and spent a year as David Marshall's law pupil. In 1962, I was admitted to the legal

---

[1] Bukit Ho Swee was a densely populated area which had thousands of squatter homes built with combustible materials such as attap and wooden boards. Between 1934 and 1968 this squatter area experienced three big fires. The second fire which occurred in 1961 was the biggest fire in Singapore (adapted from *Singapore Encyclopedia*).

profession and hired by the Faculty of Law as an Assistant Lecturer, joining my classmates, Thio Su Mien and Koh Kheng Lian. I then spent a year at Harvard Law School and another year at Cambridge University. I came home in 1965 when Singapore unexpectedly became independent, fulfilling one of my childhood dreams. Singapore was, however, faced with an uncertain future because the conventional wisdom at that time was that an independent Singapore was not viable. Singapore's independence was therefore greeted by both cheers and tears. I was one of the minority who believed that an independent Singapore would succeed.

What were my dreams for Singapore as a young man?

First, I wanted independent Singapore to survive and to be accepted by the international community as a new member state. Three years after our independence, I was sent to the United Nations, in New York, to help secure this agenda.

Second, I wanted Singapore to succeed economically, to create enough jobs for our unemployed and the young people entering the work force each year. Our economic achievements in the past forty-three years have surpassed my dream.

Third, I had hoped that we would find a socio-economic model which would achieve growth with equity. We have achieved growth but we have not done as well with equity. The disparities of wealth and income have become wider, not narrower. I find it shocking that our Gini index is worse than that of the United States[2]. In addition, as our sociologist, Tan Ern Ser[3], has warned us, we are beginning to see the stratification of our society by social class. We should not abandon our dream of achieving both prosperity and equity. We should combat all forms of social snobbery and never allow an underclass to form in Singapore.

Fourth, I wanted a better balance in our early years of nation building between the new and the old. I belonged to a group of idealistic young

---

[2] According to the 2007/2008 United Nations Human Development Report's Gini Index, the United States was ranked number 12 (40.8) and Singapore ranked number 25 (42.5). A Gini index of "0" represents perfect income equality whereas a Gini index of "100" represents perfect income inequality.

[3] Tan Ern Ser, *Does Class Matter? Social Stratification and Orientations in Singapore.* Singapore: World Scientific, 2004.

men called Singapore Planning and Urban Research group or SPUR in short. We lobbied the government to conserve some of our landmark buildings, historic neighbourhoods and streets. We did not want to lose our built heritage as we plunge headlong into the planning and building of a new Singapore. We were ahead of our time and the conservation movement did not enjoy strong support until the 1980s. I am, however, very pleased to say that, in recent decades, due to the good work of our Preservation of Monuments Board and the Urban Redevelopment Authority, we have done well in conserving our built heritage compared to other Asian cities.

Fifth, I dreamt that mutual understanding, peace and harmony would continue to prevail among Singaporeans of different races, religions, languages and cultures. In this respect, Singapore has done well. The two books[4] on ethnicity and religious diversity, edited by Dr Lai Ah Eng, confirm this impression. The Inter-Religious Organisation, Singapore (IRO), a non-governmental organisation, has made a major contribution to religious harmony in Singapore. We have developed a culture of tolerance, acceptance and respect for the faiths of others. Denigrating the faiths of others is both ethically and legally unacceptable in Singapore. I am also cheered by the growing percentage of inter-racial marriages in Singapore. Singapore should aspire to become a global centre for inter-ethnic, inter-religious and inter-cultural dialogue.

Sixth, I dreamt that Singaporeans would enjoy good governance and the rule of law. In 1960–1961, when I was the President of the University of Malaya Students Law Society, I had advocated the setting up of an ombudsman in Singapore. I did so because in Singapore, the exercise of discretionary power by the government is not subject to judicial review. Although we have an honest government and one of the best bureaucracies in the world, mistakes can and do occur. An ombudsman would be empowered to investigate and report on complaints by citizens of maladministration. I still hope that one day Singapore would have

---

[4] Lai, Ah Eng, ed., *Beyond Rituals and Riots: Ethnic Pluralism and Social Cohesion in Singapore*. Singapore: Eastern Universities Press 2004; Lai, Ah Eng, ed., *Religious Diversity in Singapore*. Singapore: Institute of Southeast Asian Studies Press, 2008.

an ombudsman although the need for one is not as great now as it was 47 years ago.

An Old Man's Dreams

I have not stopped dreaming for Singapore. What are the dreams of this old man?

First, I dream that Singaporeans would be less obsessed with money and that we would grow in kindness and graciousness. I have always heeded my mentor, Mr S. Rajaratnam's warning that Singaporeans should not become a people who know the price of everything and the value of nothing. I think we are in such danger. We seem to calculate everything in terms of money. We seem to think that a person's worth is measured by the amount of money he or she makes. We have imitated one of the worst aspects of American capitalism by paying our senior executives inflated salaries while, at the same time, stagnating the salaries of our middle and lower strata[5]. I am glad that the President recognises annually members of some of the professions which do not pay well but which make enormous contributions to our society, such as, teachers, nurses, social workers, librarians, etc. I also thank the media for showcasing selfless Singaporeans who help the poor and the disadvantaged, both at home and abroad. Money is important. We all need enough money to live in reasonable comfort and with material sufficiency. Money cannot, however, buy you good health, a happy family, good friends, peace of mind and joy. I hope that one day, Singapore's favourite film maker, Jack Neo[6] will make a new movie, entitled "Money Enough Lah".

Are Singaporeans a kind people? I am inclined to say, yes, when I remember the generosity with which Singaporeans responded to the

---

[5] See Chua Hak Bin, *Singapore Economy: The New and the Dual Economy*, in *Singapore Perspectives 2007: A New Singapore*, edited by Tan Tarn How. Singapore: World Scientific; Yeoh Lam Keong, *A New Social Compact for Singapore*. Singapore: *The Straits Times*, 23 November 2007.
[6] Comedian, actor and film director, Jack Neo Chee Keong first became a household name by being a comedian. His wrote and starred in the film *Money No Enough*, a film about the lives of working class Singaporeans who were trying to make ends meet. Neo was awarded the Public Service Medal in 2004 and the Cultural Medallion in 2005 (adapted from *Singapore Encyclopedia*).

Boxing Day tsunami, the cyclone Nargis, the earthquake in Szechuan, etc. I am constantly impressed by the letters written to the forum page of *The Straits Times*, thanking certain Singaporeans for the kindness they had shown to strangers. At the same time, I am shocked by the unkindness and even cruelty shown by some Singaporeans towards their foreign domestic workers and foreign workers more generally. Some of our foreign domestic workers are denied a decent place to sleep in, adequate food and rest and are treated as less than fellow human beings. As for the reports of wanton cruelty towards animals, I often wonder who these monsters are who commit such evil deeds. The record is therefore a mixed one. There are many kind Singaporeans but there are also many unkind Singaporeans. My good friend, Koh Poh Tiong, the Chairman of the Kindness Movements, therefore has a challenging job to do.

Are Singaporeans a gracious people? One area in which we are definitely not a gracious people is our driving manners or lack of them. From our driving practices and habits, one can infer that Singaporeans are aggressive, self-centred, inconsiderate and ungenerous. Is this an accurate portrait of ourselves? Let us hope that our driving manners, our selfish behaviour on our busses and trains, and in our elevators, do not reflect the kind of people we really are. The Minister Mentor is probably right when he said recently that we still have a long way to go to become a gracious and cultured people.

Second, I would like Singapore to become the Geneva of the East and the Venice of the 21st century. I think Singapore is a welcoming, efficient and secure meeting place for representatives of adversaries. We have already hosted some such meetings, for example, between the People's Republic of China and Taiwan in 1993, and between the United States and North Korea, more recently. Venice existed for almost 800 years as an independent city state. One of the reasons for its success and longevity was that it welcomed the merchants, artists, and other talented people of different countries and civilizations to live and work in Venice. In the same way, Singapore should continue to welcome the talented people of all nations and civilizations to live and work here. We can become the Venice of the 21st century.

Third, Singapore can be the cultural hub of South-East Asia and the home city of the Asian cultural renaissance. Singapore already has the best cultural infrastructure in South-East Asia. We have the best museums of the region. The Esplanade is the region's best centre for the performing arts. Singapore has turned necessity into a virtue. Because of our small size and short history, we have no choice but to collect the history, heritage and visual arts of the region. As a result, we have the best and most comprehensive collection in the world of the 19th century and 20th century visual arts of South-East Asia. It was fitting that the world premiere of Robert Wilson's staging of the Buginese epic, "I La Galigo", took place in Singapore. Beginning in 2008, the National Heritage Board will organise annually a festival to celebrate the civilization of an ASEAN country. The inaugural festival on Vietnam was a great success. In 2009, we will showcase the Philippines. We have also taken the initiative to organise the first conference of ASEAN's museum directors. Singapore can however serve an even larger region. Because of our ethnic composition and our vision, Singapore can bring together the civilizations of South-East Asia, China, South Asia and even Islam. The Asian Civilisations Museum is a living example of our aspiration to be the home city of the Asian cultural renaissance. The recent initiative by the Arts House to organise the conference and festival, "Asia on Edge", should be applauded. I also welcome the new President of the National University of Singapore, Professor Tan Chorh Chuan's proposal to set up a new Global Asia Institute at the University.

Fourth, Singapore can be Asia's "greenest" city. Singapore is already Asia's greenest city in the physical sense. Recently, some friends from Hong Kong, France and UK told me how impressed they were by our beautiful trees. Our beloved Botanic Gardens have been awarded three stars by Guide Michelin, putting it in the same category as the iconic Eiffel Tower of Paris. We will soon open two new gardens in Marina Bay. But, Singapore is green not just physically but in its policies towards water, sanitation, air pollution, land use, sewage treatment, etc. The book, *Clean, Green and Blue*[7] by Tan Yong Soon, Lee Tung Jean and Karen Tan (2009), tells the remarkable story of Singapore's journey in reconciling rapid economic growth with care for the environment. Singapore should also be "green" in the protection of its nature reserves and biological diversity, in the more efficient use of energy and the reduction of CO_2 emission, in the recycling of waste, and in the promotion of clean and renewable energy. I would like to see Singapore becoming a centre for the financing of green business and technology, a preferred venue for test-bedding new green technologies, products and services and for the trading of carbon credit. I am glad that a major Norwegian company has opened a plant to manufacture solar panels in Singapore. I am also encouraged by the seed money which the National Research Council has invested in research and development in solar energy. In the 21st century, with more than half of humanity living in cities, one of our greatest challenges is to make our cities as sustainable as possible. Singapore can be a role model for Asia and for the world.

Fifth, I think Singapore can become an important intellectual centre of the world. Our two leading universities, National University of Singapore and Nanyang Technological University, have been recognised as world class universities. I am confident that the Singapore Management University will soon join them. Our polytechnics, institutes of technical education, primary and secondary schools are much admired in the region. As a result, Singapore is beginning to attract a large number of foreign students to study here. There has also been a quantum leap in the percentage of our GDP invested in research and development[8]. The culture of respect for learning and research is growing and more and more young people are taking careers in research and scholarship. Our think-tanks are expanding in number and ascending in quality. Our Japanese friends have sometimes referred to Singapore as "a think-

---

[7] Singapore: Institute of Southeast Asian Studies.
[8] The gross domestic expenditure on R&D (GERD) increased from S$5,010 million in 2006 to S$6,339 million in 2007. The unprecedented year-on-year increase by 26.5% is a significant jump from the 9.3% year-on-year increase in 2006. As a percentage of GDP, GERD rose from 2.31% in 2006 to 2.61% in 2007. (*Source*: A*Star press release, 23 Dec. 2008).

tank country". What more can we do? We can invest more money in research in the social sciences and humanities. At the moment, the Ministry of Education is the only source of such funding. The National Research Council does not make grants to support such research and there is no local equivalent of the US Social Science Research Council. We can be more open in releasing data to researchers. We also need to grow the culture of tolerance for alternative and dissenting views. Without such a culture, scholarship, especially in the social sciences and humanities, will not flourish.

Conclusion

Singapore is a microcosm of the world of the 21st century. It is globalised and multi-cultural. It is both urban and green. It is situated at the confluence of the civilizations of Southeast Asia, China and India. Because of our colonial heritage, Singapore is part East and part West. It is a leading candidate for Asia's most global city. Let us make Singapore one of the most liveable cities in the world.

[Originally published in *Southeast Asian Affairs*, pp. 305–312. © 2009 Institute of Southeast Asian Studies]

Don't Knock Minimum Wage Yet

Economically, Singapore has made tremendous progress over the past 20 years. Its gross domestic product has grown from $56 billion in 1989 to $265 billion last year. Its per capita income has risen from $16,000 to $48,000. Its foreign reserves have increased from $38 billion to $263 billion.

Singapore has also done well in the Human Development Index of the United Nations Development Programme, rising from 35 to 23. A few days ago, the Legatum Institute of London ranked Singapore 17th in the 2010 Legatum Prosperity Index, ahead of Japan (18th), France (19th) and Hong Kong (20th).

But there is one area in which the situation in Singapore is sub-optimal.

Singapore believes in inclusive growth. We attach great importance to our social cohesion. We believe in the work ethic and the principle of self-reliance. We also believe that hardworking Singaporeans, no matter how humble his or her job, should earn incomes that would enable them and their families to live in dignity and material sufficiency.

This is, unfortunately, not universally the case in Singapore. Among the top 20 in the Legatum Prosperity Index, Singapore is the second most unequal country, after Hong Kong (as measured by the Gini coefficient).

The growing income disparity and the hardship of the bottom 20 percent of our citizenry are a challenge to our social cohesion and to our philosophy of inclusive growth.

According to the 2010 World Bank's Development Indicators, the lowest 20 percent of Singapore's population account for 5 percent of the country's income whereas the top 20 percent account for 49 percent.

One of the signs of the poverty at the bottom of our society is the number of children who go to school without any pocket money for lunch. The Straits Times Pocket Money Fund benefits 70,000 such children.

Professor Joel Kotkin, a scholar of cities, visited Singapore recently. In an interview with this newspaper published on Oct. 13, he said: "A third of the children in inner city London live in poverty. It is this kind of inequality Singapore should guard against."

Let us take his warning as a wake-up call. But what is to be done?

We are told not to tamper with the market in regulating wages. The truth is that the market does not work for low-skilled and semi-skilled workers because they do not have equal bargaining power and are competing against an endless supply of cheap labour in the region. I am not suggesting that we close our doors to foreign workers. We should, however, consider tighter restrictions on foreign workers in certain sectors, such as hotels and restaurants.

What would Adam Smith, the intellectual father of the market economy, say? The conventional wisdom is that Smith was against the state intervening in the market. But according to Nobel economics laureate Amartya Sen, this was not Smith's position.

Sen said that Smith was deeply concerned about the inequality and poverty that might exist in an otherwise successful economy. Smith acknowledged the importance of interventions on behalf of the poor and the underdogs of society. In his magnum opus, *The Wealth of Nations*, he wrote: "When the regulation ... is in favour of the workmen, it is always just and equitable; but it is sometimes otherwise when in favour of the masters."

The truth is that all governments regulate markets, especially the market for labour and wages. Immigration restrictions and taxes are two examples. In Singapore, the question is not whether, but how best, to regulate the labour market so that we will have a strong economy and, at the same time, enable all Singaporeans to earn a living wage.

The minimum wage is an imperfect instrument. It does not guarantee a more equal society, as is shown in the United States. It does, however, ensure that workers earn a living wage. I would prefer to rely on the National Wages Council (NWC) and Workfare Income Supplement if they can be made to work for our low-skilled and semi-skilled workers and their families, who form the bottom 20 percent of our population. We should request the NWC to consider what it can do for these workers. Workfare is an excellent Singapore innovation and we should consider how we can enhance its effectiveness.

If, however, they are less than fully effective, we should have a calm and rational discussion about the pros and cons of the minimum wage. Those who oppose the minimum wage have argued that it will increase unemployment, discourage foreign investment and reduce our competitiveness. I have reviewed the situations in Japan, South Korea and Taiwan, which adopted the minimum wage in 1959, 1988 and 1956, respectively. I have found no evidence in those three cases that the minimum wage has caused an increase in unemployment, reduced foreign investment or reduced competitiveness in those economies.

I acknowledge that the government is already doing a lot for our less fortunate citizens, in education, housing, health care, which are heavily subsidised, and through various financial assistance schemes. But existing programmes may not be enough. We should work together and think of new and innovative ideas on how to boost the incomes of the bottom 20 percent of our population.

Singapore's founding fathers envisioned building a country that would resemble an olive, with a large middle class and relatively few people at the top and at the bottom. We must not allow the olive to become a pear.

[Originally published in *The Straits Times*, 11 November 2010.]

Disagreeing with Some Hard Truths

We must thank Minister Mentor Lee Kuan Yew and the seven Straits Times journalists for sharing with us *Hard Truths to Keep Singapore Going*. Taken together with Mr Lee's two-volume memoirs, the three books constitute his intellectual legacy. The Q&A format of *Hard Truths* and Mr Lee's trenchant and unvarnished views make the book both interesting and easy to read. I also found the endnotes, at the end of each chapter, helpful.

We owe it to Mr Lee to take his views seriously. They are distilled from the experiences and reflections of an extraordinary man and leader. I agree with many of his hard truths. I agree with his assessment of the United States, of the historical importance of Deng Xiaoping and his deep belief in meritocracy and integrity.

However, we also owe him the responsibility to contest his ideas if we disagree with them. It is in this spirit and with great respect that I wish to comment on the following three points.

First, I do not agree with the Minister Mentor's view that Singapore is too small and lacks the critical mass to produce a world champion in manufacturing. His conclusion is that we will always be dependent on multinational corporations. We should accept the truth that, because of our small size, we are destined to play the secondary role of being suppliers and contract manufacturers. I am glad that Mr Michael Dee and Mr Sam Goi have expressed their disagreements with Mr Lee's view in this newspaper.

Is the view supported by the facts? I do not think so. Let us look at the achievements of some small European countries.

Switzerland, with a population of 7.6 million, has 15 companies in the Fortune Global List of 500 Companies. Sweden, with a population of 9.2 million, has five; Finland, population 5.3 million, has one; Denmark, 5.5 million, two; and Belgium, 10.7 million, five.

The point of this survey is to demonstrate that it is possible for small countries to produce world champions. In a globalised world, it is possible for small countries to overcome their limitations by borrowing the land, resources and talent of other countries. Thus Singapore builds industrial parks and new towns in other countries and welcomes foreign talent to work here.

If size were destiny, we would not have produced SIA, NOL, PSA, Changi Airport, Keppel, Sembawang, Temasek, GIC, SingTel, Tiger Beer. The Singapore Story — of which Mr Lee is the chief architect — is the story of how the people of a small country dared to dream and overcame seemingly insurmountable odds.

Second, I wish to comment on Mr Lee's assessment of the state of nation-building in Singapore. His view is that we are not yet a nation and that you cannot create a nation in 45 years. He thinks that it may take us another 100 years before we become a nation. He also thinks that Singapore is not ready for a non-Chinese prime minister.

But according to the results of surveys and polls carried out by the Institute of Policy Studies, S. Rajaratnam School of International Studies and others, it would appear that Singapore is more of a nation than Mr Lee believes. The overwhelming majority of our citizens regard themselves as Singaporeans first and, only secondarily, as Chinese, Malays, Indians, Eurasians, and so forth.

This happy state of affairs is due to the success of our proactive policy of mixing Singaporeans of different races in our schools, housing estates and in national service. It is also due to our policy of meritocracy. Finally, it is due to the evolution of a set of shared values uniting citizens of all races, religions and languages.

Again, it was Mr Lee himself who was the chief architect of these policies — and I wish to assure him that he has succeeded to a greater extent than he gives himself credit for.

I do not agree with his assessment that the surveys by our think-tanks are unreliable because the respondents were merely giving politically correct answers. I also do not agree with his view that Singapore is not ready for a non-Chinese PM. I think I speak for the majority of Singaporeans when I say that we are ready, should one emerge who is the best in his or her cohort, as all our prime ministers thus far have been. We do not regard race as a criterion for high office in Singapore.

Third, I was disappointed with the Minister Mentor's views on race. He revealed that if his daughter had wished to marry a black African, he would have had no qualms telling her: "You're mad." He also expressed reservations about inter-racial marriages.

We should not judge a person on the basis of colour, race or religion. There are good men and bad men, good women and bad women, of every colour, race and religion. I know some black Africans who are smart, kind and honourable. If I had a daughter and she had wanted to marry such a man, I would be supportive and would certainly not call her mad.

I know of many happy and long-lasting inter-racial marriages. One of the Minister Mentor's closest comrades, the late S. Rajaratnam, was married to a Hungarian. The marriage was a very happy one and endured till the end of their lives.

[Originally published in *The Straits Times*, 2 March 2011.]

Demystifying the Presidential Office

Now that the general election is behind us, the Singapore electorate is getting ready for another election.

The president's term expires on August 31. An election will therefore have to be held to elect a new president before the end of August. In this essay, I hope to demystify the office of the president and discuss some of his roles, functions and powers.

First, the president is the head of the state of Singapore. He occupies the same position as the British queen, the Malaysian king, and the Indian president — but with enhanced powers. The president is not the head of government, who is the prime minister. The president is the symbol of the country.

The reason the Constitution requires that the president belong to no political party is that he should be non-partisan and above party politics. The president should be a person who can command the support of all our ethnic and religious groups. He should, therefore, not be viewed as a chauvinist or a person who is not open to inter-faith dialogue and harmony. Under no circumstance should the office be politicised.

The president should also be able to bridge our social and economic classes. He should be admired by the poor as well as the rich, and everyone else in between. In other words, the president should be a person who can unite our nation and be a symbol of our national unity.

Second, the president plays an important diplomatic role. It would not be wrong to call him Singapore's No. 1 diplomat. All the ambassadors and high commissioners accredited to Singapore present their credentials to the president. Visiting foreign leaders normally request to call on the president, which is the universal diplomatic protocol observed by states in their relations with one another. In addition, the president can assist the prime minister and the foreign minister in expanding and deepening Singapore's external relations.

In carrying out this role, I should clarify that the president does not pursue an independent foreign policy. He has no such power. The president has to act in accordance with the advice of the Cabinet in his dealings with foreign leaders and their governments.

However, given his high status, the president can add value by undertaking visits to selected countries. These trips are not undertaken for the president's pleasure. They are carefully prepared for and undertaken only if there are key deliverables. They help to expand Singapore's economic and political space.

The president, thus, plays an important diplomatic role. Ideally, he should be knowledgeable about the world, temperamentally tactful and able to hold his own in his interactions with foreign leaders.

Third, the president can and should use the soft power of his office to champion good causes. Each president has championed causes close to his heart.

President Wee Kim Wee, who was a badminton champion in his younger days, championed sports and volunteerism. President Ong Teng Cheong championed culture and the arts, especially, music. In President S.R. Nathan's case, it is the poor, the needy and the disabled that he has championed.

President Nathan studied social studies in university and began his career as a social worker. Mrs Nathan taught in a school for the blind. As a result, both of them wished to do something in this area.

Eleven years ago, President Nathan launched the President's Challenge, in cooperation with the Ministry of Community Development, Youth and Sports and the National Council of Social Service. To date, more than $100 million has been raised, benefiting hundreds of charities and thousands of our poor, needy and disabled.

In addition, President Nathan has been tireless in helping the Community Chest and various other charities in their fund-raising activities. We must hope that the next president will also use the soft power of his office to champion good causes close to his heart and thereby help to build a better and more inclusive Singapore.

Fourth, the president is vested with executive power in five specific areas:

- He has the power to veto a proposal by the Government to spend the state's past reserves. The surpluses earned by the Government during its term of office are added to the accumulated reserves of the past, and locked away.

If, for example, a government that has just been sworn into office wishes to spend part of the surpluses accumulated during the previous five years, the president can say "no".

- Similarly, the Constitution empowers the president to veto the proposed appointment of individuals to certain key positions in the public sector. The president can also veto a proposal by the Government to remove an individual from such a key position.

The president's power in these two areas is a negative power. He can veto a Budget that proposes to spend part of the reserves, but he has no power to suggest how the reserves should be managed or to suggest an alternative Budget. Similarly, he can veto an appointment, but he cannot suggest an alternative candidate.

In exercising his veto powers, the president is required to consult the six wise people in the Council of Presidential Advisers (CPA). The president appoints two members of the CPA, including the chairman; the prime minister appoints two; and the Chief Justice and the chairman of the Public Service Commission appoint one each.

The current chairman of the council is Mr J. Y. Pillay. The other members are: Mr S. Dhanabalan, Mr Po'ad Shaik Abu Bakar Mattar, Mr Yong Pung How, Mr Goh Joon Seng and Mr Bobby Chin. Mr Lim Chee Onn and Mr Stephen Lee are the two alternate members.

The council meets monthly and advises the president on matters relating to the Budget and key public sector appointments. If the president's veto has the support of a majority of the members of the council, the veto is final. However, if the president's veto is not supported by such a majority, it can be overridden by a two-thirds majority vote in Parliament.

In choosing the next president, we should avoid choosing a person who is eager to pick a fight with the Government. In a president, we need a person possessed of equanimity, who is deliberate and calm, deeply experienced and wise. At the same time, we do not want a person who lacks the courage of his conviction or who has no convictions.

The president must not be reckless. However, if the prime minister were to propose appointing an unqualified person to be the next Chief Justice, for example, we would like the president to have the courage to veto the appointment.

The president has been vested with executive powers in three other areas. In exercising his powers in these areas, the president is not obliged to consult the CPA:

- If the advisory committee under the Internal Security Act advises that a political detainee be released and the Government disagrees, the president can order that the detainee be released.
- If the prime minister refuses to give permission to the director of the Corrupt Practices Investigation Bureau (CPIB) to continue with his investigation of an individual, the president can overrule the prime minister and allow the CPIB to carry on with its investigation.
- Under the Maintenance of Religious Harmony Act, the Government can issue a restraining order against a person deemed to be acting contrary to the maintenance of religious harmony. However, if the Cabinet's decision is opposed by the Presidential Council for Religious Harmony, the president is empowered to overrule the Cabinet.

I hope I have added clarity to the roles, functions and powers of the president. It would not be wrong to say that our president is the guardian of two of our country's core interests as they pertain to our reserves and the integrity of our public service.

In good times, his role is to maintain an "informed watchfulness" in these areas, as Ms Lydia Lim of this newspaper put it recently. However, if things go wrong, we should be able to turn to our president to protect us from the depredations of a rogue government.

[Originally published in *The Straits Times*, 15 June 2011.]

In Praise of Older Workers

In recent years, there has been much discussion in Singapore about whether to raise the retirement age. Mr Lee Kuan Yew had suggested that we do away altogether with the concept of retirement. He also famously said that retirement equals death.

The practice in Singapore is for employers, both in the public and private sectors, to retire their employees at a certain age. This could be as young as 50 if they work in our police or armed forces. The Singapore Police Force and Singapore Armed Forces do, however, help their retirees to find second careers. The normal retirement age is 62. The Government has announced that the retirement age will be gradually raised from 62 to 67.

Another common practice in Singapore is for employers to rehire some of their employees after they reach retirement age, on half or a fraction of their previous pay and with reduced or no medical benefits.

My view is that it does not seem fair to do this if the employee does exactly the same work. Employees over 62 are not covered by the Retirement Age Act, which has just come into force, and the terms of their employment are determined by mutual agreement between them and their employers.

Another common practice is to reduce the contributions of the older worker and his employers to the Central Provident Fund. This is also a questionable practice.

All these practices are based upon the assumption that, by a certain age, a person is no longer able to perform his job as competently as he could when he was younger.

I want to question this assumption. I will do so by citing the examples of my dentist, tailor and optician, all of whom are in their 80s. If they were not self-employed, they would have been retired a long time ago. Singapore would have been deprived of their contributions. Isn't it irrational — to retire such competent and productive older persons when we are very short of manpower and import over a million foreign workers to work in Singapore?

My dentist is Dr Choo Teck Chuan, a partner at the dental practice Robertson Choo Oehlers Lee & Lye. He has served as the president of the Singapore Dental Association and was instrumental in bringing the World Dental Congress to Singapore in 1990. Dr Choo is 80 years old and has the energy and competence of a much younger man. Apart from his practice in Singapore, Dr Choo has also been an active volunteer abroad. He has shared his knowledge and experience with dentists in 17 countries, including China, India and Indonesia. He was recently honoured by the American Dental Association. He works 5 1/2 days a week.

My tailor is Mr Edward Kwan of Wai Cheong. Mr Kwan is a second-generation tailor and inherited his father's business. He has been working as a tailor for 64 years. He has many famous clients, at home and abroad, including former American president Bill Clinton. Mr Kwan's eyes are sharp and hands steady and he still cuts the fabric when you order a suit from him. He works six days a week. He is 80 years old.

My optician is Mr Leow Hock Chin of Star Optical. He has been working as an optician for 54 years. I have been a client of Mr Leow for many years. I find him competent and wise. He is 83 years old and works 5 1/2 days a week.

I don't think Dr Choo, Mr Kwan and Mr Leow are unique cases. Singaporeans now live much longer than they did a generation ago. If they are blessed with good health and are of sound mind and body, there is no reason to stop them from working or to downgrade them to a lower job or to reduce their pay and benefits. Given our manpower shortage, we should have a radical, rethink about older workers and see them as assets and not liabilities. People should be judged on the basis of their ability and performance and not on age.

Those who wish to retire and can afford to do so, should, of course, be entitled to do so. But for others, who are fit and wish to continue to work, they should also be entitled to carry on.

I acknowledge that there is a tension between retaining older workers and recruiting young workers who are entering the labour market. We therefore need an economy which is growing and creating new jobs. We may also need to help some of our older workers undergo retraining so that they could work in sales or as caregivers, for example. The new trend is for individuals to have multi-careers in their lifetimes and to stop working only when they wish to and can afford to do so.

Work gives meaning to life. Work gives a person dignity and self-esteem. It is time for a mindset change. It is time to see our older workers in a new light. It is time for Singapore to recognise people like Dr Choo, Mr Kwan and Mr Leow as assets to our nation.

[Originally published in *The Straits Times*, 5 January 2012.]

Opening Eyes to Guide Dogs for the Blind

Esme and Kendra are two dogs. Esme was born in Australia and Kendra in the US. They are blond labrador retrievers. They are, however, not pet dogs, but guide dogs. Their owners are blind.

Esme belongs to Ms Cassandra Chiu, a counsellor and psychotherapist. Kendra belongs to Mr Kua Cheng Hock, a former teacher who runs a small business selling electronic devices to assist the blind.

Apart from the difficulty of securing employment, one of the biggest challenges faced by the blind in Singapore is mobility. Singaporeans are familiar with the white cane, and most of us would respond positively when we see a blind person with a white cane.

A blind person walking with a white cane would encounter problems. Because he cannot see, he could easily trip or knock against objects and hurt himself. A blind person, accompanied by a trained guide dog, would not stumble or knock against such objects because the dog would help the blind person navigate around the obstacles. A guide dog, therefore, enables a blind person to walk with confidence. It is very empowering and gives the blind greater mobility.

Esme and Kendra are the only guide dogs in Singapore. Because of their rarity, most Singaporeans are not familiar with them. Guide dogs for the blind have been around since World War I. The first guide dog training schools were established in Germany during WWI, to enhance the mobility of veterans who were blinded in combat. The United States followed suit in 1929. In 1934, Britain's Guide Dogs for the Blind began operation. The movement subsequently spread to many countries in Europe, Latin America and Asia.

In many countries, guide dogs are exempted from laws and regulations that forbid the entry of animals to public places, including restaurants. In some countries, such as the US, Australia, Brazil and South Korea, laws have been enacted to allow guide dogs to accompany their blind masters to all public places.

What about Islam, which regards dogs as unclean animals? In 2003, the Shariah Council of Britain ruled that the ban on dogs does not apply to those used for guide work. More recently, a mosque in Britain even gave permission to a blind boy to go to the mosque accompanied by his guide dog. Naturally, the dog has to wait outside the mosque for its owner.

What about Singapore? The Islamic Religious Council of Singapore (Muis) has issued a guideline allowing visually impaired customers, accompanied by guide dogs, access to halal restaurants, with certain provisos. These restaurants should have a designated area for such customers. The dog should be harnessed and kept at his side at all times. If the guide dog needs to be fed, disposable wares should be used, to prevent any cross-mixing with cutlery used for the preparation and serving of halal food. Muis is, therefore, supportive of guide dogs.

What is the policy of the Singapore Government towards guide dogs? Speaking in Parliament on Sept 19, 2005, then Minister for Community Development, Youth and Sports Vivian Balakrishnan said: "The MCYS (Ministry of Community Development, Youth and Sports) supports the use of guide dogs as another form of mobility guide for blind persons. Guide dogs can help blind persons to negotiate their way in public places, so that they can better integrate into mainstream society. The dogs also provide valuable companionship for blind persons."

Are guide dogs allowed on our trains? The answer is yes. Guide dogs are allowed access to bus interchanges. They are also allowed on public buses as long as they do not cause discomfort to other passengers due to proximity. In one instance, a bus passenger told Ms Chiu that she was not comfortable sitting near Esme. Ms Chiu moved to another seat. Is it too much for me to suggest that a sighted and able-bodied commuter should volunteer to offer his seat to the blind commuter?

The National Environment Agency has granted licensees of food establishments the discretion to allow guide dogs on their premises, so long as they are harnessed and kept at their owner's side at all times.

I would like to appeal to the owners and managers of our office buildings, shopping malls, hotels and food establishments to kindly consider allowing Ms Chiu and Esme, and Mr Kua and Kendra, access to their premises.

At the moment, there are still too many places in Singapore that do not allow entry to guide dogs. This is largely due to ignorance rather than ill will. Most Singaporeans are unaware of the rules governing guide dogs.

I am happy to report that the FairPrice and Cold Storage supermarket chains have recently decided to allow guide dogs to enter their premises. I am also grateful to the management of Tanglin Shopping Centre for allowing Ms Chiu to take Esme to work there. I hope that their decisions will encourage others to emulate them.

In the coming years, there will be many more guide dogs in Singapore. The Guide Dogs Association of the Blind is raising funds to help interested and suitable blind Singaporeans to be trained for, and acquire, guide dogs.

I would also like to appeal to the Singapore public to be kind to our disabled, including the blind accompanied by their guide dogs.

Let us make Singapore a compassionate society. A compassionate society should be sensitive to and supportive of our disabled.

[Originally published in *The Sunday Times*, 15 January 2012.]

Should Petain Road be Renamed?

In Singapore, unlike many newly independent countries, we do not have a policy of de-colonising the names of streets and places. As a result, our streets have kept the names given to them by the British colonial administration. I approve of this policy because we should not deny the past and wipe out part of our history.

There is a road in the Jalan Besar area called Petain Road. The French community has been campaigning for many years to change the name of the road. I support the campaign and would like to explain why the Street and Building Names Board, under the Ministry of National Development, should consider the request favourably.

Britain was an ally of France during the First World War. In the Jalan Besar area, there are several roads which bear the names of famous generals, such as Petain and Beatty, or famous sites of battles, such as Verdun, Marne, Jutland and Flanders. In 1928, the Municipal Government of Singapore decided to name one of the roads after the great French war hero, Field Marshal Henri Philippe Petain.

Petain was born in 1856. His father was a farmer. Young Petain joined the French army in 1876 and attended the Saint-Cyr Military Academy and the Army College. In 1911, he was a colonel and commander of the 33rd Infantry Regiment of Arras. His young lieutenant was Charles de Gaulle. His career took off in 1914, when he was already 58 years old. He was promoted to the rank of Brigadier-General. In 1915, he was given command of the Second Army and participated in the Battle of Verdun in the following year.

At the end of the First World War, Petain was regarded as one of France's greatest military heroes. In 1918, he was made a Marshal of France.

In 1922, he was appointed as the Inspector-General of the Army. The decision by the Municipal Government of Singapore to name a road after him, in 1928, was perfectly understandable.

No one in 1928 could have foreseen what Petain would do during the Second World War. The French Army had been progressively degraded after the First World War, no thanks to budgetary cuts. When the Second World War broke out in 1939, the French Army was no match for the German Army.

In May 1940, Petain, who had become the Prime Minister of France, regarded the military situation as hopeless. On the 20th of June, France signed an armistice with Germany, giving the latter control of the north and west of France, including Paris. The seat of the French government was moved to Vichy, a town located about 400 km south of Paris.

On July 10, the Chamber of Deputies and the Senate ratified the armistice, abolished the Third Republic, and adopted a new Constitution under which Petain, as the head of state, had near-absolute powers. The Petain government oppressed the French people and collaborated with Germany in suppressing the French resistance and arresting the Jews. In November 1942, Germany occupied the whole of France and Petain became a puppet of the Germans.

In 1945, de Gaulle's provisional government placed Petain on trial for treason. The three judges were in favour of acquitting him. The jury, however, disagreed and convicted him of treason and sentenced him to death. De Gaulle, who had served under Petain in 1911, commuted his death sentence to life imprisonment, on account of his age and taking into account his contributions in the First World War. Petain was stripped of all his military ranks and honours, except for the title of Marshal. He died in ignominy, in 1951, at the age of 95.

In the light of these historical facts, we must agree with the French community that it is inappropriate to continue to honour Petain by naming a road after him. The question is whether there is a precedent for changing the road's name.

I think I have found a good precedent. Chulia Street was originally named Kling Street. The word, "kling" is derived from the word, "kalinga", the name of a powerful South Indian kingdom. In the beginning, the Malays referred to all South Indians as "orang kling". However, over time, the word acquired a pejorative connotation and was used to refer to the Indian coolies.

In 1918, Rev J. A. B. Coach petitioned the municipal commissioners to change the name of the street, but his appeal was rejected. Three years later, in 1921, the commissioners acceded to the request of Dr H. S. Moonshi, who spoke on behalf of the Indian community.

I hope that the Street and Building Names Board will kindly consider the request of the French community to rename Petain Road. I propose calling it 'de Gaulle Road', to recognise the historic contributions made by the indomitable French leader in the country's history.

[Originally published in *The Straits Times*, 20 March 2012.]

What Singapore Can Learn from Europe

It is a sad reflection on human nature that when a region is faced with a crisis, it is often treated with disdain instead of sympathy. I recall that during the Asian Financial Crisis of 1997–1998, some of our European and American friends were extremely unkind and predicted that Asia would suffer a lost decade.

We must not do the same to Europe which has been faced with a serious financial and economic crisis since 2008. I have, therefore, decided to swim against the tide of anti-Europe sentiments.

I wish to highlight the fact that not all the countries of Europe are in crisis. In 2011, of the 27 EU countries, only three had a negative growth rate.

In the 2010–2011 Global Competitiveness Index of the World Economic Forum, six EU countries were ranked among the 10 most competitive countries.

I wish to make the case that Singapore has much to learn from the successful countries of Europe. I will focus on four European countries whose populations are below 10 million, namely, Denmark, Finland, Norway and Sweden.

Lesson No. 1 : Inclusive Growth

The citizens of the world aspire to live in fair societies. One important aspect of fairness is the equitable distribution of income and wealth. This is the moral force behind the economic doctrine of inclusive growth. As a result of globalisation, technological change and domestic policies, many countries have become extremely unequal.

The Occupy Wall Street movement is a reflection of the American people's sentiments against a growth model which over-rewards the top 1 percent and under-rewards the remaining 99 percent. The inequality in Singapore, as measured by the Gini coefficient, is even greater than that in America. This could partly account for the sour mood of the Singapore electorate in the two elections of 2011. Too great a gap between rich and poor undermines solidarity and social cohesion. It poses a threat to our harmony and our sense of nationhood.

Let us compare Singapore, on the one hand, and Denmark, Finland, Norway and Sweden on the other. Their per capita incomes in 2010 were as follows:

Singapore: S$59,813
Denmark: S$69,249 (€ 42,500)
Finland: S$54,584 (€ 33,500)
Norway: S$105,096 (€ 64,500)
Sweden: S$60,613 (€ 37,200)

The Gini coefficient is used universally as a summary measure of income inequality. It is based upon the difference between the incomes of the top 20 percent and the bottom 20 percent. Zero represents total income equality and one represents total inequality. What are the Gini coefficients of the five countries? In 2010, they were as follows:

Singapore: 0.46
Denmark: 0.27
Finland: 0.25
Norway: 0.24
Sweden: 0.24

In order to get a better sense of the wages earned in the five countries by the bottom 20–30 percent of the working population, I have chosen the cleaner and the bus driver. The average monthly wages of the cleaner and bus driver in the five countries are as follows:

	Cleaner	*Bus Driver*
Singapore	S$800	S$1,800
Denmark	S$5,502	S$6,193
Finland	S$2,085	S$3,910
Norway	S$5,470	S$6,260
Sweden	S$3,667	S$4,480

A few observations are in order.

First, Singapore's per capita income is roughly similar to those of Denmark, Finland and Sweden.

Second, the four Nordic countries are much more equitable than Singapore. This is reflected in their Gini coefficients as well as in the average monthly wages earned by the cleaner and the bus driver.

Third, some Nordic countries have a minimum wage and some, such as Denmark, do not. The minimum wage is, therefore, a means but not the only means to ensure that workers earn a living wage.

Fourth, the argument that the only way to raise the wages of our low-wage workers is through productivity increase is not persuasive. I would like to know, for example, how the two women who clean my office can be more productive than they already are in order to deserve higher wages? I would like to know how the Singapore bus driver can be more productive so that his income will approximate those of his Nordic counterparts?

The truth is that we pay these workers such low wages not primarily because their productivity is inherently low, but largely because they are competing against an unlimited supply of cheap foreign workers. Because cheap workers are so plentiful, they tend to be employed unproductively. In the Nordic countries, unskilled workers are relatively scarce and thus deployed more productively, with higher skills, mechanization, and better organisation.

What is the solution? The solution is for the State to reduce the supply of cheap foreign workers or introduce a minimum wage or to target specific industries, such as the hospitality industry, for wage enhancement.

Lesson No. 2: Higher Fertility

One of our challenges is our low fertility rate. For a country's population to remain stable, it needs a total fertility rate (TFR) of 2.14. Singapore's current TFR is 1.2. Our population experts tell us that our population will begin to shrink by 2025. They have, therefore, argued that, to make up the deficit, we need to import foreigners to add to our population.

Importing foreigners is the second best solution. The best solution is to raise our TFR. On this point, our policy makers seem to have run out of ideas. The various incentive schemes, such as baby bonus, do not seem to be productive. It is time to look at our four European countries for inspiration. Their 2010 TFRs were as follows:

Denmark 1.87
Finland 1.87
Norway   1.95
Sweden   1.98

The four Nordic countries have TFRs which are close to the replacement level. This achievement seems extraordinary. They do not have the benefit of maids. There are over 200,000 foreign domestic workers in Singapore. They also do not have grandparents who help with childrearing. At the same time, they have very high participation of women in their workforces. In terms of availability of time and help for childrearing, common sense would suggest that the TFR in Singapore should be higher than those in the Nordic countries. How do we explain this paradox?

Our population experts cannot explain this paradox. I will venture a hypothesis. I believe that the high TFR in the Nordic countries could be due to four factors: the availability of convenient, affordable and good childcare; good work-life balance, an excellent and relatively stress-free education system, and the relative absence of male chauvinism.

Let me say a few words on each of the four factors.

First, one of the missing links in Singapore is the inadequate supply of conveniently located, good quality and affordable childcare for infants and young children.

Second, the work-life balance in Singapore, especially for young professionals, such as lawyers, architects, teachers, etc., is non-existent. Singaporeans work one of the longest hours in the developed world. They have no other life than work and thus little time for meaningful family life. The government and our employers should reflect on whether the existing climate of encouraging or the practice of requiring our young professionals to work late into the night is necessary or desirable.

Third, sociologists like Paulin Straughan have pointed out that Singapore's highly competitive and stressful education system is also a deterrent to working parents having more children. The Nordic countries, on the other hand, is famous for its high quality, egalitarian education which fulfills the children's aspiration for a happy childhood. It is a paradox that Finland, with no streaming, no elite schools and no private tuition industry, is ranked as having the world's best education system.

Fourth, it is significant that the developed countries with low TFRs include Japan, Korea, Italy and Spain, which have a high degree of male chauvinism. Is it possible that Singapore too has a high degree of male chauvinism? The women of Singapore are often blamed for not marrying and having children. Perhaps, the main problem is not our women but our men. Perhaps, what we also need is a mindset change on the part of our men towards the status and role of our women and the shared responsibilities of the husband and wife, and father and mother in domestic chores and child-rearing.

Lesson No. 3 : Embracing Nature and Sustainable Development

Singapore is probably Asia's cleanest, greenest and most liveable city. Our air is healthy, our water is potable and our land is wholesome. In addition, we enjoy good public health and food safety. Visitors to Singapore are astonished by the fact that, in spite of our high density, 47 percent of our land is covered in greenery. In view of this, the reader will ask what can we learn from the four Nordic countries? I suggest three things.

First, people in the Nordic countries love nature and their natural heritage. They seem to have an emotional, even a spiritual, relationship with nature. They love their forests, lakes and fjords. In contrast, most Singaporeans tend to have a more pragmatic relationship with nature. They will apply a cost-benefit analysis to the destruction of a natural heritage. Pragmatism is one of our virtues. We should, however, be aware of the defects of our virtues. Not everything in life can be monetized.

Second, we can learn useful lessons from the way in which the Nordic countries have been able to reconcile economic competitiveness with a deep commitment to sustainable development. After the Earth Summit of 1992, each of them has established a national commission to mainstream sustainable development. In the case of Finland, the Prime Minister chairs the National Commission on Sustainable Development. The result is that there is a national consensus in each of those countries to internalise the ethic of sustainable development into all aspects of life.

Third, at the micro-level, there are useful lessons we can learn from the Nordic countries, in areas in which Singapore has room for improvement, for example, in energy efficiency, the use of solar energy, the recycling of waste, the use of non-polluting buses, changing unsustainable patterns of consumption and production, etc.

Lesson No. 4 : Heritage, Culture and the Arts

In the past two decades, inspired by the 1989 Ong Teng Cheong report and George Yeo's leadership at MITA, Singapore has undergone a paradigm shift in the areas of heritage, culture and the arts. The arts have blossomed in Singapore. More and more Singaporeans are interested in knowing their history and preserving their heritage. The trend is, therefore, very favourable. What can we learn from the Nordic countries?

First, we can learn the importance of giving all our children a good education in the arts. We have made good progress in recent years. The opening of the highly successful Yong Siew Toh Conservatory of Music and the School of the Arts were important milestones. We can strengthen arts education in our schools. We should consider starting courses in art history and museum studies at the undergraduate and graduate levels. This will help in the training of teachers, curators, dealers, collectors and museum administrators, which are in short supply.

Second, we can emulate the achievements of the Nordic countries in respect of museums. They have an impressive range of museums with strong collections. They have been able to harness the benefit of public-private partnership. Their museum collections extend beyond their nations to the cultures of the world. For example, the David Collection in Copenhagen is one of the world's best collections of Islamic Art. The Kiasma Museum of Contemporary Art in Helsinki has a very ambitious programming agenda, covering Western as well as Asian and African art.

Third, because of their ancient Viking past and their contemporary strength in shipping and other maritime industries, Denmark, Norway and Sweden have outstanding museums of maritime history. Given the importance of maritime trade to Singapore's past and present, it is puzzling that we do not have a museum of maritime history. I hope that one day the historic Clifford Pier, which now houses a restaurant, will be the home of a world class museum of maritime history. When that happy time comes, we can look to the Nordic countries for inspiration.

[Originally published in *The Straits Times*, 19 May 2012.]

Reflections on Immigration

One of the major themes of Prime Minister Lee Hsien Loong's 2012 National Day Rally speech is immigration. PM explained the imperative for Singapore to welcome immigrants, in order to make up for the deficit resulting from our low fertility and in order to benefit from the brain power and cultural diversity which the highly educated and talented migrants bring with them. PM called upon Singaporeans to be big-hearted in welcoming them. He also called upon the migrants to make greater efforts to integrate into Singapore. I have three reflections on the subject of immigration and integration.

First, I wish to remind ourselves that we are an immigrant nation. With few exceptions, most of us are the descendants of immigrants who have settled here from other parts of Asia and the wider world. My grandfather left his home district of Tong An, in Fujian Province, because of anarchy, poverty and the lack of opportunity. My mother was a first generation immigrant from Shanghai. On my father's side, I am, therefore, a third generation Singaporean. On my mother's side, I am a second generation Singaporean. I believe that my family's history is typical of many Singapore families. Since we are almost all the descendants of immigrants, it would be a betrayal of our history if we were to become anti-immigrants or anti-foreigners. I am optimistic that we will not become such a people. I believe that Singaporeans are generally open-hearted and broad-minded. We are one of the least xenophobic people in the world. If, in recent years, there has been unhappiness, it is because the influx of foreigners had exceeded our absorptive capacity and strained our infrastructure and social amenities. The annual intake of foreigners has to be better calibrated and managed.

Second, Singapore has become one of the world's most attractive global cities. Many members of the global elite are coming to live and work here. We should continue to welcome them because Singapore benefits from their brain power, network and cultural diversity. Singapore is, however, also a country. There are inherent contradictions between being a country and a global city. As a global city, we will inevitably become more unequal. I believe that it is possible to reconcile the contradictions. As a country, we have to worry about our cohesion and national unity. We must, therefore, ensure that Singapore is a good home for our own people as well as for the global elite. We must, therefore, narrow the widening income and wealth gaps, reinforce social mobility and work harder to achieve our vision of building a "democratic society, based on justice and equality".

Third, I support PM's exhortation to the new arrivals to try harder to assimilate. What are the values and norms of Singapore? We value integrity and the absence of corruption. We follow the law and generally observe the rules of social discipline, such as not spitting, not littering, queuing up, addressing older Singaporeans as "uncles" and "aunties". We treat members of other races, religions and languages with respect, as they are our brothers and sisters. We do not denigrate the religious beliefs of others. We enjoy eating one another's cuisines and celebrate our cultural diversity. We do not look down on those who are less fortunate than we are. We try to give back to society through volunteerism and philanthropy. We use English or Singlish as our connector language. New members of the Singapore family should try to absorb the above values and norms. If they do so, I am confident that they will be warmly welcomed into the family.

[Originally published in *The Straits Times*, 29 August 2012.]

Are Singaporeans a Kind or Unkind People?*

Minister Lawrence Wong; Mr Koh Poh Tiong, Chairman of the Singapore Kindness Movement; Dr William Wan, General Secretary of the Singapore Kindness Movement; Ms Braema Mathi, President of MARUAH; Madam Moliah Hashim, Chief Executive Officer of Yayasan Mendaki; High Commissioner Syed Hasan Javed of Pakistan; Ladies and Gentlemen

Kind Singaporeans or Unkind Singaporeans?

I have decided to review the evidence in order to answer the question: Are Singaporeans a kind or unkind people? I begin by acknowledging that there is evidence to support both sides of the proposition. Let us examine some of the evidence supporting the view that Singaporeans are not a kind people.

Facts Supporting View that Singaporeans are Unkind

First, there are many instances in which foreign workers have been subjected to unkind treatment by their employers. Some foreign workers are housed in unsanitary and inhumane circumstances. Some employers do not pay their workers promptly or at all or make all kinds of unreasonable deductions from their wages. The worst case was

---

* Keynote speech delivered at "Journeying Together for Kindness", A National Conference on Kindness, 20 October 2012, Singapore.

probably the employer who left his injured foreign worker to die on the road side.

Treatment of Foreign Maids

Second, I have often read in our newspapers about the unkind treatment of our foreign domestic workers or maids. Some maids have been sexually abused by their male employers. Other maids have been physically or psychologically abused by both their male and female employers and members of their families. Some common complaints by maids include not being given enough time to rest, food to eat and a decent place to sleep in. I was disappointed that some employers opposed the government's belated decision to grant all maids a weekly day of rest. I also think that more can be done to prevent maids from falling to their deaths by being required to clean the windows of their employers' apartments in an unsafe manner.

Abandoning Elderly Parents

Third, I am distressed by one growing trend in Singapore, which is, the abandonment of elderly parents by their children. My wife works as a volunteer in a hospital run by a group of churches. She has come across elderly women, either living alone or in institutions, who have complained to her that their children never visited them. I wonder if our cherished virtue of filial piety is beginning to wither.

Treatment of Disabled

Fourth, I think we could be kinder in the treatment of our disabled. Let me start with the education of our disabled children. I see no good reason for exempting disabled children from the law on compulsory education. The quality of education available to disabled children varies a great deal depending upon the capacity of the voluntary welfare organisation providing the service. For example, the Pathlight School for children with autism is world class. In contrast, the School for the Blind is stuck in the Third World. Employment opportunities for the disabled is another problem area. When I was the Ambassador to the US and based in Washington, DC, I took a special interest in our hearing impaired students studying at the world famous Gallaudet University. I encouraged the Singapore students to return to Singapore upon graduation. Of the group that came back, only one got a job to teach at the School for the Deaf. The rest returned to America, where employers were willing to employ them in the occupations they had studied for. Mobility is another big problem. My blind friend, Cassandra Chiu, and her guide dog, Esme, have encountered no end of problems in seeking to gain access to office buildings, shopping malls, trains, buses, restaurants, in spite of the fact that such access had been approved by MCYS, MUIS, SMRT, SBS, etc. In Korea, it is a crime for anyone to deny a blind person, accompanied by a guide dog, access to any public place.

Cruelty Towards Animals

Fifth, I think one test of the kindness of a people is how they treat their animals. As an animal lover, I am appalled by the reports I have read of cruelty towards animals. I cannot understand why there are some sadists among us who apparently enjoy torturing and killing animals. I am glad that our society, the police and our courts have taken a strong position against such offenders. Cruelty of any kind, against any sentient being, should have no place in Singapore.

Facts Supporting View that Singaporeans Are Kind

Let me now turn to examine the facts which support the view that Singaporeans are a kind people.

Treatment of Foreign Workers

First, for every unkind employer of foreign workers, there are probably several who treat their workers kindly. Some employers house their workers in very good dormitories, provide them with healthy food and social amenities. In addition, there are NGOs, such as TWC2 and HOME, which champion the rights of foreign workers. I have also come across doctors, lawyers and other professionals who volunteer their precious time to look after the welfare of these workers. There is a restaurant in Little India which provides foreign workers with free food.

Treatment of Maids

Second, the same is probably true for maids. For every unkind employer, there are probably several kind employers who treat their maids with kindness and respect. I have seen families who treat their maids as members of their families. I have also come across employers who have shown extraordinary kindness towards their maids, for example, by paying for their medical treatment or helping them with their children's education or giving them time off to further their education.

Response to Humanitarian Disasters

Third, Singaporeans always respond, with generosity, to humanitarian disasters abroad, especially those in nearby Asia. I remember the massive response by Singaporeans to the Indian Ocean tsunami in 2004, to the Cyclone Nargis in Myanmar, to the Szechuan earthquake and to the Tohoku tsunami in Japan. If Singaporeans do not have kind hearts, I do not think they would have responded so generously.

Philanthropy

Fourth, the National Volunteer and Philanthropy Centre (NVPC) has reported that, between 2004 and 2010, donations by individuals to all charities rose by 16 percent a year. For the past 10 years, 2001 to 2011, donations to charities, which can provide tax deductions for donations, rose by 9 percent each year. In 2010, Singaporeans contributed a total of $1,070 million to philanthropy. Contributions to the President's Challenge, Community Chest and The Straits Times Pocket Money Fund have increased every year. Philanthropy has taken root in Singapore and, like America, is becoming part of the culture of Singaporeans. In 2010, 85 percent of Singaporeans donated money to charity. In addition, Singapore is emerging as an important philanthropic hub of Asia. Under the leadership of NVPC, Singapore is also becoming a thought leader in philanthropy.

Volunteerism

Fifth, the good news is that Singapore is also becoming a nation of volunteers. The percentage of Singaporeans who volunteer has gone up from 15 percent in 2004 to 23 percent in 2010. The fact that some of our schools require their students to perform a certain number of hours of community service has helped to propel the trend. At my College, Tembusu College at NUS, we have some students who have adopted an orphanage in West Timor as well as many students who collect food to deliver them to needy families. I am very impressed by the spirit of our young people. Many of them are helping the poor, the disadvantaged, the marginalised, in different countries in Asia and elsewhere.

Kindness to Strangers

Sixth, I am frequently cheered by the letters in the forum page of *The Straits Times*. The letter writers are both Singaporeans and foreign visitors. All of them expressed their gratitude to Singaporeans, often unnamed, who have gone out of the way to show kindness to strangers. My foreign friends have told me that they are very impressed by the kindness of Singaporeans.

Conclusion

Let me conclude. I believe that, on the whole, Singaporeans are a kind people. In a poll conducted by SPH, in November 2011, on what virtues the Singaporeans considered important to them, kindness came in second, after honesty. There is a minority of unkind people here as there are everywhere. There are, however, areas in which we can do better. We can be kinder in the treatment of the elderly and the disabled. I appeal to our young train riders to be kinder to the elderly, disabled and pregnant commuters. We should also aspire to be kinder to all who share the spaces that we work, live and play in, regardless of age, gender and ethnicity. We should be kind to fellow workers, irrespective of rank and hierarchy. Bosses should be kinder to their staff in respect of work-life balance and profit-sharing. Neighbours should be tolerant and kind to one another. Our drivers should try to be more kind and courteous to fellow drivers, motor-cyclists, cyclists and pedestrians. We could be kinder to our cyclists and consider following the good example of New York by designating special lanes for them. We should stand up against the minority of selfish people who oppose dormitories for foreign workers, hospices, facilities for the elderly, in their neighbourhood. Let the voices of the majority of Singaporeans, who are kind, rise above those of the unkind minority.

How to be Happy

The results of the recent Gallup poll, as well as other surveys, seem to indicate that Singaporeans are an unhappy people. This surprises me because, objectively, we should be a happy people. I consider myself a happy person. I would therefore like to share with my fellow Singaporeans 10 rules which may help to make them a more happy people.

Rule No. 1

Be a positive, optimistic and kind person. Whether you are a happy or unhappy person depends largely on yourself. Negative and pessimistic people are generally unhappy people. Be kind to others. Kindness begets kindness. Try to do a good deed every day. You will find that by brightening the lives of others, you will brighten your own life.

Rule No. 2

Have a happy family. Be good to your parents. If they are elderly and living by themselves, try to visit them at least once a week and share a weekly meal with them. One of the problems encountered by our older folks is loneliness.

Be on excellent terms with your spouse. Whenever I am asked to speak at wedding dinners, I always advise the groom to do three things: Be faithful to his wife, treat her as if they were still courting and give her all his money. The last advice does not apply in cases where the wife is a spender and not a saver.

As for how to behave towards one's children, I have always liked the advice given by Kahlil Gibran: "And though they are with you yet they belong not to you. You may give them your love but not your thoughts. For they have their own thoughts."

If you are lucky enough to have grandchildren, love them with all your heart.

Rule No. 3

Find a job you enjoy doing. I think one of the reasons so many Singaporeans are unhappy is that they do not like their jobs. Since we spend so much of our lives at work, it is important to find a job which is not a chore to endure but a pleasure to do. In recent years, I have noticed a trend of many Singaporeans leaving their jobs for other jobs which pay them less but give them greater satisfaction. This is a good thing.

Rule No. 4

Treasure your friends. In your life journey, you will make many friends — at school, at university, in sports or other activities and at work. I hope you will develop a small circle of very good friends, friends who will stand by you in good times and bad times.

Rule No. 5

Exercise regularly. My wife and I try to swim every day. Exercise not only makes you healthier, it also makes you feel better. Therefore, make regular exercise a part of your lifestyle. You can't be a happy person if you are not in good health.

Rule No. 6

Enjoy eating but eat healthily and avoid the sin of gluttony. Singapore is a culinary paradise. Food is abundant, diverse and affordable.

You can eat well on any budget. Let us enjoy our food but let us also exercise some discipline when choosing what to eat. I have always tried to follow the ancient Asian wisdom of stopping when I feel 80 percent full.

Rule No. 7

Be a volunteer and support philanthropy. I once heard a speech by Mrs Barbara Bush, the wife of the 41st President of the United States. She said there was a period in her life when she suffered from depression. Instead of seeing a psychiatrist or taking medication to overcome her depression, she decided to be a volunteer. She found that by helping others less fortunate than herself, her depression gradually disappeared.

Whether we are rich or poor, we should contribute to a cause or causes close to our hearts. In spite of our favourable tax regime and the presence of many wealthy people in our society, I was very disappointed to see how lowly Singapore ranked in the table of countries for philanthropy. A wise man once said that no man could be truly happy if he lives only for himself.

Rule No. 8

Read books and listen to music. Reading is an excellent habit. Books keep me company when I am alone. Books transport me to another country, another culture, another time and into the lives of other people. Reading is an endless source of happiness. So is music. I listen to music every day. I thank Symphony 92.4FM for bringing me so much joy every day.

Rule No. 9

Take pleasure in the little things in life. My wife and I love our regular walks in the Botanic Gardens. I love to watch the sunset. I find joy in meeting an old friend, attending a concert at the Esplanade and visiting a wonderful exhibition at one of our museums. Most of all, I enjoy being with my grandson.

Rule No. 10

Don't envy others. I received this good advice from a wise man, Dr Wee Kim Wee, our sixth President. Dr Wee once told me that one of the reasons which caused people to be unhappy was that they were envious of others. Dr Wee said he never envied his friends who had a better education or earned more money or lived in bigger houses or owned more expensive cars. His rule was to be contented with what he had. I think this is a good rule. Philosophically, it would be even better if you could feel vicariously happy when you see your friends and former students doing well in life.

[Originally published in *The Straits Times*, 29 December 2012.]

Singapore's Foreign Policy
Unique Features

Introduction

I am an accidental diplomat. I had intended to spend my life teaching law. However, by a twist of fate, I was asked to be our Ambassador and Permanent Representative to the United Nations (UN) in 1968. Although I did return to the NUS Law School and served as its Dean from 1971 to 1974, I have spent most of my professional life with the Ministry of Foreign Affairs. I have been an active participant in Singapore's diplomacy for 41 years. In this essay, drawing from my experience and reflections, I will identify and discuss three unique features of Singapore's foreign policy.

Small States in a Big World

Life for small states has never been easy. It was much harder before the founding of the UN in 1945. In the pre-UN world, the fate of small States was often decided by the big States of their region or of the world. Thus, it was not uncommon for the concert of powers to arbitrarily decide to alter the boundaries of small States or incorporate parts of small States into the territories of their bigger neighbours. In extreme cases, some small States simply disappeared as a result of being forcibly incorporated into the territory of a bigger neighbour. This happened to Estonia, Latvia and Lithuania, which were incorporated by Stalin, against their will, into the Soviet Union.

Since the founding of the UN, the world has become a relatively safer place for small States. The UN Charter, the UN Security Council and the UN General Assembly are, however, unable to prevent a big State from invading a small State. The Soviet Union invaded Afghanistan, the United States (US) invaded Grenada and Iraq, Russia invaded Georgia, just to give a few recent examples. Iraq invaded and attempted to incorporate Kuwait into Iraq. Kuwait was liberated by a coalition of like-minded States, led by the US, with the approval of the UN Security Council. Kuwait was fortunate in that it is the world's 10th largest oil producer. In each of the other cases, the invasions were the subject of deliberations, either in the Security Council or the General Assembly or both. The invasions were condemned by the Parliament of Man. The UN's capacity to prevent or rectify the aggression of big States against small States is, however, uncertain and limited. The bottom line is that small States continue to live in a dangerous world.

Be Proactive

One hallmark of Singapore's foreign policy is that, although a small State, we are not passive. On the contrary, we are hyper-proactive. Small States, like small boys, are expected to be silent, passive and compliant. Small States are seldom given a seat at the top table. Small States are seldom consulted by the big States. They are usually told what to do by the big States. The norm is for small States to be reactive rather than proactive — to be the subject of the actions of the big States instead of being the actors and to accept their fate as small States. Singapore has defied the norm by being a proactive State. Let me cite three examples.

First, during the UN Conference on the Law of the Sea, Singapore found that the negotiations at the Conference were being dominated by the coastal States and the great powers. In order to gain leverage, Singapore took the initiative to establish a new grouping called the Group of Landlocked and Geographically Disadvantaged States. The group united the landlocked States and coastal countries which, like Singapore, were hemmed in by their neighbours. The group consisted of about one-third of the member States participating in the Conference. This gave us a voice and a weight which we would not have had otherwise.

A second example is the initiative which Singapore took at the UN, in 1992, to form the Forum of Small States (FOSS). The forum consists of 105 out of the 193 members of the UN. The criterion for membership is a population below 10 million. The forum has proven itself as an effective platform of small States. FOSS recently celebrated its 20th anniversary. The President of the UN General Assembly, the Secretary-General of the UN and the US Secretary of State, were among the guests who spoke at the forum. Singapore is the chairman of FOSS and the founder is Ambassador Chew Tai Soo.

Third, following the creation of G20, consisting of 20 major advanced and emerging economies of the world, Singapore feared that the interests of other States would not be taken into account. In response to this danger, Singapore took the initiative to establish a group of like-minded States, called the Global Governance Group or 3G. The group has succeeded in insisting on a linkage between G20 and the UN and has submitted policy papers to G20 for its consideration. As convener of 3G, Singapore has been invited to attend several G20 meetings. The founder of 3G is Ambassador Vanu Gopala Menon, and the group has 30 members from all regions of the world.

Be Not Afraid

Another unique feature of Singapore's foreign policy is that it is not afraid to stand up for its interests. Small States are usually reluctant to take on a bigger opponent. Singapore has no such fear. Let me cite a few examples.

First, in 1972, a young Permanent Representative to the UN, Professor S. Jayakumar, decided to take on very formidable opponents at the UN and prevailed against the odds. Let me explain the facts. At that time, many coastal States, led by the Latin-Americans, were unilaterally making extensive claims to the sea. Some wanted the territorial sea to be expanded from three miles to 200 miles. Others wanted very extensive fisheries zones. In 1972, the *US Geographer* had published a report showing that the majority of the UN's member States would not benefit from such extensive claims. This prompted Professor Jayakumar to submit a draft resolution to the UN General Assembly requesting the Secretary-General to study how the various proposals put forward by the coastal States would impact on mankind's interests. The draft resolution was vehemently opposed by the powerful coastal States. France, Canada and Malta jointly submitted an amendment which, if adopted, would have killed the resolution. In the UN, it is called a "killer amendment". Miraculously, the vote was 46 in favour, 46 against, with 27 abstentions. Under the UN's rules of procedure, the amendment failed to be adopted by one vote. The resolution was adopted. Singapore's victory made the UN take notice of this small State and its effective diplomacy.

Second, Vietnam invaded and occupied Cambodia, in December 1978. The five ASEAN countries decided to oppose Vietnam's action, not because it supported the odious Khmer Rouge regime, but because it would set a dangerous precedent. The fight in the UN General Assembly in 1979 was a cliffhanger. By taking on Vietnam, ASEAN was taking on the whole Soviet bloc as well as the leadership of the Non-Aligned Movement, including India. Many of our friends thought that our cause was hopeless. Contrary to such expectations, ASEAN prevailed. Eventually, when the Cold War ended, Vietnam agreed to withdraw from Cambodia and to seek a negotiated solution to the conflict. This resulted in the Paris Agreements of 1991.

Third, I would refer to Professor Jayakumar's book, *Diplomacy: A Singapore Experience*. In his book, the author discussed several cases in which Singapore came under tremendous pressure from the big powers, such as the US, China, United Kingdom and the European Union. In each case, Singapore refused to yield to the pressure. Singapore has shown that although we live in an unequal world, successful small countries can maintain their dignity and not give in to the unreasonable pressure of the big States.

Be Law Abiding

The third and most unique feature of Singapore's foreign policy is the priority we accord to international law. Most scholars of international affairs are puzzled by Singapore's behaviour. Singapore's leaders, from Lee Kuan Yew to the present, use a vocabulary which suggests that Singapore adheres to the Realist school, which takes a cold-eyed, unsentimental view of the world. The Realist worships power and is usually dismissive of other considerations. How can a Realist State attach so much importance to international law?

Singapore's ideology is actually not Realism, but Pragmatism. Our adherence to international law is based upon utility and not morality. Small States are better off in a world ruled by law than in a lawless world. Small States benefit from a world order in which interactions between States are based upon international law and not power. It levels the playing field. It holds all States accountable by the same rules. This is also the reason why Singapore is a strong believer in referring disputes, which cannot be resolved by negotiations, to international modalities of dispute settlement, such as conciliation, mediation, arbitration and adjudication. Small States have a better chance of winning a dispute with a bigger State in a court of law than in a contest of strength.

Singapore's adherence to international law in its foreign policy has served Singapore well. This is true in our relations with our neighbours, such as Indonesia, Malaysia and the Philippines. This is also true in our relations with the major powers.

Conclusion

Let me conclude. Singapore is a small State. Our leaders like to say that in the ocean of life, the big fish eat small fish and the small fish eat shrimp.

Singapore's first Prime Minister, Mr Lee Kuan Yew, once described Singapore as a poisonous shrimp. I prefer to see Singapore as a small fish. It is, however, an extraordinary small fish. It has organised the small fish to band together for their mutual protection. It is a fast and agile swimmer and can out-swim many big fish. The world is, however, a dangerous place and small fish will always be vulnerable to the big predators of the ocean.

[Originally published in "The Idea of Singapore", *Commentary* Vol. 22, pp. 36–40. © 2013 National University of Singapore Society.]

7 Habits of a Happy Singaporean

In two years, Singapore will celebrate its 50th anniversary as a sovereign and independent country. The Government of Singapore has appointed me to the steering committee in charge of the celebrations. In this essay, I wish to share my reflections on what makes me a Singaporean.

First, I am a Singaporean because I was born here, grew up here, went to school here, married here and live and work here.

My wife used to ask me: "Where would you like to spend your retirement years?" I would reply that I wish to work until I die and would like to die in the land of my birth. I have spent my whole life working for Singapore and, although I have never signed a bond of service, I feel bonded to Singapore.

It is, of course, true that you don't have to be born in Singapore to be a Singaporean. One of our founding fathers, Mr S. Rajaratnam, used to say that being a Singaporean is not a condition of one's birth but of one's conviction. In that spirit, we have welcomed many, who were born elsewhere, into our family. I count among our compatriots friends like Mr Asad Latif, born in India; Mr Alain Vandenborre, born in Belgium; Mr Ray Ferguson, born in the United Kingdom; Mr Simon Israel, born in Fiji; and Mr Gautam Banerjee, born in India.

Second, what makes me a Singaporean is the fact that my close friends include Chinese, Malays, Indians, Eurasians, Arabs, Jews, Armenians. I venture that hardly any Chinese, Japanese, Korean, Indian or Indonesian can make the same claim; and few even among Americans, from the land of the melting pot. In the short space of half a century, we have succeeded in achieving a level of acceptance — I would even call it celebration — of the diversity of the human family, which no older nation has done.

I believe that, if presented with a worthy Malay candidate, the electorate of Singapore would elect him or her as our President. I also believe that Singaporeans are ready for a non-Chinese Prime Minister.

Third, the Singaporean's cultural DNA includes a gene that respects all faiths.

Although Singapore is a very small country, our Inter-Religious Organisation consists of the representatives of 10 of the major religions of the world. A good Singaporean may or may not have a religion. However, he is schooled to respect all faiths, and no matter how much he may believe that his faith is the one true faith, he may not denigrate the faith of others.

This is why Singaporeans reacted so strongly when a Christian pastor was caught bad-mouthing Taoism and Buddhism. It is not only against the law to do that but it is also against our social norm. Inter-religious harmony is one of our most precious achievements.

Fourth, I believe that Singaporeans share certain core values. The Singaporean is honest, hard-working, law-abiding and reliable. We believe in meritocracy.

I know that, as imperfect mortals, we don't always reflect these virtues in our daily lives. But I would maintain that, on the whole, they are the values that Singaporeans live by. For this reason, Singaporeans are head-hunted by the private sector and sought after by international organisations. The fact that Transparency International ranks Singapore as the cleanest and most non-corrupt country in Asia and one of the top five in the world vindicates my view.

I was also very pleased by how well Singapore did in the *Reader's Digest's* exercise, in which a certain number of wallets is randomly dropped in different cities around the world. The exercise was to find out how many wallets were returned. In Singapore, seven of the 10 wallets dropped were returned by the finders. This was a high score. I am also convinced that Singapore's taxi drivers are among the most honest in the world.

Fifth, Singaporeans speak English in an identifiably unique way. I don't mean Singlish. I mean our accent and intonation.

I had a very close American friend called Miriam Levering. One day, she was on a street car in Vienna. She heard several men talking to one another in English. She went up to them and asked whether they were from Singapore. They said yes and asked her how she knew. She said: "You speak just like my friend, Tommy Koh."

Although I have spent more than 20 years of my life in America, I have not acquired an American accent. I therefore cannot understand why some Singaporeans, who have had much less exposure to the West, speak English with a fake foreign accent. We should be true to ourselves and speak English in the Singaporean way. There is no need to put on an Oxbridge accent or an American accent.

Sixth, one of the things that make me a Singaporean is my love of our hawker food. Cooking and baking are two of the greatest inventions of the human civilisation. When I was living in New York and Washington, I would often ask Singaporeans what they miss most about home. In their replies, they would always mention family, friends and food.

Our hawker food reflects the inter-racial and inter-cultural diversity of Singapore. Eating is also an arena in which Singaporeans cross many boundaries. Thus, I have Indian friends who love Chinese food and Chinese friends who love Indian or Malay food. Our hawker centres should be preserved and enhanced because they are where Singaporeans of all races, ages and incomes meet and enjoy our unique culinary achievements. I am therefore very pleased to be one of the judges, for the fourth year, of the Singapore Hawker Masters competition, sponsored by *The Straits Times* and *Lianhe Zaobao*.

Seventh, I love physical Singapore. I love our trees, parks, gardens, forests and beaches. Singapore should keep as much of our natural heritage as possible. We should also aspire to maintain a balance between heritage and modernity in our built environment. I regret that my primary school has disappeared and my high school has moved house twice. I am, however, happy that my law school has returned to its original home at Bukit Timah.

I am very encouraged by the new interest shown by Singaporeans, young and old, to preserve our memories, history and heritage. This is good because a nation is a people bound together by their collective memories of the past and their shared dreams of the future. We need to anchor our memories of the past to physical Singapore.

[Originally published in *The Straits Times*, 11 September 2013.]

Tommy and his wife Siew Aing at Kent Ridge, 1966.

◀ Tommy's mother, Madam See Tsai Ying, taken in Shanghai when she was an actress and dancer, in the 1930s.

Tommy and his father standing on the deck of his home in Washington, October 1985. Tommy's father passed away in Washington on October 30, 1985.
▼

Graduation from the University of Malaya (now National University of Singapore) with his parents, Madam See Tsai Ying and Mr Koh Han Kok. Photo taken in a studio in Kuala Lumpur, Malaysia, 1961.

Tommy *(extreme left)* with Uncle Han Thuan, mother, father, grandfather, Jimmy, Uncle Han Yean and Aunt Peck Kwee. Malcolm is in front. Picture taken at the family home at 38 Shanghai Road, in the 1950s.

Siew Aing and Tommy in 1966, taken at Tommy's parents' home.

Siew Aing and Tommy's wedding on 5 August 1967.

Aun, Wei and Siew Aing on vacation in Honolulu, Hawaii, in the 1970s.

Aun, Siew Aing and Wei when their children were at the United Nations International School, New York, in the 1970s.

Christmas at home in Washington, DC. Wei was in college and Aun in high school, taken in the 1980s.

Wei and Aun serving National Service in Pulau Tekong, taken in the 1990s.

Tommy's parents' residence at 38 Shanghai Road.

Siew Aing and Tommy's mother helping Tommy to blow out the candles on his 60th birthday, 12 November 1997. Aun looking on with amusement.

At the Institute of Policy Studies 10th Anniversary Dinner with Siew Aing, 1998.

Taken at the wedding of Aun and Su-Lyn, in Perth, on 9 September 2001.

At the Registry of Marriage on 11 November 2011.
From left to right: Aun, Su-Lyn, Toby, Tommy, Joycelyn, Wei and Siew Aing.

Tommy and Toby sharing a joke while Siew Aing looks on.

With the late President Wee Kim Wee, in Chinatown, New York, in 1977 when he was a member of the Singapore delegation to the UN General Assembly.

With the late David Marshall at the International Conference on Cambodia, 1989.
Tommy was Marshall's law pupil from 1961 to 1962. David Marshall was Singapore's Ambassador to France. He was also a member of the Singapore delegation to the UN General Assembly in 1968, when Tommy was his boss!

With former Prime Minister Lee Kuan Yew at the S. Rajaratnam Lecture organised by the MFA Diplomatic Academy, 2009. Tommy chaired the lecture by Mr Lee. [Photo credit: Ministry of Communications and Information]

With former President S. R. Nathan at the launch of *The Little Red Dot*, 2004. The book was co-edited by Tommy Koh and Chang Li Lin.

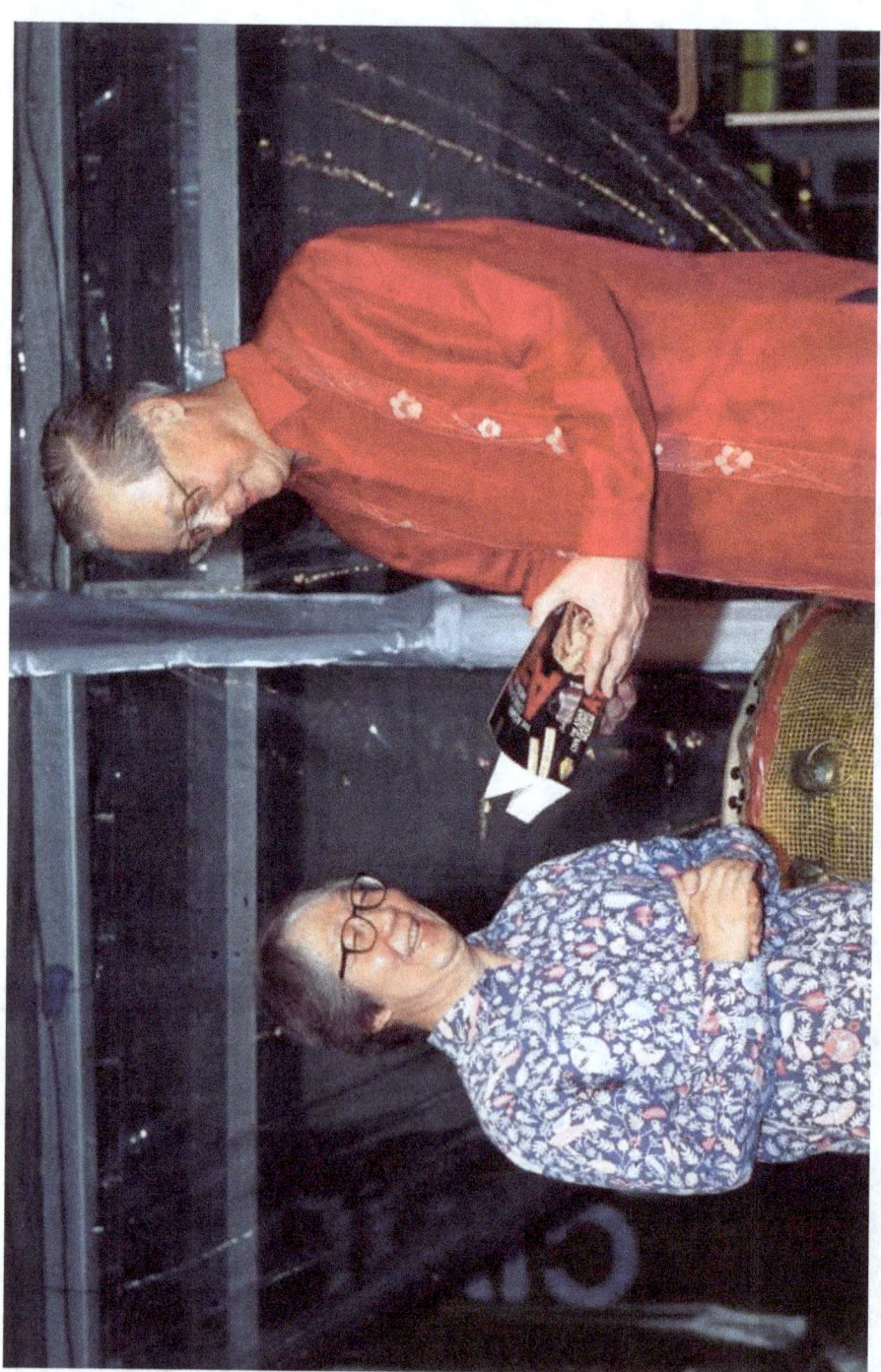

Chairman of National Heritage Board, Tommy Koh, presenting the book, *The Asian Civilisations Museum A-Z Guide*, to former Prime Minister Goh Chok Tong at the official opening of the Asian Civilisations Museum on 1 March 2003.

At the opening of the Peranakan Museum with Guest-of-Honour, Prime Minister Lee Hsien Loong, 2008. *From left to right*: Kenson Kwok, Priscylla Shaw, Michael Koh, PM Lee and Tommy Koh. Kenson was the director and Priscylla the chairman of the Asian Civilisations Museum. Michael was the CEO of the National Heritage Board.

William Burris and Tommy escorting the late President Ong Teng Cheong to visit "TRÉSORS 1993", the first international fine art and antiques fair in Singapore. President Ong was a champion of culture and the arts.

With George Yeo, then Minister for Information and the Arts, at the launch of the Festiival of Asian Performing Arts, at Raffles City in 1995.

With the late Kwa Geok Choo at Regent Hotel, on the occasion of the Asia Society's Corporate Conference, held in Singapore in 1994.

Aun, Siew Aing, Mrs Goh Chok Tong (née Tan Choo Leng) and Tommy at a book launch on Tommy's 60th birthday, 12 November 1997.

With Ho Ching, the CEO of Temasek Holdings, at an IPS lunch meeting on 29 July 2009 at Four Seasons Hotel, Singapore.

Siew Aing and Christine Dhanabalan at the FBI's firing range in Washington, DC, in the 1980s. Mr S. Dhanabalan was the second Foreign Minister of Singapore.

Tommy wearing his RI prefect's blazer at the School's 170th Founder's Day when he was the Guest-of-Honour. Mr Sat Pal Khattar, Chairman of the School, is on the left and on the right is Mr Eugene Wijeysingha, the principal of the school. The photo was taken in 1993.

The Honorary LL.D. Class of 1984 at Yale University. The President of Yale is in the front row, third from the left. Tommy Koh is in the front row, second from the right. Paul Volcker, the former Chairman of the US Federal Reserve is in the second row, third from the right.

Tommy's graduation photo from the National University of Singapore, Faculty of Law Class of 1961. Tommy is in the back row, third from the left.

National University of Singapore Faculty of Law Class of 1961 50th Anniversary reunion.
Front row *(left to right)*: Leng Fong, Devi, Aileen, Su Mien, Kheng Lian and Lakshmi.
Back row *(left to right)*: Tommy, Menon, Hin Hiong, Sachi, Sek Keong, Amarjit, Eng Tian, Yong Hong and Ronald.

New Permanent Representative of Singapore to the United Nations, Tommy Koh (right) presenting his credentials to Secretary-General U Thant at UN headquarters, New York, July 1968. [Photo credit: UNITED NATIONS]

Presenting his credentials to UN Secretary-General Kurt Waldheim, 1974.

General Assembly hears address by Prime Minister of Australia and seven statements in general debate. The delegations of Singapore headed by S. Rajaratnam (left), Minister for Foreign Affairs and Ambassador Tommy Koh, Permanent Representative to the UN, New York, September 1974. Back row *(left to right)*: Michael Cheok, Lee Cheong Giam and Peter Chan. [Photo credit: UNITED NATIONS]

35th United Nations General Assembly in New York on 16 September 1980.
Front row (left to right): S. Dhanabalan, S. Rajaratnam and Tommy Koh.
Back row (left to right): Viji Menon and Lee Yoke Kwang.

The Third United Nations Conference on the Law of the Sea, New York, March 1981.
From left: Bernado Zuleta, Under-Secretary-General, Secretariat of the Third United Nations Conference on the Law of the Sea; Tommy Koh, President of the Conference; and David L. D. Hall, Executive Secretary of the Conference.
[Photo credit: UNITED NATIONS]

The President of the Law of the Sea Conference, Tommy Koh, as guest on the United Nations public affairs programme, WORLD CHRONICLE, New York, 5 November 1982.

President of the Law of the Sea Conference, Ambassador Tommy Koh, signing the Final Act on the Third UN Conference on the Law of the Sea at Montego Bay, Jamaica, December 1982.
From left to right: Kumar Chitty, Bernado Zuleta (Secretary-General of the Conference), Roy Lee and Erik Suy (United Nations' Legal Adviser).

Reception in commemoration of the 30th Anniversary of Opening for Signature of the 1982 United Nations Convention on the Law of the Sea hosted by the Office of Legal Division for Ocean Affairs and the Law of the Sea. Secretary-General Ban Ki-moon *(second from left)* receives a book, *The United Nations Convention on the Law of the Sea 1982: A Commentary*, from John Norton Moore, Professor at the University of Virginia School of Law and Director of the Center for Oceans Law and Policy, during a reception to mark the 30th Anniversary of the UN Convention on the Law of the Sea (UNCLOS).

Also pictured: Tommy Koh *(second from right)*, Ambassador-at-Large of Singapore and former President of the Conference on the Law of the Sea, and Ambassador Satya Nandan (Fiji), former Secretary-General of the International Seabed Authority *(first from right)*. [Photo credit: UN Photo/Eskinder Debebe, New York, 2012]

Secretary-General Javier Pérez de Cuéllar met representatives of the Association of Southeast Asian Nations (ASEAN) in his UN headquarters office. *From left to right*: Zainal Abidin bin Sulong (Malaysia), Alejandro D. Yango (Philippines), Tommy Koh (Singapore), Hasjim Djalal (Indonesia), Birabongse Kasemsri (Thailand) and Rafeeudin Ahmed, the Secretary-General's Special Representative for Humanitarian Affairs in Southeast Asia. [Photo credit: UN Photo 148600/Yutaka Nagata, New York, 1982]

Singapore at the United Nations. Front row *(left to right)*: Nellie Chan, Chew Beng Yong, Viji Menon. Second row *(left to right)*: V. K. Rajan, Raymond Wong, Ong Lu King, K. Kesavapany, Geoffrey Yu and Tommy Koh.

Tommy and Siew Aing with Ann and Elliot L. Richardson. Richardson was a distinguished American who had served his country as Attorney General, Secretary of Commerce, Under Secretary of State and leader of the US delegation to the Conference on the Law of the Sea.

Tommy Koh with the 39th President of the United States, Jimmy Carter. President Carter won the Nobel Peace Prize for his life-long efforts to promote peace. He mediated the Sinai Peace Treaty between Egypt and Israel.

Siew Aing with then First Lady of the United States, Rosalynn Carter and the late Piroska Rajaratnam.

With former President Ronald Reagan and Nancy Reagan at the White House with Siew Aing, 1985.

Former Prime Minister Lee Kuan Yew and former President Ronald Reagan at the Welcome Ceremony at the White House, 1985. Tommy Koh was Singapore's ambassador in Washington from 1984 to 1990.

From left to right: Former Prime Minister Lee Kuan Yew, former President Ronald Reagan, Selwa Roosevelt (Chief of Protocol), Tommy Koh and Siew Aing, 1985.

Tommy meeting with President George H. W. Bush, his Secretary of State, James Baker and his National Security Advisor, General Brent Scowcroft, in the Oval Office of the White House, 1989. James Baker received Harvard's Great Negotiator Award in 2012.

With former President George H. W. Bush and Barbara Bush at the White House with Siew Aing, 1989.

Call on Senate Majority Leader, Bob Dole, with other ASEAN Ambassadors. *From left to right:* The ambassadors of Brunei, Singapore, Malaysia, Senator Dole, and ambassadors of the Philippines, Thailand and Indonesia.

Tommy Koh with General Colin Powell, former US Secretary of Defence, taken at the Pentagon in 1990. General Powell subsequently served as the US Secretary of State. He was the first African American to occupy those high positions as well as that of the National Security Advisor.

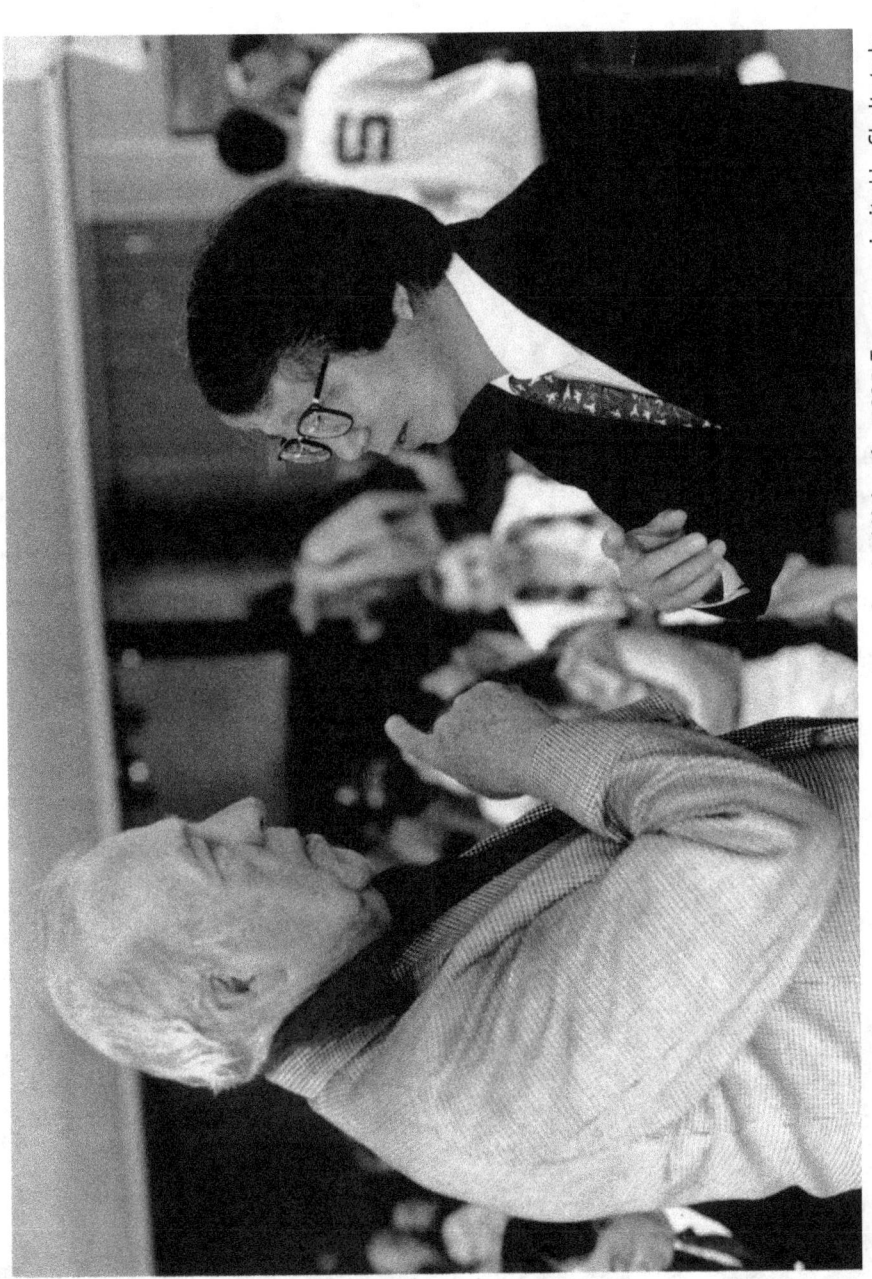

Tommy Koh and George Shultz engaged in an animated discussion at Stanford University, 1995. Tommy was invited by Shultz to be the second Frank and Arthur Payne Lecturer on the "Global Community and Its Challenges" at Stanford University in 1995.

On safari in Masai Mara, Kenya, August, 1990. Back row *(left to right)*: Khoo Seow Poh and Foong Chee Leong. Front row: Tommy Koh, Chan Heng Wing and Vanu Gopala Menon.

Practicing diplomacy with a Kikuyu woman in Masai Mara, Kenya, August, 1990. Tommy was out-negotiated by these women who would not let him go until he agreed to buy their trinklets at exhorbitant prices.

Photo taken in Ottawa, Canada, with a group of High Commissioners and Ambassadors, before they embarked on a tour of Canada's Arctic North. Tommy was the most senior member of the group and had to act as spokesman at all their stops. They visited an Inuit community in the arctic and a reservation for Canadian Indians in Yukon.

Tommy Koh chairing a meeting of the UNCED Preparatory Committee in New York, 1992. This photograph was taken just after Secretary-General Boutros Boutros-Ghali had read one of the pages of his speech twice, thus repeating a compliment which he had paid to Ambassador Koh, whereupon Ambassador Koh stopped the Secretary-General midway to tell him that he did not have to pay him the same compliment twice. It was only at that juncture that the Secretary-General realized that he had unwittingly repeated the same page of his address. The meeting broke up in laughter.

With former UN Secretary-General Kofi Annan. Taken in New York in 1997.

Tommy Koh chairing the last preparatory committee meeting of the Earth Summit, New York, April 1992.

With former US Secretary of State, Cyrus Vance, Mrs Okita, Dr Saburo Okita and Tommy Koh, the three co-convenors of the Williamsburg Conference, Gotemba, Japan, 1992. Dr Okita was one of the architects of Japan's reconstruction after the Second World War.

The Singapore delegation at the 1992 Earth Summit in Rio de Janerio where Tommy Koh chaired the Main Committee. Front row *(left to right)*: Chew Tai Soo, Ahmad Mattar, Tommy Koh, Lim Chuan Poh and K. Kesavapany. Back row *(left to right)*: Foo Kim Boon, Richard Grosse, Viji Menon, Foong Chee Leong, Khoo Seow Poh and Burhan Gafoor.

Tommy Koh, then UN Secretary-General's Special Envoy to Russia, Estonia, Latvia and Lithuania, in Moscow with the Russian ambassadors who were negotiating with Estonia, Latvia and Lithuania. Picture taken at the Ministry of Foreign Affairs in Moscow, in 1993.

With some of the judges of the International Tribunal for the Law of the Sea, Hamburg, Germany, 2003. In the second row are S. Jayakumar *(second from left)* and S. Tiwari *(third from left)*.

The IPS team in 1997. Front row *(left to right)*: Cecilia Kuek, Lee Tsao Yuan, Tommy Koh, Siew Aing, Gillian Koh, Ooi Giok Ling (deceased)
Second row *(left to right)*: Shirley Lim, Yap Mui Teng, Arun Mahizhnan, Obood Talib
Third row *(left to right)*: Angeline Lang Oi Chee, Cynthia Lin, Yeo Lay Hwee, Janice Tang Hwee Cher
Fourth row *(left to right)*: Malathi d/o Siva Raju, Angeline Yee, Chang Li Lin
Fifth row: Gwee Wee Chen

Photo taken at an IPS lunch with Ms Ho Ching, CEO of Temasek Holdings, as the guest speaker, July 2009. *From left to right*: Lito Camacho (Credit Suisse), Ho Ching, Tommy Koh, Fang Ai Lian (Great Eastern Holdings) and Kwee Liong Keng (Pontiac Land).

Leading the management team of the Asia–Europe Foundation, 2000.
From left to right: Ulrich Niemann, Terence Tan, Pierre Barroux, Tommy Koh, Peggy Kek, Cai Rongsheng and Duncan Jackman.

Tommy Koh was invited by HRH Princess Maha Chakri Sirindhorn to visit her palace and have dinner with her. The portrait behind them showed her grandparents, 2011.

Second International Advisory Board Meeting of Toyota Group, May 1997.
Front row *(left to right)*: Eiji Toyoda, Iwao Isomura, Viscount Etienne Davignon, Paul Volcker, Shoichiro Toyoda (Chairman), Tommy Koh, Hiroshi Okuda and Tatsuro Toyoda.
Middle row *(left to right)*: Akihiro Wada, Wilfried Thalwitz, Pedro-Pablo Kuczynski, Sankaranarayana Venkitaramanan, Qin Xiao, Martin Lees and Iwao Okijima.
Back row *(left to right)*: Fujio Cho, Akira Yokio, Akira Takahashi, Kosuke Yamamoto, Kanji Kurioka and Tokuichi Uranishi.

Tommy Koh *(front row, second from the right)* was a member of the board of directors of SingTel for five years. This picture of the board and senior management was taken at a retreat in New Delhi, India. The guest speaker, Sunil Mittal, Founder and CEO of Bharti Airtel, is in the front row with a tie. The then chairman of SingTel, Chumpol Naliamliang, is on his left. Then group CEO, Lee Hsien Yang, is on his right. The current group CEO, Chua Sock Koong, is in the front row, third from the right, and the current chairman, Simon Israel, is standing behind Mittal.

With former Vice Minister Xu Dunxin, leader of the Chinese delegation who negotiated the agreement to establish formal diplomatic relations between Singapore and the People's Republic of China. Picture taken at Diaoyutai State Guesthouse, Beijing, in September 1990, when the negotiation was successfully concluded. Formal diplomatic relations were established on 3 October 1990.

Members of the Singapore delegation at the Second China–Singapore Forum, in Beijing, 2006. From (*left to right*): Tommy Koh, Yeo Lay Hwee, Francis Chong, Kumar Ramakrishnan, Tan Tai Yong, Sheng Lijun, Kishore Mahbubani, Barry Desker, Kwa Chong Guan, K. Kesavapany, Wang Gungwu, Arun Mahizhnan and John Wong.

Third China-Singapore Forum

17 - 18 April 2008, Singapore

Co-organised by
East Asian Institute, Singapore and the
Chinese People's Institute of Foreign Affairs, China

Photo of the two delegations. PRC Ambassador to Singapore, Chen Baoliu, is in the front row, third from the left. The Chinese co-chair, Yang Wenchang, is seated between Wang Gungwu and Tommy Koh.

Wang Gungwu, Ambassador Yang Wenchang and Tommy Koh speaking at the public forum, following the successful conclusion of the Seventh China–Singapore Forum in Singapore, 2012.

Photo taken at the public forum on 26 April 2011, following the successful conclusion of the Eighth Japan–Singapore Symposium. *From left to right*: Masahiro Kawaii, Keiko Chino, Tommy Koh, Shotaro Yachi, Ambassador Yoichi Suzuki, and Simon Tay.

Group photo of the delegations of Japan and Singapore, at the Eighth Japan–Singapore Symposium, on 25 April 2011. The leader of the Singapore delegation, Zainul Abidin Rasheed, is seated in the front row, fifth from the right. Singapore's ambassador to Japan, Tan Chin Tiong, is seated in the front row, third from the right.

Photo taken on 26 February 2013 in New Delhi, at the public forum following the successful conclusion of the Sixth India–Singapore Strategic Dialogue. *From left to right*: Ambassador Gopinath Pillai, Jamshyd Godrej (co-chair), Indrani Bagchi (moderator), Tommy Koh (co-chair) and Ambassador Satindar Lambah (former co-chair).

Photo of the delegations from India and Singapore of the Sixth India–Singapore Strategic Dialogue, taken in New Delhi, India on 26 February 2013. The two co-chairs are Jamshyd Godrej and Tommy Koh. Singapore's High Commissioner to India, Karen Tan, is in the front row, fourth from the left.

SIGNING OF THE SETTLEMENT AGREEMENT OF THE CASE CONCERNING LAND RECLAMATION BY SINGAPORE IN AND AROUND THE STRAITS OF JOHOR

SINGAPORE, 26 APRIL 2005

Signing the Settlement Agreement of the Case Concerning Land Reclamation by Singapore in and around the Straits of Johor with Tan Sri Ahmad Fuzi bin Abdul Razak, witnessed by then Foreign Ministers of Malaysia and Singapore, Syed Hamid Albar and George Yeo, 2005. A book on the case, co-authored by Cheong Koon Hean, Lionel Yee and Tommy Koh, was launched in August 2013.

The team of lawyers who spoke on behalf of Singapore at the International Court of Justice. *From left to right*: Alain Pellet, Rod Bundy, Ian Brownlie, S. Jayakumar, Chan Sek Keong, Chao Hick Tin, Tommy Koh and Loretta Malintoppi. Picture taken at the Peace Palace, The Hague, Netherlands, in 2007 during the oral proceedings at the court.

9th Meeting of the High Level Task Force on the Drafting of the ASEAN Charter
24 – 26 August 2007, Singapore

With members of the High Level Task Force who drafted the ASEAN Charter. *From left to right:* The representatives of Indonesia, Laos, Malaysia, Myanmar, Philippines, Singapore, Thailand, Vietnam, Brunei, Cambodia, and Dr. Termsak from the ASEAN Secretariat. Tommy Koh chaired the task force in the second half of 2007. The draft of the charter was successfully concluded in October 2007 in Vientiane, Laos.

Tommy and Siew Aing visited the Neka Museum in Ubud, Bali. They were invited by the founder of the Museum, Pak Suteja Neka (*fifth from right*) and his wife, Ibu Srimin (*third from left*) to their home to meet their children.

Photo taken at the Asian Civilisations Museum on 11 March 2009, on the signing of a Memorandum of Understanding between the National Heritage Board and the Indian Heritage Centre, the Malay Heritage Centre and the Sun Yat-sen Memorial community heritage institutions.
Front row *(left to right)*: Tommy Koh, the late Balaji Sadasivan, Zainul Abidin Rasheed, and Chia Ban Seng.
Back row *(left to right)*: Michael Koh, CEO of National Heritage Board, Minister for Communications and the Arts, Lui Tuck Yew and Chairman of Singapore Chinese Chamber of Commerce & Industry, Chua Thian Poh.

Opening of the Wang Gungwu Library at the Chinese Heritage Centre, 13 September 2003. *Front row (left to right)*: Wang Gungwu, Wee Cho Yaw (founding Chairman), Washington SyCip, Tommy Koh (Chairman). *Back row (left to right)*: Liu Thai Ker and Cham Tao Soon.

Picture taken at the opening of a mini Singapore Festival at the UN Plaza Hotel in New York in 1983. The chefs from the Grand Hyatt Hotel (Singapore) came to cook Singapore food. Four musicians from the People's Association played Chinese music and two of Singapore's young artists, Ong Kim Seng (in batik, *right*) and Lee Hock Moh (in batik, *left*) exhibited their paintings.

Siew Aing and Tommy hosting the National Symphony Ball in Washington. SIA was the major sponsor of the Ball in 1985.

From left to right: Lee Hock Moh, Siew Aing, Tommy and Ong Kim Seng. Tommy invited them to visit New York to exhibit their paintings in 1983. Kim Seng had won a prize from the American Watercolor Society.

Walking with the late Kuo Pao Kun to raise funds for The Substation.
From left to right: Siew Aing, Pao Kun, Tommy and Kenneth Liang. Tommy is the Patron of The Substation since 1991. Picture taken in the early 1990s.

The National Arts Council team in 1991. *From left to right*: Corrine Wong, Lee Soon Hock, Tommy Koh, Teo Han Wue, Foo Meng Liang, Khor Kok Wah, Liew Chin Choy.

In 2003, the Singapore Government conferred on artist Tan Swie Hian, the Meritorious Service Medal. To celebrate the award, the National Heritage Board and the National Arts Council organised a major exhibition of the artist's works at the Singapore Art Museum. President S. R. Nathan was the Guest-of-Honour at the opening of the exhibition on 24 August 2004. He requested Tommy to speak on his behalf.

Tommy with the late Dr Earl Lu and Brother Joseph McNally at the Lasalle College of the Arts. Tommy was the Guest-of-Honour at the opening of the Earl Lu Gallery in 1986. Dr Lu was the first Chairman of the Singapore Art Museum.

With Singapore's Cultural Medallion winners when Tommy was Chairman of the National Arts Council. *From left to right*: Iskandar Jalil, Joanna Wong, Edwin Thumboo, Choo Huey and Goh Soo Khim.

Photo taken on the occasion of the performance by the late sitar maestro Ravi Shankar of India with the Shanghai Symphony Orchestra when Tommy was the Chairman of the National Arts Council. This is an example of using culture as an instrument to promote peace and friendship between peoples.

Accepting the donation by one of our pioneer artists, Liu Kang and his family, of his paintings and sketches to the Singapore Art Museum, May 2003. *From left to right:* Liu Thai Ker, Tommy Koh, Mr and Mrs Liu Kang and Lee Boon Yang, then Minister for Information, Communications and the Arts.

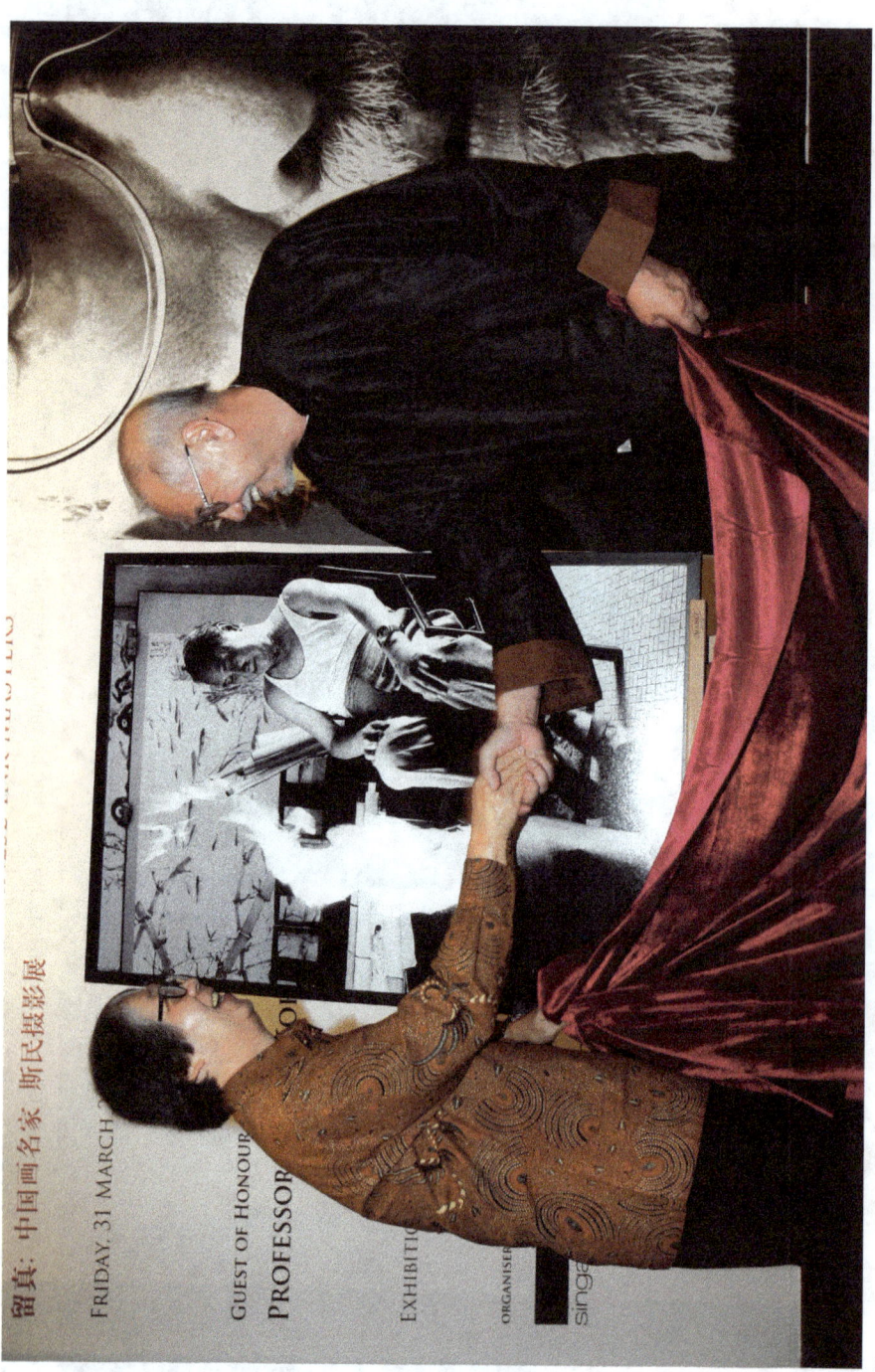

Tommy opened an exhibition "Legends: Soo Bin's Portraits of Chinese Ink Masters" at the Singapore Art Museum by Cultural Medallion winner and fine-art photographer, Chua Soo Bin, in March 2006. Singapore's pioneer artist Chen Wen Hsi is seen in the black and white photo.

A happy event at the Singapore Art Museum in April 2011, when Dr and Mrs George Quek of the Breadtalk Group (second and third from left) donated paintings by the artist, Tan Oe Pang (first on right) to the National Art Gallery of Singapore. The person on the extreme left is Kwok Kian Chow, former Director of the Gallery.

Tommy with master potter and Cultural Medallion winner, Iskandar Jalil, at his ceramics exhibition and book launch of *Images of My Pottery Travels*, in October 2011. [Photo by Ernest Goh.]

Kwek Leng Joo, Managing Director of CDL, is a talented photographer. He has published three photo art books to raise funds for the President's Challenge. Picture was taken at the Istana, in 2011, at a book launch.

Tembusu College Inaugural Dinner, 2011. Tommy is the Rector and Gregory Clancey is the Master of the College.
Back row (left to right): Tan Tai Yong, Philip Cho, Connor Graham, Tan Eng Chye, Gregory Clancey, Tommy Koh, Jerome Whitington, Prasenjit Duara, John van Wyhe, Prakash Hande, Foo Junhong, Jeremy Fernando and Kelvin Pang.
Front row (left to right): Sorelle Henricus, Sara Kuek, Danielle Henricus, Lina Lim, Catelijne Coopmans, Juliette Duara, Siew Aing, Margaret Tan and Denisa Kera.

Gregory Clancey and Tommy with the staff and students of Tembusu College who decorated the two elephants which raised over $50,000 for the conservation of the Asian elephant in its natural habitat.

Moderating a dialogue with former Prime Minister Lee Kuan Yew at the 150th anniversary of the Singapore Botanic Gardens, 2009. [Source: *The Straits Times* © Singapore Press Holdings Ltd. Reprinted with permission.]

Many happy people at the dedication of the Van Kleef Centre in January 2013. *From left to right*: Minister Grace Fu, former Queen, Princess Beatrix, Tommy Koh, King Willem-Alexander, Queen Máxima, Wong Ngit Liong (Chairman of NUS), Dr Vladan Babovic (Director of the Van Kleef Centre), Tan Eng Chye (Provost of NUS), Chew Men Leong (CEO of Public Utilities Board).

Tommy Koh moderating PM Lee Hsien Loong at the Singapore International Water Week in 2011.

Tommy Koh moderating the Administrator of UNDP, Helen Clark at the Singapore International Water Week in 2012. Ms Clark was the former Prime Minister of New Zealand, who won three successive elections.

Photo taken at the sidelines of the Second Asia–Pacific Water Summit, in Chiang Mai, Thailand in 2013. The person in front of the microphone is Yoshiro Mori, President of the Asia–Pacific Water Forum. Tommy Koh stepped down as chairman of the governing council after six years and is succeeded by the former vice-chairman, Ravi Narayanan. The other outgoing vice-chairman is Ambassador Erna Witoelar of Indonesia.

Tommy Koh having been conferred the Grand Cross of the Order of Bernado O'Higgins by Chile, 1977. Pictured with him *(from left to right)*: Siew Aing, Ambassador Francisco Tudela, Mrs Tuleda, Mdm See Tsai Ying, Jimmy Koh and Mrs Jeraldine Koh.

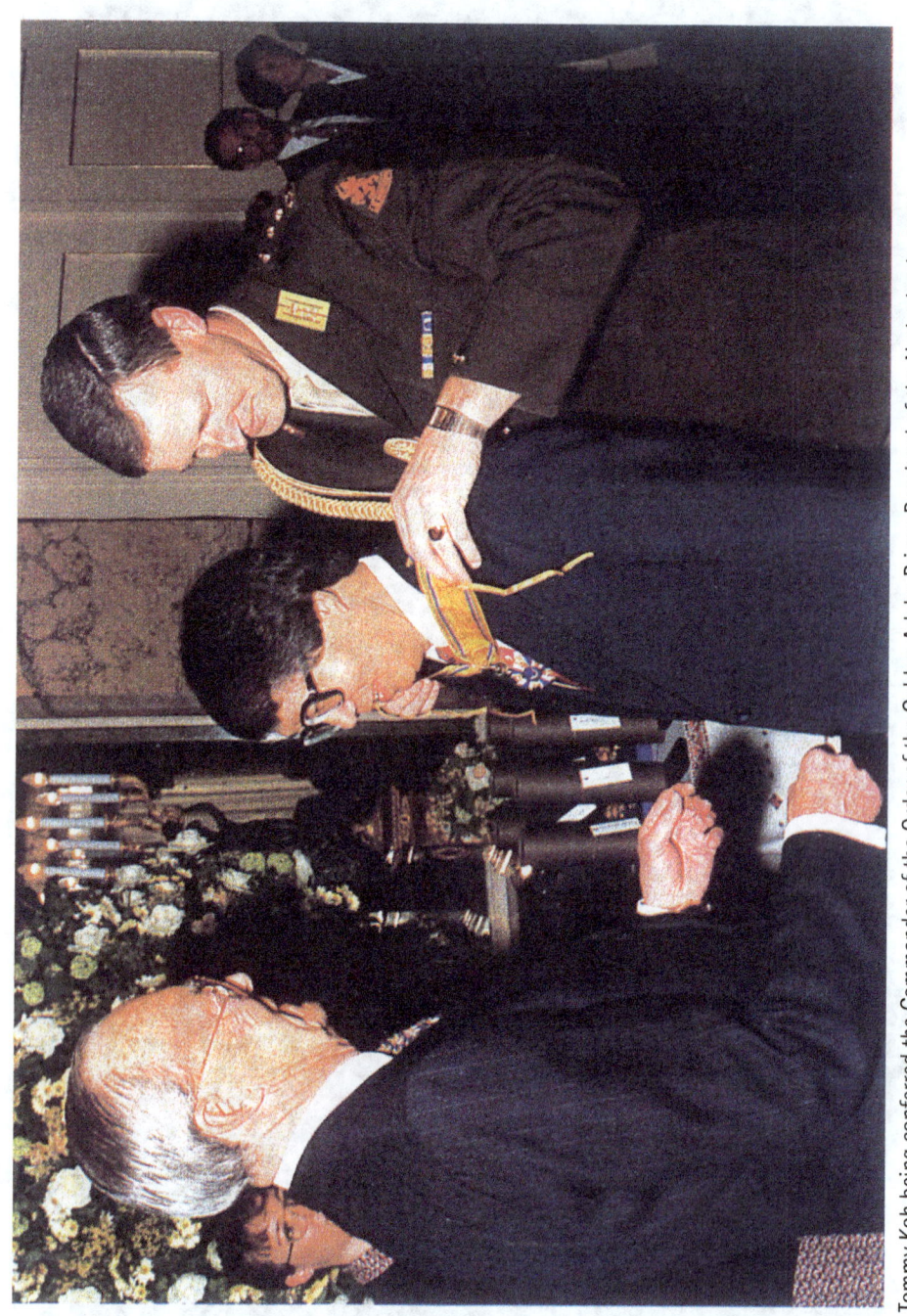

Tommy Koh being conferred the Commander of the Order of the Golden Ark by Prince Bernhard of the Netherlands, 1993.

In 2000, President Martti Ahtisaari conferred on Tommy Koh the Commander (First Class) of the Order of the Lion of Finland. Mr Ahtisaari is the former President of Finland and winner of the Nobel Peace Prize in 2008. The person on the right is Chang Li Lin, then Public Affairs Manager at the Institute of Policy Studies.

Tommy Koh receiving the Peace and Commerce Award from the US Secretary of Commerce, Donald Evans, in Washington, DC, on 6 May 2003. Tommy was Singapore's Chief Negotiator of the US–Singapore Free Trade Agreement, which was signed that day by former US President George W. Bush and former Prime Minister Goh Chok Tong. [Credit: Agence France-Presse]

Recipients of the inaugural President's Award for the Environment in 2006.
From left to right: Minister Yaacob Ibrahim, Geh Min, Tommy Koh, former President S. R. Nathan, Jeffrey Ong and Low Ping Ping.

Tommy Koh receiving the "Champion of the Earth Award 2006" from Shafqat Kakakhel, Deputy Executive Director of United Nations Environment Programme in Singapore, 2006. [Source: *Lianhe Zaobao* © Singapore Press Holdings Ltd. Reprinted with permission.]

In 2009, the Emperor of Japan conferred on Tommy Koh the Order of the Rising Sun, Gold and Silver Star. The award ceremony was held at the Japanese Ambassador's residence. *From left to right*: Ambassador Makoto Yamanaka, Tommy, Siew Aing and Mrs Yamanaka.

Tommy Koh receiving the Order of Sang Nila Utama (First Class) from former President S. R. Nathan, 2008.

4

DIPLOMACY

The Situation in Grenada*

Mr President, Singapore is one of the smallest States of the United Nations. It is a militarily weak State. Because we are small and because we are militarily weak, we therefore have a major stake in the efficacy of international law, in the principles of the United Nations Charter and the United Nations Collective Security System. It is because our national security is threatened whenever a small or militarily weak State falls victim to the aggression, intervention and interference by a bigger or militarily more powerful State, that Singapore has been so outspoken in defence of the fundamental principles of the United Nations Charter. We believe that, all small and militarily weak States share the same interest with us in protecting these principles which afford us a degree of protection in a world which is all too prone to violence.

Mr President, it is easy enough for us to demonstrate our adherence to principle when to do so is convenient and advantageous and costs us nothing. The test of a country's adherence to principle is when it is inconvenient to do so. I find myself in such a situation today. Barbados, Jamaica, the United States and the Member States of the OECS are friends of my country. It is extremely convenient for me to acquiesce in what they have done or to remain silent. To do so however will, in the long run, undermine the moral and legal significance of the principles which my country regard as a shield. This is why we must put our adherence to principle above friendship. This is why we cannot condone the action of our friends in Grenada. The stand which my country has taken in this case is consistent with the stand which we have taken in other cases,

---

*Statement delivered to the UN Security Council on 28 October 1983.

where the principle of non-interference in the internal affairs of States was also violated.

Mr President, I regret that I will have to say that some of the countries which are clamouring the loudest for the condemnation of the foreign intervention in Grenada have not demonstrated their adherence to the principle of non-interference in the internal affairs of States in other cases. Let me quote just one example. In December 1979, the Soviet Union committed aggression against Afghanistan. Soviet troops are in occupation of that country and the number of Afghans who are killed daily in resisting Soviet occupation is probably larger than all the casualties suffered in Grenada. On the 29th of November 1982, the 37th Session of the United Nations General Assembly adopted Resolution 37/37 on Afghanistan. Which countries voted with the Soviet Union against that Resolution? They were: Angola, Bulgaria, Byelorussia, Cuba, Czechoslovakia, Democratic Yemen, Ethiopia, German Democratic Republic, Hungary, Laos, Libya, Madagascar, Mongolia, Mozambique, Poland, Syria, Ukraine and Vietnam. By their support for the Soviet intervention in Afghanistan, these 18 countries have clearly shown that they owe no allegiance to the principle of non-interference in the internal affairs of States. The real basis for their opposition to the action of the United States and others in Grenada is not based upon principle but upon the fact that those who have violated the principle are their ideological adversaries and those who are the victims of foreign intervention are their ideological comrades. The world should therefore not be deceived by the opportunism and hypocrisy of these countries.

De Tocqueville Revisited
American Politics Viewed from a Foreign Perspective

Introduction

Two years ago, I was re-assigned from my post at the United Nations to the Embassy in Washington. At the UN, I had to deal with the representatives of 158 countries as well as with many key officials in the UN Secretariat — a total cast of perhaps 500 characters. When I left New York for Washington, I thought I was leaving a multilateral post for a bilateral one. However, although I am now dealing with only one government instead of 158, the US Government is, in a very real sense, a multilateral system. I do not think there is another government in the family of democractic societies in which power is so decentralized and dispersed, and in which so many institutions and individuals are involved in or have inputs into the making of policy and the implementation of decisions and programmes. The following are some of my impressions of American politics as seen from the point of view of a Singaporean whose political institutions are based on the British parliamentary model.

The Influence of Hollywood, Madison Avenue and Television

Let me begin on a relatively light note. I observe that American politics has been afflicted by three unwholesome influences. These are Hollywood, Madison Avenue and television. Hollywood exerts a powerful and pervasive influence on every aspect of American life and culture. For example, I have watched with both amusement and sadness, the annual list of the ten most admired men and women in America. Apart from the President and the First Lady, those on the list consist mostly of movie stars and other entertainers. The President of Harvard University has never made the list! The winners of Nobel and Pulitzer Prizes do not seem to enjoy the same public adulation as movie stars. Hollywood has two pernicious influences on American politics. First, it has injected "a show biz" quality into American politics. Second, as Professor Garry Orren of Harvard University has pointed out, in judging the presidential debates, "the public responds overwhelmingly to the sweat on the brow, style, manner and personality" rather than to the substance of the debate.

Madison Avenue has also had a pernicious influence on American politics. The language of advertising has infected the style and content of American political discourse. Speeches by American politicians are often characterised by bombast, hyperbole and exaggerations. The influence of television on American politics has been overwhelming. As Professor Ralph Whitehead of the University of Massachusetts has said, "Television is the language of the American people, and, in politics, if you can't use television you lack the faculty of speech."

Because television is such an expensive medium, it forces politicians to over-simplify complicated issues. As the Governor of New York, Mario Cuomo, has pointed out, "having to get your message across in 28 seconds forces you to labels, shibboleths, stereotypes and simplistics". Recently, the Democratic Party requested Senator Sam Nunn to give a two-minute response, on television, to the Administration's policy on arms control. Much to his credit, Senator Nunn declined the request on the grounds that it was impossible for him to do justice to such a complex subject in two minutes. There are, unfortunately, very few Sam Nunns in American politics.

The Separation of Powers

In Singapore, as in Britain, there is a very close nexus between the Executive and the Legislative branches of government. A government is formed by the party or by a coalition of parties which commands a majority in parliament. The moment the government loses its majority in parliament, it is obliged to resign from office. Because of the close nexus between the Executive and Legislature and because of the high degree of party discipline which exists in most parliamentary democracies, the government is normally able to get its legislative programme enacted by parliament.

The situation in the United States is entirely different. There is a clear separation of powers between the Executive, the Legislative and the Judicial branches of government. Even when the same party controls the White House, the Senate and the House of Representatives, which is not a very frequent occurrence, the Administration cannot count on the automatic support of the Congress for its legislative programme. More often, the same party does not control both the White House and the two chambers of Congress. In this case, the Administration will have to negotiate its legislative proposals with the two Houses of Congress and arrive at compromises.

Let me tell you a true story which illustrates the point I am making. The new ambassador of a major country in Asia, which will remain unnamed, arrived in Washington. He called upon a senior official in the State Department. At their meeting, the ambassador complained bitterly that the Congress had just passed a law which is contrary to the spirit of a communique which had been signed by their two governments. The State Department official explained to the ambassador that the Administration could not control the Congress and advised the ambassador to lobby its members. The ambassador was taken aback by the advice. He asked, "Wouldn't it be an interference in your domestic affairs for me to lobby members of the Congress?" The State Department official replied that unless he did so, he would not be very effective in Washington.

The Administration and the Role of the Cabinet

In Singapore, every member of the Cabinet has to be an elected Member of Parliament. In the American Cabinet, the only two elected officials are the President and the Vice-President. The Cabinet Secretaries are appointed by the President and serve at his pleasure. Under the doctrine of the separation of powers, it is not possible for a member of the Cabinet to remain a member of Congress. In the current Reagan Cabinet, only the Vice-President and the Labour Secretary, Bill Brock, has previously served in Congress.

In Singapore, the Cabinet meets every week. All important questions of policies, programmes and legislation are discussed and decided in Cabinet. Decisions are usually made by consensus but, on rare occasions, by vote. I am informed that the American Cabinet does not function in the same manner. This may partially account for the fact that the different departments and agencies of the government do not seem to work harmoniously at times. As a result, it is necessary for an ambassador in Washington to work closely not only with the State Department but also with the White House, the National Security Council, the Department of Defence, the Department of Commerce, the Office of the US Trade Representative, the Treasury Department, the Department of Transportation and others. On this Administration's policy towards Southeast Asia, we have been fortunate that the Departments of State and Defence and the National Security Council have been able to work harmoniously. Credit for this happy state of affairs must go to Assistant Secretary Gaston Sigur of the State Department, Assistant Secretary Richard Armitage of the Defence Department and James Kelly of the National Security Council.

The US Congress

The US Congress has a lower chamber called the House of Representatives and an upper chamber called the Senate. The House has 435 members and the Senate has 100 members. There are more than 300 committees and subcommittees in the two houses. In addition, there are several thousand congressional staffers.

For an ambassador to be effective in Washington, he must cultivate the leadership of the two parties in the Senate and in the House of Representatives. In addition, he must cultivate the leadership and key members of the various committees and subcommittees whose work impinges upon the interests of his country. If he is wise, he would also cultivate the key congressional staffers because they possess great influence and expertise.

There was a time in the past, when Congress was ruled by a rigid seniority system. During that era the junior members of Congress would normally comply with the requests and wishes of their seniors. A revolutionary change took place in the 1970s. By 1981, 54 per cent of the members of the Senate were serving in their first term. In the 97th Congress (1981–1982) the majority of its members had served only since 1977. This has made Congress a more democratic institution. It has led to a greater degree of decentralization of power. These changes have both a positive and a negative aspect. On the positive side, Congress today is more open and more responsive to the various social and political forces in the country than it has ever been. On the negative side, it has been criticized for being too responsive, particularly to single, narrow interests. Another negative consequence of the democratisation of Congress is that any of the 535 legislators can, through a variety of procedural manoeuvres, alter a bill, delay action, or tie the institution in knots.

The Role of Political Parties

In the United States, there are no national political parties. There are 50 state Democratic Parties and 50 state Republican Parties, each with its own views, rules and procedures. The two parties have no national leaders. They do not have strong national party committees. Although a lot of time and energy is spent in drafting the party platform, it is forgotten as soon as it is adopted. Congressmen and congresswomen are free to ignore their party's platform without fear of any sanction.

Even in Congress, it is not always easy to enforce party discipline. In one recent case, the Democratic Party's leadership in the House of Representatives attempted to discipline a congressman from Texas, Phil Gramm, who had voted against his party. Phil Gramm promptly resigned his seat in the House, joined the Republican party and won re-election to the House. Subsequently, he succeeded in winning election to the Senate.

The Influence of Money

Members of the House of Representatives have to face an election every two years. Members of the Senate enjoy a longer tenure of six years. This means that as soon as a congressman or a congresswoman is elected, he or she must immediately set about organising for his or her re-election campaign. Running for an election in this country is an extremely expensive business. In Singapore, a candidate may spend up to a maximum of S$6,000 or approximately US$3,000 for his or her campaign. This translates into approximately S$0.50 or US$0.25 per voter. In Singapore, the candidate does not have to raise his or her campaign funds as these come from the party's coffers.

The situation in the United States is different. First, there is no legal limit on how much money a candidate can spend for his campaign for election to a seat in the House or in the Senate. In 1984, Congressman Bill Green of New York spent US$1.1 million to retain his seat in the House and his unsuccessful challenger spent US$1.8 million. Campaigns for the Senate are, of course, even more costly. In the US, a candidate has to raise most of his campaign funds. He or she can expect little help from his political party. The advent of television has also increased the cost of running for elections. In 1984, the candidates spent a total of US$300 million on 30-second or 60-second TV and radio advertisements, mostly attacking their opponents.

Under current Federal Election Laws, a person or organisation may contribute the maximum of US$1,000 per election for a candidate for federal office, US$20,000 per year to national political committees and US$5,000 to another political committee. No individual or organisation may contribute more than US$25,000 directly to candidates for federal election in any one year. The federal laws, however, contain a loophole. The loophole is that there is no limit to the total amount which a political action committee (PAC) can spend on behalf of a candidate as long as the committee does not co-ordinate its activities in any way with the candidate, his or her representatives, or the campaign committee. There are approximately 4,000 political action committees in existence. In the period January 1985 to June 1986, the political action committees contributed a total of US$67 million to House and Senate candidates. Democratic candidates have reported receiving US$37 million. Republican candidates have reported receiving US$30 million. Professor Garry Orren of Harvard University has described the political action committees as phony mechanisms created to get around the finance laws. Senators David Boren and Barry Goldwater have co-sponsored a bill to deal with PACs. Senator Boren has said that, "we cannot expect members of Congress to act in the national interest when their election campaigns are being financed more and more by special interests". Senator Goldwater has stated that, "... PAC money is destroying the election process ... As far as the general public is concerned, it is no longer 'we the people', but PACs and the special interests they represent, who set the country's political agenda and control nearly every candidate's position on the important issues of the day."

The Influence of Interest Groups

Alexis de Tocqueville observed that certain American cultural values such as individuality and the need for personal achievement underlie the propensity of citizens to join groups. In a democracy, it is perfectly appropriate for a group of citizens who share a common interest or objective to form themselves into an interest group. There is nothing wrong for such groups to attempt to communicate their interests, aspirations and goals to members of the Congress or to seek to influence the course of legislation in that body. The theory is that there would be competition between various interest groups and the members of the Congress would, after taking due account of the merits of the various supplicants, decide on a policy or an issue on the basis of what is good for the nation. Unfortunately, the theory does not always accord with reality. Let me illustrate my point with the following example.

One of the thousands of interest groups which exist in this country is the tuna lobby, based in California. Due to the influence of this lobby, Congress enacted the Magnuson Act which does not recognise the rights of coastal states over tuna in their exclusive economic zones. This has caused a crisis in the relations between the United States and the island countries of the South Pacific. Many of these countries have little or no land-based resources. Their only resource is marine resource and the most valuable marine resource is tuna. Because of the refusal of the United States to recognise the rights of these countries over tuna in their exclusive economic zones, one of the countries, Kiribati, has concluded a fishing agreement with the Soviet Union and the Prime Minister of another country, Fiji, has publicly announced his intention to do the same. The South Pacific is an area of great strategic importance to the United States. It is an area in which the Soviet Union has been unable to gain a toehold for the past 40 years. It seems absurd that the policy of the United States towards the South Pacific is being controlled by the tuna lobby.

The Impact of the American Political Process on Foreign Countries

Since the United States is the leader of the free world, the choice of the US President is not only of vital importance to the United States but also to its allies and friends. The process by which the candidates of the two parties is chosen is so unpredictable and hazardous that I have once suggested, half in jest, that your allies and friends ought to have a say in the choice of your two presidential candidates.

The US system of government, characterised by the separation of powers among the three branches of government and by many checks and balances, is designed to protect the liberty of the individual. It is based upon an inarticulate mistrust of the government. The system is designed to prevent the concentration and abuse of power. It is not designed to produce a strong government, a government which has a free hand in conducting its relations with other countries.

Given the fact that power is shared between the Administration and the Congress, American foreign policy is at its best when the two institutions work in tandem and at its worse when they pull in different directions. Let me conclude my remarks by giving you two examples, one of success and the other of potential disaster. The United States played a very constructive role in assisting the peaceful transition of power which took place recently in the Philippines from President Marcos to President Aquino. One important reason for the success of US policy was that the Democrats and the Republicans, the Congress and the Administration, as well as the powerful American media were acting in unison.

My second example is in the area of trade policy. Last year, the United States suffered a trade deficit of US$150 billion. Some have estimated that the trade deficit this year could reach US$170 billion. The Administration's trade policy is based upon the following three pillars. First, to bring down the value of the US$ vis-à-vis the currencies of its major trading partners. Second, to knock down foreign barriers blocking the exports of US goods and services and to seek the removal of other unfair trade practices such as dumping and subsidies. Third, to launch a new round of multilateral trade negotiations and to include in its agenda such new items as agriculture, services, high technology, investments and the protection of intellectual property rights.

Instead of supporting the Administration's policy, Congress, especially the Democrats, has embarked upon the disastrous course of protectionism. On 6 August 1986, the House of Representatives came within eight votes of overriding the President's veto of the Jenkins Bill, which would have drastically curtailed the imports of textiles, especially from Asia, in violation of the United States' bilateral and multilateral treaty obligations. The House of Representatives has adopted by more than two-thirds majority an omnibus trade bill (HR 4800) which is blatantly protectionist and GATT-illegal. Since the Democratic Party has decided to exploit trade as an electoral issue in the November elections this year, the Republicans in the Senate, fearful of losing their slim majority, are feeling the heat and may therefore feel compelled to pass a protectionist trade bill of its own. The future of the world's trading system literally hangs in the balance. The outcome will not be decided by any rational consideration of the merits or demerits of the Administration's trade policy, but by the expediencies of party politics in an election year.

[Remarks prepared for a Symposium at the John F. Kennedy School of Government, Harvard University, held as part of Harvard's 350th Anniversary Celebration, 5 September 1986.]

Why the US Will Still be No. 1 in 2039

On 9 November 1989, the world watched the fall of the Berlin Wall with amazement. The fall of the wall led, in turn, to the re-unification of Germany, the disintegration of the Soviet Union, and the dissolution of the Warsaw Pact. After half a century, the Cold War had come to an end, and the bipolar world, with the United States and the Soviet Union as the two superpowers, was replaced by a unipolar world, with the US as the hegemon. The unipolar world, however, was short-lived and has given way to a multipolar one with the US, Europe, Japan, China, India, Russia and Brazil as the major powers.

Until recently, no one doubted that the US was the world's sole superpower and the unquestioned leader of the world. A series of reverses and self-inflicted wounds have, however, caused thoughtful individuals, in Asia and elsewhere, to ask whether the US is a declining power. At a recent meeting in Japan, a respected Japanese public intellectual asked whether we were witnessing the end of Pax America and the beginning of Pax Sinica.

I would argue that such scepticism about the US is mistaken. In my view, the US will remain No. 1 in 2039, 30 years from now. My optimism is based upon the following reasons.

First, I believe that the US economy will bounce back from the current downturn and remain the most vibrant and competitive economy in the world in 2039. The US economy was on the brink of disaster last year. Decisive action by two consecutive administrations as well as Congress saved the economy from collapse. It is in the American tradition to face up to problems, accept the painful medicine of reform and bounce back.

The US was prepared to allow two American icons, Lehman Brothers and General Motors, to fail. Post-crisis, I expect that Wall Street will be better regulated, that Detroit will produce more energy-efficient and environmentally friendly automobiles, that the US will become a world leader in clean and renewable energy technology and businesses, and the American people will spend less and save more.

Economic competitiveness in the 21st century will be increasingly driven by innovation, creativity, design, marketing, information technology and talent. These are areas in which the US excels. It is likely to continue to do so in 2039.

Second, the top American universities and research institutions are among the best in the world. They serve as magnets for some of the world's most talented students. This will likely remain so in 2039 and America will continue to benefit from a brain transfusion from the world to its top universities.

In the global war for talent, there is no country in the world that can compete with America. It has an unmatched ability to attract, retain and assimilate foreign talent. For example, over half of the tenured professors at the Massachusetts Institute of Technology are foreign-born. American universities are the best endowed and resourced in the world, with outstanding faculty and students and a culture of learning that balances freedom and discipline, encourages risk-taking and is tolerant of failure.

Competition between nations in the 21st century will depend more on brainpower and less on material factors of production. America will continue to win the global war for talent.

Third, America has the world's most attractive soft power. The young of the world listen to American music, watch American movies, wear American fashion and enjoy American food. The founders of Microsoft, Apple, YouTube and Twitter are all Americans.

At a deeper level, there is great admiration for American ideals and values. The three American values that resonate most with Asians are equality, meritocracy and opportunity.

The election of Mr Barack Obama, as the 44th President of the United States, has done more to restore the world's faith in American values and ideals than any amount of public diplomacy could have. His eloquence, his humble tone and inclusive attitude, his appeal to the Islamic Ummah and his willingness to adopt fresh diplomatic approaches to seemingly intractable problems, have greatly strengthened the appeal of American soft power.

Fourth, America's hard power or military power is unmatched. Its defence budget is the largest in the world. Its military technology — on land, at sea, in the air, in space and in cyberspace — is probably a generation ahead of its nearest rivals. America continues to lead the world in research and develoment, and in revolution in military affairs. I expect the US will remain the world's No. 1 military power in 2039.

A country's total power can be either greater or less than the sum of its parts. In the case of the US, I would argue that it is greater than the sum of its parts. Why? Because the US, as a country, is blessed with the 'X' factor.

It has an allure that adds to the sum of its military, economic, intellectual, diplomatic and cultural power. It has a youthful, optimistic and joyful attitude towards life that inspires admiration. For all these reasons — and in spite of its present travails and challenges — I believe that the sun is not setting on America.

[Originally published in *The Straits Times*, 7 October 2009.]

Can Any Country Afford a Moral Foreign Policy?*

Let me begin with a caveat and a confession. The caveat is that the views I am about to express are my own and do not necessarily reflect those of my government. The confession is that although I have spent more than 16 years in the foreign service of my country, I regard myself as an amateur in diplomacy. My formal education was in law, a fact which some adherents of the Realist school of foreign policy would regard as a disqualification rather than a qualification. I did not have the benefit of having attended a school of foreign service, such as this, or of having studied political science or international relations. I did not work my way up the ladder of my country's foreign service. Instead, I was helicoptered to the top of the ladder at a comparatively young age. I have been learning on the job. What follows is an account of a personal odyssey; the reflections of an untutored practitioner of the craft of diplomacy and an attempt to develop a framework encompassing the role of power and force, of morality and law, of conflict and negotiation in the conduct of foreign policy.

> It is necessary ... to be a great pretender and dissembler ... he who seeks to deceive always find some one who will allow himself to be deceived.
>
> — Machiavelli

I arrived at the United Nations in New York in July 1968. A few days after my arrival, Soviet and other Warsaw Pact forces invaded

---

*Speech given to the School of Foreign Service, Georgetown University, on being presented with the 1987 Jit Trainor Award for Distinction in the Conduct of Diplomacy, 18 November 1987.

Czechoslovakia and put an end to Alexander Dubcek's reform movement. On the instructions of his government, the head of the Czechoslovak delegation requested an urgent meeting of the UN Security Council and demanded the immediate withdrawal of the invading forces. During the meetings of the Security Council, the Soviet Ambassador first denied that his country had invaded Czechoslovakia. I was astonished both by his ability to tell a pack of lies with apparent sincerity and by the stupidity of his action. No one in the UN was taken in by his deceit. In December 1978, Vietnam invaded Cambodia. At first, the Vietnamese Ambassador also sought to deny that his country had invaded Cambodia. In December 1979, the Soviet Union invaded Afghanistan. Initially, the Soviet Ambassador attempted to deny the invasion. The propensity by governments and their diplomatic agents to lie is not confined to the communist countries. In my 13 years at the UN, I was appalled by the duplicitous conduct of colleagues from all parts of the world. Is it any wonder that jokesters like to say that diplomats are individuals who are sent abroad to lie for their country?

Machiavelli, in his classic work, *The Prince,* said that "he who seeks to deceive will always find someone who will allow himself to be deceived."[1] In my experience, Machiavelli's assertion is untrue. No one at the UN was deceived by the lies of my errant colleagues. In the contemporary world of instantaneous communication, of an alert and probing world press, of satellite monitoring, it is futile to lie. The truth will prevail over falsehood. Apart from a few gullible people and those who wear ideological blinkers, most people are not easily deceived.

Machiavelli also advised the prince that "It is necessary to be a great pretender and dissembler".[2] In my experience, this is bad advice. In the community of nations, some governments and diplomats acquire a reputation for duplicity and dishonesty. Is a government or a diplomat with a reputation for veracity and integrity more likely to succeed in promoting the country's interests than one with a reputation for duplicity? I think the answer is yes. I have witnessed at the UN that governments and diplomats with a reputation for veracity and integrity tend to enjoy more influence and stature and are more likely to be entrusted with leadership positions than governments and diplomats with dubious reputations. Sissela Bok was right to have pointed out in her book, *Lying: Moral Choice in Public and Private Life,* that "Trust and integrity are precious resources."³

> Whether, to consummate their enterprise, have they to use prayers or can they use force? In the first instance they always succeed badly, and never compass anything; but when they can rely on themselves and use force, then they are rarely endangered.⁴
>
> — Machiavelli

The Nuremburg Trials have made the waging of wars of aggression a crime against humanity. The Charter of the United Nations has prohibited the use of force except in self-defence. Notwithstanding these achievements in international law and in the evolving international consensus on the norms applicable to relations between states, violence and conflict are the ugly realities of our contemporary world. In view of this, it could be asked whether Machiavelli's advice to the prince to use force to consummate his enterprise is as valid today as it was 500 years ago?

Are there any limits to the efficacy of the use of force in the modern world? Let us examine this question in respect of the relations between the two superpowers, between a nuclear power and a non-nuclear power and between two non-nuclear powers. In the relations between the two superpowers, the doctrine of mutual assured destruction has practically precluded either power from resorting to force in settling disputes with the other. Both President Reagan and General Secretary Gorbachev agree that nuclear wars cannot be won and must never be fought. It is unlikely for either power to start a conventional war against the other because such a war is likely to escalate into a nuclear war.

Let us turn to look at the conflict in Afghanistan as an example of a nuclear power using force to subjugate a non-nuclear power. In spite of the Soviet Union's preponderance in firepower, it has been unable to subjugate the guerrilla forces of the Mujahideen. What lessons can one learn from Afghanistan regarding the efficacy of the use of force? First, that a tenacious guerrilla army can neutralize, to some extent, the difference in the firepower of the armies of a nuclear power and a non-nuclear power. Second, that although the international system is too weak to prevent aggression, it is capable of inflicting political and economic costs on the aggressor. The invasion of Afghanistan has diminished the influence of the Soviet Union with the members of the Non-Aligned Movement and the Organization of Islamic Conference (OIC). At the current session of the UN General Assembly, 123 states voted against the Soviet Union on Afghanistan. Third, that even a totalitarian state which professes to be unaffected by the opinion of mankind must be concerned by its standing in the eyes of the other states in the international community. General Secretary Gorbachev is reported to be anxious to find a diplomatic formula which would enable him to pull Soviet troops out of Afghanistan.

The same lessons are applicable to the case of Vietnam's invasion of Cambodia, an example of a non-nuclear power resorting to force to subjugate another non-nuclear power. The tenacity of the resistance plus the political and economic isolation of Vietnam are beginning to have an impact on the policy-makers in Hanoi. Between 1975 and 1978, Vietnam was treated like a heroic nation, especially by the non-aligned countries. Today, Vietnam is an isolated nation. I do not believe that this dramatic change in the standing of Vietnam in the world community has had no effect on the leaders of the politburo in Hanoi. Indeed, there are signs to suggest that Vietnam's leaders may soon be ready to consider non-military options to end the conflict in Cambodia.

The purpose of this excursus is not to assert the proposition that in the modern world, states can never succeed in using force to achieve their ends. The Soviet Union has, for example, succeeded in subjugating Hungary and Czechoslovakia. Other states have also succeeded in using force to occupy parts of their neighbours' territories and in incorporating foreign territories and peoples within their boundaries. The purpose of this excursus is to question the Machiavellian thesis that a state can always rely upon its superior force to consummate its enterprise. There are clearly limits to the efficacy of the use of force in the contemporary world, limits imposed by the nature of nuclear war, by the character of guerrilla war, by the political and economic costs which the international system, weak as it is, is capable of inflicting on the aggressor and, in the case of democratic societies, by domestic public opinion.

> *Saints can be pure, but statesmen must be responsible. As trustees for others, they must defend interests and compromise principles.*[5]
> — Arthur Schlesinger

In his celebrated book, *Moral Man and Immoral Society,* the Christian theologian, Reinhold Niebuhr, wrote that "Perhaps the most significant moral characteristic of a nation is its hypocrisy."[6] In *The Cycles of American History,* Arthur Schlesinger said that "Saints can be pure, but statesmen must be responsible. As trustees of others, they must defend interests and compromise principles."[7] Both Niebuhr and Schlesinger belong to the Realist school of foreign policy. They believe that the lodestar which guides a state in the conduct of its foreign policy is its national interest. But, does it follow that in pursuing its national interest, a state must be hypocritical, that it must compromise its principles? Let me explore these questions by reference to the following examples.

The first example revolves around the principle of self-determination. Spanish Sahara was a Spanish colony in North-West Africa, situated between Morocco and Mauritania. In order to pressurise Spain into decolonizing the territory, the African group at the UN asked the International Court of Justice for an advisory opinion on the right of the people of Spanish Sahara to self-determination. The court upheld the right of the people of the Spanish colony to freedom and independence. Acting contrary to the opinion of the court, Morocco and Mauritania occupied the colony and divided it between them. (Mauritania later gave up its share of the territory.) When the question came before the UN General Assembly, the then US Ambassador to the UN lobbied me to support Morocco, arguing that Morocco had always supported Singapore's and ASEAN's interests whereas Algeria (which supported the pro-independence movement in Spanish Sahara — Polisario) had not always done so. The argument was factually correct. I pointed out, however, that what was at issue was not whether Algeria or Morocco was a better friend of Singapore, but the principle of self-determination which was important to small countries such as Singapore. I explained that it was contrary to Singapore's national interest to undermine that principle. I argued that Singapore's credibility would be eroded if it failed to stand up for the principle against all violations. Therefore, I concluded that Singapore's long-term national interest was better served by supporting the principle of self-determination than by supporting a friend. I appreciate that the yardstick of national interest is imprecise and reasonable people can disagree as to what course of action is most consonant with a country's interest.

My next example concerns the US intervention in Grenada. For small countries such as Singapore, one of the most precious principles of international law and international relations is the principle of non-interference in the internal affairs of other states. The intervention by the United States, Barbados, Jamaica and the members of the Organization of Eastern Caribbean States (OECS) in Grenada posed a dilemma for me. On the one hand, I appreciated that the motive which led those states to intervene was a benign one, i.e. to rescue the people of Grenada from an oppressive communist regime and to return the country to democracy. On the other hand, the intervention was contrary to the Charter of the United Nations and to international law. I also realised that if I had not protested against the intervention in Grenada, it would have undermined my moral credibility in leading the opposition to the Soviet intervention in Afghanistan and the Vietnamese intervention in Cambodia. After wrestling with the dilemma, I came to the conclusion that the national interest of Singapore required that I put principle ahead of friendship. This is what I said to the Security Council:

> Mr President, it is easy enough for us to demonstrate our adherence to principle when to do so is convenient and advantageous and costs us nothing. The test of a country's adherence to principle is when it is inconvenient to do so. I find myself in such a situation today. Barbados, Jamaica, the United States and the member states of the OECS are friends of my country. It is extremely convenient for me to acquiesce in what they have done or to remain silent. To do so, however, will, in

the long run, undermine the moral and legal significance of the principle which my country regards as a shield. This is why we must put our adherence to principle above friendship. This is why we cannot condone the action of our friends in Grenada. The stand which my country has taken in this case is consistent with the stand which we have taken in other cases where the principle of non-interference in the international affairs of states was also violated.

Let me bring this discussion to a close. What is my lodestar? Do I subscribe to the Realist or the Moralist school of foreign policy? I reject the Realist school not because of its moral cynicism but because it does not reflect the world in which we live. The Realists believe that the only standard by which a state should conduct its foreign policy is its national interest. They believe that in pursuit of its national interest, it is necessary for a state to be hypocritical and to compromise its principles. They reject any consideration of ethics or morality in the conduct of foreign policy as being irrelevant. Although they do not say so expressly, the logical implication of the Realist stand is that we live in a world of anomie, that is to say, in a condition of lawlessness, in the absence of any governing structure, in a situation in which there are no laws, principles, rules to govern the conduct between nations. Is this an accurate description of the world in which we live?

In my view it is not. We live in an imperfect world. It is not, however, a lawless world. The world community has evolved by custom, and adopted by treaty, a very considerable body of laws, principles and rules to govern the conduct between states as well as between states and their citizens. This body of international law deals with almost every area of international relations, including the recognition of states and their admission to international organisations; trade and foreign investment; diplomatic protection of nationals; nationality; war; human rights; boundaries; territorial acquisition; the law of the oceans. There are therefore universally accepted criteria by which the conduct of a state may be judged to be lawful or unlawful, right or wrong. The Realists will say, at this point, that there is a big difference between international law and domestic law. Domestic law works because it is a command backed up by force. There is no force behind the decisions of the International Court of Justice or the UN Security Council. In his book, *International Conflict for Beginners,* Roger Fisher answered the argument in the following way:

> The [US] Supreme Court had no regiments at its command. It had no greater force vis-à-vis the government than does the International Court of Justice sitting at the Hague.[8]
>
> Law enforcement against a government involves not a command backed up by force. Rather it involves so changing the choice with which the government is confronted that their long-range interest in orderly settlement of disputes outweighs their short-run interest in winning this particular dispute.[9]

I agree with Roger Fisher that the Realist tends to exaggerate the difference between domestic law and international law. However, I concede that international law does not have the same efficacy as domestic law in a well-ordered society. Although the international legal system is weak, it is not totally ineffective. I also feel that the Realist view that in the conduct of its foreign policy, a state should act exclusively on the basis of its national interest is flawed because, in reality, no state, no matter how powerful, can entirely ignore the interests of other states, the rules of international law and international relations, the decisions and recommendations of international, regional and binational institutions and the opinion of mankind.

However, my rejection of the Realist school does not lead me to embrace the Moralist school. What is the Moralist view of foreign policy? The Moralist believes that moral values should control foreign policy. He believes that no matter how noble and virtuous the end, it never justifies the use of means that violate moral or ethical standards. Some moralists have argued that states should behave in accordance with the same high standards of morality that apply to individuals in a good society.

I have a major problem with the Moralist school. The Moralist fails to appreciate that the primary purpose of a government is to protect the independence, sovereignty and territorial integrity of the state and to promote the welfare of its people. In pursuing these objectives, a government ought to employ means which are lawful and moral. However, there will be situations, hopefully rare, when a government will be confronted by a conflict between its national interest and its fidelity to law and morality. In such situations, a government may feel compelled to subordinate considerations of law and morality to its national interest. In extreme cases, when the very survival of a state is in question, a government may even feel justified in acting beyond the law. In such situations, it is important for the politician or diplomat to have a bad conscience, to be aware of the damage that his action will inflict on the international system, so that the moral values will survive their violation.[10]

If I am neither a Realist nor a Moralist, what am I? If I have to stick a label on myself, I would quote U Thant and call myself a practical Idealist. I believe that as a Singaporean diplomat, my primary purpose is to protect the independence, sovereignty, territorial integrity and economic well-being of the state of Singapore. I believe that I ought to pursue these objectives by means which are lawful and moral. On the rare occasions when the pursuit of my country's vital national interest compels me to do things which are legally or morally dubious, I ought to have a bad conscience and be aware of the damage which I have done to the principle I have violated and to the reputation of my country. I believe that I must always consider the interest of other states and have a decent regard for the opinion of others. I believe that it is in Singapore's long-term interest to strengthen international law and morality, the international system for curbing the use of force and the institutions for the pacific settlement of disputes. Finally, I believe that it is in the interests of all nations to strengthen international co-operation and to make the world's political and economic order more stable, effective and equitable.

Notes

1. Nicolo Machiavelli, *The Prince*, Everyman's Library. Ernst Page (ed.) (New York: E.P. Dutton & Co., 1952), p. 143.
2. *Ibid.*, p. 142.
3. Sissela Bok, *Lying: Moral Choice in Public and Private Life* (New York: Pantheon Books, 1978), p. 249.
4. *Supra*, Note 1, p. 48.
5. Arthur M. Schlesinger, *The Cycles of American History* (Boston: Houghton Mifflin, 1986), p. 72.
6. Reinhold Niebuhr, *Moral Man and Immoral Society* (New York: Charles Scribner & Sons. 1932), p. 95.
7. *Supra*, Note 5.
8. Roger Fisher, *International Conflict for Beginners* (London: Allen Lane, 1971), p. 155.
9. *Ibid.*, p. 156.
10. See Gordon A. Craig and Alexander L. George, *Force and Statecraft Diplomatic Problems of Our Time* (New York: Oxford University Press, 1983), p. 278.

[Originally published in *The Quest for World Order: Perspectives of a Pragmatic Idealist*, by Tommy Koh and edited by A. Acharya, Institute of Policy Studies and Times Academic Press, 1998, pp. 1–9.]

Size Is Not Destiny*

Introduction

Singapore is one of the world's smallest countries, with a population of 5.1 million, consisting of 3.7 million citizens and permanent residents, and 1.4 million foreigners, a territory of 714 square kilometres, and no natural resources. If the power of a State in international relations is to be computed on the basis of the size of its territory, population, economy, military and natural resources, as conventional wisdom would suggest, Singapore should be an insignificant and powerless actor in the international arena. I suppose this must be the reason which led *The Economist* to write that Singapore is a country which has long punched above its weight. The purpose of this talk is to ask: (i) what is Singapore's weight in world affairs; (ii) how can small countries exert an influence in world affairs which is disproportionate to their sizes; and (iii) what should small countries do in order to succeed in the 21st century. I hope you will forgive me for talking about Singapore. I do so, not to boast about its achievements, but to use it as an example of how a small country can overcome its limitations.

Westphalian System of Nation States

The present system of nation States is often said to be about three and half centuries old. The Peace of Westphalia of 1648 has been cited as the

---

*Talk to Forum of Small States at the Singapore Permanent Mission to the United States in New York, 11 December 2012.

pivotal event which gave birth to the modern system of nation States. In the past 250 years, a corpus of scholarship has developed in the West, about the power and behaviour of States in the international system. Hans Morgenthau, in his magnum opus, *Politics Among Nations*, sought to define the power of States and the nature of international politics. According to his theory, the power of a State is derived, inter alia, from: (i) the size of its territory, (ii) the size of its population, (iii) the size of its military, (iv) the size of its economy, (v) the size of its natural resource endowment, and (vi) its national character, morale, government and diplomacy. The Morgenthau worldview is often referred to as the Realist theory of international politics. It has dominated thinking about the nature of international politics for many decades.

Concept of Territorial State

I will call the Realist concept of the State the "territorial State" concept. It emphasizes the importance of geography, size, military power and a State's war-fighting capacity. It is a concept which was useful in explaining the world when national boundaries were sacrosanct, when economies were relatively self-reliant, and before the advent of multinational corporations, information technology, a global capital market and the revolution in military affairs. In that simpler world, geography *was* destiny. The power of a State was, roughly speaking, commensurate with its size. In the totem pole of nations, a country's place in the hierarchy was determined primarily by its size. In that world, a small country, such as Singapore, would rank very low on the totem pole. The editors of *The Economist* probably had such a concept in mind when they wrote that Singapore is a country which has long punched above its weight.

We live in a world radically different from the worlds of the Prussians and of Hans Morgenthau. It is a world transformed by the revolutionary forces of economics and technology. Consider the following developments.

Trading State

First, the world has been transformed by the force of international trade. Propelled, on the one hand, by the universal wisdom that free trade brings benefits to all nations; that economic autarchy equals poverty; and by the fact that tariff barriers and non-tariff barriers to international trade have been progressively reduced over the past 50 years. This has brought benefits to consumers all over the world, expanded the markets for producers of goods and services, and enabled many developing countries to export their way out of the poverty trap. In his pioneering book, *The Rise of the Trading State*, Richard Rosencrance makes a powerful argument for his thesis that the concept of the territorial State should be replaced by the concept of the trading State. The world's five largest trading States are: the United States, China, Germany, Japan and France. This is not a surprise since they are big States. However, the WTO index does contain some surprises. For example, we find that Singapore is the world's 14th largest exporter and the world's 15th largest importer, outranking such big States as India, Indonesia, Brazil and Nigeria. I will not go so far as to say that the concept of the territorial State should be replaced by the concept of the trading State, but I will venture the more modest opinion that the concept of the power of a State should be disaggregated and that one component of State power is economic power. Free trade has enabled small countries, such as, Singapore, Belgium, Luxembourg, the Netherlands and Switzerland, to increase their economic power beyond the size of their domestic markets. The Netherlands is, for example, the world's no. 6 trading nation.

Borderless World

Second, the world has been transformed by the forces of information, technology, and global business. In his international bestseller, *The Borderless World*, Japan's management guru, Kenichi Ohmae, describes the impact of information technology, and global business on the world.

He argues that we are living in an increasingly borderless world, one in which the economies of the major regions of the world, North and South America, Western Europe and East Asia are interlinked. To prosper in this new world, governments and corporations must discard the old paradigm and embrace a new paradigm recognising the necessity to compete in a global marketplace and an interlinked economy. Therefore, countries which are outward-looking, open to the world and willing to compete in the global marketplace, will thrive. Countries which are inward-looking, protectionist, and afraid to compete in the global marketplace, will stagnate. It is not surprising that many of the countries which fall into the second category are big countries and countries blessed with abundant natural resources. In this increasingly borderless world, it is possible for the companies of a small country, such as Singapore, to become world class either by being one of the best in the business, such as Singapore Airlines, or by a policy of acquisition or strategic alliance, such as the acquisition of the American President Lines by Singapore's Neptune Orient Lines or the acquisition of the Australian company, Optus, by Singapore's telecommunications company, SingTel. After acquiring American President Lines, Neptune Orient Lines became the world's 7th largest container lines. SingTel has subsidiaries or strategic partners in Australia, India, Thailand, the Philippines and Pakistan. Switzerland has many global champions in the world of business and industry and is a role model.

World Class

Third, the world has been transformed by the force of globalisation. Globalisation has been brought about by information technology, communication, travel and trade. Globalisation is an irresistible force. It has already succeeded in tearing down walls and barriers. It has accelerated the pace at which we are progressing towards the making of a global economy and a global community. No one, whether a State, region, city, business, family, or individual, can be shielded from its impact. Whether we like it or not, we have no choice but to compete in a global race. In her book, *World Class*, Rosabeth Moss Kanter has discussed some of the implications of globalisation for businesses, cities and regions. I am fascinated by two of her observations.

The first is that globalisation has brought about the rise of a cosmopolitan elite. The members of this elite are citizens of the world. They feel at home managing businesses all over the world. They possess what Kanter calls the three Cs: concepts, competence and connections. "Concepts" means possessing the best and latest knowledge and ideas. "Competence" means the ability to operate at the highest standards anywhere. "Connections" means the best relationships, which provide access to the resources of other people and organisations around the world.

The second observation is that cities succeed in the global economy if they can achieve excellence in one or more of the following three areas: thinking, manufacturing and trading. Kanter cites Boston as an example of a city which thrives on brainpower; Spartenburg, South Carolina, as an example of a city which thrives on manufacturing; and Miami as a city which thrives on international trade. Singapore aspires to achieve excellence in all three areas. It is also seeking to recruit members of the cosmopolitan elite to work and live in Singapore. We have 1.4 million foreigners living and working in Singapore.

World Money

Fourth, in his essay, *The Global Economy and the Nation-State*, the late American management guru, Peter Drucker, wrote: "basic economic decisions are made in and by the global economy rather than the nation-state". This observation is particularly true in the area of monetary policy. The Bretton Woods agreements, which established the World Bank and IMF, adopted the gold exchange standard. In 1973, President Nixon abandoned the gold exchange standard and floated the US dollar. The theory was that floating currencies would make for stable currencies, with the market controlling exchange rates through constant small adjustments. Instead, according to Drucker, "there has been no period in peace time, ... in which currencies have fluctuated so widely and abruptly as since 1973". Drucker also described the emergence of an enormous mass of "world money" and says "(t)he volume of world money is so gigantic that its movements in and out of a currency have far greater impact than the flows of financing, trade or investment. In one day, as much of this virtual money may be traded as the entire world needs to finance trade and investment for a year ... this money also does not follow economic logic or rationality. It is volatile and easily panicked by a rumour or unexpected event." Drucker went on to describe the successive attacks on the US dollar, French franc, Swedish krona, British pound, Italian lira, Mexican peso, and concluded that, "virtual money won every time, proving that the global economy is the ultimate arbiter of monetary and fiscal policies".

Drucker made the point that currency runs are not the most appropriate cure for fiscal irresponsibility, because the cure could be worse than the disease. However, there is no other control on fiscal irresponsibility. What should a country do? Drucker answered that a country should aim to have a balanced budget and avoid having to depend on borrowing short-term, volatile world money, to cover its deficits. Singapore's record would please Drucker. It regularly runs budget surpluses. It has the world's 13th largest foreign exchange reserves. This is why Singapore was relatively insulated from the financial storm which swept through East Asia in 1997 and 1998.

Land, Labour, Capital and Knowledge

The conventional economic wisdom is that a country's economic resources consist of land, labour and capital. The new economic wisdom is that knowledge is a country's chief economic resource. Gregory F. Treverton of the Rand Corporation has written that in this period of technological revolution, the premium on knowledge is high and that of a nation's endowments, only one really matters: the quality of its people. The new economic wisdom is based upon two facts.

The first is that the highest paid jobs are to be found in the knowledge-intensive industries. This is a trend which is likely to become even more evident in the 21st century. The second is that in the contemporary world, it is possible for a country to overcome the limitations of land and labour by using the under-utilised land and labour resources of other larger countries.

Singapore has positioned itself to take advantage of the new economic realities by investing heavily in educating and training its people. In the 2011 TIMSS Survey of 45 countries, which has just been published, Singapore's students (8th grade) came in second after Korea in Maths, and our 4th grade students also came in second, after Korea, in Science. This shows that the investment is paying dividends. The lesson learnt is that small countries should give priority to the development of their human resource. Unlike big countries, they often have no other resources except their people.

A Multilateral World

One of the trends of the last 50 years is the birth and empowerment of multilateral institutions. This has happened at the global level with such institutions, as the UN, World Bank, IMF, WTO, IMO, ICAO, World Meteorological Organisation, International Telecommunications Union, WHO, WIPO, UNEP, UNHCR, playing leading roles in their respective fields. This has also happened, at the regional and sub-regional levels, as epitomised by the European Union, NATO, NAFTA, APEC, ASEAN, ASEAN Regional Forum, ASEAN+3, the East Asia Summit, etc.

In a multilateral forum, the power and influence of a country is partly determined by its importance in the world and partly by the ability of its delegation. In such a forum, it is not unusual for the delegations of small countries to outperform those of much larger countries.

The Territorial State and the Market State

We need good intellectual tools with which to understand the world in which we live. Broadly speaking, political scientists favour the concept of the territorial State. Some economists, on the other hand, have argued that the days of the sovereign State are numbered. They have put forward the alternative concept of the market State.

What is a market State? The term was apparently first used by Dr Philip Bobbit of the Rand Corporation. The market State is a State which has successfully taken advantage of the new opportunities of international trade, open borders, globalisation, information technology and human mobility. Such a State would, therefore, be a big player in international trade, be a large recipient and provider of foreign direct investment, act as an important financial centre and communication hub, host a big family of multinational corporations and foreign talent. Singapore is an exemplar of a market State.

I believe that we need both concepts in order to explain the new world in which we live. I agree with Peter Drucker when he wrote that in all probability, the nation-state would survive the globalisation of the economy and the information revolution that accompanies it. But, as Drucker went on to point out, "it will be a greatly changed nation-state, especially in domestic fiscal and monetary policies, foreign economic policies, control of international business, and, perhaps, in its conduct of war."

The Changing Nature of Power

The concept of the power of a State needs elucidation. I wish to make the argument that the power of a State is not unitary or static. It is multi-dimensional and dynamic. A State can have the following forms of power: (i) political and ideological power; (ii) military power; (iii) economic power (iv) cultural power; (v) intellectual power; and (vi) diplomatic power. Power is dynamic in the sense that it can wax and wane but also in the sense that a State may enjoy more power in some areas than in others.

Weighing a State's Power

It follows from the above that the analogy drawn by *The Economist* of comparing a State and a boxer is not a good one. Weighing a boxer is a simple task. Weighing the power of a small State is a more complex undertaking. A small State may be a flyweight nation State in terms of its geography and size of population but it could carry much more weight when it mounts the scales of economic, cultural, intellectual and diplomatic power.

Conclusion

I shall conclude with a few suggestions on how small States should prepare themselves to succeed in the 21st century.

First, the diplomacy of the 21st century is likely to have a heavy economic content. Small States should, therefore, redouble their efforts to nurture a new generation of thinkers and diplomats who could play leadership roles in important economic institutions. The challenge is not insurmountable. After all, we should be encouraged by the fact that small countries are often chosen to provide the leaders of international organisations, including the UN.

Second, culture and communications, in all its modes, will become increasingly important. Small States could develop a soft power which compensates for their lack of hard power. The internet, Youtube, Facebook and Twitter, are tools which empower small States.

Third, the globalised world needs a new architecture of governance. G20 is not the answer as it lacks legitimacy and is not representative of the world's diversity. The world capital market, the world environment, and the new threats to international security, all require institutional responses which have so far been lacking. FOSS can play a positive role. We could help the world to think creatively on how to solve a central dilemma of our time, i.e., globalisation without global governance.

Fourth, small countries can come up with new ideas which have a global impact. Bhutan's pioneering concept of gross human happiness has evolved into the concept of human well-being. It has been adopted by France, UK and the UN. Costa Rica's concept of peace with nature is another inspiring idea. Qatar is a force for peace-making and conflict resolution. Finland has the best education system in the world. Switzerland has shown that a small country can produce global champions in business as well as the unique humanitarian organisation, the International Committee of the Red Cross. Oman has shown the world that there is no contradiction between Islam and modernity. Dubai is a global hub for communications, finance and business. Abu Dhabi is re-inventing itself into a knowledge-based economy. Several small African countries, such as Burkina Faso, Zambia, Rwanda, Botswana, have achieved very impressive rates of growth in recent years. I am also very proud of the fact that, in the 2012 Ibrahim Index of African governance, 4 members of FOSS: Mauritius, Cape Verde, Botswana and Seychelles took the top 4 spots. Of the top 20, 10 are members of FOSS. New Zealand is the world's champion in rugby and is both a sporting power and movie power. Rwanda and Timor Leste have shown the world that, after a painful conflict, it is better to forgive and reconcile than to seek revenge and retribution. The Nordic countries are probably the world's best global citizens. Nauru, as Chairman of AOSIS, has made a significant impact on the world's awareness of the danger of climate change and sea level rise.

Eight Lessons on Negotiations

Introduction

I have spent 34 years with the Ministry of Foreign Affairs. During that period, I have been tasked with the responsibility to lead several delegations to negotiate with other countries. In 1990, I was asked to lead a delegation to negotiate with China for the establishment of our diplomatic relations. In 1996, I was asked to negotiate an agreement between the EU and its 10 Asian partners to establish the Asia-Europe Foundation (ASEF). In 2001, I was asked to lead a delegation to negotiate a free trade agreement with the United States. In 2003, I was asked to lead a delegation to negotiate with Malaysia to resolve a dispute over Singapore's land reclamation works in and around the Straits of Johor.

At the international level, I have also been given tasks which involve leading very substantive negotiations. In 1981, upon the sudden demise of Ambassador H. S. Amerasinghe, the UN drafted me to succeed him as the President of the Third UN Conference on the Law of the Sea. In 1990, upon the urging of Kishore Mahbubani (then Permanent Secretary of MFA) and Chan Heng Chee (then Permanent Representative to the UN), I was elected to chair the Preparatory Committee for the UN Conference on Environment and Development, also known as UNCED or the Earth Summit. When the Conference convened in June 1992, in Rio de Janeiro, Brazil, I was drafted to chair the negotiations as Chairman of the Main Committee. In 1993, the then UN Secretary-General, Dr. Boutros Boutros-Ghali, appointed me as his Special Envoy, to lead a peace mission to Russia, Estonia, Latvia and Lithuania.

Apart from those practical experiences, I have also followed the growing literature on negotiations and conference diplomacy. I have attempted to make a few modest contributions to that literature. What I would like to do in this essay is to share with my younger colleagues and interested readers the eight lessons I have learnt about negotiations.

Lesson No. 1: Treat Every Negotiation as Special and Different

Every negotiation is special and different. No two negotiations are identical because each negotiation has its own agenda, its challenges and complexities, its cast of negotiators, its tone and momentum. A good negotiator must therefore never become complacent. Just because he has successfully completed one negotiation does not mean that he will succeed in the next negotiation without putting in a major effort in learning and preparation.

Lesson No. 2: Build a Cohesive and Happy Team

Both at the national and international levels, it is the responsibility of the leader of a delegation to build a cohesive and happy team.

This is often very challenging. At the international level, you are always leading a team consisting of colleagues from many countries and cultures. At the national level, you are usually leading a team consisting of colleagues from different ministries and agencies, from different disciplines and, sometimes, from different sectors of society. In the recently concluded land reclamation case, for example, the Singapore team consisted of colleagues from three ministries, six agencies, different disciplinary backgrounds and both practitioners and scholars. As I said at the press conference on 26 April 2005, I was very proud of the fact that our engineers and biologists were able to work together and they were, in turn, able to work with our lawyers and diplomats. As a result, the Singapore team was a cohesive and happy one. It is, of course, very helpful if the collective brainpower of your delegation is superior to or, at least, equal to that of your negotiating counterpart. IQ is, however, not the only ingredient of success of a delegation. It is only one important aspect.

Lesson No. 3: Master Your Brief

Do your homework and do it well. There is no substitute for hard work and thorough and meticulous preparation. There is no such thing as a lazy but good negotiator. A good negotiator must attempt to master his brief, to understand all aspects of his case, to understand his counterpart's case, and to be ready to respond, in a cogent and persuasive manner, to questions put to him across the negotiating table or in a court of law.

Lesson No. 4: Know When and How to Use Foreign Advisers

In some cases, especially when some of the issues in dispute are very technical in nature, it is useful to consult foreign advisers. In the land reclamation case, Singapore consulted two foreign legal experts and two foreign experts in ocean engineering. They gave our Government and our delegation very good advice. We did not keep them at arm's length or subordinate our own analysis to theirs. They were successfully integrated into our team and participated, on an equal and collegial manner, in the thought process. As a result of such an approach, the distinction between foreign and local was blurred and we were able to arrive at all our decisions by consensus. The day after the settlement agreement was signed, I was very pleased to receive an email from one of our foreign advisers thanking us for treating him and his colleagues in such an inclusive manner.

Lesson No. 5: Build a Common Basis of Facts

In some disputes, such as the land reclamation case, the two parties held diametrically opposite views of the facts. The challenge for the parties is to narrow the gap and to move towards a common basis of facts. The introduction of a third party could be useful. In the land reclamation case, credit must be given to the International Tribunal for the Law of the Sea (ITLOS). In its unanimous judgement of 8 October 2003, the Tribunal ordered Malaysia and Singapore to establish a group of independent experts, to undertake a one-year study of the facts. The unanimous report of the group of experts presented the two parties with a common basis of facts. The subsequent negotiations were successful partly because the parties were negotiating on a common basis of facts. Without it, the negotiations would have been much more difficult, if not impossible, to arrive at an amicable settlement. The lesson is that where the facts are in dispute, the parties should consider using a third party procedure in order to establish a common basis of facts.

Lesson No. 6: Exercise Emotional Intelligence

I have referred to the importance of IQ in connection with Lesson No. 2. I want to refer here to the importance of emotional intelligence. This refers to a negotiator's qualities of leadership, empathy and ability to earn the trust and confidence of his own colleagues as well as those of his negotiating counterparts. Negotiations succeed best when the rapport between the negotiators is good and when they share a bond of mutual trust and confidence. I have always urged my colleagues to build rapport with their negotiating counterparts and to conduct themselves in such a way as to earn their respect and trust. I have always practised "makan" diplomacy or "dining" diplomacy because I have found that eating together is a bonding experience.

Being a lover of the arts and of museums, I have also practised cultural diplomacy. When we were negotiating with the US on the free trade agreement, I took my counterpart, Mr. Ralph Ives, who loves Indian food, to Apollo Banana Leaf for dinner and took him on a tour of Little India. On the day when the land reclamation settlement agreement was signed, I invited the whole Malaysian delegation to the ceremonial opening of a lovely nyonya kebaya show at our Asian Civilisations Museum. The fact that the opening was co-officiated by the wives of the Prime Ministers of Malaysia and Singapore made the occasion and the 26th of April 2005 a memorable one.

The lesson I wish to share is the importance of showing your negotiating counterpart respect, friendship and courtesy. Never make your negotiating partner "lose face". You will find that your goodwill will be reciprocated by their goodwill, thereby creating a positive environment for the negotiation.

Lesson No. 7: Cultivate Cultural Intelligence

To negotiate successfully with another country, a good negotiator should study that country's history, culture and negotiating style. In other words, in addition to IQ and EQ, a good negotiator should also cultivate his cultural intelligence. The beginning of wisdom is to understand that we all live in our own cultural box. We should therefore make an attempt to understand the content of the cultural box of our negotiating counterpart. This will help us to avoid violating cultural taboos such as serving pork to American Jews or food which is not halal to our Malaysian or Arab friends. At a deeper level, it will help us to understand how our American, Chinese and Malaysian friends think and how they negotiate. Armed with this understanding, we will be able to customise our negotiating strategy and tactic to suit each negotiating partner. I am always astonished by the fact that ministries of foreign affairs pay so little attention to historians and cultural anthropologists. This is a mistake. The lesson I wish to share is the importance of understanding the history, culture, mindset and negotiating style of the different countries we negotiate with. An ideal negotiator, in my view, should have IQ, EQ and CQ.

Lesson No. 8: Think Win-Win

The outcome of a good negotiation should be an agreement which is fair and balanced. It is not and cannot be a zero sum. Instead, it must be a win-win outcome. To arrive at such an outcome, negotiators on both sides should focus on solutions which encompass the fundamental interests of both parties. I have always found it useful to put myself in the shoes of my negotiating partner and to understand what his interests are and what his bottom line is. Negotiations can only succeed if there is a spirit of give and take on both sides. This means, for example, that I should be willing to give some comfort language when my negotiating partner has indicated that he needs such language in order to satisfy his political masters or a domestic constituency. It also includes my willingness to make a small concession, in a matter of secondary importance to my country, in order to achieve an agreement on a package deal which is of fundamental interest to my country. In other words, I must be willing to be flexible and accommodating. However, when my fundamental interest is at stake, I must be firm and let my negotiating partner know that it is a point on which I have no flexibility. The lesson I wish to share is that a negotiation is not a zero sum game. It is a game in which the challenge is to find a win-win outcome.

Conclusion

Negotiation permeates a diplomat's life. However, no one teaches a diplomat how to be a good negotiator. I hope that the eight lessons I have distilled from my experiences and reflections will be useful to my younger colleagues and other interested readers.

[Originally published in *The Little Red Dot: Reflections by Singapore's Diplomats*, edited by Tommy Koh and Chang Li Lin, World Scientific, 2005, pp. 199–205.]

The Art of Chairing Conferences
Lessons Learnt

Introduction

I wish to distil some useful lessons from having chaired two of the most challenging conferences convened by the United Nations (UN): the Third UN Conference on the Law of the Sea (UNCLOS) and the Preparatory Committee for the UN Conference on Environment and Development (UNCED) and the Main Committee of the Conference itself (the Earth Summit). I hope that some of these lessons will be useful to colleagues who may have the opportunity to chair other major international conferences.

Lesson No. 1: Master Your Brief

It is not possible to be a good chairman of a conference if you do not master your brief. By this I mean mastering the rules of procedure of the conference as well as its content. This is not easy to do as most conferences have a long and complex agenda. Some items on the agenda may also be highly technical. During the conference on the law of the sea, for example, I had to understand and be able to make good judgements on such matters as the financial terms of mining contracts, the geomorphological structure of the continental shelf and margin, the life cycles of different species of fish, etc. In order to increase my knowledge and that of my colleagues in the conference, I requested some of my friends in the non-governmental organisations, to arrange briefings, workshops, retreats for us by acknowledged experts in those areas. The lesson is that the chairman of a conference must be sufficiently knowledgeable so that he is able to guide the negotiations and make good compromise proposals, if the need should arise.

Lesson No. 2: Use Your Bureau

Every conference has a bureau. If the bureau is small, the chairman should use it as the steering committee of the conference. If the bureau is large, as was the case of UNCED, the chairman should treat it as a microcosm of the conference. I did not ignore the large bureau but invented a smaller *de facto* bureau to help me in steering the conference. I called it the "collegium", which consisted of myself, the chairmen of the three committees, the rapporteur and the eight persons I had appointed to chair the eight negotiating groups I had established. At the Earth Summit, I invited the chairmen of the regional and interest groups to join the expanded collegium. Both during the Preparatory Committee and at the Earth Summit, in Rio de Janeiro, I would meet with the collegium every day. At the same time, I kept the large bureau reasonably happy by meeting with it at regular intervals and submitting all procedural proposals for its approval. If I had not done so, there would have been a revolt by the bureau against the collegium. The chairman of a conference has to reconcile the competing needs of democracy and efficiency.

Lesson No. 3: Work with the Secretariat

All international conferences are serviced by a secretariat. Not all secretariats are of the same quality. However, my philosophy is to work with the secretariat. I regarded the secretariat as my strategic partner. The Secretary-General of UNCED was the remarkable Canadian, Maurice Strong. Twenty years earlier, I had helped Maurice Strong to prepare for the 1972 Stockholm Conference on the Human Environment, of which he was also the Secretary-General. From March 1990 till June 1992, I worked in tandem with Maurice Strong, Nitin Desai and the other members of their able team. I invited Strong, Desai and other senior members of their team to join the daily meetings of the collegium. I kept no secrets from them. There were no tensions or conflict between Strong and me, unlike Strong's relationship with the UN Secretary-General, Dr Boutros Boutros-Ghali. Maurice Strong was good with the media and I was happy to let him be the public face of the Earth Summit to the world.

Lesson No. 4: Be a Team Player and Team Builder

A good conference chairman must be a team player and a team builder. Those who like to work alone or to work in secret should not aspire to chair conferences. A chairman will not succeed in his enterprise if he is a solo player. As a conference chairman, you are the leader of a team. The other members of your team are the chairmen of the committees of the conference, the rapporteur of the conference and the head of the secretariat. Both during the Preparatory Committee and at the Earth Summit, I was constantly talent-spotting. I was looking for able men and women, from all the regional and interest groups, to whom I could delegate part of my responsibility. I established eight negotiating groups and appointed eight able colleagues to lead them. However, if they failed to deliver, I did not hesitate to replace them. If the negotiations on a specific text hit an impasse, I would ask the interested parties to meet under the chairmanship of one of the intellectual leaders of the conference. In every case, they succeeded in finding a compromise text.

Lesson No. 5: No Secret Negotiating Groups

The UN has 192 member States. Most international conferences are attended by all the member States of the UN and sometimes, even more.

It is difficult to conduct negotiations with so many interlocutors. It is, therefore, always tempting for the chairman to set up a smaller negotiating group. One should always resist this temptation unless one has the blessings of the plenary to do so. During the fourth and final session of the UNCED Preparatory Committee, the Committee requested me to take over the negotiations of the text of the Rio Declaration of Principles from the chairman of the Third Committee. I agreed to do so on the condition that the negotiations be conducted in a group of 16, 8 each from the Group of 77 and OECD. The plenary agreed and the 16 members of the negotiating group were chosen, not by me, but by the two interest groups. We completed our negotiations in two days and the result of the small group was subsequently ratified by the plenary. In Rio, all the negotiations were conducted in the presence of all delegations. It was hard, but we succeeded in negotiating and adopting by consensus, the 500 pages of Agenda 21. My advice to conference chairmen is to avoid setting up small negotiating groups in secret. Why? Because the secrecy will be exposed, the product of the small negotiating group will be repudiated and your credibility will be destroyed.

Lesson No. 6: Create an Inclusive, Transparent and Orderly Negotiating Process

It is the responsibility of the conference chairman to create, with the approval of the conference, an inclusive, transparent and orderly negotiating process. The process must be both transparent and inclusive in order to have legitimacy. The process must be orderly in the sense that there should be a rational structure linking the different negotiating bodies and a hierarchy of accountability. The conference chairman is both the master planner of the negotiating architecture and the commander-in-chief. He has to hold every conference officer to account. However, he is the captain of the ship. He must hold himself accountable to the plenary of the conference for the fate of the conference.

Lesson No. 7: The Importance of Timing

In negotiations, as in life, timing is very important. A conference chairman must intervene when the time is ripe. If he intervenes prematurely, he will be rebuffed. During the first session of the UNCED Preparatory Committee, the Committee was very polarised and could not even agree on the agenda. After an all night session, sometime in the early hours of the morning, the exhausted delegates asked me to make a compromise proposal. With the help of about a dozen colleagues, representing the different regional and interest groups, I was able to draft a compromise proposal, which was adopted. During the fourth session of the UNCED Preparatory Committee, the chairman of the Third Committee put forward a compromise text of the Rio Declaration. Although it was a good proposal and he meant well, he had acted prematurely. The Group of 77 rejected his proposal and accused him of being biased in favour of the developed countries. I had to take over the negotiations from him. The lesson is that a good conference chairman should be skilful in judging when the conference is ready to accept a compromise proposal from him.

Lesson No. 8: The Quest for Consensus

The decision-making process of most UN conferences is by consensus. The concept of consensus means adopting a decision in the absence of any objection. A conference chairman must work very hard to garner support for a proposal and to seek to accommodate all those who have legitimate concerns or objections to the proposal. A proposal is usually revised many times until all such legitimate concerns have been taken care of. What do you do if you are faced with one solitary delegation which is determined to block the adoption of the proposal? If you think that the delegation has a legitimate concern, you should try to accommodate that concern. However, if you judge that the delegation is acting unreasonably, you must have the courage to confront that delegation. At the fourth session of the UNCED Preparatory Committee, Israel was the only delegation which opposed the adoption of the Rio Declaration of Principles. At the Earth Summit, Saudi Arabia insisted on deleting the whole chapter, on Climate, from Agenda 21. I overruled Israel and Saudi Arabia and requested them to challenge my ruling which I was prepared to put to the vote. They were angry, but declined to challenge my ruling because they knew that they did not have the support to overturn my ruling. What is the lesson? The lesson is that a conference chairman must be patient and fair, but he must be prepared to be firm and, if necessary, ruthless when confronted with a solitary delegation which is determined to block consensus.

Lesson No. 9: How to Deal with the NGOs

Both during the Conference on the Law of the Sea and during the UNCED preparatory and negotiating processes, I had a positive relationship with most of the representatives of the accredited non-governmental organisations (NGOs). Several of the representatives became my good friends. During UNCLOS, there was a group of NGOs which called themselves the Neptune Group. I worked very closely with them. Through their good offices, I was able to obtain the expert advice of MIT on the financial terms of mining contracts and the advice of leading American oceanographers on the continental shelf and margin, etc. During UNCED, I was very close to a group of NGOs, which put out the Earth Summit Bulletin. The bulletin was an accurate summary of the various negotiations which took place on the previous day. What is the lesson learnt? It is that, wisely used, the NGO community can be very helpful to a conference and to its chairman. However, if not properly managed, the NGOs can have a negative and disruptive influence on a conference.

Lesson No. 10: Qualities of a Good Chairman

To succeed as a conference chairman, one should be humble and respectful of all his conference colleagues. He should treat all colleagues fairly, whether they represent big or small countries. He should be transparent and trustworthy. He should be a good listener and be willing to take into account the interests and concerns of all delegations. He should be pro-active in reaching out to the various regional and interest groups. He should be optimistic. He should be calm, especially when faced with a crisis. He should have courage and be prepared to confront those who are determined to block progress and isolate them. He should be a good mediator and bridge builder. Ideally, a good conference chairman should be able to unite his colleagues and inspire them with their common vision.

[Unpublished paper prepared for the MFA Diplomatic Academy.]

Two Financial Crises: Five Truths from Asia

In 1997 and 1998, East Asia suffered a serious financial crisis that wiped out decades of progress. Unemployment and poverty increased substantially in countries such as Indonesia and the Philippines. The political leaders of Indonesia, South Korea, and Thailand lost their mandates and were replaced.

Although Thailand is an ally of the United States, it is not as important an ally as Mexico, where the United States provided a bailout to prevent a surge in immigration. To the disappointment of the Thai government and its people, the United States declined to come to its rescue. This may be one of the reasons why Thailand has drawn closer to China and downgraded its relationship with the United States.

The International Monetary Fund (IMF) worked closely with the US Treasury in the rescue of Indonesia, South Korea, and Thailand. The IMF prescribed bitter medicine: distressed financial institutions would be allowed to fail in order to avoid a "moral hazard". In the case of Indonesia, the IMF prescription went beyond the financial crisis. It forced President Suharto to accept a humiliating wholesale reform of the political economy. Many Asian leaders suspected that the IMF-American agenda actually included regime change.

The United States, supported by Europe, lectured Asia during its financial crisis. Asian governments were told to avoid becoming overleveraged, to strengthen regulations, to increase transparency, to reduce the role of the state in their economies, and to pursue responsible macroeconomic and fiscal policies.

Some of my American and European friends were unsympathetic during the Asian financial crisis. A few even gloated over Asia's misfortunes, displaying some of the West's worst prejudices toward Asia.

A decade later, fortunes have been reversed. Asians have watched the Western financial crisis — including the staggering government bailouts in the financial sector — with disbelief. The crisis in America spread rapidly to Europe, where governments had to nationalize or inject capital into banks to prevent bankruptcies. Two European countries, Iceland and Hungary, have sought the help of the IMF.

Unlike their Western counterparts a decade ago, no Asian leader or pundit has gloated over the misfortunes of America and Europe, or presumed to lecture. Instead, Asians have tried to be helpful where possible and where our help is welcomed. We realise that we live in the same global village, and when the mansions of the two wealthiest families are on fire, the prosperity and security of all are threatened. We, Asians, uphold the following truths:

- *First*, be humble and refrain from lecturing. I would respectfully point out that the United States did not practice what it preached. It is overleveraged at all levels. Its regulatory structure is weak. Its financial products, especially the securitized products, lack transparency. It has not pursued responsible and prudent macroeconomic and fiscal policies.
- *Second*, practice the virtue of thrift and follow the simple rule that one should live within one's means. Thrift has largely disappeared in America. Households save only two percent of their income; the average American household has nine credit cards and a debt of $17,000; the American government owes the world more than $10 trillion. It has become the world's largest debtor nation.
- *Third*, we must find the courage to confront our problems rather than pointing the finger at scapegoats. Instead of facing up to America's problems of low savings and overconsumption, some US leaders are blaming others. For example, US Federal Reserve Chairman Ben Bernanke has attributed the current financial crisis to "global

imbalances" and the "excessive savings" of Asia. Strangely, we Asians get blamed both when we have too much debt and also when we have too much savings.
- *Fourth*, it is to be hoped that this crisis has diminished the attractiveness of Wall Street's style of capitalism. Unfortunately, the "greed is good" culture has infected some Asian countries; excessive pay for senior management, for example, has become fashionable in certain parts of Asia. This is not consistent with our communitarian values or our emphasis on team work and equity.
- *Fifth*, the latest crisis has reinforced the fact that global economic and financial power is slowly and ineluctably moving east. This makes forums such as the Group of 7 (G-7) and G-8 moribund. Without the presence of China and India, these forums do not reflect the realities of our contemporary world.

[Originally published in *What Matters*, a publication of McKinsey and Company, 23 February 2009.]

Australia Must Respect Asean's Role

Australian Prime Minister Kevin Rudd has proposed an Asia-Pacific community (APc). He spoke of the idea in Singapore last June and again at last month's Shangri-La Dialogue.

The region, he has argued, needs a body "with a mandate to engage across the breadth of the security, economic and political challenges we will face in the future".

Among other things, he has been at pains to emphasise that:
- Though there is no appetite for additional institutions, our current structures do not provide a single forum for all relevant leaders to discuss a full range of issues;
- The Australian initiative is to begin a conversation about where we need to go; Canberra has no prescriptive view on the matter;
- The APc would, over time, emulate Asean's success in community-building in South-east Asia; and
- Australia would convene a Track 1.5 conference to further explore its initiative at the end of this year.

My initial reactions to Mr Rudd's proposal are as follows.

First, I welcome Canberra convening an inclusive process of discussions on our regional architecture. For the discussion to be useful, it should focus on the challenges and opportunities facing the Asia-Pacific region, the existing structure for dealing with them and whether there is a need to renovate that structure in order to enable the region to respond more effectively to future challenges and opportunities.

Second, I think it is relevant to remind ourselves that there are in existence three parallel community-building processes in our region, each covering South-east Asia, East Asia and the Asia-Pacific, respectively.

The Asean story in South-east Asia does not need repetition here. The wider East Asian community has also embarked on a community-building process, driven by Asean+3 (China, Japan and South Korea) and the East Asia Summit (EAS), which is in effect Asean+3+3 (India, Australia and New Zealand).

The fact that we are also committed to building an Asia-Pacific community through the Asia-Pacific Economic Cooperation (Apec) forum does not make either Asean+3 or EAS superfluous. I was therefore surprised when I heard an Australian friend say recently that with an APc we would not need either Asean+3 or EAS. Such a view shows that he was out of touch with Asian sentiments and realities.

Third, I think, implicit in Prime Minister Rudd's remarks was the view that, while admirable, Asean's role should be confined chiefly to South-east Asia. Such a view disregards the important role that Asean has played and continues to play as convener and facilitator of Asean+3, EAS and the Asean Regional Forum (ARF). Asean's role has never been confined to South-east Asia.

Indeed, due to its cohesion, neutrality and acceptability to all stakeholders, Asean has been often called upon to play the role of the region's neutral chairman. Australia should respect this and not seek to divide Asean or to diminish its role.

Fourth, one troublesome element of Australia's proposal — articulated by Mr Rudd's special envoy, Ambassador Richard Woolcott, and never publicly repudiated by the Australian government — is the idea that the APc will have a core group or bureau. This group would consist of key countries in the region: the United States, China, India, Japan and Indonesia. Some Indonesian commentators have added three more to the list — Australia, South Korea and Russia. That would make for a total of eight, a sort of G-8 for the Asia-Pacific.

I think such an idea is anti-democratic and elitist. It would also have the effect of marginalising Asean. As a practical matter, I do not see how the Asia-Pacific region can be led by a group of countries with such competing interests and agendas.

Fifth, it could be useful to review the existing institutions and processes in the region. In doing so, we should be aware that each piece of the structure has its own history and logic. We must avoid destroying a structure that has taken years to build. This is not say we cannot consider improvements.

For example, we could consider holding the annual meetings of Apec and ARF back-to-back. This can be done by moving a few chairs around as the compositions of the two organisations overlap though they are not identical. We should also consider whether to elevate ARF participation to the summit level.

Another idea worth exploring is whether to freeze the composition of the EAS at the current 16 or to admit both the US and Russia. There are cogent arguments in favour and against such an expansion and they deserve our serious consideration.

Those who favour the inclusion of the US in the EAS have argued that the regional initiative is unlikely to prosper without the participation of the US. Those opposed have pointed out that admitting the US and Russia to the EAS would be analogous to admitting both into the European Union.

These are some of my thoughts as I reflect on the Australian initiative. The last thing we want is to create a new forum or organisation on top of the structure we already have. I hope my remarks will be viewed by my Australian friends as a constructive contribution to their initiative to begin a dialogue about where we need to go.

[Originally published in *The Straits Times*, 24 June 2009.]

In Defence of Europe

The financial crisis, which began in the United States in 2008, has moved across the Atlantic. It is now centred on Europe, especially the euro zone. In recent months, readers of this newspaper have had a steady diet of negative reports and commentaries by mainly British and American sources on the euro, the euro zone and the European Union (EU). There is very little empathy with or understanding of the European integration project in those two countries. We wish to give a more balanced and positive view of the situation. We will do so by answering a number of frequently asked questions.

What Is the Historical Significance of the European Union?

The European Union may be seen by many today as mainly an economic and monetary union, but in fact, it had its origins first and foremost as a peace project.

Europe in the first half of the 20th century was the killing fields of the world. Conflict between European nations led to World Wars I and II, the most destructive in human history.

Following World War II, visionary leaders such as Jean Monnet, Robert Schuman and Konrad Adenauer decided to put an end to war and took the first steps towards peace by launching the European integration project. They proceeded step by step beginning with the creation of the European Coal and Steel Community in 1952. The success of this experiment led to bolder attempts to create the European Economic Community in 1958, with the signing of the Treaty of Rome. In 1967, the customs union binding the original six member states was completed.

The community became a Union in 1993 when the Maastricht Treaty (formally known as the Treaty of the European Union) came into force in 1993. With the admission of new members, the membership gradually increased from the original six to 27 today. What is remarkable in the past 60 years is that no member of the EU has gone to war with another.

Has the EU's Economic Integration Been a Success?

The EU's economic integration is a success story. In 1993, a single market was created by abolishing all internal barriers to trade in goods and services. The four freedoms — freedom of movement of goods, services, capital and people — are guaranteed.

The EU is the world's largest economy and biggest investor. It has a combined population of 501 million and a combined gross domestic product (GDP) of €12,268 trillion (S$21 trillion) accounting for 28 percent of the world's GDP and 21 percent of world trade.

The EU is China's and India's top trading partner and Singapore's second-largest trading partner. The importance of the EU to the global economy and Asia cannot be underestimated.

What Led the EU to Create the Euro?

The completion of the single market in 1993 created the conditions necessary for the European leaders to embrace the goal of monetary union. A single currency would ensure macroeconomic stability, avoid the volatility of exchange rates, reduce transaction cost and act as a catalyst for the integration of European financial markets, which benefit European businesses.

To give up a country's national currency is to give up an important symbol of that country's sovereignty. This must have been an especially difficult decision for the Germans because the deutschemark was such a strong currency.

Germany joined the other EU countries in adopting the Maastricht Treaty in 1993, which contains the Stability and Growth Pact as an informal institution to guarantee responsible fiscal behaviour.

Under the treaty, a country had to comply with the following five criteria in order to join the euro zone:

(a) Low inflation;
(b) Low long-term interest rates;
(c) Stable exchange rates;
(d) Government budget deficit of less than 3 percent of GDP; and
(e) Total public debt of less than 60 percent of GDP.

In the run-up to the launch of the euro, the original 11 members of the euro zone accepted extraordinary macroeconomic and fiscal discipline to qualify for membership in the euro zone. The euro was launched on Jan 1, 1999.

Who Sets Monetary Policy in the Euro Zone?

There are three institutions which together shape policy in the euro zone. First, the European Central Bank (ECB), which sets monetary policy for the 17 countries within the euro zone.

Second, the ECB works with the national central banks within what is called the European System of Central Banks (ESCB). The ESCB is analogous to the US Federal Reserve System. Decisions are taken by the Governing Council of the ECB.

National central banks participate actively in the preparation and implementation of the decisions. The Governing Council of the ECB consists of the president of the ECB, the heads of the central banks of the 17 euro zone countries and five other full-time members of the Executive Council.

Third, the Stability and Growth Pact, an institution for close mutual surveillance and coordination to ensure fiscal responsibility. It, however, lacks teeth and failed to sanction the countries which violated the Pact, including Germany and France. From the very start, the target of not having public debt above the 60 percent limit has not been strictly enforced. The public deficit target (the condition that the budget deficit should not exceed 3 percent of GDP) has also been violated early on not only by Greece, Italy and Portugal but also by Germany between 2002 and 2005, France in 2003 to 2004, Austria between 2004 and 2006 and The Netherlands in 2003.

What Caused the Current Crisis in the Euro Zone?

The crisis was in part an indirect outcome of the success of the euro. The introduction of the euro, which is accepted as a safe and stable currency, allowed countries in the euro zone to borrow at very low interest rates. This led to excessive borrowing by some euro zone countries and failure to comply with the criteria of the Stability and Growth Pact, in respect of the limits set on budget deficit and total public debt.

Sanctions were not imposed against these violations. The result is that countries such as Greece, Portugal and Italy are carrying enormous sovereign debt. The market has responded by refusing to continue extending loans to those countries or is charging them exhorbitant rates for such loans.

Will the Recent Decisions Taken by the EU Leaders Solve the Problem?

The recent decisions taken by the EU leaders do address the fundamental weakness of the system, that is, how to enforce fiscal discipline. Except for Britain, all the EU leaders agreed on a new inter-governmental "fiscal compact", which allows for automatic sanctions on budget rule-breakers, and calls on governments to amend their national Constitutions to prevent profligacy and ensure budgets that are balanced.

They also agreed that draft national budgets will be submitted to the EU before they are adopted by their national parliaments.

These proposals agreed in the summit in Brussels, if adopted and faithfully implemented, will ensure that the euro zone's fiscal house will be in order.

Will National Legislatures and Voters Accept the Fiscal Compact?

It is a little hard to predict if all the national legislatures will accept the fiscal compact. There are several elections coming up early next year in countries such as France, and this may inject partisan politics into the process. The voters' mood may also be soured by the various austerity measures already in place.

However, by opting for an inter-governmental pact rather than treaty changes, governments may be able to avoid holding referenda to approve it. The prospect of approval by national parliaments is reasonably good. The proponents of the pact will emphasise that national parliaments are still primarily responsible for drawing up the rules and procedures that would then be monitored by a euro-watchdog for consistency and implementation.

Will the Euro Survive and Continue to be a Strong Currency?

The euro is and will continue to be a strong currency. Launched on Jan 1, 1999, on a par with the US dollar, the euro is, today, trading at one euro to US$1.30. It is, therefore, a stronger currency than the US dollar. We have no doubt that the euro will survive the current turmoil. The 17 countries of the euro zone, led by Germany and France, are determined to ensure that the euro succeeds and they will do whatever it takes to prevent its failure.

We have faith in the future of the euro, of the euro zone countries and of the EU. The EU will restore its fiscal house to order and unleash the energies of its creative people and businesses to generate growth, create jobs and reduce unemployment. Further structural reforms will ensure a return to competitiveness and confidence.

We must not forget that 10 out of the top 20 most competitive economies in the World Economic Forum Global Competitiveness Index 2010–2011 are EU member states. The EU will emerge from this crisis more disciplined and more competitive.

Asia, with strong trade and investment ties with the European Union, has a stake in the success of the euro and the EU.

[Co-authored with Yeo Lay Hwee. Originally published in *The Straits Times*, 15 December 2011.]

China and the World

I wish to begin my essay with a caveat. I am neither a China expert nor a historian. My views are those of a generalist, I have, however, had several happy encounters with China. In 1990, I was Singapore's chief negotiator in the successful negotiations to establish diplomatic relations between our two countries. In 2004, I was Singapore's representative in the ASEAN–China Group of Eminent Persons, established at the suggestion of Chinese Premier Wen Jiabao, to take stock of ASEAN–China relations and to recommend a roadmap to the future. Since 2006, I have co-chaired the China–Singapore Forum, an annual track 1.5 process, together with the President of the Chinese People's Institute of Foreign Affairs, Ambassador Yang Wenchang.

1. History as a Guide to the Future

I believe that if we want to understand China's worldview, we must begin by understanding China's history. I believe that a country's past often provides one with a key to interpreting its present and predicting its future. What strikes me is that in the course of China's long history, the country was often invaded and ruled by the invaders.

During the Northern Song dynasty (960–1127), Northern China was invaded and ruled by the Khitans, a nomadic people of proto-Mongol stock. The Khitans established the Liao dynasty (907–1125) and subsequently, the Western Liao (1124–1211).

During the Southern Song dynasty (1127–1279), the Khitans were defeated by another group of nomadic people called the Jurchen, who established the Jin dynasty (1115–1234). In 1127, the Jurchen army took Bianjing, the capital of the Northern Song and captured the Song rulers.

From 1279 to 1368, China was ruled by the Mongols who established the Yuan dynasty. From 1644 to 1911, China was ruled by the Manchus, who established the Qing dynasty.

Of greater salience, of course, is China's recent history. Many Chinese today remember the 19th century and the first half of the 20th century as a period of great humiliation for China. It was invaded by the Western imperial powers and Japan and subjected to the unequal treaties. Chinese sovereignty and territorial integrity were compromised. This unhappy period ended only in 1949, with the establishment of the People's Republic of China.

2. China as Victim and as Aggressor

China was not, however, always the victim of aggression. During the Yuan dynasty, the Mongolian rulers of China conquered Korea and, using Korea as the launching pad, tried to conquer Japan twice, but unsuccessfully. The Mongols destroyed Pagan in Myanmar sad invaded both Vietnam and Java. Although those invasions were undertaken by the Mongols ruling China and not by a Han Chinese dynasty, the victims of the invasion did not make such a distinction. To them, the invaders came from China. After the passage of so many centuries, these invasions continue to linger in the memories of the peoples of Korea and Southeast Asia. Even the seven maritime expeditions, led by Admiral Zheng He, during the Ming dynasty, have recently come under some revisionist analysis. The majority of historians view the seven voyages as peaceful and pathbreaking, in their scale and scope. A minority view has recently emerged, which views them as a display of Chinese power, meant to intimidate and reinforce the tributary system.

3. What China Wants

My reading of Chinese history leads me to conclude that what the Chinese people want is for China to be a strong nation-state, able to defend Chinese sovereignty and territorial integrity and, increasingly, its far-flung interests. China wants to be respected by the world. China wants a seat at the top table. I do not think China is a revolutionary power which is seeking to export Chinese communism or the Chinese model of development (the so-called Beijing consensus). I do not have the impression that China is seeking hegemony, whether at the global or regional level. I find no evidence to support the allegations that China is trying to impose a Chinese version of the Monroe doctrine on East Asia or that it is trying to re-establish the tributary system of the Ming dynasty. I am also not persuaded by the view that China is scheming to exclude the United States from Asia or the Asia-Pacific.

China wants and needs a peaceful external environment to concentrate on internal development. China would, however, oppose any attempt by any country or group of countries, to contain or impede China's rise. China wants to work within the framework of the international system but expects that the same rules would apply to her as to other countries. China wants to have access to resources in the world market and would perceive any attempt to restrict such access as hostile. China would resent any attempt to manipulate existing rules governing trade and investment to deny her access to markets for her exports or block investment opportunities to Chinese companies and investors.

4. How Powerful Is China Today?

China is a rising power. Many countries have benefitted from China's rise and welcome it. But there are those who fear its rise. Most great economic powers in history are developed countries. China is not. It is a big but developing country. An over-emphasis on the size of China's economy would result in an exaggeration of the power of China. But simply focussing on China's low per capita GDP would cause us to underestimate China's global influence. It is, therefore, useful to assess, as objectively as possible, China's economic, military and soft power.

5. China's Economic Power

How big is the Chinese economy? What are some of the vital statistics?

In 2008, the Chinese economy was about US$4.4 trillion, just behind Japan, at $4.9 trillion. China is expected to overtake Japan this year and become the world's No. 2 economy. China is, however, still quite a distance behind the United States, at $14.2 trillion, and the EU at $18.4 trillion, If China continues to grow at 7+% per annum, China will catch up with the US in 20 to 30 years. China is, however, still a relatively poor country. China's per capita income is only $3,414, compared to over $45,000 for the US.

China is a major player in international trade, accounting for 7.31% (2009) of world trade. It has replaced Germany as the world's No. 1 exporter. China is both a recipient of FDI and an exporter of FDI. The size of FDI hosted by China is estimated at $92.4 billion (2009). Chinese FDI abroad is estimated at $55.9 billion (2009). China enjoys both a trade surplus of $348.9 billion (2009) and a current account surplus of $426 billion (2009), China's foreign exchange reserves, of $2.4 trillion (2009), is the largest in the world. China has become USA's largest creditor country.

China's manufacturing industries have made tremendous progress and, as a result, it is often referred to as the factory of the world. For example, China is responsible for 40% of the world's total output of steel and cement. In 2009, China manufactured 13 million automobiles, surpassing the US.

To sum up, we can say that China has become the world's second largest economy. Barring an unforeseeable internal upheaval or a hostile external environment, China should be able to continue to grow at or above 7% per annum in the next 20 to 30 years. In time, the size of the Chinese economy will catch up with that of the US. We should, however, remember that, when we divide China's GDP by 1.3 billion people, China's per capita income is relatively low and will not attain the OECD average, let alone that of the US, for many years to come. We should regard China's economic progress and growing prosperity as beneficial to China's neighbours and to the world economy, as long as China continues to be open to the world and play by the international rules governing trade, investment, monetary policy, etc.

6. China's Military Power

Since 1989, China has been devoting significant resources to the modernisation of its armed forces. In 2010, China's declared military budget is $78 billion. The US has alleged that this does not capture the totality of China's military expenditure. The Stockholm International Peace Research Institute (SIPRI) has suggested that China's total military expenditure could be as high as $84.9 billion. The equivalent numbers for the US is $607 billion, for France $65.7 billion, for the UK $65.3 billion and for Russia, estimated at $58.6 billion. This puts the US in a totally different league. The US alone accounts for 41.5% of total world military expenditures.

China's total military personnel is 2.3 million. China's nuclear warheads are estimated by SIPRI to be between 100 and 400. The US Defence Intelligence Agency has estimated that China has between 1,330 and 1,660 ballistic and cruise missiles, mostly deployed near Taiwan. China's space technology has made several major breakthroughs. In 2003, China sent the first astronaut into space. In 2007, China shot down a satellite using sophisticated space technology.

In its 2009 annual report to the US Congress, the US Department of Defence stated that although China has increased its capabilities for local and regional operations in certain areas since 2000, a number of limitations have persisted. These include the PLA's air and amphibious lift capacity.

According to the Pentagon, the PLA is only capable of the sealift of one infantry division and the delivery of 5,000 parachutists in a single lift. The Pentagon also pointed out that although China has a few aerial refuelling aircraft, it does not have the number of tankers, properly equipped combat aircraft or sufficient training to employ this capability for power projection. After reading the Pentagon's report, I do not have the impression that China's military power is catching up with that of the US.

7. China's Soft Power

I will use the term "soft power" in an expansive way to include a country's cultural, political, diplomatic and brand power. The concept seeks to capture all the aspects of a country's power and influence which are not economic or military. The purpose of projecting a country's soft power is to gain the admiration, respect and following of other countries and peoples.

In recent years, China has done an excellent job in projecting its soft power to the world. The spectacular success of the 2008 Beijing Olympic Games not only earned the admiration of the athletics and countries participating in those games but also of millions of people who watched them on television. I am sure the 2010 Shanghai Expo will make a similar impression. Taken together, they could rightly be said to constitute China's coming out party, in much the same way as the Tokyo Olympic Games did for Japan and the Seoul Olympic Games for South Korea.

China is blessed with a rich and ancient civilisation. China has started the Confucius Institute to disseminate its language and civilisation to the world, similar to the British Council, Alliance Française and Goethe Institut. There are 282 Confucius Institutes in 88 countries. It is estimated that 40 million foreigners are learning the Chinese language. There are 223,000 foreign students studying in China. Two of China's universities, Tsinghua University and Peking University, are ranked No. 49 and 52, respectively, in the 2009 *Times Higher Education* Index of the world's top 200 universities.

China has tried to be a responsible global citizen. It provides help to other developing countries. The US Department of State has estimated that China's official development assistance is between $1.5 and $2 billion. China's influence could be seen at the China–Africa Summit in Beijing and the China–ASEAN Summit in Nanning. China has 2,157 personnel serving in 12 UN peacekeeping missions. A few Chinese nationals have assumed leadership roles in international organisations, such as Dr Margaret Chan at the WHO, Dr Justin Yifu Lin at the World Bank and Mr Sha Zukong at the UN.

Finally, China has produced some global icons in sports, film and music, such as Yao Ming, Jackie Chan and Zhang Yimou and Tan Dun.

I want to make an important point here about China's soft power. China's hard power, namely, economic and military power, will continue to develop and expand. In this context, the wise use of soft power by China will soften her image and make a more powerful China less threatening and more inviting and attractive.

8. My Wish List

I want to conclude with three wishes.

First, I wish that as China becomes a more powerful country, it will continue to practise a policy of good neighbourliness and refrain from any temptation to bully her smaller neighbours. The future of China's relations with the world depends as much on how China chooses to interact with the world as on how the world chooses to deal with China. One litmus test of China's sincerity and the credibility of the doctrine of peaceful rise is China's relations with Southeast Asia. In the past two decades, China has earned the goodwill and support of the members of ASEAN through its generous and benign policies. Much is, therefore, at stake in the manner in which China manages its disputes with the claimant states of Southeast Asia, in the South China Sea. I would urge all the claimant States to observe the "self-restraint" commitment in the ASEAN Agreement on the Code of Conduct of States in the South China Sea and refrain from building new facilities on the disputed maritime features. I would also urge them to consider taking confidence-building measures in order to pave the way for negotiations on joint development of the disputed areas.

Second, I wish that China will continue to play a constructive role in the various international organisations, in global governance, and in upholding the rule of law in the world. China has benefitted from the rule-based multilateral system and should support the system. I welcome the constructive role which China is playing in combating piracy off the coast of Somalia and in working with Indonesia, Malaysia and Singapore and other like-minded states, in the Straits of Malacca and Singapore. I also hope that China will take a more positive attitude towards third party dispute settlement institutions and procedures. In addition to using the WTO's dispute settlement procedures, I hope that one day, in the not too distant future, China will refer one of her legal disputes either to the International Court of Justice or the International Tribunal for the Law of the Sea or both. As China's power grows, the world has a right to expect that it will shoulder a greater burden of international responsibility. China will be expected to help in finding solutions to international conflicts, tensions and challenges.

Third, I wish that China will redouble its efforts to deal with its many environmental problems and to embrace sustainable development. At present, China suffers from serious air, water and land pollution in many cities and regions of the country. China has made impressive progress in harnessing solar and wind energy and in developing clean and green technology. The success of China's transition to a low carbon economy would not only benefit the people of China, but the people of the world. A clean, green and environmentally friendly China would further augment China's growing soft power.

Jia you!

[Orignally published in *China in the Next 30 Years*, MoraQuest, Chicago, IL, pp. 200–208. © 2011 Central Compilation & Translation Press.]

Japan's Prospects and Challenges
A View from Southeast Asia*

Most of my friends, both Asians and Westerners, have a pessimistic view about Japan's future. They think that Japan is in terminal decline. They point to the facts that Japan has a shrinking population, a stagnant economy, an insular mindset, a huge public debt, an unstable political system and weak leaders. As a contrarian, I do not subscribe to this conventional wisdom. I believe that Japan can overcome its challenges. I believe that Japan has many strengths which are under-estimated. I believe that Japan can still have a bright future. The following are the reasons for my optimism.

My Faith in the People of Japan

First, I believe in the people of Japan. I believe that they will overcome the many challenges which beset their country. The strengths and virtues of the Japanese people were on display when the Northeast of Japan (Tohoku) was struck by a devasting earthquake and tsunami on 11 March 2011. There were no panic and lawlessness. There were no scenes of looting. Instead, the people reacted with calm, courage, discipline, unity and civic-mindedness. The world had never seen a people behave in such an exemplary manner in the face of such a great tragedy. The recovery from the triple disasters has taken place smoothly and rapidly. This has given the Japanese people a new spirit of self-confidence which had been missing for a long time.

---

*Speech at the International House of Japan on the occasion of its 60th Anniversary Celebrations, 3 October 2012, Tokyo, Japan.

The Quality of the Japanese Workforce

Second, I believe in the high quality of the Japanese workforce. I was a member of Toyota's International Advisory Board for five years (1996–2001). I was, therefore, able to observe the workers of Toyota. What I saw was a workforce which was one of the best educated, trained and diligent in the world. This is one of the core strengths of the Japanese economy. The competitiveness of an economy depends, in part, on the quality of its human resource. Japan should, however, raise its labour productivity. According to the 2011 report of the Japan Productivity Center, Japan's labour productivity ranked no. 20 among the 34 OECD countries. The low labour productivity is due largely to the retail sector and overstaffed corporate headquarters.

Work Ethic and Culture of Excellence

Third, I admire the Japanese work ethic and the pervasive culture of excellence. The people of Japan are extremely hardworking. It must be the only country in the world in which people actually die of over-work! The work ethic is a core value of the Japanese people. So is the culture of excellence. Every Japanese worker, no matter what his or her job or occupation, seeks to achieve excellence. We see this in the attitudes of the sushi chef at his counter, the potter at his kiln, the interpreter in her booth, the worker on the factory floor, etc. I suspect that this culture of excellence has contributed to the high reputation of the Japanese brand and products.

Science, Technology, Innovation

Fourth, the competition among the advanced economies is increasingly driven by technology and innovation. Japan has a strong track record of innovation and new technology. Japan used to dominate the world in consumer electronics and white goods. In recent years, Japan seemed to be falling behind the United States and Korea, in such areas as electronics and mobile phone technology. Japan remains, however, a world leader in automotives, robotics, game technology, anime, photographic technology and green technology. Japan spends 3.8 percent of its GDP on Research and Development (R&D), outspending the US (2.7 percent) and Germany (2.6 percent). 21 percent of all patents granted by the US in 2009 were to Japanese inventors. According to the World Intellectual Property Organization (WIPO), Japan's share of patent applications globally has risen from 10 to 20 percent in the past 10 years. Japan should do more to exploit its investments in R&D and its innovation by translating its new inventions into products and services for the world market.

Global Champions

Fifth, in the corporate world, Japan has produced some notable global champions. There are 68 Japanese companies in the Fortune Global 500. Many of these companies are world class. Other companies, such as, Rakuten and Uniqlo, are likely to join this club. These two companies are using English as one of their working languages. This will make them more competitive internationally. It is important for Japan to produce more global champions because such companies are profitable, attract talented employees, generate innovation and good jobs, as Heang Chhor, the former head of McKinsey in Japan, has argued in the book, *Reimagining Japan* (2011, page 430).

Japan's Soft Power

Sixth, Japan has a very attractive soft power. The world admires Japan as a peaceful and beautiful country. It is immaculately clean and takes excellent care of its environment. It has a long and rich history and its heritage in the arts and crafts has been carefully preserved. Japanese design, fashion and architecture are much admired. Japan is viewed as both prosperous and egalitarian. There is a high level of social trust and harmony. The quality of life is high and various aspects of Japan's popular culture, such as its cuisine, ikebana, judo, manga, anime, J-Pop, have been embraced by the world. The Japanese people are viewed as polite, cultured and considerate. They are also admired for their inner strength and never-say-die attitude. This was best exemplified by the victorious Nadeshiko Japan, which, in spite of the relative small size of its players, defeated the bigger-sized US team in the final of the FIFA World Cup in 2011. The same team won the silver medal in the 2012 Olympic Games in London, losing to the US in the final. I wish also to praise the contributions which Japan has made, under UN auspices, to peace-keeping and nation-building, in Cambodia, Timor Leste, Aceh, and Mindanao. Japan has also played a positive role in the reconstruction of Sri Lanka, after the conclusion of the civil war. I would encourage Japan to do more in the pursuit of peace.

Japan's Five Challenges

What are Japan's biggest challenges? I will comment on the following challenges:

(a) Demography;
(b) Gender;
(c) Education;
(d) Business; and
(e) Leadership.

The Demographic Challenge

First, Japan's demographic challenge. There are two aspects to this challenge: (i) Japan has the world's fastest ageing population; and (ii) Japan's population has been shrinking since 2005 because the Japanese are not reproducing themselves. Japan's total fertility rate is 1.4. Singapore is afflicted with the same problems. In spite of many financial incentives and more generous maternity leave, the total fertility rate of Singapore hovers around 1.2. There is an ongoing national debate in Singapore on how to raise our fertility rate to the French and Nordic levels. We are re-examining our policies relating to maternity and paternity leaves, subsidised childcare for infants and young children, early or pre-kindergarten education, the role of the father in child-rearing, the work-life balance, etc. Without prejudging the outcome of this review, I must confess that I am not very optimistic about the prospect of raising our fertility to or near the replacement level of 2.1. I suspect the same is true of Japan.

Making up the Deficit

In order to make up the deficit, Singapore imports people through its immigration policy. As a result, our population has grown progressively from 2 million in 1970 to 4 million in 2000, to its current level of 5 million. The optimum size of the Singapore population has not been settled, but I suspect it will be around 6 million.

Singapore's capacity to absorb immigrants is due, partly, to our history as an immigrant nation and, partly, to our diversity. Our population consists of citizens whose forefathers had migrated to Singapore from China, South Asia, Southeast Asia and West Asia. As a result, we have developed a culture of accepting diversity. Multiculturalism is in our DNA. There is very little xenophobia in Singapore. However, in recent years, especially during the boom years, Singapore had taken in too many foreigners. The influx was greater than our absorptive capacity, straining our infrastructure and amenities and causing great discomfort to Singaporeans. The Singapore Government has since recalibrated its policy. According to the opinion polls, 70 percent of Singaporeans are in favour of immigration.

Can Japan Accept Immigrants?

The question I wish to pose to my Japanese friends is whether Japan can liberalise its immigration policy in order to prevent its population from shrinking? Can the Japanese people, who are used to living in a homogenous society, accept foreigners? Is Japan willing to assimilate talented foreigners into the Japanese family? If the answers to these questions are no and if the fertility rate remains low, then we are faced with the scenario of a Japan with a shrinking population. This will have many implications for Japan and for the world. If the answers to my questions are yes, then we face an entirely different scenario, of a global Japan, energised by the infusion of new talent from the rest of Asia.

In Praise of Older Workers

The Japanese people enjoy the longest life span in the world of 83 years. By 2030, people over the age of 65 could account for one-third of Japan's population. This is going to be the trend in the developed world as people live longer, but it will happen in Japan first. Demographers and economists generally view this in a negative light as they assume that the older people will stop working and become dependants. Hence, they talk about the worsening dependency ratio of ageing societies.

I would like to urge Japan to become the world's thought leader on ageing. Instead of viewing older people as a liability, we should view them as an asset. A few years ago, Mr Lee Kuan Yew, the first Prime Minister of Singapore, caused a consternation in Singapore when he proposed that the concept of mandatory retirement be abolished. He has often said that retirement equals death. I agree with his philosophy. We should encourage older people, who are fit and who wish to work, to continue to do so. I am very proud of the fact that my dentist and tailor are both 80 years old and my optician is 82 years old. We need a radical re-think about ageing. Can Japan be our thought leader?

The Gender Challenge

Second, I want to refer to Japan's gender challenge. The Japanese society is viewed by us in Southeast Asia as a male-dominated society. We note that 30 percent of women drop out of the workforce after marriage. Another 20 percent drop out after the birth of the first child. As a result, women's participation in the workforce, at 50 percent, is relatively low. We have also noticed the under-representation of women in policy-making and senior positions, both in the public and private sectors. Japan was ranked no. 94 out of 134 countries in the 2010 Gender Gap Index of the World Economic Forum. In the UN Human Development Index, Japan is ranked 8 in the world. However, in the Gender Empowerment Measurement, Japan is ranked 59. As a generalisation, I would say that there is greater gender equity in Southeast Asia than in Japan. Japan should seriously consider how to empower its women so that this talented and well-educated human resource can make a bigger contribution to the country. I suspect that the solution lies both in improving the child-care infrastructure and in changing the mindset of the Japanese men towards women. The fact that women are treated as second class citizens was brought home to me by the way Japan treated its male and female football teams on their way to the Olympic Games. The medal-winning women's team was flown to London in economy class whereas the men's team, which has not won a medal of any colour, was in business class.

The Education Challenge

Third, I want to comment briefly on Japan's education challenge. Japan has good schools and universities. Tokyo University is regularly ranked among the top 10 or top 20 in the world. What then is the problem? One problem which Japan shares with others in East Asia is that, because of their Confucian heritage, their education systems tend to emphasise rote-learning and respect for authority. Without undermining our strengths, we need to produce more independent and critical thinkers. Another problem is that Japan's education system is not producing global citizens. Unlike the trend in Southeast Asia, the trend in Japan is that fewer students are going abroad to study. Is it too radical to suggest that Japanese universities should consider requiring their students to study one year abroad? There are very few universities in Japan which offer degrees, either at the undergraduate or post-graduate levels, in English. I am an academic adviser to the Ritsumeikan Asia-Pacific Univeristy, located in Beppu, Oita Prefecture. The university teaches in both Japanese and English and 50 percent of the students are non-Japanese. Japan needs more such universities. Japan's elite universities have the potential to re-make themselves into Asia's leading centres of learning, in areas in which Japan has excelled. The question is whether Japan's leaders have such a vision. Do the leaders of Japan envision a future in which Japan's elite universities will compete with those of the United States for the best and brightest students of Asia?

The Business Challenge

Fourth, the challenges faced by Japanese business. Japanese business face challenges at home and abroad. Let me begin with the challenges they face at home. According to Dr Klaus Schwab, the Executive Director of the World Economic Forum, the three biggest obstacles encountered by business in Japan are: (i) policy and government instability; (ii) tax rates and regulations; and (iii) inefficient government bureaucracy. Dr Schwab wrote that, "The macroeconomic environment is challenging enough; the larger problem, though, is that Japanese politics is in disarray. There have been six Prime Ministers since 2006. This kind of churning makes such reforms difficult to implement." (*Reimagining Japan*, pages 125–126).

Japanese business also face many challenges abroad. According to Gordon Orr, Brian Salsberg and Naoyuki Iwatani of McKinsey, "Japan's biggest companies have been losing relative market share over the past 10 years: their proportion of the Fortune 500's total revenues decreased to 13 percent, from 35 percent, between 1995 and 2005 …. [Japan's] share of the world's export value of electronic goods has fallen from 30 percent in 1990 to less than 15 percent today .... Many Japanese companies have no alternative to globalisation if they hope to continue growing." (*Reimagining Japan*, page 151).

It will be culturally very challenging for great Japanese companies to transform themselves into great multinational companies. The boards of most Japanese companies do not have any foreigners. The same is true of their senior management and their talent pools. Most Japanese executives are not proficient in English, the business language of the world. Although difficult, such a transition can be made. Companies such as Nissan, Komatsu, Takeda, Shiseido, Uniqlo and Rakuten, have successfully embarked on such a journey.

My question to the leaders of business in Japan is whether they are convinced that their companies have no alternative but to globalise. If they are convinced, do they have the will to bring about this transformation. As Shinzo Maeda, the Chairman of Shiseido, has written, "There is a Japanese saying that change starts at the top and cascade to lower levels. That is true for us. Once we made the commitment to embrace diversity at the top, everything else began to cascade in the right direction. Now we are pushing for diversity at every level." (*Reimagining Japan*, page 162).

The Leadership Challenge

Fifth, perhaps the most difficult challenge facing Japan is the leadership challenge. For over three decades, the leadership of Japan was provided by a golden triangle, consisting of the political leaders of the Liberal Democratic Party (LDP), the leaders of the bureaucracy and the leaders of the business community. This governance structure has been broken. As a result of scandals and growing incompetence, the LDP has lost the confidence of the Japanese people. For the same reasons, the public has also lost its trust in the bureaucracy. The leaders of the bureaucracy used to provide the country with both ideas and stability. They can no longer play that role. There is no other institution which has filled the policy vacuum. Japan does not have great think-tanks like those in the United States which are constantly throwing up new ideas and policy proposals. There are also few public intellectuals in Japan of national stature who can provide the country with intellectual leadership.

Politically, things seem to be in a state of a flux. After the LDP lost power, Hosokawa, Hata and Murayama, from the left, provided Japan with an alternative leadership. They were, however, not successful and have since faded away. In the meantime, the Democratic Party of Japan (DPJ) has emerged as the new alternative to the LDP. The DPJ is suspicious of the bureaucracy and has unwisely chosen to govern without its support. In the short time that it has been in power, the DPJ has changed the leadership of the government from Hatoyama, to Kan, and to Noda, in quick succession. At a time when Japan needs strong and visionary leaders, neither party seems able to fulfil this need.

Professor Gerald Curtis at Columbia University, an expert of Japan, has written that: "The public's disappointment with the DPJ is matched by a lack of enthusiasm for the LDP, or for any of the several small parties that have recently been created by defectors from the LDP. Japanese politics, like the economy itself, has fallen into a deep funk with no clear way out." (*Reimagining Japan*, page 129).

A new generation of younger Japanese has entered politics. Many have been elected to the Diet in the 2009 elections. The question is whether these new leaders will rise to the challenge. Will they be able to envision a new future for Japan that will capture the people's imagination and support? Will they have the wisdom to forge a new partnership with the bureaucracy, business and civil society? Will they re-energise existing political institutions or build new political institutions? Will all these happen soon so that Japan will stop drifting?

Conclusion

Let me conclude. Japan has played a very important role in the rise of Asia. Japanese investment, technology and Official Development

Assistance (ODA) have enabled the countries and peoples of ASEAN/Southeast Asia, to make rapid progress in their social and economic development. The Fukuda Doctrine of 1977 continues to be a beacon guiding Japan and ASEAN in their engagement. The ASEAN-Japan partnership is strong, substantive and trouble-free. It is a partnership founded on shared interests, common objectives and a high level of mutual trust. ASEAN has a vested interest in a vibrant, prosperous and self-confident Japan. We wish Japan success in meeting its historic challenge of re-making an inward-looking Japan into a global Japan. History has shown us that Japan has the capacity to make such historic transformations. The Meiji Restoration and Japan's post-war reconstruction are two such examples. A global Japan will be a boon to Japan, to Asia and the world.

China and Japan: Frenemies?

Having just visited Japan, I came away with the disturbing impression that most of the Japanese public intellectuals I met have a negative attitude towards China, perceiving its rise as a threat to Japan. They think that as China grows in power, it will seek to impose its will on its neighbours.

They believe China has abandoned Deng Xiaoping's policy of "tao guang yang hui" (meaning "not to show off one's capability but to keep a low profile"). Instead, they believe that China is seeking to impose its hegemony on the region.

My Chinese interlocutors, on the other hand, blame Japan for causing the current tensions.

They feel that by nationalising three of the disputed islands which are also claimed by China, Japan has violated the understanding reached by then-Prime Minister Kakuei Tanaka and China's leaders in 1972. Both sides at that time reached a tacit "understanding" to shelve the dispute for a future solution and get on with the more urgent normalisation of diplomatic relations.

The Chinese are angry that Japan is not willing to even acknowledge the existence of a dispute. They suspect that Japan is being made use of by the United States in an alleged attempt to contain China.

Many Shared Affinities

In this essay, I wish to remind the leaders of China and Japan not to allow the current impasse over the Senkaku/Diaoyu and the passion generated by the accusations and counter-accusations to blind them to the many affinities which they share and the common interests which bind them.

Geographically, China and Japan are destined to live next to each other until the end of time. Since there is nothing they can do to move away from each other, they have no choice but to learn to get along as good neighbours.

Historically, relations between China and Japan go back at least 2,000 years. For most of that time, the two countries lived at peace with each other.

The four exceptions were: the war between Tang China and the Paekche, on the Korean peninsula in 663; the two unsuccessful attempts by Yuan China under the Mongols to invade Japan, in 1274 and 1281; the Japanese war against Qing China in 1894–1895; and Japan's war against China from 1931 to 1945.

Culturally, there has been much mutual learning.

In ancient times, Japan received from China the Chinese written script, *kanji*, Confucianism and Buddhism. In the past century, however, Chinese students and intellectuals have gone to Japan to learn science, medicine and engineering, and how to remake China into a modern state. There are at present over 69,000 Chinese students studying in Japan, comprising more than 50 percent of the foreign students in Japan.

Friendship Pact Signed

Following then-United States President Richard Nixon's historic visit to Beijing, Japan lost no time in normalising its relations with China. In September 1972, then-Prime Minister Kakuei Tanaka visited China and met Chairman Mao Zedong and Premier Zhou Enlai. Diplomatic relations were established on September 29, 1972. A treaty of peace and friendship was concluded on August 12, 1978.

During the past 41 years, relations between China and Japan expanded in all spheres of activities. For example, China is today Japan's largest trading partner.

Japan, too, has been helpful to China during the past 40 years.

- First, from 1972 until 2004, China was a major recipient of Japan's official development assistance estimated at over US$40 billion.
- Second, Japan is the largest investor in China. By the end of 2012, Japan had invested US$83.9 billion (S$104 billion) in over 43,000 projects.
- Third, Japan is China's third-largest trading partner.
- Fourth, Japan strongly supported China's accession to the World Trade Organisation.
- Fifth, Japan was the first Group of Seven (G-7) country to resume high-level contacts with China, following the 1989 Tiananmen incident. In short, Japan has played a pivotal role in China's development since 1972.

Japan, too, has benefited from China.

- First, China is Japan's largest export market and top trading partner, accounting for 20 percent of Japan's total trade value.
- Second, China is an important source of tourism. In 2011, 1.04 million Chinese tourists visited Japan, representing 17 percent of the total number of tourists who visited Japan that year.
- Third, China is one of the largest markets for Japanese cars, a key industry of Japan.
- Fourth, China is Japan's biggest national debt holder. By the end of 2011, China held a total of US$230 billion of such debt.

Complementary Economies

In conclusion, it would not be wrong to say that China has become an indispensable economic partner of Japan. The outcome of Prime Minister Shinzo Abe's "three-arrow" economic reform strategy is, in part, dependent on the continuation of their good bilateral economic ties. He had called for monetary, fiscal and structural reforms to generate growth.

The Chinese and Japanese economies are fundamentally complementary and not competitive. The relationship is therefore mutually beneficial. Japan needs China and China needs Japan if both are to succeed. It makes good sense for them to cooperate and no sense to view each other as enemies.

In a joint statement that then-Chinese President Hu Jintao and Japanese Prime Minister Yasuo Fukuda issued on May 7, 2008, the two leaders pledged to work together to make the East China Sea into a "Sea of Peace, Cooperation and Friendship".

Today, we have a disagreement between Japan and South Korea over Dokdo/Takeshima, and another between Japan and China over Senkaku/Diaoyu. The East China Sea is in danger of becoming a theatre of conflict.

I hope the leaders of China and Japan remember the commitment their respective predecessors made in 1978 to leave the dispute to future generations. They should lower the temperature and tone down the rhetoric. They should pull back their armed forces since there is a risk of miscalculation.

Explore Non-Legal Options

Although China, Japan and South Korea all purport to uphold the rule of the law and although they have nationals who are judges in the International Court of Justice and the International Tribunal for the Law of the Sea, their governments seem unwilling to refer their disagreements to arbitration or adjudication.

This being the case, they should therefore explore other non-legal options to solve or manage their disagreements.

The options include negotiating a code of conduct, setting up a sub-regional fishery organisation and applying the concept of joint development to the resources in the areas of disagreement.

North Korea's planned missile launch, which may take place as early as today, will be a wake-up call for Japan and China to truly understand the meaning behind a Japanese proverbial story known as "The Three Arrows" — one arrow is easily broken, but three arrows bundled together are harder to break. Interestingly, there is a Chinese proverbial tale which uses chopsticks to deliver the same message.

[Originally published in *The Straits Times*, 10 April 2013.]

My Faith in India

Growing up in a British colony, after the Second World War, I could not accept the right of the British to rule over us. I supported the anti-colonial struggle then taking place in Asia, Africa and elsewhere. I was inspired by the moral crusade of Gandhi against the British in India. It seemed miraculous that the non-violent struggle led by this man, whom Churchill had grossly underestimated and dismissed as that "naked Kafir", would defeat the might of the British empire. Gandhi was one of my childhood heroes.

Nehru's Legacy

India's first Prime Minister, Jawaharlal Nehru, was another hero. His enduring legacy to India consists of democracy, secularism and the rule of law. Nehru had championed Indonesia's struggle against the Dutch, Myanmar's struggle against the British, Vietnam's struggle against the French, and the freedom movement everywhere. In 1947, two years before India's independence, Nehru had convened the Asian Relations Conference, in New Delhi, to promote the idea of a federation of Asian States. He was also an architect of the Bandung Conference of 1955, which sought to unite Asia and Africa. Nehru was a visionary and a man ahead of his time. His 1947 statement that "the future is bound to see a closer union between India and Southeast Asia" is coming true.

Hindu Rate of Growth

Like many leaders of his generation, such as Nkrumah of Ghana, Nyerere of Tanzania and Kaunda of Zambia, Nehru embraced socialism. He believed in central planning and heavy industries. His economic strategy was based on a policy of import-substitution, a fixed exchange rate for the rupee and massive power given to the bureaucracy to control imports and exports. As a result, the Indian economy grew at a very modest rate between 1947 and 1991, and was barely able to keep up with the population increase. Indians had come to accept the under-performance of the Indian economy as normal and referred to the low growth rate as the Hindu rate of growth.

Second Tryst with Destiny

An economic revolution took place in 1991. India found itself in dire circumstances. The economy was stagnant and the country was faced with a balance of payment crisis. The country was at a crossroads. Under the leadership of Prime Minister P. V. Narasimha Rao, Finance Minister Manmohan Singh and Commerce Minister P. Chidambaram, India had a second tryst with destiny. It decided to change course and to embrace reform and to open up the economy. It decided to unleash the private sector and to enable Indian enterprise and talent to flourish.

India's Achievements

From 1991 to 2000, the average annual rate of growth of the Indian economy was 5.6 percent. For the decade, 2001 to 2011, the economy grew at the average annual rate of 8.2 percent. In 2005, 2006, 2007 and 2010, the growth rate exceeded 9 percent. India's external trade has increased from US$37.3 billion in 1991 to US$411.4 billion in 2011. As India's economic prospects have improved and the business environment has become more conducive, foreign direct investment received by India has gone up from US$73 million in 1991 to US$46 billion in 2012.

World Class Indians

Liberated from the unreasonable restrictions of the past, the Indian private sector has boomed. Several Indian companies have become global champions. Lakshmi Mittal's Arcelor is one of the world's largest steel companies. Tata has acquired the British steel company, Corus, and owns the prestigious Jaguar and Land Rover. Bharti Airtel has expanded into Africa. Wipro, Infosys and other Indian companies rank among the best in the information and communication technology industry. India's largest IT company, Tata Consultancy, has a large development centre in Singapore and an even bigger one in China. Bangalore is linked to Silicon Valley. Talented Indians have headed such leading companies and institutions as Pepsico, Citibank, McKinsey, Standard Chartered, etc. Indian professors are present at all the top universities of the world. The Nobel Laureate, Dr Amartya Sen, is one of the world's most admired economists. Fareed Zakaria is a global icon in journalism. Narayana Murthy, Nandan Nilekani and Azim Premji are pioneers of the IT industry and philanthropists.

India's Challenges

Although India has made tremendous progress in the past 20 years, it has still a long way to go to become a First World nation. Hundreds of millions of Indians continue to live in abject poverty, without access to clean water, sanitation, housing and healthcare. 37 percent of Indians are illiterate. 42 percent of children under the age of 5 in India are malnourished. The infant mortality rate is 44 per 1,000 live births. The maternal mortality rate is 212 per 100,000 live births. The discrimination against girls is reflected in the child sex ratio of 914 girls per 1,000 boys. The UNDP's Human Development Index ranks India No. 134 out of 187 countries. India will fail to meet several of the Millennium Development Goals and Targets. I hope that Indian leaders will reduce their tolerance for poverty. Law enforcement is weak. Indian women are not treated with sufficient respect and equity.

The Journey Is Incomplete

India's journey to economic reform and opening is incomplete. Several sectors of the Indian economy remain closed to foreign participation and competition. The infrastructure is inadequate. The bureaucracy and regulators often have a protectionist mindset. The World Bank has ranked India No. 132 for ease of doing business. Corruption is pervasive and Transparency International has ranked India No. 94 out of 174 countries. Approvals could take years to obtain. To get a judgement from a court could take years and, in some cases, even decades. Sometimes, changes of policy, legislation and taxation are applied retrospectively.

Conclusion

India's leaders know that, after centuries of stagnation and decline, India has a historic opportunity to catch up with the West. They also know that India faces many challenges. They are determined to overcome those challenges. As an old friend and admirer of India, I am optimistic about India's future. I believe that India will succeed in becoming one of the world's largest economies and a middle-income country.

[Originally published in *The Straits Times*, 9 March 2013.]

China and India
Chini Hindi Bhai Bhai?*

The new premier of China, Li Keqiang, chose India as the first country to visit in his first trip abroad. This is symbolically significant. The message is that China accords India a very high priority in its foreign policy. Good relations between China and India, two countries of continental size, with a combined population of over 2.5 billion and possessing two ancient and rich civilizations, is desirable and achievable. This is the second most important bilateral relationship in the world, exceeded only by the US-China relationship.

Historical Links

Most contemporary observers believe that the mighty Himalayan mountains constitute a natural barrier between China and India. As a result, there have been minimal interactions between their two peoples. This is historically wrong. In fact, as Amartya Sen has pointed out in his book, *The Argumentative Indian*, "intellectual links between China and India, stretching over much of the first millennium and beyond, were important in the history of the two countries".

---

*The author is the co-chairman of the China-Singapore Forum and the India-Singapore Strategic Dialogue.

Buddhism and Mutual Learning

Buddhism played a central role in initiating the movement of people and ideas between the two countries. In the 5th century, the Buddhist monk, Faxian, spent a decade studying at Nalanda University in today's state of Bihar. In the 7th century, an even more famous monk, Xuanzang, spent 17 years at Nalanda. In addition to Buddhism, China benefitted a great deal from India in science, mathematics, medicine, architecture, music and literature. In the 8th century, an Indian scientist, Gautama Siddhartha, (Qutan Xida) was appointed by the Chinese emperor as the President of the Board of Astronomy. It is wonderful that members of the East Asia Summit are building a new Nalanda University, with Amartya Sen as the head of its governing board and Singapore's George Yeo and China's Li Zaoxing, playing an active role in the initiative. The rebirth of Nalanda University reminds us that, 1,000 years ago, there was an Asian community and Asians were studying together and learning from one another. Our current efforts to form an Asian community therefore have ancient roots.

Positive Historical Legacy

There is therefore a positive historical legacy on relations between China and India. Skipping forward to the 20th century, the contacts between them have been less substantive and significant. However, as Asad Latif has pointed out in his article, "Sino-Indian ties: Looking back to the future" (*The Straits Times*, 30 May 2013), there were some positive exchanges. Latif recalled that a young Indian doctor, Dwarkanath Kotnis, volunteered to look after the communists in Yan'an and the Eighth Route Army and is celebrated in China as a hero. Acknowledging this link, Premier Li met with Kotnis' relatives during his visit to Mumbai earlier this month. In 1928, Rabindranath Tagore established a Chinese Studies Institute at his school at Santiniketan.

1962 Border War

In 1962, however, China and India fought a brief border war. Although the victorious Chinese forces unilaterally withdrew from the territories they had occupied, Nehru felt humiliated and betrayed. Memories of that war continue to rancour in the hearts and minds of many of the Indian intelligentsia.

Sweet and Sour Relationship

What is the current state of relations between them? Do they share more convergent or divergent interests? Is a rising China a boon or a threat to India and vice versa? The current state of bilateral relations is both sweet and sour. There are both points of convergence and points of divergence.

Convergent Interests

China and India share the following convergent interests.

First, the two economies are both competitive and complementary. China needs India's exports of iron ore, cotton, other commodities, steel and other intermediate goods. India needs China's exports of machinery, electronics goods and other manufactured products. India has a competitive edge over China in software, pharmaceuticals and services. China has an edge over India in manufacturing. There are many complementarities between the two economies.

Trade

Second, trade is booming between China and India. China has become India's largest trading partner. The two-way trade has reached US$70 billion. The agreed target is US$100 billion by 2015. This is achievable as both economies are expanding in spite of the poor economic environment in the West and because they have started from a very low base and only recently.

Investment

Third, provided some political sensitivities can be removed or eased, there is tremendous scope for more Chinese investment in India and more Indian investment in China. At present, China has only invested US$278 million in India, ranking it no. 30 on the list of India's foreign investors. China has invested in India's automobile, power, metallurgical, construction, and services industries. India has invested US$422 million in China, ranking it no. 20 on India's list of investment destinations. Leading companies from China and India, such as Huawei and Tata, respectively, are showing the way. Huawei currently employs 500 Indians in Bangalore and Tata employs 4,000 Chinese in 10 companies in China.

Cooperation in Multilateral Forums

Fourth, China and India share many common interests in international trade negotiations and climate change negotiations. China and India cooperate in many multilateral institutions, such as, the UN, WTO, G20 and BRICS. They see themselves as the champions of developing countries and of the emerging economies. I would like to see China and India joining the US and EU in protecting the freedom of navigation and defending the global commons.

Divergent Interests

China and India do, however, have many points of divergence. The following is a list of the most important: (i) border dispute; (ii) trade deficit; (iii) international rivers; (iv) Tibet and the Dalai Lama; (v) Pakistan;

(vi) the so-called Chinese string of pearls; (vii) competition for natural resources; and (viii) deficit of trust. I will comment on what I consider to be the four most important issues.

Trust Deficit

First, there is a deficit of trust between Beijing and New Delhi. In the 2013 India Poll, conducted by the Lowy Institute and the Australia India Institute, it was revealed that 83 percent of the Indians polled perceive China as a security threat to India. Only 31 percent of Indians agree that China's rise has been good for India. Because of the deficit of trust, each side tends to misinterpret the policies and actions of the other. For example, India regards the ports which China is building in Bangladesh, Myanmar, Sri Lanka and Pakistan, the so-called string of pearls, with suspicion. President Xi Jinping has recently proposed, as one of his five principles of co-existence between China and India, the strengthening of cultural ties and to increase mutual understanding and friendship between the two peoples. Increasing mutual understanding and reducing mutual distrust is an imperative.

Border Dispute

Second, the border dispute is largely a legacy of British imperialism. China claims the Indian state of Arunachal Pradesh as South-eastern Tibet. One of the most important temples of Tibetan Buddhism is located in Tawang, which is part of Arunachal Pradesh. India claims that China is occupying Indian territory in the Himalayan frontier, in the Ladakh region, called Aksai Chin. Any solution will require political will and compromise on both sides. Zhou Enlai and Deng Xiaoping had proposed one possible compromise. Prime Minister Manmohan Singh has recently stated, as one of his five principles, that India is willing to show accommodation on the border issue but that accommodation must take into account "ground realities". I am confident that the border dispute can be solved when there is sufficient political will to do so in Beijing and New Delhi. I note that China has resolved all her land border disputes except those with India and Bhutan. I am heartened by the recent declaration of both countries not to allow these disputes affect their overall bilateral relations. The speedy resolution of a recent border standoff demonstrates the determination and desire of the leaders of the two countries to achieve this.

Water

Third, in Asia, unlike Europe, the upper riparian states and the lower riparian states do not have a culture of consultation and cooperation. India is concerned that the building of dams by China on the Yarlung Zangbo/Brahmaputra, will adversely affect those who live downstream. This is a legitimate concern. Asians should learn from the positive experience of Europe in this respect. For example, the 19 riparian states of the River Danube consult and cooperate with one another in the management and use of that river system. The same regime should apply to all the great river systems of Asia.

Trade Deficit

Fourth, the growing trade deficit suffered by India has become a political problem. India's trade deficit with China has ballooned from US$9.38 billion in 2007 to US$28.87 billion in 2012. Premier Li Keqiang and PM Manmohan Singh have agreed to take energetic actions to increase Indian exports to China and to reduce the deficit. Indian companies should overcome their fear of China and establish themselves in China in order to take advantage of the booming Chinese market.

Rising Together

Can a rising China and a rising India live at peace with each other? I agree with Prime Minister Manmohan Singh and former Chinese Premier Wen Jiabao, when they said that the world is big enough to accommodate both. I also agree with Kishore Mahbubani who, in his book, *The Great Convergence*, wrote that: "Both China and India were entering into one of the most promising periods of civilizational rejuvenation. It would be sheer folly for China and India to waste this precious moment by engaging in a zero-sum geopolitical competition." Relations between China and India in the 1950s were very good. Nehru had extended India's hand of friendship to the People's Republic of China, at a time when some in the West, were hostile to it. When Zhou Enlai visited New Delhi, he was greeted with banners proclaiming that, "Chini hindi bhai bhai", meaning Chinese and Indians are brothers. I hope that one day in the near future that sense of brotherhood will return to the Sino-Indian relationship.

[An edited version was published in *The Straits Times*, 15 June 2013.]

The ICRC at 150: Reflections of an Asian Admirer

I thank the *International Review of the Red Cross* for inviting me to contribute an essay to its special issue on the auspicious occasion of the 150th anniversary of the International Committee of the Red Cross (ICRC).

I have served twice as Singapore's Permanent Representative to the United Nations. It was during my second posting (1974–1984) that I had the opportunity to work closely with the ICRC to save Cambodian lives. I have also served as an adviser to the ICRC for several years. I regard myself as an old friend and admirer of the ICRC. In this reflective essay, I will touch on its past, present and future.

The Founding Principles

I recall the fact that it all started in 1863, when a group of five members from a pre-existing charity from Geneva, led by Henry Dunant, were so horrified by what had happened on the battlefield of Solferino, that they decided to do something about it. Their simple idea of providing humanitarian relief to wounded soldiers was founded on the three principles of humanity, neutrality and impartiality. The success of their initiative is an example of the power of an idea whose time has come. It is also an example of a private initiative which has changed the world. I look forward to the day when Asian visionaries will also promote initiatives which will have such a benevolent impact on the world.

ICRC's Unique Role and Functions

I regard the ICRC as a unique and indispensable international organisation. I attach very high value to its functions which include the following;

(i) the progenitor, custodian and promoter of international humanitarian law (IHL);
(ii) the provision of relief supplies to prisoners of war and detained civilians;
(iii) visiting persons deprived of their liberty;
(iv) the provision of relief supplies to people affected by humanitarian emergencies, caused either by man-made or natural disasters;
(v) being present on the ground in conflict situations in order to ensure compliance with IHL;
(vi) tracing missing persons;
(vii) using quiet diplomacy to raise awareness on the needs of those affected by humanitarian emergencies, and to persuade decision-makers to alleviate their suffering and to respect IHL; and
(viii) acting as the partner of the International Federation of the Red Cross and Red Crescent Societies (IFRC).

War Will Always be with Us

War is inherently a cruel and destructive enterprise. However, given the nature of Man, war will always be with us. According to the book, *50 Facts that Should Change the World*, by Jessica Williams, there are 32 armed conflicts in 27 countries, affecting 2.3 billion people. Since it is impossible to banish wars, we should do what we can to reduce their cruelties by promoting and strengthening IHL which, inter alia, prescribes rules prohibiting the use of certain weapons, such as chemical and biological weapons, and the targeting of civilians, and provides for the protection of prisoners of war, the protection of women and children.

The Association of Southeast Asian Nations (ASEAN) and International Humanitarian Law (IHL)

When my colleagues and I, in the High-Level Task Force, were drafting the ASEAN Charter, in 2007, we agreed to include in Article 2, para (2) (i), a reference to IHL. In other words, ASEAN and its member states shall uphold the UN Charter and international law, including IHL. My impression is that, in Asia, there is insufficient knowledge, understanding and ownership of IHL. The ICRC should consider enhancing its engagement with ASEAN to promote the better understanding of and adherence to and ownership of IHL in ASEAN and the wider Asian region. I note with approval what the ICRC is currently doing with ASEAN and Asia, for example, the annual Southeast Asia Teaching Session on IHL for government officials and academics, the national and regional moot court competitions and the fact that, for the first time, the Pictet competition will be held in an Asian country (Thailand) this year. We should, however, aim to raise the bar. The ICRC should work more closely with the Secretariats of ASEAN and SAARC. The ICRC should work harder to earn the trust of the governments in Asia. The ICRC should offer its help to those governments in a way which is culturally acceptable.

Saving Cambodian Lives

The ICRC is an activist organisation. Its delegates are present, on the ground, in almost all the conflict situations in the world. Some of the conflict situations are highly dangerous. As a result, some brave and dedicated men and women have lost their lives in the line of duty. I want to refer to a case in which no ICRC lives were lost but many Cambodian lives saved. In 1979, the world was shocked by the sight of hundreds of thousands of starving, sick and dying Cambodians, arriving at the Thai-Cambodian border. The UN and ICRC sprang into action.

Tribute to ICRC Delegates

In a joint operation, co-led by the ICRC and UNICEF, with the legendary Sir Robert Jackson, acting as the Special Representative of the UN Secretary-General, the Cambodian refugees were given shelter and safety, food and medical care, both along the border and in special camps built on Thai territory. I visited one such camp at Khao I Dang, and was immensely impressed by what I saw. What was accomplished on the ground would not have been possible if not for the skilful diplomacy of three ICRC delegates at the UN, namely, Jean-Pierre Hocke, Jacques Moreillon and Michel Veuthey. Although many years have passed since those critical years when we worked closely at the United Nations to save the Cambodians, I wish to remember their contributions and pay them my respect. The success of the ICRC is due, in no small part, to the excellence of its people.

The Singapore Red Cross Society

I wish to conclude by referring to the Singapore Red Cross Society. The national societies and the ICRC have common origins. The ICRC delegation in Kuala Lumpur, Malaysia, has been very supportive of the Singapore Red Cross Society. The Society plays an active role inside Singapore. However, equally important is the role they play in responding to appeals for help by sister societies. The Singapore Red Cross Society is trusted both by the government and the public. It has a proud record of responding promptly, generously and competently to appeals for help.

The Indian Ocean Tsunami

In the aftermath of the Indian Ocean tsunami of 2004, the Singapore Red Cross Society received an outpouring of support, both in cash and in kind. The Society also coordinated the activities of many non-governmental organisations which rushed in to help. The money contributed by the public was used to rebuild infrastructure, housing, an orphanage and to supply the people with an easy to use devise to turn polluted water into safe drinking water in Indonesia, Sri Lanka and the Maldives.

Myanmar, China and Japan

The Singapore Red Cross Society also responded promptly and effectively to assist the victims of the earthquakes in Sichuan and the Cyclone Nargis in Myanmar. In the aftermath of the Tohoku earthquake and tsunami in Japan in 2011, there was also an outpouring of public support for Japan. The Singapore Red Cross Society has used the money raised to build community facilities in three of the affected areas. I am happy to observe that the Singapore Red Cross Society has become extremely active and, in response to humanitarian crisis situations, especially those in Asia, has stepped up to the plate to help raise funds and emergency supplies for the victims.

Promoting IHL

The Singapore Red Cross Society also plays an active role in promoting IHL. For example, it organises the regular IHL Debate series and assists our law students in participating in the Jean Pictet IHL moot competition and in the Hong Kong Red Cross IHL moot competition. The Society also works with the Ministry of Defence in the dissemination of IHL to members of our armed forces.

Looking to the Future

Looking ahead, I am confident that the International Red Cross and Red Crescent Movement will have a bright future. The future will bring new challenges as well as new opportunities. The new media and social media are examples of new opportunities. One of the challenges for the ICRC is to keep up-to-date with developments in the field of armed conflict, such as the complicated role of non-state actors, revolutionary developments in defence technology and paradigm shifts in global geopolitics.

In an increasingly globalised world, the ICRC should also reflect on how it can become a more globalised organisation. In some parts of Asia, the ICRC is viewed as a white man's organisation. Given the unhappy colonial history of these countries, this perception is an impediment to ICRC's acceptance and effectiveness. The ICRC should reflect deeply on what it can do to shed this image. Certain things, however, should not change. The ICRC's core principle of neutrality must not change. It is the basis on which trust is built. In conflict situations, trust is a rare and precious asset.

Happy Anniversary!

[Originally published in *International Review of the Red Cross*, Vol. 94, No. 888, Winter 2012. © 2012 International Committee of the Red Cross]

5 LAW

Reflections on the Negotiating Process of UNCLOS*

The Third United Nations Conference on the Law of the Sea is said to be the biggest international conference ever held. At its first substantive session held in Caracas in the Summer of 1974, there were 143 participating delegations with over 2,000 delegates. In the subsequent 8 years, the number of participating delegations rose to almost 160. The conference had a long and complex agenda. The subjects and issues on the agenda involved important economic, strategic, environmental, scientific and other interests of States as well as of the international community as a whole. In the years ahead, the international community will, no doubt, hold other global conferences, dealing with other important questions on the planetary agenda.

It may, therefore, be useful to look back on the negotiating process of the conference and to ask whether we could learn any valuable lessons from it. Does the experience of the Law of the Sea Conference teach us anything on how to manage a large multilateral conference? Does it tell us anything about how to structure negotiations, what rules of procedure to follow, what methods of work are likely to be the most productive and what pitfalls to avoid?

---

*This article is Lecture 4 of *The 1982 Stimson Lectures: Building a New Legal Order for the Ocean*, delivered at Yale University, 1982, unpublished.

Rules of Procedure

One of the most important innovations of the conference is its rules of procedure. The rules of procedure contain an appendix which, inter alia, states:

> The Conference should make every effort to reach agreement on substantive matters by way of consensus and there should be no voting on such matters until all efforts at consensus have been exhausted.

Consensus

The letter and spirit of this 'gentleman's agreement' was scrupulously observed by the Conference. Not a single article in the Convention was adopted by vote. All the provisions of the Convention were negotiated until satisfactory accommodation was reached between the competing interests and there was general agreement on the provisions.

Cooling Off

Another interesting feature of the rules of procedure is the provision in Rule 37 for a cooling off period before a vote is taken. Under Rule 37, paragraph 2, when a matter of substance comes up for voting for the first time, either the President or 15 delegations may request a deferment of a vote for a period not exceeding 10 days. During the period of deferment, the President shall make every effort to facilitate the achievement of general agreement. At the end of the period, the President shall inform that Conference of the results of his efforts. A vote on the proposal may be taken only after the conference has determined that all efforts at reaching agreement have been exhausted.

Required Majority

The majority required for the adoption of a proposal by vote is also of interest. On all matters of substance, the decisions of the conference shall be taken by a two-thirds majority of the representatives present and voting provided that such majority shall include at least a majority of the States participating in that session of the conference. What this means is that even though there may be a two-thirds majority in favour of a proposal, it will not be adopted unless the number of positive votes is greater than half the number of delegations attending that session of the conference.

How did the rules of procedure work in practice? In practice, the rules of procedure worked very well. When the gate was opened for the submission of amendments to the draft Convention, altogether 33 amendments were submitted. The President invoked Rule 37 and declared a cooling off period of 10 days. During this period, he and his colleagues in the Collegium, contacted the co-sponsors of all the amendments in order to do two things. *First*, they tried to see whether any of the amendments enjoyed widespread and substantial support and which, if accepted, would enhance the prospects of achieving general agreement. Of the 33 amendments, only one fell into this category. This was an amendment submitted by the Council of Namibia concerning its right to become a party to the Convention. Following consultations conducted by one of the vice-presidents, from Ireland, a compromise proposal was accepted by the conference. *Second*, after the President had ascertained that the other amendments did not satisfy the two criteria stated above, he tried to persuade their co-sponsors to withdraw or, at least, not to insist on putting them to the vote. After much persuasion, he succeeded in respect of all the amendments except three. Spain insisted on putting its amendments to Article 39 and Article 42 to the vote. Both amendments were not adopted. The second Spanish amendment obtained the required two-thirds majority but not the second requirement of a majority of the delegations attending that session of the conference. Turkey also insisted on putting its amendment to Article 309 to the vote. Turkey's amendment was also rejected. The rejections of these amendments, especially of Spain's amendment to Article 42, which had considerable merit, confirmed the conference's commitment to the consensus procedure.

Reconciling the Package Deal with a Broad Agenda

The conference had an extremely long agenda. It contained no less than 25 subjects and issues. At the same time, delegations insisted that both because the different aspects of ocean space are interrelated, as well as for tactical reasons, all the subjects and issues on the agenda must be dealt with together in a package and a single Convention must be adopted. A problem similar to this will arise when the global economic negotiations are launched. How did the conference on the Law of the Sea deal with this problem? The conference decided that it was simply impossible to deal with all these subjects and issues in one negotiating forum. The conference decided that the package deal approach did not preclude the allocation of the different subjects and issues to different negotiating bodies, so long as their interrelatedness was always borne in mind and so long as it was understood that the solutions to the different subjects and issues must be brought together into a single convention. Therefore, the conference established 4 principal fora to deal with the subjects and issues: the Plenary, which dealt with the preamble, the final clauses and disputes settlement; the First Committee which dealt with Part XI of the Convention and related annexes; the Second Committee which dealt with Parts I to X of the Convention and related annexes; and the Third Committee which dealt with the preservation and protection of marine environment, marine scientific research and marine technology. The point to be made here is that the package deal approach does not preclude the allocation of different subjects and issues on an agenda to different negotiating fora so long as the negotiators in the different fora bear in mind their interrelatedness, and so long as the different components will be welded together at a later point.

Miniaturising the Negotiating Groups

A conference with 160 participants is obviously a large and unwieldy body. It is impossible to conduct meaningful negotiations in such a large body. The problem is how to transform such a large conference into small, efficient and representative negotiating groups. This is by no means an easy task. In the Law of the Sea Conference, all delegations felt that they had important national interests at stake. They, therefore, wanted to participate directly in the negotiations so as to promote or to protect their national interests. They resisted the idea that they should allow others to represent their interests. The conference eventually solved this problem in the following way. Let us take, as an example, the negotiations on the financial terms of mining contracts. The Chairman of the Negotiating Group first held meetings at the level of the plenary so that all delegations could participate in them. The second step he took was to establish an open-ended group of financial experts. Although the meetings were open to all, the very name of the group intimidated many from coming and the group of financial experts had a regular attendance of approximately 30 delegations, or one-fifth of the membership of the conference. To miniaturise this further, when the Chairman considered that the time was ripe for negotiating an agreement, he invited the representative of the United States to represent all the market-economy countries, and three representatives of the Group of 77, one each from Africa, Asia and Latin America to represent the developing countries. Simultaneously, the Chairman conducted negotiations with the Soviet Union, representing the centrally-planned economies. The results of these negotiations were subsequently ratified by the conference. The technique of miniaturising the negotiating groups requires political finesse, obtaining the trust of the interest groups, good feedback from the negotiators to their interest groups and good judgement on timing.

Negotiating Groups

Reference has already been made to the fact that the conference had 4 principal negotiating fora: the Plenary, the First, Second and Third Committees. At various times, informal negotiating groups were established within each of these fora. Within the Third Committee, for example, two working groups were established, one dealing with the protection and preservation of the marine environment and the other dealing with marine scientific research.

In addition to the above, the conference also established 7 negotiating groups to deal with 7 hardcore problems. Negotiating Group 1 dealt with the international regime for the exploration and exploitation of the international area of the seabed and ocean floor and was chaired by Francis Njenga of Kenya. Negotiating Group 2 dealt with financial arrangements and was chaired by Tommy Koh of Singapore. Negotiating Group 3 dealt with the organs of the International Seabed Authority and was chaired by Paul Bamela Engo of the Cameroon. Negotiating Group 4 dealt with the relationship between coastal States and landlocked and geographically disadvantaged States with respect to the living resources of the exclusive economic zone and was chaired by Satya Nandan of Fiji. Negotiating Group 5 dealt with the disputes settlement aspect of the subject of Negotiating Group 4 and was chaired by Constantin Stavropoulos of Greece. Negotiating Group 6 dealt with the continental shelf and was chaired by Andres Aguilar of Venezuela. Negotiating Group 7 dealt with the question of sea-boundary delimitation and was chaired by Judge Manner of Finland.

A remarkable feature of the conference was that some of the most important and intractable problems were negotiated and resolved, not in any of the principal fora or negotiating groups established by the conference, but in informal negotiating groups which were privately convened. Jens Evensen of Norway convened a group which dealt with the exclusive economic zone and with marine pollution. Jorge Castaneda of Mexico, convened a group which resolved the difficult question concerning the status of the exclusive economic zone. A group was convened, under the joint initiative of Fiji and the United Kingdom, to negotiate the question of passage through straits used for international navigation. At the initiative of Professor Louis Sohn of the United States, a group was convened under the co-chairmanship of Australia, El Salvador and Kenya, on the question of disputes settlement.

The experience of the conference has been that both the formal and the informal negotiating groups were extremely useful. Sometimes, when a problem eludes a solution in a formal negotiating gorup, it is necessary to take it into a smaller and more informal negotiating group. If the private negotiating group is to succeed in getting its result ratified by the conference, it must comprise all those who have a real interest at stake as well as those who are regarded as the leaders of the conference. The fact that such an effort is being made should not be kept secret from the conference because secrecy tends to breed suspicion.

Interest Groups

Some commentators have characterised the Third United Nations Conference on the Law of the Sea as primarily a North–South negotiation. This characterisation is incorrect. On most issues before the conference, the interests and positions of a country were determined not by its development status or its ideological orientation, but by geography. Hence, most negotiating groups were not composed along North–South lines. Part XI of the Convention, dealing with deep seabed mining, was the only area in which the delegations were polarised between North and South.

Delegations at the conference belong to a whole variety of groups. With a few exceptions, they belong to regional groups. Of the 5 regional groups, only the East European Group was able to work with a high degree of coherence on all issues. The African group was usually able to take a unified position on First Committee matters. Members of the other regional groups were split on most of the issues before the conference. The Group of 77, consisting of nearly 120 developing countries, was effective only in the area of the mining of the deep seabed. Some of the most important interest groups established at the conference were the following:

(1) the coastal States Group;
(2) the group of landlocked and geographically disadvantaged States;

(3) the territorialist group consisting of coastal States which have claimed 200 miles territorial sea;
(4) the group of straits States;
(5) the group of archipelagic States;
(6) The group of coastal States with broad continental margins, sometimes referred to as the "margineers";
(7) the group of island States;
(8) the European Economic Community;
(9) the group favouring the mediumline or equi-distance principle in sea-boundary delimitation;
(10) the group favouring equitable principles in sea-boundary delimitation;
(11) the group of land-based producers;
(12) the Western gang of 5 consisting of the United States of America, the United Kingdom, France, the Federal Republic of Germany and Japan called the coordinating group of 5;
(13) The East-West gang of 5 consisting of the United States of America, the USSR, United Kingdom, France and Japan called the group of 5; and
(14) the two super-powers.

What purpose did these interest groups serve? The establishment of the interest groups was an important prelude to serious negotiations. It took some time for countries to identify their own interests and for those with kindred interests to form coalitions or groups. It was only after the interest groups had been established, that negotiations could be held between the representatives of the competing interest groups.

Were there any disadvantages to the group system? There were two disadvantages to the group system. *First*, it was often difficult for the groups to come to an agreed position. Negotiations were often held up for days in order to allow the Group of 77 to come to a common position. Once they had done so, the groups tended to get locked into that position and it was often difficult for them to reconsider their positions and to modify them in the course of negotiations. The *second* disadvantage was that the groups often gave a very narrow mandate to their negotiators. This often meant that the negotiators had little or no flexibility and were not able to give and take in the course of the negotiations. The conclusion is that, although the group system serves a useful function and will probably be a feature of any major multilateral conference, it should be used with flexibility. When an impasse occurs, the group system should not prevent the emergence of sub-groups of delegations in the competing groups which could seek to build bridges between the groups.

Role of Conference Leaders

The principal officers of the conference were the President, the Chairmen of the First, Second and Third Committees, the Chairman of the Drafting Committee and the Rapporteur General. These six officers comprise the Collegium. The Special Representative of the Secretary-General attended all meetings of the Collegium as an observer. The Collegium worked extremely well during the conference and provided it with the administrative, managerial, political and negotiating leadership. The conference would have floundered if the Collegium was not united and if it had failed to provide the conference with leadership. The conference conferred extensive powers on the principal officers of the conference. This came about by accident and not by design. The conference had commenced without a basic text. At the second substantive session of the conference held in Geneva, in 1975, the conference requested the chairmen of the 3 main committees to produce a negotiating text which came to be known as the Informal Single Negotiating Text. The President of the conference contributed a text on disputes settlement. The Informal Single Negotiating Text underwent many revisions culminating in the Convention. These revisions were undertaken by the Collegium in accordance with certain criteria established by the conference. The criteria were that the modifications must be based upon compromise proposals emerging from negotiations and consultations which, when presented to the plenary, were found to enjoy widespread and substantial support and which would substantially improve the prospects of achieving consensus.

The leaders of the conference did not, however, consist only of the members of the Collegium and of the Chairmen of the 7 negotiating groups. A handful of other individuals, by virtue of their knowledge, ability, negotiating skill and initiative, were recognised by their peers as leaders of the conference. These include Jens Evensen of Norway, Jorge Castaneda of Mexico, Keith Brennan of Australia, Elliot Richardson of the United States, Joseph Warioba of Tanzania, Alfonso Arias-Schreiber of Peru, S. P. Jagota of India, Alvaro de Soto of Peru, Christopher Pinto of Sri Lanka, Inam Ul-Hag of Pakistan, Fernando Zegers of Chile, Karl Wolf of Austria and Semyon Kozyrev of the Soviet Union.

The Role of Personality in Multilateral Negotiations

In a multilateral conference, the importance and effectiveness of a delegate depends on both the weight and influence of his country and on his own qualities. In the case of the 5 major powers, the United States, the Soviet Union, the United Kingdom, France and the Federal Republic of Germany, the power of the country is probably more important than the personal attributes of its representative. This is not the case with the other countries. In a multilateral conference, apart from the Big 5, the personal qualities of a delegate determine his influence and effectiveness. Let me give the following example. Fiji is a relatively small developing country, and yet its chief representative to the conference, Satya Nandan, played one of the most important roles in the conference. He co-chaired the negotiating group on passage through straits. He was instrumental in negotiating the compromise text between the archipelagic States and the major maritime powers. He chaired the difficult negotiations between coastal States and landlocked and geographically disadvantaged States with respect to the living resources of the exclusive economic zone. He chaired the negotiations on the provisions of the Convention dealing with production limitation. Finally, he assisted the President in resolving the problem of sea-boundary delimitation.

Making Negotiations Succeed

The first pre-condition for successful negotiations is to establish mutual trust and confidence. If the two sides are separated by mutual mistrust and suspicion, it is very difficult to make the negotiations work. This was the situation prevailing in the First Committee between 1974 and 1976. The developed countries suspected that the developing countries were out to prevent them from having access, under reasonable terms and conditions, to the resources of the deep seabed. The developing countries suspected that the developed countries were determined to exploit the common heritage of mankind without their participation and without the equitable sharing of the benefits. The fog of suspicion and mistrust lifted when Elliot Richardson was appointed as the leader of the United States delegation in 1976. He was able to win the trust and confidence of his negotiating adversaries. He was able to convince them that solutions could be found which could accommodate the interests of both sides.

Qualities of Negotiators and Chairmen

The second pre-condition for a successful negotiation is the quality of the negotiators and of the chairmen of negotiating conferences. A good negotiator should be a person possessing technical competence, negotiating skills, personal integrity, a calm temperament and a likable personality. A good chairman should possess, in addition to those qualities, objectivity, a judical temperament, a capacity to reconcile differences, the ability to think of creative solutions to seemingly intractable problems and the courage to put forward compromise proposals.

Third, it is helpful if the two or more sides to a negotiation could agree on what the facts were. In the difficult negotiations on the financial terms of mining contracts, for example, the chairman was able to convince the negotiators to accept a computer model developed by a team of scholars at the Massachusetts Institute of Technology, as a means of comparing the economic performance of a hypothetical seabed mining system under different conditions. The acceptance of the model contributed greatly to the success of the negotiations. In establishing the facts on which the negotiations are to be conducted, the use of experts is sometimes helpful. In the Law of the Sea Conference, the non-governmental organisations contributed a great deal to the education of the delegates on many technical issues, such as the financial terms of mining contracts, transfer of technology, the continental shelf, by bringing experts to talk to the delegates.

Techniques of Chairmanship

There are many different techniques of chairing a negotiation. Some chairmen are good at shuttle diplomacy. Others prefer to have the negotiating adversaries meet face-to-face. Some chairmen listen to the negotiators without putting a single question to them. Others prefer to play a more active role by analysing the issues and putting questions to the negotiators. The different techniques of chairmanship all seem to work. The choice of the technique and style must depend upon each chairman's cultural and intellectual preference and on his personality. Whatever the technique of the chairman, he must understand that each party to a negotiation has certain irreducible minimum interests. He must try to meet those interests and to think of a solution which accommodates the interests of both parties. He should try to create a good negotiating atmosphere and control the tempers of the negotiators. He should try to win the trust and confidence of the negotiators. He should have a creative mind and not be afraid to think of novel solutions to seemingly intractable problems. He could prevent delay and prevarication by setting strict time-limits. Finally, when an important breakthrough occurs, he should maintain the momentum and persuade the negotiators to continue, if necessary, skipping meals, working late into the night and over the weekend. Very often, one breakthrough will lead to another and it is important for the chairman to understand this and to practise the doctrine of "hot pursuit" in negotiations.

Conclusion

I have tried to describe the complex process by which the new Convention on the Law of the Sea was negotiated and adopted. What were the unique features of that process? What were the procedural rules, arrangements, innovations which made the process succeed? What generalisations can be drawn from that experience about the art and science of negotiations? The negotiating process succeeded for a whole variety of reasons. *First*, I woud point to the rules of procedure and the "gentleman's agreement" which laid primary emphasis on the objective of achieving consensus. The cooling off period before voting and the double majority requirement for substantive decisions served to reinforce the commitment of the conference to the goal of achieving consensus. *Second*, we have learnt that it is possible to reconcile the package deal approach with the allocation of different subjects and issues to different negotiating bodies. *Third*, we have seen the importance for the leadership of the conference, the collegium, to work as a cohesive team and to provide the conference with its managerial, diplomatic and negotiating leadership. *Fourth*, it is absolutely essential to transform a large, unwieldy conference of 160 players into small, representative and efficient negotiating groups. Although efforts to miniaturise the negotiating fora will encounter resistance, they are essential and can be done. *Fifth*, a conference needs formal, informal and even privately convened negotiating groups. As a general rule, the more informal the nature of the group the easier it is to resolve a problem. However, secrecy must be avoided and if the results of a negotiating group are to have a chance of winning the support of the conference, the group must include all those who have a real interest at stake and the conference leaders. *Sixth*, interest groups play a useful function and is probably a permanent feature of any global negotiation. The group system should, however, be operated with flexibility. We must avoid the twin dangers of groups adopting rigid positions which cannot be modified and giving their negotiators a mandate with no room for give and take. *Seventh*, negotiation is both an art and a science. There are probably some qualities of a negotiator which are in-born and cannot be taught. There are other attributes, skills and techniques which can probably be identified, analysed and taught. A good negotiator should possess technical competence, negotiating skills, personal integrity, a calm and likeable personality. A good chairman should possess, in addition to those qualities, objectivity, a judicial temperament, a capacity to reconcile differences, the ability to think of creative solutions to seemingly intractable problems and courage. In the final analysis, the Third United Nations Conference on the Law of the Sea succeeded because it brought together a group of negotiators and chairmen who possess many of these qualities. They did not regard one another as the enemy which had to be conquered. They regarded the issue or question under negotiation as the enemy which had to be conquered. While pursuing the interests of their respective countries, they also felt inspired by the fact that what they were doing was no less than writing a constitution for the oceans.

The Quest for a World Order*

Introduction

It is a very great honour to have been invited to deliver the inaugural Tun Mohamed Suffian Public Lecture. Tun Suffian is my favourite Malaysian. During the years when I was Dean of the Faculty of Law of the National University of Singapore, Tun Suffian was the only person I had nominated for the conferment of the honorary degree of doctor of laws. My heart was filled with pride and joy when I was asked to be the public orator at the 1972 convocation of the then University of Singapore at which the honorary LLD degree was conferred on him. I shall quote some passages from my citation.

The Roots of Mohamed Suffian bin Hashim

Mohamed Suffian springs from a humble origin. He was born on 12 November 1917, the son of a kathi, on the banks of the Perak River, at Kota Lama Kiri. As a child, he attended the Malay school at Kampong Masjid, Lenggong. Four years later, he was sent to an English-medium school, the Clifford School at Kuala Kangsar. Suffian was a brilliant pupil. He received three double promotions and consistently topped his class. With school completed, Suffian was advised by his principal not to apply to the Malayan administrative service as he lacked sufficient social connections, but to compete for a Queen's Scholarship.

---

*Text of the Inaugural Tun Mohamed Suffian Public Lecture delivered at the Institut Pengajian Tinggi, University of Malaya. The views expressed are the author's and do not necessarily reflect those of his government.

Suffian the Queen's Scholar

Suffian won a Queen's Scholarship and attended Cambridge University from 1936 to 1940. He was graduated with the degree of Bachelor of Arts, with honours, in 1939 and, in the following year, he was conferred the degree of Bachelor of Laws. In 1941, he was called to the English Bar.

The Second World War

War had, however, intervened and Suffian found himself in India. Here, he was to display the resourcefulness and versatility that were already evident in his career at the Clifford School where he was captain of the school, editor of the school magazine and a King's scout. In India, he worked as a radio broadcaster and became the Head of the Malay section of the British Broadcasting Corporation. When the war ended, Suffian resigned from this position and entered the Malayan Civil Service. He returned home in 1948, 12 years after leaving her shores. He did not, however, return alone. In 1946, he had married Bunny Grange, a lovely, intelligent and highly spirited woman. Theirs has been a long and a very happy marriage.

Suffian's Legal Career

Suffian's career has been so varied and eventful that time would not permit a complete recital of all the high posts he has filled and the many honours that have been bestowed upon him. I will just mention a few landmarks in his versatile career, a career that is distinguished by many firsts. He was the State Secretary of Pahang. He was the first Malaysian to be appointed the Legal Advisor of that State. He was a Constitutional Adviser to both the Malaysian Conference of Rulers and to the Sultan of Brunei. He was the first Malaysian Solicitor-General of the Federation of Malaya. In 1961, at the comparatively young age of 44, Suffian was appointed a Judge of the High Court of Malaysia. In 1968, he was appointed a Judge of the Federal Court of Malaysia. In 1973, he was appointed the Chief

Justice of the High Court of Malaysia. On 1 May 1974, he was appointed the Lord President of the Federal Court of Malaysia. He retired as Lord President on reaching his 65th birthday, on 12 November 1982. Suffian is such a man of principle that he declined the government's request to stay on unless the retirement age for judges contained in the Constitution was amended.

Suffian the Educator and Scholar

Suffian's contributions to higher education span the two sides of the Causeway. He was, for many years, an external examiner in law of the National University of Singapore. He has served as the Pro-Chancellor of the University of Malaya for many years. He was the Chairman of the Advisory Council on Higher Education. He played an important part in the conception and birth of the University of Science in Penang and the National University. Suffian has also made important contributions to legal scholarship. In 1963, he published the first official translation of the Malayan Constitution into Malay. In 1972, he published *An Introduction to the Constitution of Malaysia*. In 1978, he co-edited with Professor Francis Trindade and Mr H.P. Lee, a book entitled *The Constitution of Malaysia — Its Developments, 1957–1977*.

Suffian the Man and Judge

As a lawyer and judge, Mohamed Suffian has always practised his belief that the law must serve the cause of justice. The technicalities of the law have never prevented him from interpreting and applying the law to yield a just result. He has been particularly concerned with the interests of the humble folk. The high judicial offices that he has occupied has not lengthened the distance between Suffian and the people or reduced his empathy for them. It is therefore a signal honour for me to devote this lecture to Mohamed Suffian, a just judge, a brilliant scholar, a man whose modesty, integrity and honour have never been affected by office or power.

The Quest for World Order

I have chosen as the topic of my lecture, "The Quest for a World Order". The quest for an international order is as old as the advent of national states. However, in the old days, relations between states were governed less by law than by might. Small nations were often preyed upon by militarily more powerful nations. Even during the nineteenth century in Europe, small nations were often sacrificed to maintain peace among the more powerful states. Lord Castlereagh, one of the architects of the Concert of Europe, which resulted from the Congress of Vienna, frankly stated that he "could not harbour any moral or political repugnance" against the act of handing Saxony over to Prussia, since the King of Saxony had "put himself in the position of having to be sacrificed to the future tranquility of Europe."[1]

The League of Nations

The first major attempt to create a world order was made immediately following the end of the First World War. Although the US President Woodrow Wilson, was an ardent advocate of the League of Nations, the United States failed to join the new world organization because of the isolationist sentiments in the US Congress and because of the uncompromising attitude adopted by President Wilson towards his domestic critics. The failure of the United States to join the League of Nations is thought by some to be one of the reasons for its eventual failure.

The Principle of Collective Security

The League of Nations had been created to implement the principle of collective security. The idea was that wherever an act of aggression

---

[1] Guglielmo Ferrero, *The Reconstruction of Europe: Tallyrand and the Congress of Vienna, 1814–1815* (translated by Theodore R Jaeckel): 1941, New York, GP Putnam & Sons, p. 178.

occurred, the whole international community would combine to defend the victim. By doing so, the League would be defending not only the victim of aggression but peace itself. Article 11 of the Covenant declared that "any war or threat of war, whether immediately affecting any of the members of the League or not, is hereby declared a matter of concern to the whole League". When an act of aggression took place, the League's Council was to "advise upon the means by which this obligation should be fulfilled". Under art 16, members were under an absolute obligation to apply economic and communications sanctions against another member which had gone to war in disregard to its covenant. But they were under no obligation to take any stronger action. If economic sanctions were to fail, the Council might recommend armed action to defend the victim. But no member was automatically obliged to respond.

An Epidemic of Lawlessness

When put to the test, the League of Nations failed to defend the victims of aggression against their aggressors. Italy attacked and colonized Ethiopia. Japan conquered Manchuria. Germany annexed the Rhineland, Austria and Czechoslovakia. In none of these cases did the League impose economic sanctions against the aggressor or recommend armed action to defend the victim. In 1939, when Russia attacked Finland, the League finally acted to expel the former from its membership. But, as George Scott commented, "... when viewed against the omissions, the erosions, the failures of the past, and the reality of the world scene at that moment, the incident [of expelling Russia from the League] must seem like no more than an irrelevant piece of play-acting".[2]

Causes of the League's Failure

Why did the League of Nations fail?

---
[2] George Scott, *The Rise, and Fall of the League of Nations:* 1974, New York, McMillan, p. 398.

Evan Luard the author of *A History of the UN*, has suggested the following reasons for the failure of the League. *First*, "A purely voluntary commitment to go to the defence of other States if they were attacked was far too feeble to be of any value ... Clearly, a far more specific obligation, based on collective and not individual judgment, would be required."[3] *Second*, "The League had collapsed because it had no 'teeth.'[4] It was thus almost universally concluded that, to be effective, any subsequent organization must be equipped with some more substantial military power to implement its decisions."[5] *Third*, "Most of the disputes of the time were essentially political rather than legal in character; and it was political procedures rather than legal which were required to resolve them effectively. International law, and the legal procedures which applied it, might have their part to play in resolving certain kinds of international dispute, though usually not the major ones. But they were unlikely to be able to maintain for long a peaceful and harmonious order unless they were supplemented by procedures which were political rather than legal in style."[6]

The Second Try at World Order

While the Second World War was still raging, the leaders of the three principal allies, Roosevelt, Churchill and Stalin, were already planning to set up a new world organization after the war. Their representatives met at Dumbarton Oaks in Washington, DC to hammer out the salient features of the new organization. The Charter of the UN, approved in San Francisco, was based essentially upon the accord reached at Dumbarton Oaks.

The UN's Collective Security System

There were certain similarities and differences between the UN and the League of Nations. Like the League, the UN would have an Assembly

---

[3] Evan Luard, *A Hisory of the UN*, Vol. 1, 1982, New York, St. Martin's Press, p. 6.
[4] *Ibid*.
[5] *Ibid*. at p. 8.
[6] *Ibid*. at p. 10.

consisting of all its members, a smaller council, a secretariat and a court. The Charter of the UN was designed to avoid some of the defects of the League's covenant. For example, the League had to make all its decisions by unanimity, thus giving every member a veto. In the UN, the General Assembly would decide by either a simple majority or, for important questions, a two-thirds majority. In the Security Council, the five great powers were given permanent seats and the power of veto. Member states were under an obligation to respond to a demand of the Security Council to use force to resist aggression. A force, in the form of earmarked units made available by member States, was to be permanently available to the Security Council for this purpose. Finally, the five great powers which were allies in the Second World War, the United States, USSR, UK, France and China were members from the beginning and were pledged to work together in maintaining the peace of the world.

The UN Paralysed by the Cold War

The efficacy of the collective security system of the US was based upon the assumption that the war-time allies would continue to work together after the war. The assumption proved fallacious as the alliance between the Western powers and the Soviet Union broke down as soon as the war ended and the era of the Cold War began. The polarization between the East and West became so pervasive and intense that almost every dispute or conflict, anywhere in the world, became tainted by the East–West confrontation. As a result, with very rare exceptions, the collective security system enshrined in the UN Charter, was paralysed.

Is the Cold War Over?

In recent months, both President Mikhail Gorbachev of the Soviet Union and President George Bush of the United States have declared that the Cold War is over. The words have been backed up by deeds. The first achievement was the INF Treaty which, for the first time in the history of disarmament, wiped out a whole class of intermediate-range nuclear weapons. The two superpowers have resumed their Strategic Arms Reduction Talks (START) in Geneva. The sticking point in these negotiations is to work out a verification procedure for sea-launched cruise missiles. If the START talks succeed the two superpowers are likely to agree to reduce their strategic missiles by 50 percent. A third hopeful development is in the field of conventional arms in Europe. As is well known, the Warsaw Pact allies possess a preponderance over NATO in conventional arms. The Soviet Union has accepted the principle of asymmetrical reductions. Both the Warsaw Pact and NATO have submitted radical proposals to the Vienna talks on conventional arms (CFE) which would drastically reduce every category of conventional weapons including the number of US troops stationed in Western Europe and the Soviet troops in Eastern Europe. The two sides are also engaged in a series of confidence-building measures as well as in the reconsideration of defence doctrines and defence postures. Their mutual goal seems to be to achieve security at vastly reduced numbers.

Impact on Regional Conflicts in the Third World

Have the positive developments between the two superpowers and their respective military alliances in Europe, had a beneficial impact on the regional conflicts in the Third World? The answer is yes. The two superpowers are seeking to extricate themselves from such conflicts and are even cooperating to resolve them. Let me just cite a few examples. The Soviet Union has withdrawn its troops from Afghanistan. The United States and the Soviet Union cooperated to negotiate the implementation of Security Council Resolution 435, which would enable Namibia to accede to independence and which led to the withdrawal of Cuban troops from Angola. The influence of the Soviet Union was probably one of the factors which led Vietnam to decide to withdraw its troops from Cambodia by the end of September this year. The Soviet Union has informed the United States that it has stopped the supply of arms to the Sandinista government in Nicaragua and was prepared to work with the

United States to bring peace to Central America. Even in the Middle-East, the Bush administration has expressed its willingness to work with the Soviet Union to resolve the Arab–Israeli conflict.

Regional Conflicts Likely to Continue

I would like, however, to strike a note of warning. One should not assume that regional conflicts in the Third World will disappear just because the two superpowers will cease to inject their rivalry into them. The fact is that most of the conflicts in the Third World have indigenous causes — tribal, racial, religious and linguistic conflicts, disputes over boundaries and the hegemonic ambitions of regional powers. Superpower involvement has often exacerbated these conflicts but it was seldom the cause of the conflicts. As one of my esteemed African friends said to me recently: "Very soon, we will not have the excuse of blaming our conflicts on the two superpowers. We will have to confront the unpleasant reality that most of the conflicts in the Third World are of our own making."

Strengthen Regional Unity

If I am correct in predicting that regional conflicts are likely to endure, is there anything that can be done about them? I would like to suggest one possible approach. Let us use Southeast Asia as an example. During the past 22 years, one of the most remarkable achievements in Southeast Asia has been the formation and progressive strengthening of ASEAN. The six member states of ASEAN have woven a tapestry of cooperative arrangements which bind them. They have developed a habit of consulting one another and of taking the others' interests into account when deciding on a policy. Because of ASEAN, bilateral differences between member states have either been resolved or tranquilized. Because of the progress which ASEAN has made in these past 22 years, mutual confidence has increased, mistrust and misunderstanding have dissipated, and the danger of conflict has grown more remote.

Southeast Asia

In September this year, Vietnam has pledged to withdraw its troops from Cambodia. If the Vietnamese withdrawal is accompanied by an internationally acceptable comprehensive political solution, leading to a quadripartite interim coalition, a credible international peace-keeping force and free elections to enable the Khmers to exercise their right to self-determination, the principal source of tension in Southeast Asia for the past ten year will disappear. I can then foresee the normalization of relations between ASEAN and the states of Indochina. In time, as mutual confidence grows and trade and investment expand, the countries of Southeast Asia could learn to live with one another as good neighbours. When that happens, a Southeast Asian forum, like the CSCE in Europe, consisting of all ten states of the region, could well be a helpful development which would enable the countries of Southeast Asia to enhance their cooperation and to reduce misunderstanding through the process of dialogue and conciliation.

The Third Try at World Order

The end of the Cold War and the emergence of Mikhail Gorbachev as the new Soviet leader have raised the tantalizing thought that the UN may be about to enter into a new and creative phase of life. New Soviet thinking about the UN began on 17 September 1987 by the publication of an article by Gorbachev in Pravda. In it, Gorbachev embraced Hammarskjold's vision of the UN as a "place for the mutual search for a balance of differing, contradictory, yet real, interests of the contemporary community of states and nations". He called for "drastic intensification and expansion of the cooperation of states in uprooting international terrorism" and proposed the creation under the UN aegis of a tribunal to investigate acts of international terrorism. He indicated agreement with the proposition that "the world cannot be considered secure if human rights are violated in it" and held it "necessary that national legislation and administrative rules in the humanitarian sphere everywhere be brought in accordance with international obligations and standards". He observed that one "should not forget the capacities of the International Court either" and proposed that the General Assembly and the Security Council approach it more often "for consultative opinions on international disputes". "Its mandatory jurisdiction," he added, "should be recognized by all on mutually agreed upon conditions. The permanent members of the Security Council, taking into account special responsibility, are to make the first step in that direction."

Soviet Proposals to Strengthen the UN

One year later, on 22 September 1988, the Soviet Union circulated an aide-memoire entitled "Towards comprehensive security through the enhancement of the role of the United Nations". The aide-memoire proposed the "extensive use of UN peace-keeping operations' and the affirmation of the primacy of international law in interstate relations". The memorandum also proposed that UN observers could be stationed along "frontiers within the territory of a country that seeks to protect itself from outside interference at the request of that country alone". The memorandum proposed granting the Secretary-General the right, without further authorization, to dispatch military observer missions and fact-finding missions to a state or states where a conflict, or outside interference, threatens the peace. It also envisaged fact-finding and truce observation on the authority of the General Assembly with the consent of the state or states on whose territory these activities are to be carried out. As an onus of its good faith, the Soviet Union has begun to pay, in convertible currency, its UN budget arrears and even to pay for UN peacekeeping operations.

Will the West and NAM Respond?

The new proposals and suggestions of the Soviet Union to strengthen the UN are nothing short of revolutionary. They represent a complete reversal of the policies and postures which the Soviet Union had pursued in the past. How will the West, especially the United States, respond? According to Thomas M. Franck, the United States has accepted the challenge presented by these Soviet initiatives and the State Department is authorized to prepare counter proposals.[7] Franck is also of the view that the new mood in Moscow and Washington is generally viewed by the governments of the Third World as being beneficial to them.[8]

A Unique Moment in History

I agree with Professor Franck when he wrote:[9]

> There thus exists at this moment a unique opportunity, a rare conjunction of the principal tendencies in the international system. For the first time since the creation of the United Nations, the United States, the Soviets and the Non-Aligned Movement appear able to form a common view of the organization's systemic capabilities: a view neither excessively optimistic nor mired in cynical pessimism. Moreover, all three groupings are moving away from fear-based, or ideology-driven policies toward pragmatic politics of overlapping national self-interest. Above all, the three principal tendencies appear to understand that the system offers sound machinery ... for negotiating and administering agreed responses to humanity's recognized common enemies of poverty, illness and environmental degradation.

Conclusion

We are living in a unique moment of world history. Man's first try for a world order, the League of Nations, foundered in an epidemic of lawlessness which led to the Second World War. At the end of the Second World

---

[7] Thomas M Franck, Vol. 83, 1989, *American Journal of International Law*, p. 540.
[8] *Ibid.*
[9] *Ibid.*

War, the international commmunity made a second try at world order by establishing the United Nations. The Charter of the UN was intended to cure the deficiencies of the League's covenant. The Charter envisaged a system of collective security to maintain world peace and gave the Security Council the teeth to enforce its decisions. The Charter was not drawn up by a group of utopianists but by Roosevelt, Churchill and Stalin. The UN has not, however, been able to function effectively because of the Cold War and, less importantly, by the occasional irresponsible behaviour of the Third World majority in the General Assembly. Now that the Cold War is coming to an end we are faced with a new opportunity to breathe life into the provisions of the UN Charter. Let us, the East, the West, and the non-aligned, seize this opportunity to make the third try at world order a success. History may not present us with another opportunity.

[Originally published in the *Malayan Law Journal*, 25 August 1989.]

Will There be a Clash of Cultures Between the US and East Asia?*

Introduction

The collapse of the Soviet Union, the liberation of Eastern Europe and the end of the Cold War were events which brought one epoch of world history to an end. For almost 50 years, the world was divided into two ideological camps, one led by the United States, the other by the Soviet Union. When the Cold War suddenly ended there was joy in the world. Humankind hoped that there would be a new era of world peace.

In the United States, the mood among many intellectuals was one of triumphalism. Francis Fukuyama captured that mood in his famous essay, "The End of History".[1] Fukuyama did not mean the end of history in the literal sense but in the Hegelian sense. His thesis is that with the demise of communism there is no alternative coherent system of belief capable of challenging the Western concepts of democracy and capitalism. For a time, this view seemed to enjoy much support.

However, in the summer of 1993, Harvard Professor, Samuel P. Huntington, published an essay in *Foreign Affairs,* entitled "The Clash of Civilizations?".[2] In this famous essay, Huntington expressed the following hypotheses:

1. the fundamental source of conflict in this new world will not be primarily ideological or primarily economic;
2. the great divisions among humankind and the dominating source of conflict will be cultural;

---

*This is the third of three lectures delivered by Tommy Koh, in 1995, at Stanford University in his capacity as the Second Arthur and Frank Payne lecturer on the Global Community and Its Challenges.

3. the principal conflicts of global politics will occur between nations and groups of different civilizations; and
4. a central focus of conflict for the immediate future will be between the West and several Islamic-Confucianist states.

East Asia consists of societies such as China, Japan, Korea, Vietnam, Taiwan, Hong Kong and Singapore, which are often described as Confucianist, and others, such as, Indonesia, Malaysia and Brunei, which are predominantly Muslim. If Huntington's hypotheses are right, then we are likely to see, in the future, conflicts between the United States and East Asia based upon their cultural or civilizational differences. Is Huntington right?

America as a Beacon to the World

Many Asians do not understand America. America is not a normal country. From the time of its birth, Americans have believed that their country was founded with a divine mission. Owen Harries, the editor of the journal, *The National Interest,* has described that mission as follows:

> A concern for promoting democracy and liberty and what we have come to call "human rights" is bred in the American bone. From Thomas Jefferson's proclamation of the newly formed country as the "Empire of Liberty" onwards, it has been an article of faith that the country exists, not only to promote the freedom of its citizens, but to serve the cause of freedom throughout the world. Disagreement has centered mostly on how best to do that — whether by example alone, or by active crusading.[3]

Since this belief is an article of faith, it is like America's secular religion. A believer in a faith would not normally subject his beliefs to intellectual analysis or to the empirical test. Thus, Americans have never hesitated in their proselytizing mission abroad in spite of the vast discrepancies between American ideals and American realities at home. Slavery, the mistreatment of native Americans, discriminations against minorities, the many imperfections of the American democracy never shook the American people's belief that God had intended their country to be a beacon to the world. Asians must understand this historical background or they will often be puzzled by American rhetoric and behaviour and they may misconstrue American motives.

Democracy and Human Rights in United States Foreign Policy

The promotion of democracy, human rights and, to a lesser extent, capitalism, will always be part of United States foreign policy. It is, of course, not possible for any country to construct a foreign policy on a single issue. The importance of this issue has to be weighed against the importance of other interests, such as, security, economics, etc. The weightage given to democracy and human rights will vary from one country to another and from one administration to another. There is also a constant struggle in Washington between the ideologues and pragmatists. Does the Clinton Administration seek to promote democracy and human rights in East Asia? The answer is yes. Let me cite three sources to support my answer.

First, in his statement to the Senate Foreign Relations Committee on 31 March 1993, the Assistant Secretary for East Asia and the Pacific, Winston Lord, said:

> ... as President Clinton has emphasized, promoting democracy must be one of the central pillars of our foreign policy ... Thus, even as we deal pragmatically with authoritarian governments we should press universal principles. Whenever possible, we should work with others to expand the frontiers of freedom.

Second, in an address to the Center for Asian Pacific Affairs of the Asia Foundation, on 28 June 1994, the Assistant Secretary for Democracy, Human Rights and Labour, John Shattuck, said:

> Protecting human rights and promoting democracy are integral elements of US foreign policy ... some Asian governments see

democracy as a threat to their sovereignty and authority. These governments attack the very idea that human rights are universal. As a result, there are more tensions in our bilateral relations with some Asian governments over human rights than with governments elsewhere.

Third, in an address to the Overseas Development Council, in Washington, DC, on 13 October 1993, National Security Adviser, Anthony Lake, said, "the successor to a doctrine of containment should be a strategy of enlargement — a strategy of American efforts to enlarge the community of market democracies".

A Critique of United States Foreign Policy

Owen Harries has expressed the view that United States foreign policy suffers from three defects.[4] He calls them the three "Cs": consequences, circumstances and capacity.

What does Harries mean by the problem of "consequences"? His argument is that "Politics is about consequences, not about purity of intention, not about therapy and good feeling".[5] He quotes Max Weber's view that whilst an individual is free to follow the ethic that one must always do what is right regardless of consequences, a government has an obligation to take into account foreseeable consequences in deciding its actions. In other words, once human rights "enters the realm of politics, the promotion of human rights has to take its place in a hierarchy of interests and values, including such basic concerns as the promotion of security, peace, order, prosperity. The place of human rights ... in that hierarchy will vary from occasion to occasion, and no responsible government will ever be able to put them always at the top ... This way of thinking is uncongenial to Americans. They are inclined to approach politics in terms of an ethic of absolute ends, one that scorns discrimination and compromise and demands consistent rectitude".[6]

Harries goes on to say that, "insofar as a country's rhetoric and posture are absolute and moralistic in character, it inevitably leaves itself open to the charge of hypocrisy and double-standard. Because in the real world such a posture is unsustainable and in practice it has to discriminate. Thus the difference in the American approach to human rights in China and human rights in, say, Saudi Arabia has provided Asian critics with an easy target".[7] Also, "when push comes to shove, the United States cannot sustain the position it has taken".[8] The reversal of Clinton's position on China's MFN status is a case in point.

The second problem with United States foreign policy, according to Harries, is the problem of "circumstances". His criticism is that Western liberals in general tend to work on the maxim that "one size fits all", ignoring the specific circumstances of each country. Harries quotes, with approval, the following quotation from the British philosopher and statesman, Edmund Burke:

> circumstances ... give in reality to every political principle its distinguishing color and discriminating effect. The circumstances are what render every civil and political scheme beneficial or noxious to mankind.[9]

The third problem is "capacity". Harries argues that "no country has the capacity to impose democracy on another. Democracy is essentially a do-it-yourself enterprise not an export commodity or a gift to bestow. Before intervening in the affairs of another country in the name of human rights and democracy, therefore, a government should consider carefully its capacity to achieve intended purposes, rather than to create unintended ones ... American understanding of other societies and cultures is not profound, its experience of dealing with them is not extensive ... its attention span tends to be short. And once engaged in an enterprise it is impatient for quick results and eager to move on to something else".[10] The result is that, "[i]t is very easy to create, and leave, an unstable mess which others have to live with. In other words, it is easy to behave irresponsibly".[11]

Do Asians and Americans Share the Same Values?

David Hitchcock, a retired member of the United States Foreign Service, who knows East Asia well, wrote a most interesting report in 1994, entitled "Asian Values and the United States, How Much Conflict?".[12] In 1994, Hitchcock interviewed over 100 persons in Singapore, Kuala Lumpur, Jakarta, Bangkok, Shanghai, Beijing, Seoul and Tokyo. The persons interviewed were think-tank experts, officials, businessmen, journalists, religious and cultural leaders. What were the principal results of Hitchcock's survey?

First, he found a surprising degree of congruence between the personal and societal values of Northeast Asians and Southeast Asians (see Annex I). On personal values, Asians from the two sub-regions gave equal emphasis to the importance of hard work, respect for learning, honesty, self-reliance, self-discipline and the fulfilment of obligations. On societal values, the two groups of Asians agree on the importance of orderly society, harmony, respect for authority, official accountability and consensus.

Second, he found both similarities and differences between Americans and Asians on personal values and societal values (see Annex II).

Third, on personal values, there were two, self-reliance and hard work, which were listed by both Asians and Americans among the five most important personal values. What were the differences? Asians emphasized the importance of respect for learning, honesty and self-discipline whereas Americans emphasized achieving success in life, personal achievement and helping others.

Fourth, on societal values, there were also similarities and differences. Asians and Americans agree on the importance of accountability of public officials and freedom of expression. What were the important differences? They were:

(a) orderly society (71 percent of the Asians versus 11 percent of the Americans);
(b) personal freedom (82 percent of the Americans versus 32 percent of the Asians); and

(c) individual rights (78 percent of the Americans versus 29 percent of the Asians).

Hitchcock's survey findings confirm my impression that there are significant differences between the personal and societal values of Asians and Americans. To recapitulate, Asians emphasize the importance of orderly society whereas Americans emphasize the importance of personal freedom and individual rights. Asians emphasize the importance of respect for learning and self-discipline whereas Americans emphasize the importance of success, personal achievement and helping others. Given these differences it is therefore not surprising that East Asia and the United States do not hold identical views on Democracy and Human Rights.

Asian and American Perspectives on Democracy

In a paper presented to a conference on "Democracy and Capitalism: Asian and American Perspectives", held in Singapore in January 1993, Sam Huntington offered the following definition of "democracy":

> A modern nation-state has a democratic political system to the extent that its most powerful decision-makers are selected through fair, honest, periodic elections in which candidates freely compete for votes and in which virtually all the adult population is eligible to vote ... According to this definition, elections are the essence of democracy. From this follow other features characteristic of democratic systems. Free, fair, and competitive elections are only possible if there is some measure of freedom of speech, assembly and press, and if opposition candidates and parties are able to criticize incumbents without fear of retaliation. Democracy is thus not only a means of constituting authority, it is also a means of limiting authority.[13]

In his book, *The Third Wave,* Huntington also made the point that a democracy has not passed the test until it has experienced two turnovers of power.[14] In the same book, Huntington acknowledges that democracy takes different forms in different cultures. He also argues that American democracy differs in its origins, theory, development and institutions from European democracy. American democracy, Huntington states, is a very distinctive, even peculiar phenomenon, which in practice has little relevance to other societies. Huntington quoted James Bryce who, in the 1890s, summed up the central elements of the American political creed as follows:

1. the individual has sacred rights;
2. the source of political power is the people;
3. all governments are limited by law and the people;
4. local government is to be preferred to national government;
5. the majority is wiser than the minority; and
6. the less government the better.[15]

In her paper presented to the same conference, Chan Heng Chee argued the view that not all democracies must resemble the Anglo-American version. Could we not have Asian democracies and African democracies? She wrote, "curiously, when we discuss Asian art, literature and architecture, we readily look for and appreciate the difference between the West and non-Western countries. But when we come to examine political institutions and political development, there is an expectation of parallel developments as well as end products".[16]

Chan Heng Chee also pointed out the arbitrariness with which the West classifies countries as democratic or non-democratic Taking Singapore as an example, she pointed out that the Freedom House Survey, 1991–1992, classifies Singapore as "partly free",[17] Huntington classifies Singapore as "non-democratic",[18] and Fukuyama classifies Singapore as a "liberal democracy".[19] So, depending on which Western authority you consult, Singapore is described as "non-democratic" on the one extreme and as a "liberal democracy" on the other.

Chan agrees with Huntington that the holding of free and fair elections to select political leaders is the litmus test of a democracy. She contends, however, that Asian democracies, unlike Western democracies, possess the following four characteristics:

1. A communitarian sense which teaches that the individual is important as part of a group or society rather than the notion that the individual is the centrepiece of democracy and society;
2. A greater acceptance of and respect for authority and hierarchy whether it is India, China, Japan or the countries of Southeast Asia;
3. The dominant party can remain in power for two or three decades or more as long as they continue to perform effectively as the ruling party; and
4. Nearly all the Asian democracies have a centralized bureaucracy and a strong state.[20]

Huntington agrees with Chan that, if "democratic institutions take root in Asia they will result from very different forces and are likely to take very different forms from those of American democracy".[21] Huntington is, however, not sure to what extent the culture in East Asia will prevent or postpone the movements towards democracy that economic development encourages. Huntington is also not sure whether, apart from Japan, the other Asian democracies satisfy the "first criterion for democracy ... equitable and open competition for votes between political parties with an absence or minimal levels of government harassment or restriction of opposition groups".[22] These are, in my view, legitimate questions.

Culture and Democracy

There is no consensus, either among Asians or Americans, on whether East Asia's culture will prevent or postpone the development of Western-style democracy. Among the Americans, Huntington seems to think that it will. Richard Shifter, Special Assistant to the President and Counsellor in the National Security Council, disagrees.[23] Shifter argues that there is no reason why the ideas of the Enlightenment should not become universal. He quotes, with approval, the view of the West Indian novelist, V. S. Naipaul, who has argued that Western civilization is the universal civilization that fits all men.[24]

At the 1993 Singapore Conference, one American participant expressed the view that, "cultural differences are real and do matter. In many Asian countries the Confucian heritage remains a strong barrier to liberal democracy ... Thus, although many in the West remain hopeful about the political consequences of economic development in China, it is more likely that an authoritarian pluralist model will emerge than a system akin to the liberal Anglo-American model".[25]

There is also no consensus among Asian intellectuals. Singapore's Senior Minister, Lee Kuan Yew, has expressed the view that:

> The system of government in China will change. It will change in Korea, Taiwan, Vietnam. It is changing in Singapore. But it will not end up like the American or British or French or German systems. What are we all seeking? A form of government that will be comfortable, because it meets our needs, is not oppressive, and maximizes our opportunities.[26]

The Korean leader, Kim Dae Jung strongly disagrees. In a reply to Lee Kuan Yew, he states:

> Asia should lose no time in firmly establishing democracy and strengthening human rights. The biggest obstacle is not its cultural heritage but the resistance of authoritarian rulers and their apologists ... Culture is not necessarily our destiny. Democracy is.[27]

The report of the Commission for a New Asia, entitled "Towards A New Asia", came down somewhere between Lee Kuan Yew and Kim Dae Jung. It stated that:

> if democracy that is resilient and durable is to take strong and permanent root in Asian societies, it must be deeply embedded in Asian values and mores and embrace institutions and processes

special to specific culture. This must not be made into an excuse for foot-dragging and for the adoption of democratic forms without democratic substance. We must see through attempts to equate regime stability with national stability ... Yet the proposition holds: each society must find the most fitting form of democracy for its peoples.[28]

In his interesting paper, entitled "Democratic Transition in Asia: The Role of the International Community", Dr Muthiah Alagappa of the East-West Center, urged that:

Promotion of democracy will be more successful if the effort is directed towards strengthening long-term forces that will make democratic principles a durable part of the domestic political discourse rather than demanding a quick transition by the governing elite ... the focus should be on promoting socioeconomic development, strengthening civil society, and building political institutions.[29]

Asian and American Perspectives on Human Rights

In the debate on human rights one finds the same divisions as in the case of democracy. Not all American intellectuals and officials share the same view. Some are more willing to recognize the merit in the arguments of some Asian governments and intellectuals than others. In the same way, some Asian officials and intellectuals have put forward a coherent alternative view to that of the West whilst other Asians strongly support the views of the West. Yash Ghai, of Hong Kong University, has, for example, written a paper for the Asia Foundation, in November 1994, entitled "Human Rights and Governance: The Asia Debate" (Occasional Paper No. 4), in which he criticized the views of Asian governments on this subject. There is, however, a majoritarian view on each side. Prior to the 1993 United Nations Conference on Human Rights in Vienna, the Asian governments held their regional meeting in Bangkok. With the exception of Japan, they were able to agree on a common stand which was embodied in the Bangkok Declaration.

The Prime Minister of Thailand, Chuan Leekpai, spoke for most of his Asian colleagues when he observed that although "there is only one set of fundamental human rights for whatever part of the world", it is only natural that the implementation of these rights should "vary because of differences in socio-economic, historical and cultural backgrounds". Also, at Bangkok, most Asian representatives gave special emphasis to the view that would place economic growth and community development ahead of individual freedoms.[30]

In Vienna, the West was furious with the Asians, accusing them of trying to undermine the principle of universality and of seeking to subordinate civil and political rights to social and economic rights. How were the differences resolved? According to one Asian representative in Vienna:

> The result after weeks of wrangling was a predictable diplomatic compromise ambiguous enough so that all could live with it, but that settled very few things. There was no real dialogue between Asia and the West, no genuine attempt to address the issues. If anything, the Vienna Conference may only have hardened attitudes on both sides and increased the deep skepticism with which many Asian countries regard Western posturing on human rights.[31]

Let me try to disaggregate the issues and deal with some of the more important ones.

First, is there a core of human rights which are universal in character and from which there must be no derogation? The answer is yes. Asians and Americans agree that genocide, murder, torture and slavery should be universally condemned. The problem lies outside this core. Is it ever justifiable to infringe on the liberty of the individual? Is it ever justifiable to impose curbs on the freedom of the press? Is it true that human rights and economic progress are inseparable companions? What should the East Asians do to promote the cause of human rights in their own countries? What, if anything, should the United States do to promote the cause of human rights in East Asia?

Second, is it ever justifiable to infringe on the liberty of the individual in the interest of his society? Let us take the fight against the drug menace as an example. In his interview by *Foreign Affairs,* Lee Kuan Yew, said:

> Let me give you an example that encapsulates the whole difference between America and Singapore. America has a vicious drag problem. How does it solve it? It goes around the world helping other anti-narcotic agencies to try and stop the suppliers. It pays for helicopters, defoliating agents and so on. And when provoked, it captures the President of Panama and brings him to trial in Florida. Singapore does not have that option. We can't go to Burma and capture the warlords there. What we can do is pass a law which says that any customs officer or policeman who sees anybody in Singapore behaving suspiciously, leading him to suspect the person is under the influence of drugs, can require that man to have his urine tested. If the sample is found to contain drugs, the man immediately goes for treatment. In America if you did that it would be an invasion of the individual's rights and you would be sued.[32]

The issue can be generalized. Every society needs to strike an appropriate balance between, on the one hand, the rights of the individual and, on the other hand, the rights of the community. If an Asian country decides that in the interest of fighting the drug menace, it is appropriate for the state to have the right to ask an individual for a sample of his urine, why should the West condemn such a decision as a violation of the individual's liberty?

Third, is it ever justifiable to impose curbs on the freedom of the press? The freedom of the press is protected by the United States Constitution. The United States Supreme Court has, over time, elevated that right to almost an absolute right. The Supreme Court, for example, struck down a law of Florida giving individuals, who have been attacked by the press, a right of reply even though such a right is enshrined in the American Convention on Human Rights. The Court has made it almost impossible for an American, in public life, to sue the press for libel because he or she will have to prove actual malice. In addition, the freedom of speech is stretched to such an extent that it is deemed to protect speeches preaching religious hatred and racial hatred.

Many of the countries in Southeast Asia are plural societies in which race, religion and language are emotionally explosive issues. These countries are relatively new and fragile. Many Asians have experienced in the past three decades, rioting and murder, resulting from racial and religious misunderstandings. Given this background and present reality, is it wrong for these countries to curb the freedom of speech and of the press, to forbid statements advocating racial or religious hatred, in order to preserve social harmony?

I should also point out that not all Asians or Americans regard the American press as a model to emulate. Let me quote from two Americans. Carl Bernstein, one of the two *Washington Post* reporters of Watergate fame, said recently:

> The monster that ate the media — ravenous sensation-and-scandal machine — is consuming decent journalism and relegating reporting and respect for context to an adjunct of the new porn-journalism, an adjunct used by many of our giant media corporations to clothe themselves in respectability as they increasingly make their real bucks off thrash. Since Watergate and the resignation of Richard Nixon, the American Press has been engaged in an orgy of self-congratulation. No attitude, it seems to me, is more unjustified.[33]

George Stephanopoulos, the former White House Communications Director and currently Special Adviser to President Clinton, stated that:

> The working, day-to-day political press is neither liberal nor conservative. They are adversarial. Certainly, that is a noble tradition in American journalism. But, today it is fair to question whether the adversarial stance has gone too far in its obsession with conflict, controversy and scandal. The only way to break through into the realm of public attention is with controversy. As a result, less and less factual news gets out every day.[34]

Stephanopoulos goes on to say:

> The deeper social problem, I agree, is that the adversarial media culture is the enemy of community. You can't build a consensus or coherence in the society around anything if the automatic stance of the media towards any person or movement is that "they are morally corrupt, don't believe anything they say" ... it is ... corrosive in a free society because it devalues everything.[35]

Fourth, is it true that human rights and economic progress are inseparable companions? John Shattuck thinks so. He said, "the interrelationship between economics, security, and human rights means that policies in those three areas not only should but must proceed in tandem — that these issues are, ultimately, all of a piece", Aryeh Neier, the former Executive Director of Human Rights Watch has argued that:

> Open societies around the world are flourishing economically to a far greater extent than closed societies or societies that were closed recently. There are, of course, exceptions. They demonstrate that political freedom, by itself, is no guarantee of prosperity and that the denial of political freedom does not ensure economic failure.[37]

Bilahari Kausikan does not agree with the view of the two Americans I have cited. He argued that the American dogma does not accord with East Asia's historical experience. He wrote:

> That experience sees order and stability as preconditions for economic growth, and growth as the necessary foundation of any political order that claims to advance human dignity ... The Asian record of economic success is a powerful claim that cannot be easily dismissed.[38]

The empirical evidence does not support either view. There are societies which have a good record in human rights and a poor record in economic development. On the other hand, we also have societies which enjoy political order and stability and have failed economically. The economic success or failure of a country would appear to depend less on its human rights record than on the degree of its economic freedom.

Fifth, what, if anything, should the United States do to promote the cause of human rights in East Asia? I have two suggestions. My first suggestion is "Physician, heal thyself". America should set its own house in order if it wants its prescriptions to be taken seriously by East Asia. The fact that America is in serious trouble is admitted by leaders of both parties.

The new Speaker of the House of Representatives, Newt Gingrich, in an address to the nation, on 7 April 1995, said:

> ... I believe we must remake Government for reasons much larger than saving money or improving services. The fact is, no civilization can survive with 12-year-olds having babies, with 15-year-olds killing each other, with 17-year-olds dying of AIDS, with 18-year-olds getting diplomas they can't even read ... As a father of two daughters, I can't ignore the terror and worry parents in our inner cities feel for their children. Within half a mile of this Capitol, your Capitol, drugs, violence and despair threaten the lives of our citizens.

Speaking on 13 November 1993, in the church in Tennessee where Martin Luther King junior preached his last sermon, President Clinton asked what Dr King would have said, had he lived to see that day. President Clinton said:

> He would say, I did not live and die to see the American family destroyed. I did not live and die to see 13-year-old boys get automatic weapons to gun down 9-year-olds just for the kick of it. I did not live and die to see young people destroy their lives with drugs and then build fortunes destroying the lives of others.

Gertrude Himmelfarb, in her new book, *The De-Moralization of Society*,[38] gave the following report on the state of social pathology in America:

1. the rate of illegitimate birth in the United States rose from 3 percent in 1920, to 5 percent in 1960, to 11 percent in 1970, to 18 percent in 1980 and to over 30 percent in 1991;

2. the rate of illegitimate birth in the African-American community in 1991 was 68 percent;
3. the United States has the highest incidence of teenage pregnancy among the industrialized societies, at 10 percent in 1990; and
4. crime is the major concern of the American people. In 1987, the Justice Department reported that eight out of every ten Americans would be a victim of violent crime at least once in their lives. As for non-violent crime, in 1992 alone, one in every four households experienced a crime.

The family is under siege in America as it is in Britain. The restoration of the moral health of society will depend, in part, on the success or failure in preserving the institution of family in those societies. These are the wise words of Jonathan Sacks, the Chief Rabbi of the United Hebrew Congregation of the Commonwealth:

> The family is not one social institution among others, nor is it simply one lifestyle choice among many. It is the best means we have yet discovered for nurturing future generations, and for enabling children to grow in a matrix of stability and love ... It is where one generation passes on its values to the next and ensures the continuity of civilization. For any society, the family is the crucible of its future.[39]

My second suggestion is for the United States to heed the advice of the wise Professor, Robert A. Scalapino, of University of California at Berkeley. He said:

> Multilaterization ... offers the best possibility for advancing the human rights agenda ... While there is a growing consensus on the desirability of universal values and a set of primary rights, there is considerably less agreement about the means to attain these goals. Multilateralism is preferable to bilateral activism because the latter approach heightens tensions and as a result is less effective and perceived to be less just.[40]

Don Emmerson, one of America's foremost scholars on Southeast Asia would agree with Scalapino. He wrote:

> Far from persuading the ASEAN states that they really ought to adopt American-style democracy or American-style notions of the sanctity and precedence of the individual over the community, economic growth had emboldened some Southeast Asia leaders, notably in Singapore, Kuala Lumpur, and Jakarta, to defend an alternative, putatively "Asian way" emphasizing order, social discipline, and the priority of the community over the individual. Far from pushing the region away from authoritarian temptations, American *moralpolitik* had in the end helped to trigger into being a counterimage of itself.[41]

Sixth, what should East Asia do to promote the cause of human rights in their respective countries? I will begin my answer by stating what East Asia should not do. It should not cease to uphold the traditional virtues of strong family, hard work, thrift, reverence for education, respect for elders, responsibility for the consequences of one's actions, self-discipline, self-reliance and social harmony. Some of these are not uniquely Asian virtues. They used to be called "Victorian" values in England. They were part of the "Protestant" ethic of America. As Margaret Thatcher has recalled:

> We were taught to work jolly hard. We were taught to prove yourself; we were taught to live within our income. You were taught that cleanliness is next to godliness. You were taught self-respect. You were taught always to give a hand to your neighbour. You were taught tremendous pride in your country. All these things are Victorian values. They are also perennial values.[42]

The governments of East Asia need to make further progress in their respect for the rights of their citizens. They also need to level the playing field between the governing and the opposition parties. The Commission for a New Asia enumerated 28 economic, social, cultural and religious human rights in its report. The Commission said, "In the Asia of today, many of these 28 most important fundamental human rights are being fully respected.

But no single nation state has an unblemished record. In every nation much progress needs to be made."[43] I agree. The Commission went on to say:

> We need to remind ourselves that personal rights are sacrosanct, but in most instances they are not absolute, only relative. Rights may flow from the very nature of individuals themselves, but they impose equally essential responsibilities on them for the promotion of the common good. Thus, every insistence on individual rights comes with a call for individual self-discipline and self-restraint. We believe the best safeguard for the continued enjoyment of rights is the conscientious exercise of their corresponding responsibilities.[44]

I also agree with Kausikan when he wrote:

> Most East and Southeast Asian governments sincerely want to protect and advance the human dignity of their citizens, even if they must do so within the constraints of their circumstances. Their good faith is less likely to be questioned if they accept the framework of the two UN human rights covenants.[45]

East Asian governments which have not already done so, should consider acceding to the two United Nations human rights covenants. Let the dialogue between the United States and East Asia on human rights be conducted in a multilateral forum and on a level playing field.

Why Is Asia Talking Back?

For several centuries, the West has dominated Asia and the world. The West has regarded itself as economically, culturally and morally superior to Asia. The Asians had accepted their subordinate position. Recently, the East Asians are talking back. What has caused this change? How has the West reacted to the change?

The East Asians are talking back to the West for the following reasons.

First, for the first time in several hundred years, many of the economies of East Asia have caught up with the West. They are playing in the same league. Therefore, they no longer regard themselves as inferior to the West. They want the West to treat them as equals.

Second, as Kausikan has pointed out, "East and Southeast Asian countries are increasingly conscious of their own civilizations and tend to locate the sources of their economic success in their own distinctive traditions and institutions".[46]

Third, East Asians feel that they should have the right to find their own social and political arrangements, consistent with their history, culture, and particular circumstances. They do not expect the West to adopt those arrangements but they do ask the West to acknowledge their right to find their own path to Nirvana.

Fourth, as former United States Ambassador, Stephen Bosworth, has rightly pointed out:

> The moral authority of US leadership was founded on the attraction of American ideals and the unique successes of the American political and economic system. Generations of Asians saw the United States as a model toward which they should strive in their own efforts at nation building. The durability and underlying equity of America's social contract, the nation's economic dynamism and expanding middle class as well as its confidence in the principles on which its government was founded were all once widely admired. But, today America's inability or unwillingness to summon the national resolve to address serious social and economic problems corrodes its ability to exercise effective international leadership.[47]

How has the West reacted to an East Asia which talks back? Some have not reacted very well. An Australian professor, Eric Jones, for example, warned that:

> East Asia ... will not simply dominate the world economy within a generation but become the model of choice for less-developed countries, in social mores as well as policies. The Less Developed

Countries will look East, not West, in ways unwarranted since the Ming dynasty.[48]

Eric Jones' alarmist view has earned him a retort from Kausikan, who asked, "And why not? Did God anoint the West the only valid model? Or is the assumption that only the Great-White-Masters are worthy of attention?".[49]

A Plea for Mutual Respect and Mutual Learning

Is there going to be a culture clash between East Asia and the United States?

I do not think so. For one thing, many Asians like me continue to admire America (see Annex III). David Hitchcock[50] reported that the Asians he interviewed readily admitted that their countries had benefited from the following Western influences and values in their development:

1. science, technology, business and public administration;
2. modern capitalist economies;
3. the concept of contracts;
4. equal opportunity;
5. the rule of law;
6. an equal role for women;
7. democracy;
8. a willingness to adapt to new ideas;
9. a sense of rationality; and
10. social mobility.

Second, we are living in an increasingly integrated, interdependent and globalized community and economy. The process is being driven by transnational business, information, technology and the market place of ideas. As a result, the United States and East Asia are heading towards greater convergence not greater divergence.

Third, in the Pacific, we are engaged in the historic enterprise of building a Pacific Community. I agree with my colleague, Kishore Mahbubani, when he said that:

> The Pacific Community will be a completely new creation. It will not be an Asian Community, nor will it be an American community. If the Pacific has emerged as the most dynamic region in the world, it is because it has drawn on the best practices and values from many rich civilizations, Asian and Western. If this fusion continues to work, there will be explosive creativity on a scale never before seen.[51]

Finally, in order to avoid a culture clash, East Asians and Americans should adopt towards each other an attitude of mutual respect and mutual learning. We can and should learn from each other and adopt each other's best practices. The trends are favourable. The United States is moving back to its traditional values or virtues. East Asia is moving towards greater political openness. Since there will never be complete convergence between the United States and East Asia, it is important for us to respect each other. Our lodestar should be: unity in diversity.

Notes

1. Francis Fukuyama, "The End of History?", *The National Interest,* Summer 1989, pp. 3–18.
2. Samuel P. Huntington, "The Clash of Civilizations?", *Foreign Affairs,* Summer 1993, p. 22.
3. Owen Harries, "Huntington and Asia: Prediction or Warning?", Paper delivered at the Eight Asia-Pacific Roundtable, Kuala Lumpur, 5–8 June 1994, pp. 11–12.
4. *Ibid.,* p. 12.
5. *Ibid.*
6. *Ibid.,* p. 13.
7. *Ibid.*

8. *Ibid.*
9. *Ibid.*, p. 15.
10. *Ibid.*, p. 16.
11. *Ibid.*, p. 17.
12. David I. Hitchcock, *Asian Values and the United States, How Much Conflict?* (Washington D.C.: Centre tor Strategic and International Studies, 1994).
13. Samuel P. Huntinglon, "American Democracy in Relation to Asia", in *Democracy and Capitalism: Asian and American Perspectives* (Singapore: Institute of Southeast Asian Studies, 1993), p. 28.
14. Samuel P. Huntington, *The Third Wave: Democratization in the Late Twentieth Century* (Oklahoma: University of Oklahoma Press, 1991).
15. *Supra*, note 13, p. 35.
16. Chan Heng Chee, "Democracy: Evolution and Implementation, An Asian Perspective", *supra*, note 13, p. 7.
17. *Ibid.*, p. 3.
18. *Ibid.*, p. 3.
19. *Ibid.*, p. 4.
20. *Ibid.*, pp. 21–24.
21. *Supra*, note 13, p. 38.
22. *Ibid.*, p. 41.
23. Richard Shifter, "Is There a Democracy Gene?", *The Washington Quarterly*, Vol. 17, No. 3, 1994, pp. 121–127.
24. *Ibid.*, p. 121.
25. *Capitalism and Democracy, Asian and American Perspectives* (New York: Asia Society, 1993).
26. Fareed Zakaria, "Culture Is Destiny (A Conversation with Lee Kuan Yew)," *Foreign Affairs*, Vol. 73, No. 2, pp. 109–126.
27. Kim Dae Jung, "A Response to Lee Kuan Yew", *Foreign Affairs*, Vol. 73, No. 6, p. 194.
28. *Commission for a New Asia, Towards a New Asia* (Kuala Lumpur: Institute of Strategic and International Studies. 1994), p. 35.
29. Muthiah Alagappa, *Democratic Transition in Asia: The Role of the International Community* (Honolulu: East-West Center, 1994), p. 32.
30. *Supra*, note 12, p. 9.
31. Bilahari Kausikan, "Asia's Different Standard", *Foreign Policy*, Fall 1993, No. 92, p. 32.

32. *Supra*, note 26, p. 112.
33. *The Straits Times*, 20 March 1995.
34. *Ibid.*
35. *Ibid.*
36. Aryeh Neier, "Asia's Unacceptable Standard", *Foreign Policy*, Fall 1993, No. 92, pp. 43–44.
37. *Supra*, note 31, p. 35.
38. Gertrude Himmelfarb, *The De-moralization of Society* (New York: Alfred A. Knopf, 1995).
39. Jonathan Sacks, *Faith in the Future* (London: Darton, Longman and Todd, 1995).
40. *Supra*, note 25, p. 44.
41. Donald K. Emmerson, "US Policy Themes in Southeast Asia in the 1990s", Paper to be published in David Wurfel and Bruce Burton (eds.), *Southeast Asia in the "New World Order": Rethinking the Political Economy of a Dynamic Region*, p. 24.
42. *Evening Standard*, 15 April 1983.
43. *Supra*, note 28, ch. 3.
44. *Ibid.*
45. *Supra*, note 31, pp. 38–39.
46. *Ibid.*, p. 34.
47. Stephen W. Bosworth, "The United States and Asia", *Foreign Affairs*, America and the World 1991/1992, pp. 127–128.
48. Eric Jones, "Asia's Fate", *The National Interest*, Spring 1994, p. 21.
49. Bilahari Kausikan, "The 'Singapore School'" (Letters), *The National Interest*, Summer 1994, p. 107.
50. *Supra*, note 12, p. 4.
51. Kishore Mahbubani, "The Pacific Way", *Foreign Affairs*, January/February 1995, p. 107.

Annex I

(a) Personal Values: East Asians and Southeast Asians

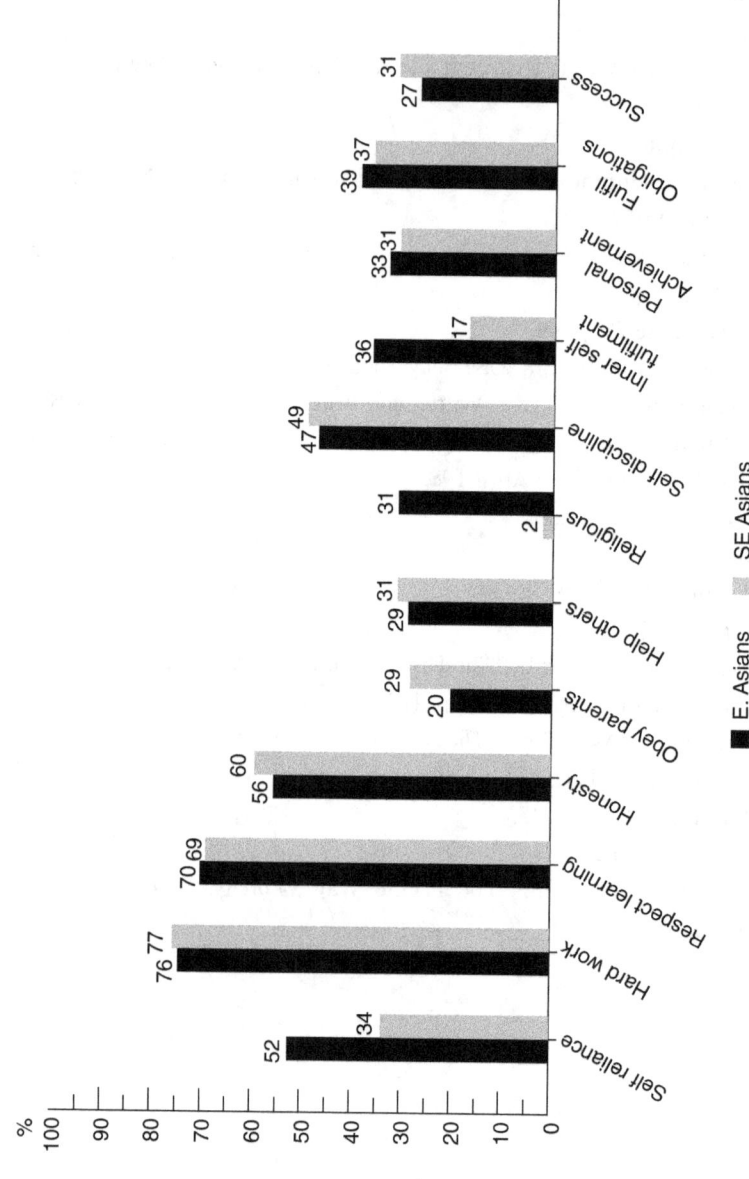

Note: Respondents asked to choose up to five of 12 values shown.

(b) Societal Values: East Asians and Southeast Asians

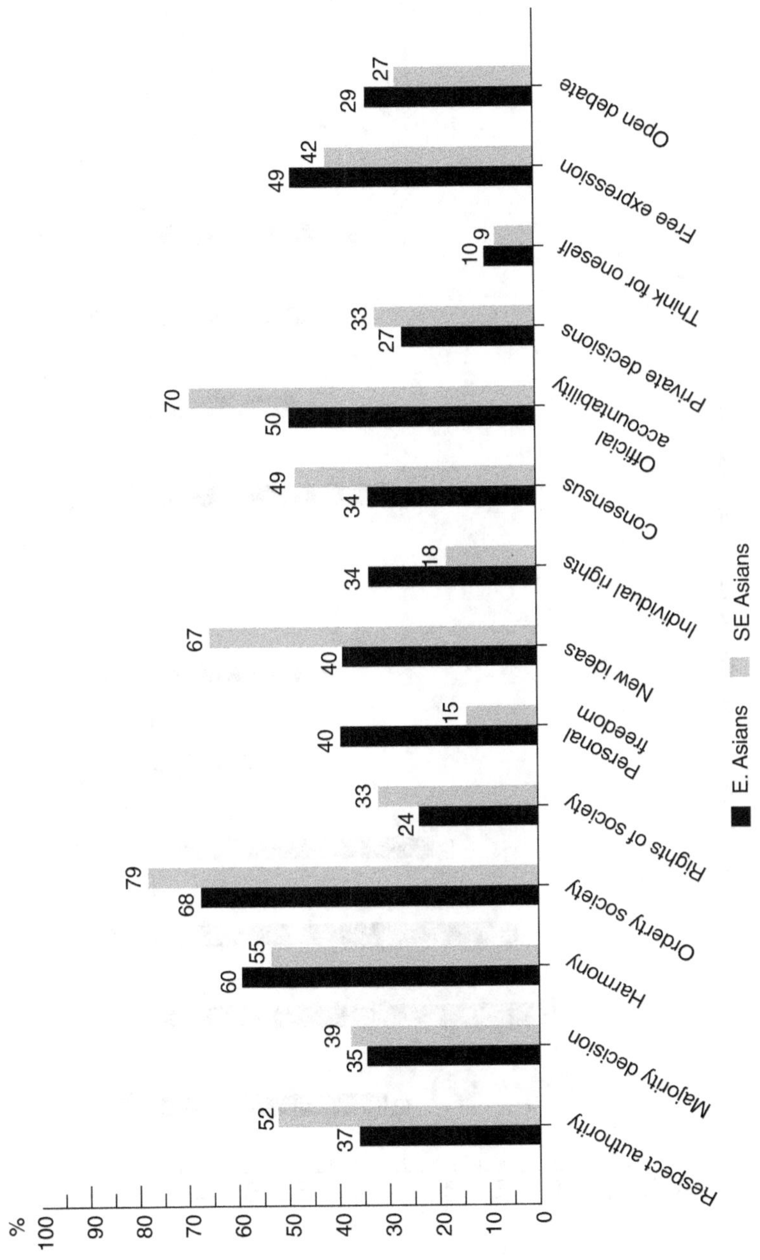

Note: Respondents asked to choose up to six of 14 values shown.

Annex II

(a) Personal Values: Asians and Americans

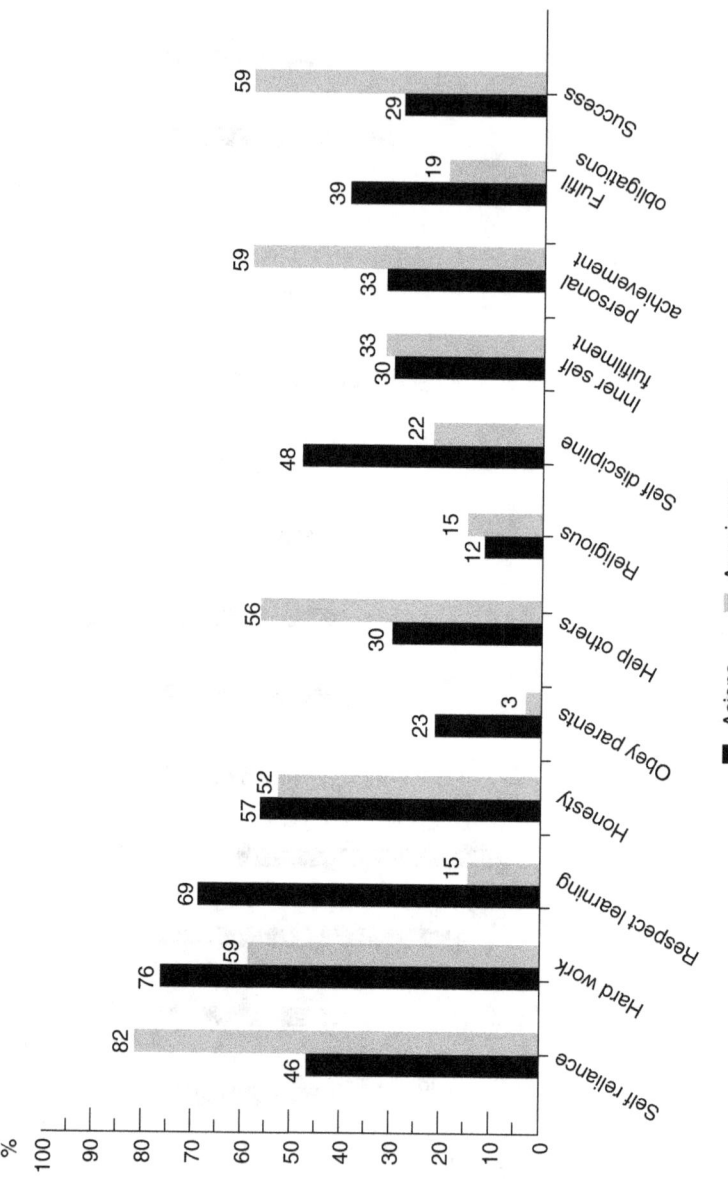

Note: Respondents asked to choose up to five of 12 values shown.

(b) Societal Values: Asians and Americans

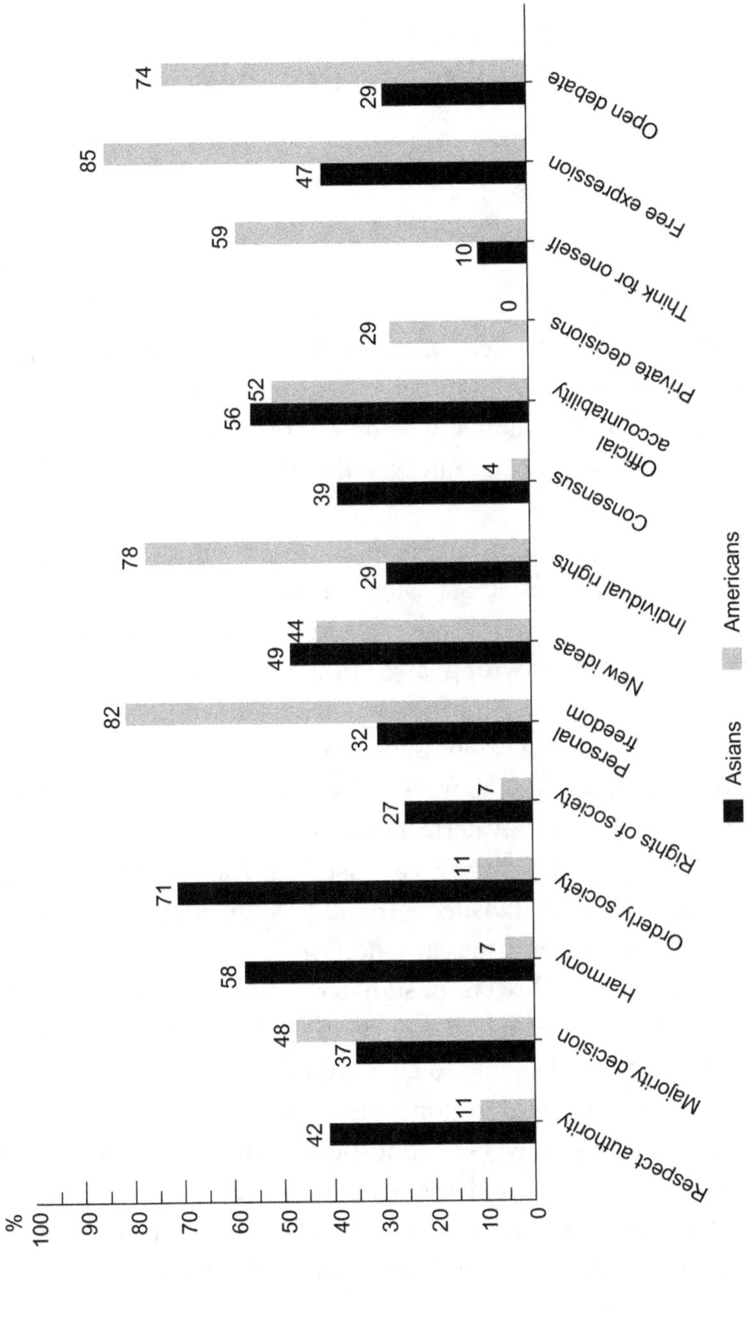

Value	Asians	Americans
Respect authority	42	11
Majority decision	37	48
Harmony	58	7
Orderly society	71	11
Rights of society	27	7
Personal freedom	32	82
New ideas	49	44
Individual rights	29	78
Consensus	39	4
Official accountability	56	52
Private decisions	0	29
Think for oneself	10	59
Free expression	47	85
Open debate	29	74

Note: Respondents asked to choose up to six of 14 values shown.

Annex III

Reports of America's Sorry Demise May Just Be a Bit Exaggerated

by Tommy Koh

Singapore — The United States has been getting bad press recently, at least in parts of Asia. Almost daily we read stories about its shortcomings: falling educational standards, a deteriorating attitude to work, a rising drug menace and crime rate, an alarming number of births to single mothers.

America's problems are real. But they should be seen in proper perspective. The United States has many strengths and virtues.

East Asians often think of Americans as individualistic and self-centred. This is wrong, as I know from the 19 years I lived in the United States, first as Singapore's ambassador to the United Nations in New York and then as ambassador to Washington.

In Singapore, only about 1 person in 10 does volunteer work. But more than 80 million Americans donate time to a cause.

The neighborhood library I used in Washington was staffed by volunteers. One day I visited a friend in a hospital. I noticed that many staff workers were wearing carnations in their lapels. I asked one of them why. He said the flowers designated volunteers. I was amazed that the hospital had so many volunteers. I have often wondered when Singaporeans will become so civic-minded.

There is a strong tradition in the United States of giving money to schools, colleges, universities, hospitals, libraries, churches, museums, symphony orchestras and opera and ballet companies.

Last year Americans contributed $126.2 billion to educational and charitable institutions. Most came from individuals. An additional $9.6

billion was donated to artistic, cultural and humanitarian organizations. As chairman of the Singapore National Arts Council, I would leap with joy if I could raise even a small fraction of that.

As a proportion of their incomes, the poor in America gave more to charity than the rich. The spirit of voluntarism and private contributions, two pillars of American communities, are as alive today as when Alexis de Tocqueville, the perceptive French social observer, took notice of them in 1830.

There is a strong spirit of entrepreneurship in America. (The 1994 World Competitiveness Report ranks the US economy as the most competitive in the world.) Unlike Singaporeans, Americans are encouraged to take risks. Society rewards those who succeed but just as importantly, it does not stigmatize those who fail.

American culture nurtures original thinking and pioneering research. Each year, more Nobel prizes are awarded to Americans than to scientists from any other nation. And Asian scientists who have won Nobel prizes have been based in America.

No nation has welcomed so many immigrants and refugees, and none has assimilated them so well, as the United States. Since the Vietnam War ended in 1975, America has taken in over 850,000 refugees from the region. Many of their children have topped their classes in American schools and been awarded scholarships to study at the most prestigious US colleges and universities.

Today, Asian-Americans are the fastest growing community in the United States. Because of the relative absence of racial or class barriers, many Asian-Americans have risen to the top of their professions. In the United States, a child, no matter what his ethnic origin or family circumstances, can aspire to the American dream.

As a superpower, the United States has shared its wealth, technology and markets with others. It has shed the blood of its sons and spent its treasures in defence of others. After World War II, America, the victor, treated Japan and Germany, the two vanquished nations, with a magnanimity unparalleled in human history. As a result, Japan and

Germany are today the two most powerful economies in the world, after the United States.

No other nation has been so generous as the United States in sharing its technology with others. This has, among other things, enabled Japan to catch up with America and, in some areas, to surpass it in the technological race. And US capital, technology and markets have enabled the economies of East Asia to grow.

On a personal level, I have been the fortunate beneficiary of many kind-hearted American friends. When I studied at Harvard Law School, a host family was appointed to look after me. They made sure that I was not lonely and invited me home for dinner on festive occasions.

In spite of its shortcomings, the United States is the most admired nation on earth. This is not only because of its size, wealth, military power of its extraordinary accomplishments in business, science, technology and higher education. America is the most admired nation because of its ideals, altruism, magnanimity and generosity. An Asia-Pacific region without the United States would be a poorer and more dangerous place.

Source: Comment contributed to the *International Herald Tribune*, October 8–9, 1994.

[Originally published in *The United States and East Asia: Conflict and Co-operation*, The Institute of Policy Studies & Times Academic Press, 1995, pp. 90–116.]

My Adventure with International Law

1. Introduction

I studied international law in my final year in the academic year of 1960 to 1961. The course was taught by a part-time teacher. We followed a very conservative curriculum based on a standard British textbook. I remember that I wrote a paper on humanitarian intervention which was published in a student magazine. I did not imagine that 18 years later, I would have to refute Vietnam's invocation of the doctrine of humanitarian intervention to justify its invasion and occupation of Cambodia. Nor could I have foreseen my subsequent involvement with the practice of international law.

The course I took at the University of Malaya was not well taught. It was taught in a very didactic manner. It focused too much on the learning of black letter law. There was no attempt to relate the law in the book to the real world in which we lived. The course was not exciting and challenging. I was so disenchanted that when I went to Harvard Law School, I did not take any courses in international law even though I became acquainted with some of that Law School's legendary teachers in international law, such as, Louis Sohn.

The reason which led me to study international law was my desire to help build a world ruled by law. The quest for a just world order would dominate my thinking for the rest of my life. But, my interest in international law was rekindled only when I accepted a posting to the UN in 1968. At the UN, international law was relevant to so many of our daily pre-occupations, everything from the Soviet invasion of Czechoslovakia, to war and peace in the Middle-East, to the right to self-determination and the right to development, to the prohibition of genocide, torture, racial discrimination and gender discrimination. The UN was, however, both an exciting and a frustrating arena for an international lawyer. On one occasion, I remember the Soviet Ambassador telling me that international law should be supportive of Soviet foreign policy and not the other way around. The interrelationship between international law and foreign policy has been a constant refrain in my work.

2. Vietnamese Hijackers: To Extradite or Not to Extradite?

In 1977, a Vietnamese civilian airline was hijacked by four Vietnamese and flown to Singapore. The hijackers surrendered to the Singapore authorities and asked for political asylum. The government of Vietnam demanded that the aircraft be returned and the hijackers be extradited to face trial in Vietnam. The Singapore government returned the aircraft and rejected the appeal of the hijackers for political asylum. It had, however, to decide on the fate of the hijackers.

Singapore and Vietnam did not have an extradition treaty between them. Singapore was, therefore, not legally bound to extradite them to Vietnam. Under international law, Singapore had two options: first, to extradite them to Vietnam; and second, to prosecute them in Singapore.

I was then serving as Singapore's Permanent Representative in New York. I decided to canvass the opinions of my colleagues at the UN. The sample I constructed was a microcosm of the UN membership. By a big majority, my UN colleagues were of the opinion that the hijackers should not be extradited to Vietnam, but should be tried in Singapore. The reason for their preference was their perception that the hijackers would not receive a fair trial in Vietnam. The hijackers were, in fact, tried and convicted in Singapore.

3. The Law and Politics of Recognition

When Singapore seceded from Malaysia and became an independent country, one of Singapore's pre-occupations was whether other States would recognise Singapore as a new sovereign and independent State. Our early fears proved to be unfounded as no State withheld its recognition. Singapore's membership of the United Nations, the Commonwealth and other international organisations helped to give it legitimacy.

The recognition of the government of a State is usually not controversial. Controversy can, however, arise if there is more than one party claiming to be the lawful or legitimate government of a State. Often, the issue is brought up at the UN in New York in the form of the question, who is entitled to occupy the seat of the country in question. When debated at the UN, especially during the Cold War, the question becomes highly politicised. International law is often subordinated to the primacy of realpolitik.

4. Cambodia's Representation at the UN

The question of Cambodia's representation at the UN came up twice. The first time was in 1970, when King (then Prince) Norodom Sihanouk was overthrown by General Lon Nol. While my personal sympathies were with Sihanouk, who had been a good friend of Singapore, Singapore had no choice but to vote for Lon Nol. Why? Because under international law, the issue is not whether Lon Nol had achieved power lawfully, but whether his government was in control of the country. In this respect, international law is based upon reality not morality. Lon Nol ruled Cambodia from 1970 to 1975, when his government was overthrown by the Khmer Rouge. The Khmer Rouge government, which styled itself as the government of Democratic Kampuchea, occupied Cambodia's seat at the UN from 1975.

5. Choice of Two Evils

On Christmas Day, 1978, Vietnam invaded and occupied Cambodia. Vietnam overthrew the Khmer Rouge and installed a new Cambodian government in Phnom Penh. At the UN General Assembly in 1979, a huge fight took place over the representation of Cambodia. The world was faced with an invidious choice between two evil options: the murderous regime of the Khmer Rouge or the puppet government of Vietnam. I had the unenviable task of leading the ASEAN team in arguing that allowing the Khmer Rouge to retain Cambodia's seat was the lesser of two evils. My argument was that the other option was worse because it would condone Vietnam's invasion and occupation of her smaller neighbour, Cambodia, and establish a bad precedent in international law and practice. My involvement with Cambodia, which began in 1965, would continue until 1991, when the Paris Agreement was signed. Today, the Khmer Rouge threat is gone. Cambodia is, once again, sovereign and independent. The country is at peace and the government and people are busy rebuilding their country after 20 years of war and destruction. The Cambodian story could be a source of inspiration to the people of Afghanistan.

6. Establishment of Diplomatic Relations with China

I had one other experience with the practice of recognition. In 1990, I was asked to lead Singapore's delegation to negotiate with China on the establishment of diplomatic relations between our two countries. Although Singapore and China did not have formal diplomatic relations, the two countries enjoyed a warm and substantive friendship. Also, Singapore had no diplomatic relations with Taiwan or the Republic of China. The only reason for the delay in establishing diplomatic relations with China was that, because of Singapore's ethnic composition, it preferred to wait until Indonesia had re-established its diplomatic relations with China.

The negotiations with China were successfully completed after three rounds of talks, one in Singapore and two in Beijing. What were the sticking points in the negotiations? There were three. First, Singapore did not want to humiliate our old friend, Taiwan. Second, Singapore wished to retain the right to send its national servicemen to Taiwan for training. Third, Singapore was unwilling to downgrade certain agreements which it had concluded with Taiwan. Given the tremendous goodwill existing and the benign intervention of leaders on both sides, the two delegations successfully concluded the negotiations in September. A ceremony was held at the UN in New York, on 3 October 1990, to witness the establishment of diplomatic relations between the two countries. In the past 19 years, the relationship between China and Singapore has flourished in all fields.

7. The Law of the Sea

Singapore has one of the world's two busiest ports. Singapore lives on its trade with the world. The bulk of world trade is seaborne. It is therefore logical for Singapore to be interested in the law of the sea. The opportunity for Singapore to play an active role in the evolution of the law of the sea arose in the late 1960s, when the UN began the preparatory process leading to the convening of the Third UN Conference on the Law of the Sea. Several distinguished Singaporeans, including Professor S. Jayakumar, Justice Chao Hick Tin and Mr S. Tiwari, were members of our delegation to the Conference. By a stroke of fate, I was drafted to serve as President of the Conference during the two concluding years. The point I wish to make here is that this was not a mere codification conference. In addition to codifying pre-existing law, the Conference also made new law. Concepts such as the exclusive economic zone, transit passage, archipelagic sea-lane passage, common heritage of mankind, etc., are new in international law. I have written extensively on the 1982 UN Convention on the Law of the Sea as well as on the negotiating process leading to its adoption. Professor S. Jayakumar and I co-authored a comprehensive chapter on the negotiating process of the Conference in Volume 1 of the Commentary by the University of Virginia (1985).

8. International Maritime Organisation

The international organisation identified by the 1982 UN Convention on the Law of the Sea as "the competent authority" is the International Maritime Organisation (IMO). The IMO's vision is safe ships and clean seas. Towards that end, it encourages States to become parties to treaties to promote the safety of navigation and to combat marine pollution. Our own Maritime and Port Authority of Singapore (MPA) works closely with the IMO. Together, they run many training courses in Singapore.

9. The Straits of Malacca and Singapore

One of my ambitions was to implement Article 43 of the 1982 Convention, with respect to the Straits of Malacca and Singapore. Article 43 enjoins coastal States and user States to cooperate to ensure the safety of navigation and to prevent and combat pollution in the international straits. The three straits States — Indonesia, Malaysia and Singapore — have cooperated closely through the Tripartite Technical Experts Group (TTEG). Of the user States, only one, Japan, had been cooperating with the straits States, both financially and in other ways, such as, by undertaking hydrographical surveys of the straits. I had convened two conferences, in 1993 and 1996, and had succeeded in bringing together all the stakeholders. I was, however, unsuccessful in forging a consensus at those two conferences. The parties were not ready. In 2007, I had the great pleasure of chairing a conference convened by the IMO, at which the three straits States adopted a cooperative mechanism which has given life to Article 43 of the Convention.

10. International Environmental Law

In 1990, the UN decided to convene, in 1992, the sequel to the historic 1972 Stockholm Conference on the Environment. The 1992 Conference would be known as the UN Conference on Environment and Development (UNCED) or the Earth Summit or the Rio Summit, in short. The UN set up a preparatory committee for the Summit. I was persuaded by my good friends, Chan Heng Chee, our then Ambassador to the UN, and Kishore Mahbubani, our then Permanent Secretary, to make a bid to chair the preparatory committee. Proceeding on the false assumption that the job would be easy compared to the Law of the Sea Conference, I agreed. I subsequently found that the issues were highly politicised and it was extremely difficult to forge a consensus in Rio. An account of the Earth Summit's negotiating process is contained in my *Singapore Law Review* lecture, delivered on 15 December 1992, and published in the *Singapore Law Review*.

Chairing the UNCED negotiations gave me an opportunity to contribute to the development of international environmental law. I chaired the drafting of the Rio Declaration of Principles, which can be described as "soft" law. I also chaired the negotiations on the monumental document known as Agenda 21, setting out an agreed programme of work in each sector for the next 20 years. Two environmental treaties, on Climate Change and Biodiversity, were opened for signature in Rio. Subsequently, a good friend, Parvez Hassan, and I were able to play a modest but catalytic role in the founding of the Asia Pacific Centre for Environmental Law (APCEL), which is based at the National University of Singapore's Law Faculty.

11. International Trade Law

My involvement with the World Trade Organization (WTO) and international trade law came about accidentally. In 1996, the WTO held its first Ministerial Conference in Singapore. I was one of a group of officials, from the Ministry of Trade and Industry and the Ministry of Foreign Affairs, assisting our then Minister for Trade and Industry, Mr Yeo Cheow Tong. By tradition, the Minister of the host country was elected Chairman of the Conference. The then Director-General of the WTO was Mr Renato

Ruggiero. One of the reasons for the success of the Conference was the seamless way in which the Chairman and the Director-General and their officials worked together. For an account of the negotiating process, see my lecture, "The WTO's First Ministerial Conference: The Negotiating Process", delivered on 19 March 1997, at the book launch of the Singapore Society of International Law.

12. Helms-Burton Act

Since the 1996 WTO Ministerial Conference, I have been appointed three times to serve on WTO dispute panels, twice as Chairman. The first case was a dispute between the European Union, as complainant, and the United States, as respondent. The European Commission had requested the WTO for a ruling on the legality of the Helms-Burton Act, which imposed sanctions against Cuba. The European Commission argued that the Act's extra-territorial effect contravened both WTO law and international law. The case was political dynamite and was fortunately settled before the panel met.

The second case was brought by the US and New Zealand against Canada. The two complainants argued that Canada had acted in contravention of WTO law by subsidising its milk and dairy exports. The legal issue of subsidies in agriculture was a very important one. The panel ruled in favour of the complainants and was upheld on appeal.

The third case was brought by Australia and New Zealand against the US. The US had invoked its domestic safeguards law against the import of lamb meat from Australia and New Zealand. The legal issue was whether the US law was consistent with the WTO law on safeguards. The panel found in favour of the complainants and was upheld on appeal. I have written a paper on my experiences with the WTO dispute settlement process. The paper will be published in a forthcoming book, co-edited by Margaret Liang and Lim Chin Leng.

13. The Land Reclamation Case

Because of its small size and growing population, Singapore has been reclaiming land from the sea since the beginning of colonial Singapore. The reclamation works carried out over the last 30 years have enabled Singapore to increase its land area from 580 to 680 square kilometres. However, Singapore has always respected its international boundaries and adopted the international best practices in order to minimise marine pollution.

In 2002, Malaysia began to voice its displeasure at Singapore's land reclamation works in Tuas and Pulau Tekong. On 4 July 2003, Malaysia invoked Article 286 of the 1982 UN Convention on the Law of the Sea and initiated arbitral proceedings against Singapore. In its response, Singapore reminded Malaysia that, under Article 283 of the said Convention, the two parties had an obligation to exchange views and to attempt to settle the dispute through negotiations. Malaysia agreed to meet Singapore on 13 and 14 August 2003 in Singapore. I was appointed as the leader of the Singapore delegation. Although the negotiations made progress, Malaysia refused to hold a second round of the negotiations. Instead, it applied to the International Tribunal for the Law of the Sea (ITLOS) on 4 September 2003 for provisional measures under Article 290(5) of the 1982 Convention. In essence, Malaysia requested the Tribunal for an order for Singapore to suspend all its reclamation activities until the Arbitral Tribunal had issued its decision.

Singapore appointed me as its Agent in the case. On 20 September 2003, Singapore submitted its response to Malaysia's request. Oral hearings were held at five public sittings from 25 to 27 September 2003 in Hamburg. On 8 October 2003, the Tribunal delivered its unanimous judgement. The Tribunal did not accede to Malaysia's request for provisional measures. Instead, the Tribunal required the two parties to establish a group of independent experts to determine, within a year, the effects of Singapore's land reclamation works and to propose appropriate measures to deal with any adverse effects. This was a brilliant move by the Tribunal because it required the two parties to return to a cooperative mode and to resolve their differences on the basis of an objective study by independent experts.

The group of independent experts submitted its unanimous report to the two governments on 5 November 2004. The study found that Singapore's land reclamation works had not caused any serious impact. The report recommended that Singapore should take mitigation measures to eliminate 17 impacts.

The report was accepted by the two governments. Three rounds of negotiations were held to arrive at an agreement to implement the report and settle the dispute. On 20 April 2005, the settlement agreement was signed by the two agents, in Singapore, in the presence of the two Foreign Ministers. I have co-written an article on this case, with Jolene Lin, in Volume X (2006) of the *Singapore Year Book of International Law*.

14. Pedra Branca

Since Professor S. Jayakumar and I have co-written a book on the Pedra Branca case (NUS Press, 2009), I will not write in any detail about it here. I was appointed as Singapore's Agent in that case. I was a member of the team, led by Chief Justice Chan Sek Keong, which drafted Singapore's memorial, counter-memorial and reply. I was also a member of the team which appeared before the International Court of Justice (ICJ) in November 2007. As an international lawyer, the privilege of appearing before ITLOS in 2003 and the ICJ in 2007, was a dream come true. Those experiences have strengthened my commitment to international law and the peaceful settlement of disputes.

15. ASEAN Charter

Professor S. Jayakumar and I were given the opportunities to make two modest contributions to the making of the ASEAN Charter. Prof Jayakumar represented Singapore in the Group of Eminent Persons (EPG) which was constituted by the 11th ASEAN Summit in Kuala Lumpur in 2005. The EPG's report was presented to the 12th ASEAN Summit in Cebu in January 2006. The Summit appointed a High-Level Task force (HLTF) to draft the Charter, to be ready for signature at the 13th ASEAN Summit in Singapore in November 2007. Ambassador Rosario Manalo of the Philippines was Chair of the HLTF from January until August and I held the chairmanship from August until November. I have co-edited a book, with Ambassador Manalo and Attorney-General Professor Walter Woon, on *The Making of the ASEAN Charter* (World Scientific, 2009).

The ASEAN Charter is regional law, rather than international law. The Charter has the potential to transform ASEAN, from a regional body which has evolved by what is often called "The ASEAN Way", to a new regional organisation which will rely more on laws, rules and institutions. ASEAN will also establish a new commission on human rights and a system for the compulsory settlement of disputes.

16. The Torres Strait

The Torres Strait is a strait lying between Papua New Guinea in the north and Australia in the south. It is a strait used for international navigation and Part III of the 1982 UN Convention on the Law of the Sea is applicable to it.

The Torres Strait is hazardous to navigation because of the strong currents and the narrowness of the strait at some critical points. It is also close to the Great Barrier Reef. In order to prevent accidents in the strait, the governments of Australia and Papua New Guinea (PNG) decided to impose compulsory pilotage on all ships transiting the strait, whether or not they are heading for an Australian port. A ship which does not take on an Australian pilot can be penalised financially on any subsequent visit to an Australian port.

Singapore, the US and other user States objected to Australia's action, both at the IMO and at the UN General Assembly. There were two issues in the dispute. First, whether the IMO had authorised the imposition of compulsory pilotage. Australia said yes, but, except for PNG and New Zealand, the other members of the IMO said no. Second, is the imposition of compulsory pilotage in a strait used for international navigation consistent with UNCLOS? Again, Australia, PNG and New Zealand said yes, while the rest said no.

Singapore and Australia have held two rounds of bilateral consultations on the dispute relating to the Torres Strait. I led the Singapore delegation to the second round which was held in Singapore on 4 March 2009. Although the atmospherics were good, no progress was made on substance. The two sides have basically agreed to disagree.

In my view, the best writing on the Torres Strait is by Professor Robert Beckman in "PSSAs and Transit Passage — Australia's Pilotage System in the Torres Strait Challenges the IMO and UNCLOS", published in *Ocean Development and International Law*, 38: 325–357, 2007.

17. Conclusion

Looking back on the last 50 years, I have three concluding thoughts. First, I am struck by the vast expansion in the scope of international law. The international law I studied as a law student did not adequately prepare me for my subsequent career. In the past five decades, the law has grown and changed in so many areas. For example, in the field of human rights, international humanitarian law, international criminal law, law of treaties, law of the sea, air and space law, trade and technology law, intellectual property rights, refugees and internally displaced persons, inter-State and intra-State conflicts, etc. The curriculum of law schools should reflect the revolution which has taken place in international law.

Second, the teaching of international law should be modernised. Teaching should not focus on the regurgitation of black letter rules. Instead, international law should be taught as a dynamic body of rules which is constantly growing. Greater reliance should be made of case classes so that students can appreciate the relevance to and impact of the rules on real life situations. Whenever possible and appropriate, law teachers should attempt to use current legal problems in their classes. Students should be encouraged to do attachments with foreign ministries, defence ministries, international organisations, non-government organisations, and other agencies in order to experience, at first hand, the interactions between law and practice.

Third, international law teachers have an important job to do in educating the legal profession, the judiciary and the general public on the relevance and importance of international law. There is, at present, a huge gap of knowledge between the international lawyers and the rest. Let me illustrate my point with a personal anecdote. One of my good friends, who has held one of the highest offices in Singapore, wrote me a series of letters. In those letters, he contended that there is no such thing as international law. The arrest and extradiction of Milosevic to the Hague to stand trial for war crime redoubled his conviction that the world is ruled by power, not by law. His letters have convinced me that we, the teachers and practitioners of international law, have a lot to do in convincing a sceptical world that, however imperfect, international law exists and that it impacts many aspects of our lives. We must continue to believe in a world ruled by power and law, and not by power alone.

[Originally published in *Singapore Journal of International & Comparative Law*, Vol. 5, No. 2, 2001, pp. 277–283, updated October 2009.]

The Negotiating Process of the ASEAN Charter

I was a member of the Singapore delegation to the 12th ASEAN Summit, held at the Shangri-La Hotel on Mactan Island, Cebu, The Philippines. I attended the meeting, held on Friday, 12 January 2007, at which the Chairman and members of the Group of Eminent Persons (EPG) presented their report to the ASEAN Leaders. Foreign Minister George Yeo observed to me, after the meeting, that we had just witnessed a historic event. On the next morning, 13 January, the 10 members of the High Level Task Force (HLTF) held an informal meeting, on the sidelines of the Summit, to get acquainted with one another and to organise our work.

HLTF's Mandate

The HLTF received its mandate from the ASEAN Leaders as contained in the Cebu Declaration on the Blueprint of the ASEAN Charter (Annex 1). The mandate was to complete drafting the ASEAN Charter in time for the 13th ASEAN Summit, to be held in Singapore in November 2007. On what bases would the Charter be drafted by the HLTF? It would be drafted on the bases of the:

(i) directions of our Leaders given at the 11th and 12th ASEAN Summits;
(ii) relevant ASEAN documents; and
(iii) recommendations of the EPG.

Directions from 11th Summit

What directions from ASEAN's Leaders were contained in the Kuala Lumpur Declaration on the Establishment of the ASEAN Charter (12 December 2005) (Annex 1) and the said Cebu Declaration? The Kuala Lumpur Declaration contains four specific directions. The Leaders declared that the Charter should:

(i) serve as a legal and institutional framework of ASEAN to support the realisation of its goals;
(ii) codify all ASEAN norms, rules, and values and reaffirm that ASEAN agreements signed and other instruments adopted before the establishment of the Charter shall continue to apply and be legally binding where appropriate;
(iii) reaffirm principles and ideals contained in ASEAN's milestone agreements, in particular, the ASEAN Declaration (1967), the Treaty of Amity and Cooperation in Southeast Asia (1976), the Treaty on Southeast Asia Nuclear Weapon Free Zone (1995), the ASEAN Vision 2020 (1997) and the Declaration of ASEAN Concord II (2003), as well as the principles contained in the UN Charter and international law, including 18 selected principles; and
(iv) confer a legal personality to ASEAN and determine the functions, develop areas of competence of key ASEAN bodies and their relationship with one another in the overall ASEAN structure.

Directions from the 12th Summit

What directions were contained in the Cebu Declaration? It contains only two directions:

(i) to make the ASEAN Charter the crowning achievement of ASEAN on its 40th Anniversary; and
(ii) that the Charter will enable ASEAN to meet its future challenges and opportunities, serve as a firm foundation to achieve one ASEAN

community by providing an enhanced institutional framework as well as by conferring a legal personality to ASEAN.

No Reference to Role of Foreign Ministers

Neither the Kuala Lumpur nor the Cebu Declarations gives a role to the Foreign Ministers. Their role evolved by practice and necessity. The 10 members of the HLTF were appointed by their respective Foreign Ministers. It was, therefore, natural for the HLTF to turn to the Foreign Ministers for their advice and guidance and because the HLTF was accountable to the Foreign Ministers.

No Requirement to Consult

The HLTF's mandate, unlike that of the EPG, did not require it to meet with ASEAN senior officials, representatives of civil society, parliamentarians or to undertake study trips. However, when requests and invitations were received and in order not to offend, but, instead, to earn the goodwill of the various stakeholders, the HLTF agreed to visit the EU at Germany's invitation and to meet with ASEAN senior officials, parliamentarians and members of the civil society. The HLTF held two meetings, in Manila and Singapore, to meet with representatives of the civil society, private sector, academia and the media. The HLTF's meetings with the Senior Officials from the three pillars, HLTF-EI, ASCCO and SOC-COM, were intended to solicit their inputs for the drafting of the Charter.

EPG's Report

The EPG's report is a bold and visionary one. It was drafted by 10 ASEAN elder statesmen, led by Tun Musa Hitam, a former Deputy Prime Minister of Malaysia. They were appointed to serve in their individual capacities and not as representatives of their respective governments. This enabled them to think out of the box and to make some radical recommendations on how to strengthen ASEAN and for the Charter. Unlike the EPG, the HLTF consisted of 10 representatives of the 10 ASEAN Governments, working under the supervision of the Foreign Ministers. Also, the EPG's report was not the only basis, but one of the bases on which the HLTF drafted the Charter. Some members of the EPG do not understand this and have therefore expressed disappointment with the Charter. They should not feel disappointed because, with only a few exceptions, most of their recommendations have been reflected in the Charter. The HLTF held the EPG in high regard and constantly referred to its report in the course of drafting the Charter. In fact, the HLTF invited Tun Musa Hitam and members of the EPG to speak to us at our first meeting, held in Jakarta on 5 February 2007.

HLTF's Informal Meeting on 13 January 2007

The informal meeting of the HLTF was chaired by Ambassador Rosario Manalo of the Philippines, the then Chair of the ASEAN Standing Committee. As agreed by member States, this meant that the chairmanship of the HLTF would pass to Singapore, at the end of the ASEAN Foreign Ministers' Meeting in July. The HLTF agreed to hold their first meeting at the ASEAN Secretariat, on 5 and 6 February 2007 and to invite the Chairman and members of the EPG to address us. The HLTF requested the ASEAN Secretariat's Special Assistant to the Secretary-General, Dr Termsak Chalermpalanupap, to prepare the following documents:

(i) a summary of the Leaders' instructions on the Charter;
(ii) a draft outline of the Charter, based upon a paper prepared by the Indonesian member of the EPG, Pak Ali Alatas, and known as the Alatas paper;
(iii) a list of issues on which the ASEAN Leaders had expressed divergent views at the Cebu Summit; and
(iv) a proposed timeline for HLTF's work.

First Meeting of HLTF

The first order of business of the HLTF's meeting on 5 February 2007 was to listen to the views of the EPG. In response to the HLTF's invitation to all EPG members, Chairman of the EPG, Tun Musa Hitam and his colleagues from Cambodia and Laos, Aun Porn Moniroth and Khampanh Simmalavong, respectively, attended the first meeting of the HLTF. It was a useful meeting, although the EPG delegation refrained from giving direct answers to the many questions posed by members of the HLTF. The Secretary-General made many useful points to the HLTF. The atmosphere of the meeting was good and the 10 members of the HLTF were able to work cooperatively with one another.

What else did the HLTF achieve at its first meeting? The meeting had the following deliverables:

(i) It adopted nine guidelines on the drafting of the Charter;
(ii) It authorised the Singapore delegation to redraft the preamble and the chapters on objectives and principles;
(iii) It agreed to accept an invitation from Germany (the then Chairman of the EU) to visit Germany and Brussels and to attend a workshop to exchange views with representatives of the German government, parliament and think-tanks;
(iv) It agreed to meet with representatives of civil society organisations at the beginning of the third meeting in Manila; and
(v) It agreed to request a meeting with the ASEAN Foreign Ministers during their retreat in Siem Reap in March.

Second HLTF Meeting

The second HLTF meeting was held in Siem Reap on 28 February and 1 March 2007. The meeting advanced the work of the HLTF by:

(i) adopting an agreed skeletal outline of the chapters and articles of the Charter;

(ii) adopting a comprehensive work plan for the period, March to November;
(iii) agreeing that the deputies and other colleagues would help the Secretariat to vet the draft summary records and prepare the documents for the HLTF's consideration; and
(iv) agreeing to meet with the HLTF on economic integration as well as with the coordinating committees of the three pillars of ASEAN.

First Meeting with Foreign Ministers

With the help of the Secretariat, the Chair prepared the HLTF's first progress report to the Ministers. All the 10 members of the HLTF met with the Ministers on the early evening of 1 March 2007. Rosario Manalo read the progress report and requested the Ministers' guidance on 10 points. The Ministers did not pose any questions to us. Instead, they discussed our progress report during their working dinner. After the dinner, the Secretary-General gave us a copy of his written notes containing the Ministers' decisions on the 10 points.

The Ministers decided, inter alia :

- that the term "ASEAN Union" should not be mentioned in the Charter;
- that there is no need to mention suspension, expulsion and withdrawal in the Charter;
- that the basic principle of decision-making is consensus;
- that there must be an appropriate provision in the Charter to deal with serious non-compliance and when consensus cannot be achieved;
- that there is no need to make specific provisions on funding the Special Fund;
- that the HLTF should draft an enabling provision to allow appropriate dispute settlement mechanisms to be established; and
- to include a draft provision on an ASEAN Human Rights Commission as an organ.

Third HLTF Meeting

The third HLTF meeting was held in Manila on 28 and 29 March. The HLTF held a dialogue session with representatives of non-governmental and civil society organisations. The meeting implemented the decision taken at the second meeting to create a working group of assistants. They would meet one day before the HLTF and would vet the draft summary records, and with the help of the Secretariat, attempt to merge the various texts into a single text and prepare the ground for the HLTF to meet. The HLTF completed its discussions of the Preamble and the Principles (Chapter I). Working in parallel, the group of assistants managed to produce merged texts for Purposes (Chapter II) and Membership (Chapter III).

Fourth HLTF Meeting

The fourth meeting of the HLTF was held in Yangon on 9 April 2007. The group of assistants met on 8 April. The HLTF on the Charter held a meeting with the HLTF on Economic Integration. The latter offered to draft paragraphs for inclusion in the Preamble, Purposes and Principles, based on key documents and agreed language. They requested an advance copy of the first draft of the Charter. They also requested the Charter HLTF to consider:

(i) whether the ASEAN minus X principle could be expanded to become "policy";
(ii) that the AEM should remain as the coordinating body for the economic pillar and retain its right to report directly to the Summit;
(iii) to strengthen the role of the Secretary-General and the ASEAN Secretariat in coordinating implementation, monitoring and reporting compliance of ASEAN economic agreements, commitments, and plans of action; and
(iv) that the EDSM should be enshrined in the Charter as the mode of dispute settlement for the economic pillar.

The response of the Charter HLTF was somewhat sceptical. My sense is that there was a certain lack of empathy between some of the members of the Charter HLTF, all of whom are from their foreign ministries, and our colleagues from the economic track. This could have been due to the fact that in some ASEAN countries, coordination between them is not optimal and there is also considerable rivalry between them.

The HLTF did not make much progress during their half-day meeting in Yangon. This was largely due to the lack of discipline as several HLTF members insisted on revisiting texts which had already been agreed. As a result, the only new ground covered was a cursory discussion of six paragraphs from Purposes.

Fifth HLTF Meeting

The fifth meeting of the HLTF was held in Hanoi on 19 and 20 April 2007, preceded by a meeting of the group of assistants on 18 April. Unlike the previous meeting, the HLTF worked with a greater sense of urgency and managed to complete its discussions of four chapters of new texts on Legal Personality, Membership, Privileges and Immunities, and Decision-Making. The HLTF also began a preliminary discussion on the organisational structure of ASEAN. The HLTF decided that all its future meetings would be extended from two to three days.

Sixth HLTF Meeting

The sixth HLTF meeting was held in Penang on 17, 18 and 19 May 2007, preceded by a meeting of the group of assistants on 16 May. The HLTF also held a dialogue with a delegation from the ASEAN Inter-Parliamentary Assembly (AIPA). The meeting made good progress and completed its discussions of several key chapters, on dispute settlement, budget and finance, and administration and procedure. Professor Walter Woon made a major contribution to the chapter on dispute settlement.

The Secretary-General, Ong Keng Yong, presented a revised organisational structure, in diagrammatic form, taking into account the roles of the proposed four deputy secretaries-general.

Seventh HLTF Meeting

The seventh HLTF meeting was held in Bali on 26, 27 and 28 June 2007, preceded by a meeting of the group of assistants on 25 June. The HLTF held a two-hour long consultation with the four heads of the national human rights commissions from Indonesia, Malaysia, Philippines and Thailand, and with the Chairman of the ASEAN Human Rights Mechanism Working Group (a network of human rights NGOs from ASEAN countries), Pak Marzuki Darusman of Indonesia. The meeting was useful, especially on the question of defining human rights in the ASEAN context, and on the possible role and function of an ASEAN human rights mechanism.

The HLTF (without their staffers, but with Dr Termsak) devoted two half-days, in a retreat format, to the discussion of two issues: the enabling provision for establishing an ASEAN human rights mechanism and its terms of reference. The HLTF agreed that the terms of reference would specify that it:

(i) would be inter-governmental in composition;
(ii) would not be a finger-pointing body;
(iii) would define human rights in an ASEAN context;
(iv) represent ASEAN's views at international forums; and
(v) should have consultative status.

At the request of Myanmar, it was also agreed that the paper containing the views of the HLTF would be treated as a Secretariat concept paper.

Apart from human rights, the HLTF focused on the nomenclature and functions of the key organs (Chapter IV), especially the Summit, ASEAN Executive Board, Foreign Ministers' Meeting, ASEAN Standing

Committee and the Permanent Representatives. In the meantime, the assistants had revised the text of the Chapter on External Relations.

Eighth HLTF Meeting

The eighth meeting in Manila was a long meeting, taking place from 22 to 26 July, 28 July, and 30 and 31 July 2007. The HLTF completed its discussions on the Chapter on External Relations and the Chapter on General and Final Provisions. The HLTF also discussed the major elements of the remaining Chapter on Organs. Singapore's innocuous proposal to insert an enabling provision for the Leaders to task the relevant Ministers to deal with emergency situations as well as with crosscutting issues, consumed one and a half days of discussion before it was finally accepted.

The most contentious issue was the human rights mechanism. On the evening of 26 July, the 10 members of the HLTF were divided into three camps:

(i) Cambodia, Laos, Myanmar and Vietnam were opposed to the creation of an ASEAN Human Rights Commission;
(ii) Indonesia, Malaysia, Philippines and Thailand in favour; and
(iii) Brunei and Singapore occupying the middle ground.

The meeting adopted, on an ad referendum basis, the following text:

> ASEAN shall/may establish an ASEAN human rights body, at a time acceptable to all ASEAN member states to promote and protect human rights and fundamental freedoms of the people of ASEAN.

On 28 July, the Chair informed the HLTF that her Foreign Minister had rejected the ad referendum formulation. Indonesia, Malaysia and Singapore also informed the meeting that their Foreign Ministers had also rejected the ad referendum formulation as falling below their instruction given in Siem Reap. Philippines then put forward a new proposal that ASEAN shall establish a Human Rights Commission and ASEAN countries would participate when they were ready to do so. The proposal was supported by Indonesia, Malaysia and Thailand and rejected by Cambodia, Laos, Myanmar and Vietnam. Strong words were exchanged and emotions ran high. Ong Keng Yong saved the day by putting forward the following innocuous text:

> In conformity with the purposes and principles of the ASEAN Charter relating to the promotion and protection of human rights and fundamental freedoms, ASEAN shall cooperate to establish an ASEAN human rights body.

This and other contentious issues on which the HLTF was unable to arrive at a consensus were referred to the Foreign Ministers for their guidance.

Second Meeting with Foreign Ministers

On the morning of 30 July, the HLTF held its second meeting with the Foreign Ministers. The HLTF submitted its second progress report, a first draft of the Charter and a request for guidance on 14 points. The Foreign Ministers considered our report, the draft Charter and answered each of our 14 requests. The HLTF Chair was present at the Foreign Ministers' Meeting as a resource person. Following the meeting, the Secretary-General provided the HLTF with his written summary of the Ministers' decisions. The decision of the Ministers to establish an ASEAN human rights body was received by some of my colleagues with disbelief. The Foreign Ministers confirmed the correctness of the Secretary-General's and the Chair's reports.

The HLTF met briefly on the evening of 30 July and at breakfast on 31 July to receive and discuss the decisions made by their Ministers.

Apart from the human rights issue, the Ministers had also instructed the HLTF to inter alia:

(i) include the principles of democracy and constitutional government, in place of the principle of rejecting undemocratic and unconstitutional changes of government;
(ii) state that the Summit may make its own rules of procedure, and acting as a committee of peers, decide how specific decisions may be made;
(iii) enshrine the ASEAN minus X principle for economic commitments;
(iv) delete the principle of non-discrimination and the repatriation of foreign workers; and
(v) delete the provision on Special Funds.

Ninth HLTF Meeting

The HLTF held its ninth meeting in Singapore from 24 to 26 August 2007. At a brief ceremony held on the morning of 24 August, Rosario Manalo passed the gavel of chairmanship to Tommy Koh. Singapore decided to separate the chairmanship and its national position. Tommy Koh would act as the neutral chairman, Walter Woon would represent Singapore's national position and Andrew Tan would succeed the able Luis Garcia as chairman of the group of assistants. Walter Woon would also chair the group of legal experts to undertake the legal scrubbing of the draft Charter. Chan Sze-Wei would assist Walter Woon in the HLTF and Deena Bajrai would assist him in the group of legal experts.

The focus of the Singapore meeting was on the outstanding organisational issues, namely, the Community Councils, the Committee of Permanent Representatives, the National Secretariats, and a new article on sectoral ministerial bodies. The key points of the discussion were the composition and reporting lines of the Community Councils and sectoral ministerial bodies, whether to include provisions for the various bodies to consult with stakeholders, and how to reflect the role of the Senior Officials' Meeting.

The Secretariat introduced a paper containing feedback from the ASEAN Senior Economic Officials and another paper containing follow-up on inputs from ASEAN Economic Ministers on the ASEAN Charter. On 26 August, the Secretariat was requested by the ASEAN Economic Ministers, who were meeting concurrently in Manila, that they be put in charge of the ASEAN Economic Community Council.

Tenth HLTF Meeting

The tenth HLTF meeting was held in Chiangmai from 10 to 14 September 2007. The HLTF completed its discussion of all the outstanding articles of Chapter IV. The group of assistants, chaired by Andrew Tan, prepared the first draft of the third progress report to the Foreign Ministers.

Most of the time in Chiangmai was spent on human rights. There was no disagreement with the fact that in Manila, our Ministers had agreed to include in the Charter an enabling provision to establish an ASEAN human rights body. The disagreement was over:

(i) the function of the human rights body;
(ii) whether the Ministers had instructed the HLTF to draft the terms of reference; and
(iii) whether the terms of reference should be completed before the signing of the Charter.

The meeting was deadlocked. The Philippines, supported by Indonesia, Malaysia and Thailand, said that the item on the terms of reference of the human rights body should be deleted from the agenda. Rosario Manalo also said that the body's function would include monitoring and that its terms of reference should be taken up by a group of experts after the Charter has been signed. On the other hand, Cambodia, Laos, Myanmar and Vietnam took the position that the terms of reference must be finished by the HLTF as a package with the enabling provision and that the human rights body would only have consultative status.

In the hope of breaking the impasse, the Chair organised a working dinner on 12 September, hoping that colleagues would feel more relaxed in a dinner setting. This was not the case. Strong words were exchanged with one colleague threatening to pack his bag and go home. Rosario Manalo was so worked up that she went into the men's toilet by mistake! The dinner adjourned in a bad mood and without any common ground. Our Thai host, Khun Pradap, decided to lighten the atmosphere with some durian therapy. He treated us to some wonderful Thai durian, which we had to eat on the deck beside the river.

On the morning of 13 September, the Chair found that colleagues had gathered themselves into two different rooms: with Cambodia, Laos, Myanmar and Vietnam in a room on the ground floor and Brunei, Indonesia, Malaysia, Philippines and Thailand in another room on an upper floor. The Chair and Walter Woon spent the whole morning commuting between the two groups, trying one compromise text after another. Finally, at around noon, the two sides agreed to accept a compromise consisting of two elements:

(i) the inclusion of an additional paragraph in the Charter on the Human Rights Body that:
"The ASEAN human rights body shall operate in accordance with the terms of reference to be determined by the ASEAN Foreign Ministers";

and

(ii) an informal discussion on the ASEAN Secretariat's concept paper on "Possible Elements for Inclusion in the Terms of Reference of an ASEAN Human Rights Body."

Eleventh HLTF Meeting

The HLTF held its 11th meeting at the Permanent Mission of Brunei to the UN in New York on 26 September 2007. The focus of the meeting was to prepare the third progress report and draft Charter for submission to the Informal ASEAN Ministers' Meeting (AMM) on 27 September. At the request of the Foreign Minister of Singapore, the HLTF was requested to submit not more than two issues to the IAMM. The HLTF agreed that the two issues would be the human rights body and the frequency of summit meetings. On the first issue, the HLTF posed four questions:

(i) what is the nature and function of the HRB;
(ii) who should draft the TOR;
(iii) when should the TOR be completed; and
(iv) where should the HRB be placed in the Chapter on Organs.

The one-day meeting was very productive as the HLTF was able to clean up several outstanding questions.

Third Meeting with Foreign Ministers

On the morning of 27 September, all 10 members of the HLTF met the Foreign Ministers in one of the conference rooms at the UN. The Chair read the third progress report and requested the Ministers' guidance on the issues discussed above. Unlike previous occasions, the HLTF was allowed to remain in the room while the Ministers discussed and agreed on answers to the questions posed to them. The Secretary-General's written notes on the decisions of the IAMM were given to HLTF later that day. On the HRB, the Ministers decided that it should be located in Chapter IV, after ASEAN National Secretariats and before the ASEAN Foundation. The Ministers also decided that the HLTF should draft the TOR, which need not be included in the Charter. If the TOR cannot be completed before the Summit, it should be regarded as work-in-progress. Interestingly, the Chairman of the IAMM stated that, "ASEAN is in favour of the promotion and protection of the human rights of its citizens … ASEAN should therefore view human rights in a positive light, and not adopt a defensive attitude."

Twelfth HLTF Meeting

The HLTF held its 12th Meeting in Bandar Seri Begawan from 3 to 5 October 2007. The intention in Brunei was to produce a clean text of the Charter. This intention could not be realised because a few colleagues insisted on re-opening agreed texts. There was also no agreement on how to streamline the lengthy Preamble and Purposes. The HLTF managed to deal with the brackets and footnotes in 11 out of the 13 Chapters. The legal scrubbing of Chapters 1 to 13 progressed smoothly.

Thirteenth HLTF Meeting

The 13th and final meeting was held in Vientiane from 18 to 20 October 2007. In order to speed up the work of the HLTF, the Chair introduced the ground rule that any amendment which is met by even a single objection would not be accepted. With this procedure in place, the work was accelerated but it also meant that attempts to remove repetitive language from the Preamble, Purposes and Principles were not possible.

A lot of time was spent on how to respond to the requests of the ASEAN Economic Ministers. They were resisted by several members of the HLTF who, probably for domestic reasons, had no empathy for the AEM. Because of their resistance, compromise language had to be negotiated between those who were supportive and those who were unsympathetic to the requests of the AEM. I would respectfully request our Foreign and Economic Ministers and their respective senior officials to meet together and to do so more frequently in order to bridge this gap.

In order to complete our work on time, the final meeting was held in the evening of 20 October, after a short break for dinner. The pace of progress picked up as the night wore on. Soon, all the remaining disputed texts were settled. The report of the chairman of the group of legal experts, Walter Woon, was accepted without any reservation. The chairman of the group of assistants, Andrew Tan, submitted the four annexes and accumulated summary records to the plenary and they were rapidly approved. The letter of transmittal was also approved. At the magic hour of midnight, the HLTF succeeded in completing its work by adopting a clean text of the ASEAN Charter, legally scrubbed, consisting of a Preamble and 13 Chapters, with four annexes and a letter of transmittal, for submission to the ASEAN Foreign Ministers on 19 November 2007. Everyone was tired but happy that, after ten months of very hard work, our collective endeavour had been successfully concluded.

Reflections

First, I would like to pay a tribute to our Foreign Ministers. Although their role was not mentioned in the Cebu Declaration, they played an indispensable role. All the difficult issues were resolved, not by the HLTF, but by our Foreign Ministers.

Second, I would like to give a big bouquet to Ong Keng Yong and Termsak Chalermpalanupap. Keng Yong was a fountain of wisdom and, with his unique combination and candour and humour, he was able to tell us unpleasant truths in a palatable manner. Termsak was a walking encyclopaedia and a prodigious worker. He was ably assisted by his three staffers, Ms Teh Lip Li, Ms Carla Budiarto and Ms Serena Wong.

Third, the traditional ASEAN spirit of solidarity and of seeking mutual accommodation, in the constant quest for consensus, prevailed and helped to keep the family together, especially on those occasions when strong words were exchanged and tempers had got out of control. When it was all over, I believe that we have remained friends and proud of our historic achievement.

Fourth, I think I made the right decision to act as a neutral chairman and to ask Walter Woon to represent Singapore. If I were not a neutral chairman, I do not think it would have been possible for me to act as an honest broker in Chiangmai and to broker a compromise acceptable to the two opposing groups of colleagues.

Fifth, it is never easy to chair a multi-national meeting, even one consisting of only the representatives of 10 countries. I had to reconcile the competing interests of the 10 countries, the strongly held beliefs of some and the highly restrictive mandates of others. I had also to build a team of 10 very senior colleagues, some of whom have very strong personalities. My strategy was to follow Buddha's teaching and to be ego-less. I decided to endure the difficulties with a smile, a dose of humour, and to be always polite, respectful and calm.

Sixth, the successful exercise of drafting the ASEAN Charter in less than a year was a difficult, challenging and ultimately, inspiring experience. The 10 of us were conscious of our historic mission. Although each of us fought hard to protect our respective national interest, we were always ready to compromise for the common good. I hope that this account of our negotiating history will, on the one hand, inform the outsiders how difficult the process was and, on the other hand, inspire the people and officials of ASEAN with our strong collective will to build a brighter future for ASEAN and Southeast Asia.

Finally, I wish to express my deep gratitude to my Singaporean colleagues, Walter Woon, Andrew Tan, Chan Sze-Wei and Deena Bajrai. Without them, I could not have got the job done.

Note added: Annex 1 is not reprinted here. See pp. 167–196 of *The Making of the ASEAN Charter*.

[Originally published in *The Making of the ASEAN Charter*, edited by T. Koh, R. G. Manalo and W. Woon, World Scientific, 2009.]

Advice to Law Freshmen*

Dean Tan Cheng Han, Members of the Advisory Board, Members of the Faculty, Ladies and Gentlemen

On behalf of the Advisory Board, and on my own behalf, I join Dean Tan in extending a warm welcome to the members of the 2008 freshmen class.

This occasion brings back for me many happy memories of my first day as a law student 51 years ago. I know that some of you will be thinking, "Gee, my parents weren't even born then!" As a freshman, my mind was filled with hopes and anxieties, dreams and aspirations and, most of all, with many questions. What I intend to do is to share with you 10 rules which may help to answer some of your questions.

Rule No. 1: Learn to Work Smart

The Dean has advised you to work hard. I don't disagree, but I would add that it is more important to work smart. What do I mean by working smart? I mean, for example, learning to speed read, which all freshmen at Harvard have to do. I mean learning how to read a book, how to take notes, how to store and retrieve information, and cultivating the discipline of total focus and high productivity. The objective is to complete an assignment in the shortest possible time without sacrificing quality.

---

*Speech delivered at NUS Law Freshmen Inauguration Ceremony, 4 August 2008, NUS Bukit Timah Campus.

Rule No. 2: Cultivate Your Thinking Skills

In law school, you will have a very heavy reading load. In every course you take, you will have to learn and remember the major principles, statutes, case law, and the views of learned scholars. There is no escaping the need to memorise some of the information in order to pass your exams. But, in my view, what is more important is to develop your thinking skills: the ability to separate the relevant from the irrelevant, the ability to analyse a problem, the ability to identify and frame the issues, the ability to apply the relevant principles to the facts and the ability to exercise good judgement. The cases you will forget, sometimes, as soon as the exams are over, but your thinking skills will stay with you forever.

Rule No. 3: Learn to Write Well

It is important for a lawyer, indeed for the graduate of any discipline to write well. By writing well, I mean writing clearly, succinctly and persuasively. I also mean acquiring the skill to draft good letters, proposals, counter-proposals, agreements, etc.

Rule No. 4: Learn the Skills of Presentation, Negotiation and Advocacy

In addition to writing well, a good lawyer must also learn to speak well. Speaking well is a skill which can be acquired and polished with practice. I hope that you will learn the arts of presentation, negotiation and advocacy. As you know, the NUS Law School holds the world record for having won the Jessup Moot Court Competition four times. Let us not lose that record to another Law School.

Rule No. 5: Develop Your Emotional Intelligence

To succeed in this world, it is not enough to have high cognitive intelligence. You should also have high emotional intelligence, a concept made famous by Daniel Goleman. What do I mean by developing your EQ? I mean developing your ability to work with others as a team, your ability to motivate people, your ability to empathise and to lead. Learning to be a good team player is one of the most important skills you should learn. You should also learn to treat your peers with civility and your subordinates with dignity.

Rule No. 6: Develop Your Cultural Intelligence

We live in an increasingly globalised world. Whether you are a lawyer, diplomat, business person or belong to another profession, you will cross many boundaries in the course of your work. The boundaries may be geographical, linguistic, ethnic, religious or cultural.

You should learn enough about the history, religion and culture of the country you are working with or in so that you will be able to work smoothly and productively in that cultural box. This is what I call cultural intelligence. If you have a chance to study in another country as an exchange student, grab it.

Rule No. 7: Develop Good Values

You will not be a happy and successful lawyer and human being if you do not have sound values. The two most important values are integrity and kindness. Without integrity, no employer will hire you and no client will entrust his case to you. The world would be a much better place if all of us would embrace the value of kindness — a virtue taught by all the great religions of the world.

Rule No. 8: Form Enduring Friendships

Friends are very important to most of us. Some of the friendships you make at law school will last a lifetime. This is true in my case and I hope it will be true in your case. You should, therefore, invest some of your time in making friends, especially those with whom you share a common interest. You could consider joining or forming a study group, book club, art club, music club, nature club, a club to tutor under-privileged children, volunteer to be a nature or museum guide, to help a particular VWO or charity, etc. If you are lucky, you may find the love of your life at law school.

Rule No. 9: Be Passionate About Justice

Remember that the law is a noble and learned profession. We should not treat it as simply a service industry. Remember too that the ultimate purpose of law is to render justice. Be passionate for justice and against injustice. We should not stand silent if the law is used as an instrument of oppression or in order to secure an unjust end.

Rule No. 10: Have a Great Time

Your four undergraduate years should be a golden period of your life. Don't spend all your time studying or in the library. Have a great time and good luck.

WTO Dispute Settlement System: Some Reflections

Introduction

Under the General Agreement on Trade and Tariff (GATT), the dispute settlement process was based upon the concept of conciliation. Therefore, a party whose trade practices had been challenged could block the establishment of a dispute panel. It could also block the adoption of an adverse panel report.

From Voluntary to Mandatory

One of the enduring achievements of the Uruguay Round is the adoption of a mandatory system of dispute settlement. In 1995, at Marrakesh, the WTO adopted the Dispute Settlement Understanding on Rules and Procedures Governing the Settlement of Disputes, known by the acronym, DSU. The DSU is administered by the Dispute Settlement Body (DSB) consisting of all WTO members.

Dispute Settlement Body

The DSB is the sole WTO body with authority to establish panels, to adopt their reports and those of the Appellate Body, to maintain surveillance of the implementation of the rulings and recommendations it adopts, and to authorise the suspension of concessions or other obligations under

WTO agreements if its rulings or recommendations are not acted on by members in a timely fashion.

1996 WTO Ministerial Meeting

I had never served at GATT or the WTO. My involvement with the WTO happened accidentally. In 1996, the WTO held its first Ministerial Meeting in Singapore. I was a member of the Singapore delegation led by our then Minister for Trade and Industry, Mr Yeo Cheow Tong. My job was to help the Minister in chairing the various negotiations and meetings.[1] As a result, I got to know the then WTO Director-General, Dr Renato Ruggiero, and other members of the WTO Secretariat as well as the members of some of the delegations. I could not have foreseen, in 1996, that in the following four years, I would be called upon to serve on three dispute panels, twice as chairman.

How the System Works

If a member of WTO has a trade dispute with another member, the former could make a formal request to the latter for consultations concerning the subject of the dispute. If the consultations do not succeed in resolving the dispute, the complaining member can request the DSB for the establishment of a panel to examine the dispute. A panel normally consists of three persons, none of whom should be a national of the complaining or responding members or of a third party which has intervened in the proceedings before the panel.[2] The panellists serve in their individual capacity. One of the three panellists would be chosen as chairman. The panellists are usually chosen by the WTO Secretariat, with the consent

---

[1] I have said something about this meeting elsewhere — Tommy Koh, *The Quest for World Order: Perspectives of a Pragmatic Idealist* (Singapore: IPS/Times Academic Press, 1998), pp. 120–126.
[2] This rule precluding national panelists does not however apply to persons serving on the Appellate Body.

of the parties. If either party disagrees with the proposed composition of the panel, it could, within 20 days of its establishment, ask the WTO Director-General to name the panel. Sometimes, the parties take the initiative to propose to the Secretariat, the composition of a panel.

Once a panel has been composed, the panel would be informed of the identity of the person from the WTO Secretariat who would serve as the panel's secretary. This person is usually from the division of the WTO Secretariat most relevant to the subject of the dispute, eg, agriculture or rules. The panel would also be served by a lawyer from the Legal Division. The team therefore usually consists of the three panellists and the two Secretariat officials. The gang of five would work very closely on the dispute for the ensuing six to nine months.

The first order of business is for the panel to discuss its terms of reference, settle the working procedures, timelines, dates for the two substantive meetings with the parties, date of the meeting with third parties, etc. The panel would usually request one of its members to hold an organisational meeting with the parties in Geneva to settle these procedural matters.

The panel would then study the written presentations submitted by the parties. The presentations, together with their annexes and exhibits, could be quite voluminous. The panel would then meet in Geneva and hold the first substantive meeting with the parties. The panel would hold a special session with the third parties. If there are preliminary applications, the panel would arrange to hear them first and then decide whether to dispose of them immediately or defer its decisions on them.

The parties would submit their second written presentations to the panel. After studying them, the panel would hold the second substantive meeting with the parties. I would have something more to say about how the second panel which I chaired, changed the format of the second meeting in order to extract more value from it.

Following the second substantive meeting, the panel, with the help of the Secretariat, would begin drafting its interim report. The report is in two parts. The first part is factual and descriptive and is subject to the amendments of the parties. The second part of the report is substantive. The panel would issue its interim report to the parties and request for their comments. The panel would take their comments into account before issuing its final report.

After receiving the final report of the panel, a party could request the panel to hold a meeting to review its report. In the two cases, which I chaired, no such meeting was requested. However, in both cases, the unsuccessful party appealed to the Appellate Body. We waited anxiously for several months before we heard the good news that the Appellate Body had upheld our decisions. The whole process, from the beginning to the end, could take about a year. The time taken by the dispute panel is about six months.

First Dispute Panel

US — The Cuban Liberty and Democratic Solidarity Act or Helms-Burton Act

On 17 February 1997, I received a telephone call from the WTO's Director-General, Dr Renato Ruggiero. He informed me that the European Commission (EC) had brought a complaint against the United States, on the extra-territorial effect of the Helms-Burton Act, which imposed sanctions against Cuba. The EC requested the WTO to establish a dispute panel to which the US was opposed. The DSB had agreed to establish such a panel on 20 November 1996. The two sides had been unable to agree on the composition of the panel. The EC had requested the Director-General to name the panel. Dr Ruggiero informed me that Mr Arthur Dunkel of Switzerland (former Director-General of GATT) had agreed to chair the panel and Mr Edward (Ted) Woodfield of New Zealand had agreed to be a panellist. Dr Ruggiero would like me to be the third panellist. He wanted my reply by 20 February as he intended to announce the composition of the panel on that day. Because of the importance of the panel and its possible impact on Singapore's relations with the US, I told Dr Ruggiero that I had to obtain the permission of my government. I was given approval to accept the appointment by Dr Ruggiero's deadline.

Helms-Burton Act

Cuba had shot down two planes piloted by Cuban-Americans. This caused great anger in the US Congress. In retaliation, the US Congress enacted the Cuban Democracy Act and the Cuban Liberty and Democratic Solidarity Act, also known as the Helms-Burton Act. The Act aimed at deterring non-US persons and companies from doing business with Cuba. The Act provided, inter alia, for any US citizen, with more than US$50,000 worth of expropriated property in Cuba, to sue, in US courts, any foreign company or person which buys, leases, or profits from these properties. The law also directs the US Administration to deny visas to and exclude from the US, such persons and corporate officers and controlling shareholders of those companies, along with their spouses and minor children.

EC Requested US for Consultations

The Helms-Burton Act attracted protests from many US allies and friends. The EC alleged that the Cuban Democracy Act and the Helms-Burton Act, contain six objectionable measures. The EC therefore requested the US for consultations pursuant to the DSU, GATT and the General Agreement on Trade in Services (GATS).[3]

Consultations were held on 4 June, 2 July and 23 September. The consultations were, however, not successful in resolving the dispute between the two parties.

EC Requested Establishment of Panel

On 3 October 1996, the EC requested the DSB to establish a panel. The EC requested the panel to find that eight of the US measures were inconsistent with its obligations under the GATT, WTO and GATS.

---

[3] Request for Consultations, US — The Cuban Liberty and Democratic Solidarity Act (Helms-Burton Act), WT/DS38/1, 13 May 1996.

The DSB agreed to establish such a panel on 20 November 1996. As the two parties could not agree on the composition of the panel, the EC requested the Director-General to name the panel.

EC and US Reactions to Panel

On 20 February 1997, Dr Ruggiero met with the representatives of the EC and the US to inform them of the composition of the panel. The EC representative said that it was a very good panel. The US representative kept silent.

On the same day, the US announced in Washington, DC, that it would boycott the panel on the ground that it lacked jurisdiction.

Also, on the same day, the EC's Commissioner for Trade, Sir Leon Brittan, issued a statement in Brussels stating that the EC would continue to negotiate with the US in spite of the establishment of the panel.

Panel's Teleconference

The panel had a teleconference on 27 February 1997. We agreed on the following:

(a) that the establishment of the panel was exerting pressure on the two parties to reach a settlement;
(b) that the panel would send its proposed time-table to the parties;
(c) that we would give the parties three months to settle the dispute;
(d) that we did not know whether the US would invoke the defence of national security (GATT Article XXI) and requested the Secretariat to undertake research on the topic; and
(e) to hold the first meeting with the parties on 12 May 1997 and the second meeting on 16 June 1997.

Communication to EC, US and Third Parties

On 27 February 1997, Chairman Dunkel wrote to the EC and US, conveying our proposed time-table and working procedures.

On 3 March 1997, EC replied accepting the Panel's proposals. The US did not respond.

On 12 March 1997, the panel wrote to the Third Parties (Japan, Thailand, Malaysia, Canada and Mexico) informing them of the proposed timetable and affording them with an opportunity to be heard on 13 May 1997 at 10.00am.

EC Requests Delay and Suspension

On 14 April 1997, the EC requested the panel for a one week extension for the filing of its first written submission to 21 April 1997. The panel agreed.

On 21 April 1997, the EC requested the panel to suspend its proceedings pursuant to Article 12.12 of the DSU in order to allow the parties to bring their negotiations to a successful conclusion. The EC, however, reserved its right to resume the panel's suspended proceedings within the next 12 months. The panel acceded to the EC's request on 21 April 1997.

US-EU Understanding on Helms-Burton Act

On 18 April 1997, a Washington-based publication, "Inside US Trade", published the text of the US-EU Understanding on the Helms-Burton Act (Vol. 15 No. 16). This text was never officially communicated by the two parties to the panel or to WTO.

Panel Lapsed on 21 April 1998

The panel's proceedings were suspended on 21 April 1997. It could remain in suspension for 12 months. Thus, at midnight, on 21 April 1998, the authority of the panel lapsed and it ceased to exist.

Thanks from Ruggiero and Dunkel

On 5 May 1998, Dr Ruggiero wrote to thank me for serving on "this very controversial and sensitive panel". On 19 June 1998, Mr Arthur Dunkel wrote to say that the "Dispute Settlement Body was taken seriously by both parties, and I believe that it has helped to enforce the multilateral trading system".

Concluding Thoughts

As this was my first experience of serving on a dispute panel, I treated it as a learning experience. What did I learn? I learnt the rules and procedures of the WTO dispute settlement system, especially the DSU and DSB. I learnt how a panel works with the Secretariat, the parties, the third parties, etc. I learnt from Mr Dunkel the role and responsibility of the chairman of the panel. I came to know and admire the two members of the Secretariat who were assigned to assist the panel: Ms Gabrielle Marceau and Mr Joost Pauwelyn. I took comfort in the fact that although our panel was suspended, its very existence had imposed tremendous pressure on the two parties to negotiate in good faith and to arrive at an amicable compromise.

Second Dispute Panel

Canada — Measures Affecting the Importation of Milk and the Exportation of Dairy Products

On 28 July 1998, I received a fax from Mr Paul Shanahan, Counsellor of the WTO's Division on Agriculture and Commodities. The fax recalled that on 25 March 1998, the DSB had established a panel to examine the complaints brought by New Zealand and USA against Canada. The WTO Secretariat, in consultation with the three parties, was in the process of establishing the panel and wanted to know whether I was willing to be a member. Permission was given for me to accept the appointment.

Background

The US and New Zealand alleged that Canada was providing subsidies, in particular, export subsidies, on dairy products through its national and provincial pricing arrangements for milk and other dairy products. Specifically, the two complaining countries alleged that Canada had established and maintained a system of special milk classes through which it maintained high domestic prices, promoted import substitution, and provided export subsidies for dairy products going into world markets. They alleged that the Canadian measures were inconsistent with GATT (1994), the Agreement on Agriculture, the Agreement on Subsidies and Countervailing Measures and the Agreement on Import Licensing Procedures.

Consultations

USA and New Zealand requested Canada for consultations pursuant to Article 4 of DSU. Consultations were held between the US and Canada on 19 November 1997 and between New Zealand and Canada on 28 January 1998. The consultations were not successful in resolving the dispute.

Requests for Panel

Following the failure of consultations, the US requested the DSB for a panel on 2 February 1998. New Zealand did likewise on 12 March 1998. The DSB acceded to the two requests on 25 March 1998 and merged the two panels into one.

Composition of Panel

On 12 August 1998, I received another fax from Mr Paul Shanahan confirming that I had been selected by the three parties to serve on the panel and to be its chairman. I was also informed that my two colleagues on the panel were Professor Ernst-Ulrich Petersmann of Germany and Mr Guillermo Aquilar Alvarez of Mexico. Professor Petersmann was formerly with the WTO Secretariat and, after his retirement, was teaching in Geneva. Mr Aquilar was a lawyer in private practice and was a member of the Mexican delegation which negotiated the North American Free Trade Agreement (NAFTA).

Secretariat

Mr Shanahan served the panel as its secretary. We were also assisted by a lawyer from the Legal Division, Mr Joost Pauwelyn. Both of them did a splendid job. The other members of the Secretariat who helped us with the case were: Mr Jeffrey Gertler, Mr Erik Wijkstrom and Mr William Davey.

Organisational Meeting

The panel accepted the Secretariat's proposed timetable for the work of the panel and its working procedures. Professor Petersmann chaired an organisational meeting with the parties on 18 August 1998. The parties accepted the panel's proposed timetable and working procedures.

First Substantive Meeting

The first substantive meeting was held on 19 and 20 October 1998. On the first day, the panel heard oral presentations by the US, New Zealand and Canada. On the second morning, the panel heard the presentations of the two third parties, namely, Australia and Japan. In the afternoon of the second day, the panel allowed the three parties to pose questions to each other. The panel also posed questions to the three parties.

Second Substantive Meeting

The second substantive meeting with the parties was held on 17 and 18 November 1998. On the first day, we heard the rebuttal submissions by the three parties. On the second afternoon, we heard the concluding statements of the parties.

Interim Report

The interim report was divided into two parts: the first part was descriptive and the second substantive. The panellists and the Secretariat met in Geneva in October and November to brainstorm on the issues presented by the case and the panel's findings on each of the issues. The process was interactive. Following the discussions, the panel would request the Secretariat to put up drafts which would then be commented upon by the panellists. The drafts would be amended until all the panellists were satisfied with them.

On 5 February 1999, the interim report of the panel was conveyed to the parties.

Final Report

Comments on the interim report by the parties were carefully considered by the panel and the Secretariat. The Secretariat sent the panel a memorandum on the comments received, discussed their merit, and proposed how the panel should respond to them in its final report. Following the exchange of many emails, the panel and the Secretariat agreed on the content of the final report.

In its final report,[4] the panel found that Canada was in violation of its obligations under the Agreement on Agriculture, specifically Article 9.1(a) and 9.1(c) and, in the alternative, Article 10.1.

Canada did not ask the panel for a review meeting but appealed to the Appellate Body.

Upheld by Appellate Body

On 13 October 1999, seven months after the panel's final report, the Appellate Body upheld the panel's finding that Canada was providing subsidies, in violation of Article 9.1(c) of the Agreement on Agriculture.[5]

---

[4] Report of the Panel, Canada — Measures Affecting the Importation of Milk and the Exportation of Dairy Products, WT/DS103/R, WT/DS113/R, 17 May 1999.
[5] Report of the Appellate Body, Canada — Measures Affecting the Importation of Milk and the Exportation of Dairy Products, WT/DS103/AB/R, WT/DS113/AB/R, 13 October 1999.

Significance of This Case

The legal significance of this case was that it was the first case which involved the substantive provisions of the Agreement on Agriculture relating to export subsidies. The Appellate Body upheld the panel's finding that the provision of milk to processors/exporters, although it is not financed directly with government funds, was, nevertheless, "financed by virtue of governmental action", within the meaning of Article 9.1(c) of the said Agreement.

Third Dispute Panel

US — Safeguard Measures on Imports of Fresh, Chilled or Frozen Lamb Meat from New Zealand and Australia

On 24 February 2000, I received a fax from Mr Jan Woznowski, Director of the Rules Division of WTO. He informed me that Australia, New Zealand and the US had nominated me to chair a dispute panel to examine a dispute between Australia and New Zealand, as complainants, and the US, as respondent. The issue was whether the US had violated its obligations under WTO's Safeguards Agreement. I was given permission to accept the appointment.

Background

For over 50 years, the sheep industry in the US had been on the decline. The downsizing of the industry was accelerated by the phasing out, in 1996, of US subsidies to sheep farmers. The US alleged that in 1997 and 1998, there was an unexpected surge of imports of lamb meat from Australia and New Zealand. The US alleged that because of the progress of technology, it became possible for Australia and New Zealand to export fresh and chilled lamb meat instead of frozen meat to the US. As a result, there was direct competition between the imports and domestically produced lamb meat. The US contended that its domestic industry was faced with the threat of serious injury from the increased imports. The US imposed safeguard measures to protect its domestic industry for a period of three years, by a combination of tariff and quota, and by providing the industry with a grant of US$100 million in order to bring about adjustment and to regain competitiveness. Australia and New Zealand complained that the US had acted in violation of the Safeguards Agreement and GATT (1994).

Consultations

On 16 July 1999, New Zealand requested the US for consultations pursuant to Article 4 of DSU and Article 14 of the Agreement on Safeguards. Consultations were held on 26 August 1999, but they failed to resolve the dispute.

On 23 July 1999, Australia requested the US for consultations. Consultations were held on 26 August 1999 but they also failed to resolve the dispute.

Panel

On 14 October 1999, New Zealand requested the DSB to establish a panel to examine the dispute. On the same date, Australia made a similar request.

At its meeting on 19 November 1999, the DSB agreed to establish a single panel to deal with the two disputes.

On 21 March 2000, the three parties agreed to compose the panel with me, as chairman, and with Professor Meinhard Hilf of Germany and Mr Shishir Priyadarshi of India as the other two panellists. Professor Meinhard Hilf was a professor of law at Hamburg University. Mr Shishir Priyadarshi was an Indian diplomat and Counsellor in the Permanent Mission of India to the WTO.

Secretariat

Ms Clarisse Morgan of the Rules Division served as the able secretary to the panel. Mr Werner Zdouc, a lawyer from the Legal Division, was also assigned to assist the panel. The five of us worked very hard and harmoniously.

Organisational Meeting

Mr Shishir Priyadarshi chaired the organisational meeting with the parties on 28 March 2000. The meeting adopted the timetable and the working procedures.

First Substantive Meeting

The panel held the first substantive meeting with the parties on 25 and 26 May 2000.

On the morning of 25 May, the panel first heard two preliminary applications from the US and one from Australia. The first preliminary application by the US was for a ruling on the alleged insufficiency of the panel's requests of Australia and New Zealand. The second preliminary application was for a ruling on exclusion of the US Safeguards Statute from the panel's terms of reference. The panel rejected both applications.

Australia requested the panel to make a preliminary ruling on the disclosure by the US of confidential information excluded from the US International Trade Commission's report and information covering the process after the USITC had reported to the President. The panel declined to make such a ruling.

After disposing of the three preliminary applications, the panel heard the oral presentations of the three parties.

On the morning of 26 May, the panel allowed the parties to respond to each other's presentations made on the first day and to post questions to each other. The panel posed eight questions to the US and six questions to Australia and New Zealand.

The panel also held a session to hear the three third parties: Canada, EC and Iceland. Although Japan had intervened as a third party, it did not submit a written or oral statement to the panel.

Second Substantive Hearing

The second substantive hearing was held on 26 and 27 July 2000. On the first day, USA, Australia and New Zealand made very long statements. The panel felt dissatisfied as no new value had been added. It therefore decided to change the format for the second day.

On the second day, and with no prior notice, the panel informed the parties that it was grappling with four clusters of issues and it would like to hear the parties' views on them. The four issues were:

(a) Was the surge in imports foreseeable?
(b) What was the definition of the term "industry"?
(c) What was the proof of serious injury?
(d) Was the remedy imposed by the US President consistent with the WTO Agreement on Safeguards?

The change of format produced the intended result. We got the three parties away from reading scripted statements. We got them to think on their feet, to engage each other and to focus on the issues.

Interim Report

The descriptive part of the interim report was prepared by Ms Clarisse Morgan. The panel reviewed and approved it. It was conveyed to the parties for their comments and amendments.

The substantive part of the interim report was more carefully considered by the panel. A conference call was held on 10 October 2000 to go over a draft of the interim report.

The interim report was issued to the parties on 2 November 2000.

Final Report

The panel took the comments of the parties into account in preparing its final report. In its final report, the panel held, inter alia:

(a) that the US had acted inconsistently with Article XIX:1(a) of GATT (1994) by failing to demonstrate as a matter of fact the existence of "unforeseen developments";
(b) that the US had acted inconsistently with Article 4.1(c) of the Agreement on Safeguards because the USITC failed to obtain data in respect of producers representing a major proportion of the total domestic production by the domestic industry as defined in the investigation; and
(c) that the US had acted inconsistently with Article 4.2(b) of the Agreement on Safeguards because the USITC's determination in the lamb meat investigation in respect of causation did not demonstrate the required causal link between increased imports and threats of serious injury. Because of the above violations of Article 4, the US had also acted inconsistently with Article 2.1 of the Agreement on Safeguards.

The final report of the panel was issued on 6 December 2000, and circulated on 21 December 2000.[6]

Appellate Body

The US appealed to the Appellate Body. On 1 May 2001, the Appellate Body upheld the panel's findings, on most points, in its report (AB-2001-1).[7] This was a huge relief coming five months after our report.

---

[6] Report of the Panel, US — Safeguard Measures on Imports of Fresh, Chilled or Frozen Lamb Meat from New Zealand and Australia, WT/DS177/R, WT/DS178/R, 21 December 2000.
[7] Report of the Appellate Body, US — Safeguard Measures on Imports of Fresh, Chilled or Frozen Lamb Meat from New Zealand and Australia, WT/DS177/AB/R, WT/DS178/AB/R, 1 May 2001.

Final Reflections

Based upon my three experiences, I have formed several reflections.

First, I believe that the WTO dispute settlement system is an admirable one. It is mandatory and not voluntary. No member of the WTO, no matter how powerful, can block the establishment of a panel or the adoption of a panel's report. The system is speedy, low cost and fair. In practice, the Appellate Body ensures that a consistent jurisprudence is being followed by the different panels.

Second, I have formed a very favourable view of the quality, dedication and productivity of the WTO's small Secretariat. The personnel assigned to assist the three panels of which I was a member were uniformly excellent.

Third, the WTO is very fortunate to be able to find so many well qualified "volunteers" to serve as panellists. Each assignment is extremely intense and takes about six to nine months. The panellists are not paid for their contributions. They do it because they believe in the WTO, in the rule of law and in the peaceful settlement of disputes between States.

Fourth, in the case of the two panels which I had the good fortune to chair, I was very pleased that although the panellists had never worked together before, they worked well as a team. I was also very happy to see the symbiotic relationship which developed between the panellists and the Secretariat officials assigned to work with us.

Finally, I wish I had more time so that I could assist the WTO by serving on other panels. On three subsequent occasions, I had to reluctantly turn down the WTO's requests and recommended three able colleagues, Ambassador Vanu Gopala Menon, Ambassador K. Kesavapany and Mr S. Tiwari, who subsequently served on these panels.

[Originally published in *Economic Diplomacy: Essays and Reflections by Singapore's Negotiators*, eds. C. L. Lim and M. Liang, World Scientific, 2010, pp. 141–155.]

Is There a Role for Law in a World Ruled by Power?*

In this essay, I wish to discuss one of the most controversial questions in international relations: the relationship between international law and power. The Realists like to say that the world is ruled by power. They tend to be dismissive of international law. I want to argue that even in a world ruled by power, States need international law.

The Nature of Power

I shall begin by elucidating the concept of power. The Realists often mistakenly think that power equals military power. This is not the case. In his 2009 book, *Power Rules: How Common Sense Can Rescue American Foreign Policy*, Leslie H. Gelb disaggregates power into its three components: military power, economic power and foreign policy power. Another American thinker on US foreign policy, Professor Joseph Nye, has suggested a fourth component of power, namely, soft power. The current US Secretary of State, Hillary Clinton, has said that the Obama Administration will use the concept of smart power, which is to use the optimum combination of the four components of power, depending on the context and the circumstances. The Obama Administration is not against the use of military power, but it will only use it as a last resort and when the war is just. My first point is, therefore, that when the Realists say the world is ruled by power, the term power includes

---

*Presented at the Indonesian Society of International Law 8th Anniversary Seminar on "International Law as a Political Instrument?", 10 June 2010, Constitutional Court, Jakarta.

not just military power, but also economic power, diplomatic power and soft power or cultural power.

Do We Live in a World Ruled by Force?

The second point I wish to make is that we do not live in a world ruled by force. To be sure, States do, from time to time, resort to force to achieve their objectives. Many had hoped that, with the end of the Cold War, the world would enter a more peaceful phase. According to the Stockholm International Peace Research Institute (SIPRI), there have been more armed conflicts in the world, since the end of the Cold War, than during it. My conclusion is that we will never live in a word without wars.

It would, however, be a mistake to jump from this fact to the conclusion that we live in a world ruled by force. On the contrary, I would argue that, we live in a relatively peaceful world and that the resort to the use of force to resolve inter-State disputes is a minority phenomenon. I would go on to make the argument that, even for militarily powerful States, there are limits on the use of force to secure their objectives. It may seem paradoxical, but it is a historical fact that militarily powerful States do not always prevail over their less powerful adversaries. The two most famous recent examples are Vietnam and Afghanistan. The United States did not prevail over Vietnam and the Soviet Union did not prevail over Afghanistan.

Do We Live in a Lawless World?

My third point is that we do not live in a lawless world. We live in an increasingly inter-connected and inter-dependent world. It is a world bound together, not just by State interests, but also by international organisations, regional groupings, international law, customs and practices. The United States is, without question, the most powerful State in the world. But, even the most powerful State in the world cannot act alone. It needs allies and friends. It cannot ignore the interests and opinions of other States.

Let me use trade as an example. The US has to trade with other countries in order to promote its prosperity and to create jobs. The US is a member of the World Trade Organization (WTO). The US has to accept the laws and rules governing international trade which has been enacted by the WTO and its predecessor, GATT. Weaker States, such as Australia and New Zealand, can refer a trade dispute with the US to the dispute settlement body of WTO for resolution. The US cannot block the WTO from establishing a dispute panel. I chaired a WTO dispute panel dealing with a dispute brought by Australia and New Zealand against the United States. If the dispute panel finds in favour of Australia and New Zealand, will the US comply? As the most powerful State in the world, can the US disregard the decision and walk away. In theory, it could, but in practice the US has always complied. Why? Because it is in the enlightened self-interest of the US to do so. If the US decides to defy the decisions of the WTO's dispute settlement body, other States would be tempted to emulate the US. The result is that the whole system would be undermined.

It is in the interests of all states, including the US, to uphold the rule of law in the world. All states benefit more from a peaceful, orderly and rules-based world, than a chaotic, lawless and violent world.

The Limits of Military Power

Some Realists may object to my example taken from the world of trade. Let me, therefore, cite another example. In 1990, Iraq decided to invade Kuwait and incorporate it into Iraq. Iraq was militarily superior to Kuwait and had no trouble overwhelming the Kuwaiti defence. Was Iraq successful in using military force to conquer and acquire the territory and resources of its weaker neighbour?

Iraq was not successful. The UN Security Council condemned the invasion and demanded the withdrawal of Iraqi forces from Kuwait. When Iraq refused to comply, the UNSC authorised the use of force by a coalition of countries, led by the US. Diplomatically, Iraq was almost totally isolated. Militarily, the Iraqi forces suffered a humiliating defeat and withdrew from Kuwait. Kuwait recovered its sovereignty and independence.

I am not using the Kuwait case to say that the UN will always come to the rescue of a small State, which is the victim of aggression by a more powerful State. But, the historical record since the founding of the UN in 1945, suggests that the unilateral use of force seldom leads to a successful outcome. Let me cite the following examples to support my contention: North Korea failed to conquer South Korea, the US withdrew from Vietnam, the Soviet Union withdrew from Afghanistan, Vietnam withdrew from Cambodia, Iraq withdrew from Kuwait and the US will soon withdraw from Iraq. Because the US did not obtain the second UNSC resolution, it did not get the support of the world. As a result, although the US succeeded in invading Iraq militarily, it did not succeed in its post-invasion agenda because it did not have international law on its side and many of the allies and friends of the US were unwilling to help.

Is There a Role for Law in a World Ruled by Power?

Is there a role for law in a world ruled by power? My answer is yes. I have already demonstrated that we do not live in a lawless world.

States interact with one another in many areas. Trade is just one of them. Others include investment, tourism, aviation, shipping, telecommunications, the internet, banking, tax, mobility of workers, refugees, terrorism, weapons of mass destruction, non-proliferation of nuclear weapons, human rights, women's rights, children's rights, etc. What is not very well known to the public is that in all these areas as well as in others, there are applicable international law, conventions, rules and institutions.

This is a reality which has an impact on States as well as on individuals. Let me cite one example. Mobile phones have become a necessity and not a luxury. All of us make calls to friends at home and abroad on our mobile phones. When we make such a call to a foreign friend, the call is carried either by a submarine cable (95 per cent of the time) or by a satellite. The submarine cables of the world are governed by international law, especially by the UN Convention on the Law of the Sea. The satellites are governed by air and space law and regulated by the International Telecommunications Union (ITU).

Conclusion

The inescapable conclusion is that international law permeates many aspects of our lives. It provides the framework for international cooperation. It helps to make this a rules-based world. International law supports the civilisation we enjoy. It is hard to imagine the kind of world this would be if we did not have any international law. It would be a nightmarish Hobbesian world.

It is, of course, true that unlike a domestic legal system, there is no officer empowered to enforce the judgements and decisions of the International Court of Justice, the International Tribunal for the Law of the Sea, WTO's dispute settlement body, etc. But, does this mean that they have no force and are not complied with? The truth is that most States choose to comply most of the time. Why? Because they consider it to be in their own self-interest to do so. What the Realists sometimes do not understand is that all States, including the US, choose to abide by international law because it is in their core interests to have a peaceful, orderly, rules-based world. I would hope that the two rising giants of Asia, China and India, will support this view.

Mapping Out Rival Claims to the South China Sea

During the past two years, tension has been rising in the South China Sea. As a result of a deadline set by a United Nations body for coastal states to submit their claims to extended continental shelves, there was a flurry of claims and counter-claims in 2009, including a joint submission by Malaysia and Vietnam and a response by China.

There have also been several incidents at sea, between China and Vietnam, over fisheries; and between China, on the one hand, and the Philippines and Vietnam, on the other, over the collection of seismic data and exploration for hydrocarbons by oil companies.

At the Asean Regional Forum, held in Hanoi in July last year, there was a sharp exchange of words between the foreign ministers of China and the United States.

Much has been written about the South China Sea, but the salient questions of law and fact involved remain unclear. I will attempt to answer 10 of the most frequently asked questions.

Question 1: What and where is the South China Sea?

The South China Sea is a semi-enclosed sea, bounded by China in the north, the Philippines in the east, Vietnam in the west, East Malaysia and Brunei in the south-east, and Indonesia and West Malaysia in the south-west.

This body of water is about 3.5 million sq km. It forms part of the Pacific Ocean, one of the global commons.

Question 2: What is the significance of the South China Sea?

First, it is the highway for trade, shipping and telecommunications. Eighty percent of world trade is seaborne. One-third of world trade and half of the world's traffic in oil and gas pass through the South China Sea. Freedom of navigation in the South China Sea is, therefore, of critical importance to China, Japan, South Korea, Asean and other trading nations and maritime powers.

Second, it is rich in fish and other living resources. Fish is a principal source of protein and fishing is a source of employment for millions of Asians who live in coastal communities.

Third, it is presumed that there are significant deposits of oil and gas in the continental shelves underneath the South China Sea.

Question 3: Is there a law governing the South China Sea?

It is governed by international law, particularly the UN Convention on the Law of the Sea (Unclos), which was adopted in 1982 and came into force in 1994. China, Japan, South Korea and all the 10 Asean countries are parties to this convention and thus bound by its provisions.

Question 4: Which are the claimant countries and what have they claimed?

Two groups of geographic features located in the South China Sea are subject to competing claims of sovereignty, namely the Paracel Islands, located in the northern part of the South China Sea, and the Spratly Islands, located in the central part of the South China Sea. In particular, the sovereignty dispute over the Spratly Islands is a continual source of conflict and tension in the region.

China, Brunei, Malaysia, the Philippines and Vietnam are the claimant states. Taiwan is also a claimant but not recognised by the international community as a sovereign and independent state. It is, therefore, not a party to the UN Convention.

Brunei reportedly claims part of the area of waters in the Spratly Islands adjacent to it, including two maritime features, namely Louisa Bank and Rifleman Bank, as part of its continental shelf.

The Philippines reportedly claims 53 of the maritime features in the Spratly Islands which it calls the Kalayaan Island Group as well as Scarborough Shoal.

Malaysia reportedly claims sovereignty over 11 maritime features in the Spratly Islands.

Vietnam claims sovereignty over all the maritime features in the Paracel Islands and the Spratly Islands.

China claims sovereignty over all the maritime features in the South China Sea.

Taiwan's claims are identical to those of China. Taiwan is, however, in physical possession of the largest maritime feature in the South China Sea, namely Itu Aba or Taiping.

Question 5: Are the claims consistent with Unclos?

The convention does not contain any new law on how to determine a state's claim to sovereignty over territory. The question has to be determined by customary international law.

Disputes over sovereignty can be resolved by negotiation, conciliation, arbitration or adjudication. It is, thus, not possible for one to say whether the sovereignty claims by the five claimant states are valid or not. They have not been tested in a court of law or arbitral tribunal.

The Chinese claim is not clear. The ambiguity is caused by a map which was attached to a Chinese official note to the UN on the outer limits of its continental shelf under Unclos in May 2009. The map contains nine dashed lines forming a U, enclosing most of the waters of the South China Sea. The map was first published in 1947 by the Republic of China under the Kuomintang, prior to the founding of the People's Republic of China.

What is not clear is whether China is claiming sovereignty over the maritime features enclosed by the lines or to both the features and the waters so enclosed. If the former, this is consistent with the convention. However, if the latter, then China's assertion of rights, based upon history, to the waters, is not consistent with the convention. The convention does not recognise such rights.

When China acceded to the convention, it agreed to be bound by the new legal order set out in the convention. Under the law of treaties, when a state becomes a party to a treaty, it is under a legal obligation to bring its laws and conduct into conformity with the treaty.

Question 6: What maritime zones are the features entitled to?

There is considerable confusion about the answer to this question. First, there is no authoritative study of the different maritime features which make up the Spratly Islands group. Such a study should classify them into: islands, rocks, low-tide elevations and artificial islands.

Second, under the convention, artificial islands are not entitled to any maritime zones except for a 500m safety zone. A low-tide elevation is not entitled to any maritime zone but can be used as a base point in measuring the territorial sea. A low-tide elevation is submerged at high tide.

A rock is entitled to a 12-nautical mile (22 km) territorial sea. An island is entitled to a territorial sea, a 200-nautical mile exclusive economic zone and a continental shelf.

Under Article 121 of the convention, the difference between a rock and an island is that an island is capable of sustaining human habitation or economic life.

Third, the policies and pronouncements of the claimant states show little regard for the law and are self-serving.

To put it crudely, they seem to be saying that 'my rock is an island and your island is only a rock'. In its submission to the UN in 2009, Indonesia contends that all the features in the South China Sea are rocks and not islands.

Question 7: What is Asean's position on the South China Sea?

Asean, as a group, does not support or oppose the claims of the four Asean claimant states. The group has also not taken a position on the merits of the disputes between China and Asean claimant states. Therefore, any perception that the claims of Brunei, Malaysia, the Philippines and Vietnam are backed by Asean is incorrect.

Asean is, however, a stakeholder in the South China Sea. First, it wishes to maintain peace in the region. Second, it wishes to promote good relations between China and Asean. Third, it is committed to the peaceful settlement of disputes. Fourth, it wishes to ensure that all interested parties act strictly in accordance with international law, especially Unclos.

In 2002, when tensions were high, Asean drafted a Declaration on the Conduct of Parties in the South China Sea (DOC). The DOC was signed by Asean and China. In July this year, the Asean Regional Forum adopted a set of implementing guidelines. Both the DOC and the guidelines are non-binding.

Although they are not unimportant, the fact is that some claimant states have violated both the letter and spirit of the DOC by acting unilaterally to expand and fortify the features they occupy.

Asean and China should work together to formulate and adopt a binding code of conduct as their next goal.

Question 8: What is the US position on the South China Sea?

The US is not a claimant state or a littoral state. It is, however, a stakeholder. Why? First, the US is a major trading nation and maritime power.

It has a legitimate interest in ensuring that the freedom of navigation and other lawful uses of the sea are respected by the claimant states and littoral states.

Second, the US has an interest in ensuring that the claimant states act strictly in accordance with international law, including the Unclos, of which it is, unfortunately, not a state party.

Third, while the US has not endorsed the claims of the Philippines and Vietnam, it is concerned that the disputes should be resolved peacefully, without resort to force.

Fourth, the US is concerned about the Chinese map and would oppose any attempt by China to assert rights to the waters enclosed by the nine dashed lines.

Fifth, the US has a treaty alliance with the Philippines but it has been ambiguous over whether and under what conditions that alliance might apply to an armed conflict in the South China Sea involving the Philippines and another claimant.

Question 9: What could China and the Asean claimant states do to bring about an amicable settlement to their disputes?

They have two fundamental choices. The first option is to try to resolve their sovereignty disputes through negotiations, both bilaterally and multilaterally.

However, if the negotiations prove to be fruitless, the parties should consider whether to resort to other modalities of dispute settlement, such as conciliation, arbitration and adjudication.

However, sovereignty disputes cannot be referred to any form of third-party dispute settlement without the consent of the parties.

Also, China has exercised its right, under Article 298, to opt out of compulsory binding dispute settlement, for disputes concerning its maritime boundary delimitation. So, a claimant state, such as the Philippines, cannot refer maritime boundary delimitation disputes with

China to arbitration under Annex VII of Unclos or adjudication before the International Tribunal for the Law of the Sea.

However, the Philippines could, for example, frame the issue as one relating to other Unclos provisions, such as its rights to explore and exploit the natural resources in its exclusive economic zone or whether certain disputed features are rocks or islands.

The second choice is for the parties to put aside their sovereignty disputes and to apply the concept of joint development to the disputed areas. Joint development has worked in other cases, for example, between Malaysia and Thailand (1979–1990), between Malaysia and Vietnam (1992) and between Australia and Timor Leste (2002).

However, we face a major obstacle. The concept of joint development must be applied in the context of a disputed area. But, until China is prepared to clarify its claims, we will not be able to determine what are the disputed areas.

Question 10: What is Singapore's position?

Singapore is not a claimant state. It does not support the position of any of the claimant states. On the merits of the various claims, Singapore is neutral.

Singapore is, however, not neutral on the need by all the claimant states to strictly adhere to international law, in general, and Unclos, in particular. Singapore is also insistent that the disputes must be resolved peacefully. Any threat or use of force would be unacceptable. Singapore shares Asean's aspiration to maintain peace in the region and to promote good relations between Asean and China.

Pending the resolution of the dispute, Singapore supports the effort by Asean and China to implement the DOC that would serve as a guide for the behaviour of the claimant states in order to avoid confrontation and reduce tensions.

As a neutral party, trusted by all the claimants, Singapore seeks to play a helpful role, especially through the National University of

Singapore Centre for International Law, to bring the parties together, elucidate the issues, research the facts and the law, and help the parties to find ways to achieve an amicable settlement to their disputes.

[Originally published in *The Straits Times*, 13 September 2011.]

A Tribute to Lee A. Sheridan

The University of Malaya, as it was then called, decided to establish a Department of Law in 1957. The University appointed as its first Professor of Law, a young man called Lee A. Sheridan. He was under 30 years at the time.

I first met Lee Sheridan in the later part of 1956. I was then preparing to sit for my HSC 'A' Level examinations. I had already decided to study law and on the advice of one of my English teachers at Raffles Institution, I had set my heart on going to Oxford University. One fateful day, I invited Professor Sheridan, in my capacity as the President of the Literary and Debating Society, to speak to its members on the new law department at the local university. I remember that he spoke very well and made a deep impression on me. After the meeting, I confided in him that I was planning to take up the study of law in England. It did not take long for Lee Sheridan to persuade me that it would be preferable to study the laws of Singapore in Singapore rather than in England. I have never regretted my decision.

Lee Sheridan did a fantastic job in founding our Law School. He had to recruit a teaching staff, comprising both full-time teachers such as Alice Tay, Bernard Brown, Harry Calvert and Geoffrey Bartholomew, as well as part-time teachers such as Tan Boon Teik, Punch Coomaraswamy and Harry Wee. Apart from Bashir Mallal's invaluable *Malayan Law Journal*, there were no published legal materials which could be used by the students. Sheridan and his colleagues set about collating local legal materials to supplement the English textbooks. The curriculum which Lee Sheridan devised was unique in several ways. First, he insisted that law should be taught in the grand manner suggested by Oliver Wendell Holmes. Thus, we had to take courses in logic, in moral philosophy and in legal history. On both teaching and examination techniques, Lee Sheridan was extremely unorthodox. He thought that there was no point for teachers to inflict magisterial lectures on their students when the students could obtain the information from books. He used the case class method of teaching, a method pioneered by Harvard Law School. On examination techniques, he put us through a whole battery of tests ranging from short objective-type questions to the conventional essay-type questions, to a take-away examination.

I remember Lee Sheridan as a man of boundless energy. He not only taught a heavy load but he also published a great deal. In addition, he always found time to help the members of the legal profession and served the community. He and his wife, Margaret, made it a habit to invite a few law students home every week either for drinks or for a meal at which they would have the opportunity to meet with members of the legal profession and other leaders of the Singapore community. I have always been amazed by how Lee managed to do so many things at the same time.

I have maintained contact with Margaret and Lee Sheridan during the many years which have elapsed since they left Singapore. I admire them a great deal and remember with gratitude and pleasure the years I spent with Lee, first as his student and then, later, as his colleague.

18 May 1984

A Tribute to Punch Coomaraswamy

One of Singapore's most distinguished sons, Punch Coomaraswamy, passed away on 8 January 1999.

I want to pay a sincere tribute to my good friend and teacher. When the University of Malaya started to teach law in 1957, Punch Coomaraswamy volunteered to teach, part-time, at the University. I was one of his fortunate students. He was a very good teacher. He was knowledgeable about the law, especially the law of evidence. He was clear in his explanations and he brought to his classes, his enthusiasm for his subject, patience, warmth and kindness. All his students liked and admired him.

He took a particular liking to me. One day, as I was about to begin my final year as a law student, he took me aside for a chat. He told me that when he was a student at the University of Nottingham, in England, he was also very active in student politics. He confided in me that in his final year, he had been over active in student politics. As a result, his studies had suffered. He told me not to make the same mistake. Based on his fatherly advice, I gave up all my student activities, excepting that of President of the Students' Law Society, in order to concentrate on my studies. If not for Punch Coomaraswamy's good advice, I would probably not have topped my class, earned a first class honours degree, and my career might have taken a different turn.

Later, Punch Coomaraswamy served as the Speaker of the Singapore Parliament. When the Singapore Government offered me my first appointment as Ambassador to the United Nations in 1968, I sought his advice. He counselled me to accept the appointment.

Punch Coomaraswamy had served his country, with distinction, in many capacities: as a lawyer in private practice; as a part-time teacher of law at our University; as a Speaker of the Singapore Parliament; as our Ambassador to India, Australia and the United States of America; as a judge of the Supreme Court; and as a Chairman of the Institute of Southeast Asian Studies.

I would also like to pay a tribute to Punch Coomaraswamy as a good man. He was a loving husband to his wife, Kaila, and a good father to their three children, Mohan, Shoba and Vinodh. He was a very filial son to his mother, Chellam.

Punch Coomaraswamy had touched my life and the lives of many, in Singapore and abroad. I shall always remember him in my heart and be grateful to him for his friendship, advice, support and kindness.

[Originally published in the *Singapore Law Gazette*, February 1999. © 1999 Law Society of Singapore]

A Heartfelt Tribute to a Remarkable Man: Chan Sek Keong*

Today, Chief Justice Chan Sek Keong will celebrate his 75th birthday and retire. This is an appropriate moment for us, who have known him for 55 years, to pay him a tribute.

Childhood

Sek Keong was born and grew up in Ipoh, Perak. His father was a clerk in a bank and the family had very modest means. Sek Keong was a very good student and topped the whole of Perak in his Cambridge Overseas School Leaving Certificate examinations. He came to Singapore in 1957, to join the pioneer batch of law students at the then University of Malaya, in Singapore (now the National University of Singapore, or NUS).

Law Student

There was a special *esprit de corps* which united our class. We were very close to one another and to our teachers, who were in many cases only a few years older than the students. The three of us belonged to a study group which met almost every day to review our work. Sek Keong was the "tutor" of the group and would explain the intricacies of the laws of property and trust when our teachers could not. When he typed a case note, he would make extra carbon copies to give to the rest of us. His understanding of the law, his lucidity and unselfish nature were some of

---

*Co-authored with T. P. B. Menon.

his positive attributes. He was a kind, fair-minded and courteous person. He has remained true to the values and beliefs of his student days.

Legal Career

He was in private law practice in Singapore for 23 years, from 1963 to 1986. In 1986, he was appointed as a judicial commissioner. Two years later, in 1988, he was appointed a judge of the Supreme Court. Four years later, his career took a different trajectory. He served as the attorney-general from 1992 to 2006, a total of 14 years. In 2006, he was appointed as the chief justice. To sum up, Sek Keong spent 23 years in law practice, 14 years as the attorney-general and 12 years on the Bench, six of which as the chief justice. The NUS Law School is very proud of him because he is the first local graduate to be appointed as judicial commissioner, judge, attorney-general, and chief justice. We, his old classmates from the Law School, salute him for the following reasons.

A Modest and Humble Man

First, we salute him because he is unspoilt by power, status and wealth. He has never forgotten his humble roots. He leads a simple and frugal life. He remains a modest and humble person.

A Man of Integrity

Second, he is a man of integrity. As a result, he is trusted by all who have dealings with him. He had an excellent reputation with his clients when he was in legal practice. As chief justice, he has earned the trust and respect of the government, the legal profession and the public. In an opinion poll, commissioned by *Reader's Digest*, he was picked by the Singapore public as the person they trusted the most.

A Fair-Minded Person

Third, he is fair-minded and believes strongly that the law should render justice. When he became the chief justice, he was aware that there was a concern that efficiency was being pursued to such an extreme that it could jeopardise the dispensation of justice. In his first speech as the chief justice, he said: "Both justice delayed and justice hurried can cause injustice … Judges must not judge in haste or prejudge disputes in order to dispose of cases faster … no litigant should be allowed to leave the courtroom with the conviction or feeling that he has not been given a fair or full hearing because it was done hurriedly." (April 22, 2006)

Courtesy and Patience

Fourth, he is always courteous and patient. Young lawyers often fear appearing before the Supreme Court. They fear that the judges would expose their ignorance and humiliate them, in front of their clients and the public. In the same speech referred to above, he said: "I assure the Bar that young lawyers who appear before me and my fellow judges should not feel stressed and should have no fear of being stressed." Although he could have demolished a bad argument addressed to him in court, he has never humiliated or belittled the lawyer putting forward the argument. His philosophy is to "live and let live". During his tenure as chief justice, he has developed a more cordial and harmonious relationship between Bench and Bar.

Legal Scholar

Fifth, Sek Keong has a profound knowledge of the law. This is evident in all his written judgments, which are a joy to read. His judgments are always based on sound legal reasoning. They are lucidly and elegantly written as he is an accomplished wordsmith. It would be true to say that "there are few areas of the law which he did not touch and little that he touched which he did not adorn". The chief justice leaves a substantial legacy of world-class judgments which have enriched our jurisprudence.

In conclusion, we wish to say that Chan Sek Keong has served Singapore with great distinction, both in the private and public sectors. As attorney-general and as the chief justice, he has carried out his responsibilities with integrity and fairness. He has enhanced the reputation of the Singapore judiciary and reinforced Singapore's commitment to the rule of law.

[Originally published in *The Business Times*, 5 November 2012.]

A Tribute to Satya Nandan

The Third UN Conference on the Law of the Sea was unusual in many respects. First, it was unusually long, beginning in 1973 and ending in 1982, a total of nine years. Second, it began even though the preparatory process had failed to produce a basic negotiating text. Third, all decisions were taken by consensus which required lengthy and often very acrimonious negotiations. It also required skilful chairmen or facilitators who were able to forge a consensus from seemingly irreconcilable positions. Fourth, the conference had the usual regional groups but many coalitions and special interest groups. Fifth, there were many big egos in the delegations. Clashes of personalities sometimes obstructed the progress of our work. Sixth, it was a treaty making conference. Delegates who were good lawyers, with an excellent command of the English language and with drafting skills, were more effective than other delegates. Seventh, the power and influence of a delegate is not necessarily commensurate with the power and influence of the country he represents. I think the so-called Realists would find this hard to understand.

The US delegation was very ably led by Ambassador Jack Stevenson and, subsequently, by Ambassador Elliot L Richardson. They were excellent lawyers as well as men of great integrity and goodwill. I remember that, on one occasion, Ambassador Richardson surprised his audience when he said that at the conference, the representative of the small country, Fiji, had more influence than those much bigger countries. The representative of Fiji was Satya Nandan.

In this essay, I want to try to understand why he was so effective.

First, Satya Nandan is a good lawyer. He has an excellent command of the English language. He can draft very well. In other words, he has many of the qualities of a good lawyer.

Second, unlike some of his colleagues at the conference, Satya has no ego. He was quite happy to remain in the background and not seek the limelight. He was focused on getting the work done and did not mind that other people took the credit for it. He is a very modest and humble person.

Third, he is a sincere, honest and trustworthy person. His colleagues at the conference liked and respected him. They felt that they could trust him to do his best to find a formula which would accommodate their countries' interests. He has the personality and character of an ideal chairman or facilitator.

Fourth, he has a strategic mind and is willing to take an initiative if he felt that he could make a contribution. Let me cite an example. In 1975, at the third session of the conference, he and his British colleague co-convened a private group on straits. They hand-picked the 13 countries which were invited to join the group. They deliberately excluded both the US and the Soviet Union. They also excluded those straits states, such as Indonesia, Malaysia and Spain, which, in their views, took an extreme view. This private group succeeded in agreeing on a set of draft articles on passage through straits used for international navigation which were incorporated into the Single Negotiating Text, by the Chairman of the Second Committee, Ambassador Reynaldo Galindo Pohl. Part III of the Convention, on Straits Used For International Navigation, is largely based upon the text produced by the private group.

Fifth, he was called upon twice by the UN Secretary-General to help. Satya Nandan undertook negotiations, lasting 16 months, which culminated in the adoption of UN General Assembly Resolution A/48/L.60, on 27 July 1994, amending Part XI of the Convention. This enabled the US to declare that it would support the convention. Satya Nandan was also instrumental in negotiating the agreement on straddling fish stock and highly migratory species of fish.

Sixth, I will conclude by talking about two of Satya's qualities which are partly responsible for his extraordinary achievements. These are his unflappability and his patience. He is always cool and self-controlled. He remains calm when faced with an adversity. He has tremendous patience and never gives up. I suspect that because of his patience and other good qualities, he succeeds in wearing down his opponents until they give up their resistance and join the consensus.

Summer 2013

ART, CULTURE AND HERITAGE

10 Stops Along a Singapore Historical Trail

This essay is inspired by a book that I launched recently. The book is entitled *Singapore's Heritage Through Places of Historical Interest*. The author, Dhoraisingam S. Samuel, is 86 years old.

The book describes 160 places of historical interest in Singapore. Using the book as a resource, I will take the reader on a journey through the history of Singapore by visiting 10 of the places described in the book.

First, let us start at Fort Canning. Its original name was Bukit Larangan (Forbidden Hill). According to the Sejarah Melayu (Malay Annals), when Prince Sang Nila Utama from Palembang founded Singapura in 1297, he built his palace on top of the hill. When Stamford Raffles founded modern Singapore, he also built his residence on the hill, renamed Government Hill. It was only in 1859 that it was named after George Canning, then the British Governor-General of India. During World War II, the British general Arthur Percival had his headquarters in underground bunkers at the fort. During the Japanese occupation, the fort became the headquarters of the Japanese Imperial Army. In 1926, gold ornaments were found at the site during excavation works. These objects are on display now at the National Museum. They were made in Java in the 14th century, during the Majapahit period, and confirm the view that Singapore has been inhabited since the 14th century.

Second, let us visit the Eurasian Community House at 139, Ceylon Road. Although the house is relatively new, the community is old and can trace its roots back to the Portuguese conquest of Malacca in 1511. In commemoration of the 500th anniversary of that historic event this year, the Eurasian Association and National Heritage Board (NHB) will co-organise an exhibition in November on the Portuguese heritage of the Eurasian community.

Next, I will combine the two statues of Raffles at Empress Place and the Istana Kampong Glam at 85 Sultan's Gate. Taken together, they remind us of the remarkable story of how modern Singapore was founded by a young official of the British East India Company. The Istana was the seat of Sultan Hussein Shah. The current building, now the home of the Malay Heritage Centre, was built by Hussein's son, Sultan Ali, between 1840 and 1843.

Fifth, I will take the reader to the Armenian Church of St. Gregory in Armenian Street. On March 26 this year, we celebrated the 175th anniversary of the consecration of the church. It is the oldest surviving Christian church in Singapore and has been designated a national monument.

Sixth, let us visit the Nanyang Memorial Hall at 12, Tai Gin Road. The man who overthrew the Qing dynasty, put an end to the rule of emperors and founded the Republic of China — Sun Yat Sen — received critical support from the Chinese community in South-east Asia. He visited Singapore nine times and stayed at this house on three occasions. On the occasion of the 100th anniversary of the 1911 revolution in October, the Singapore Foreign Minister will officiate at the opening of a new Zhongshan Park and the re-opening of the hall, now managed by NHB.

Seventh, my next choice, the Goodwood Park Hotel, will be a surprise to many readers. What is the historical significance of the hotel? The significance is that it was built in 1900 by the German residents of Singapore as their club house, the Teutonia Club. When World War 1 broke out in 1914, the British government requisitioned the place as enemy property. Another interesting historical fact is that the British Military Administration used the premises to conduct the war crime trials in 1947.

Eighth, let us go a little out of town to visit the Ford Motor Works in Bukit Timah Road. Ford used to assemble its cars in this factory. On Feb. 15, 1942, Lieutenant-General Percival surrendered to General Yamashita Tomoyuki in this building. The building is now a national monument, under the management of the National Archives. It houses a small museum on World War II and the Japanese occupation of Singapore.

Ninth, in order to be even-handed, we should go next to visit the place where the Japanese surrendered to the British in 1945. It was at the City Hall that Lt-Gen Seishiro Itagaki surrendered to Admiral Lord Louis Mountbatten. The City Hall, like Fort Canning, is loaded with history. It was here that Indian independence leader Subhas Chandra Bose addressed the Indian National Army. It was here that Mr Lee Kuan Yew proclaimed Singapore's self-government in 1959, its merger with Malaysia in 1963, and its independence in 1965. The first and second prime ministers of Singapore were sworn in here. The City Hall and the adjoining building, the old Supreme Court, are currently being renovated. They will be reincarnated in a few years as our National Art Gallery.

Finally, I will conclude this journey at a happy place, the Singapore Botanic Gardens. Raffles started the first Botanic Gardens in 1822 in Fort Canning. The park was closed in 1829. After an interregnum of 30 years, the new Botanic Gardens was opened in 1859 in Napier Road. Henry Ridley, director of the gardens, successfully planted the rubber seeds smuggled out of Brazil, in the gardens. This was the start of the rubber industry in Malaya. In 2009, the Singapore Botanic Gardens celebrated its 150th anniversary. It is a jewel in our crown.

Note added: In December 2012, the Singapore government applied to UNESCO to list the Singapore Botanic Gardens as a World Heritage Site.

[Originally published in *The Straits Times*, 27 April 2011.]

Karel van Kleef: The Man Who Loved Singapore

On June 18, 1930, a Dutchman died in the city of Haarlem (now part of Amsterdam), in the Netherlands. In his will, he left his whole estate to Singapore. Who was this man?

His name was Karel Willem Benjamin van Kleef. He was born on Nov. 20, 1856, in Batavia (now Jakarta). His father was Salomon Benjamin van Kleef, a gynaecologist. His mother was Geetruida van Hogezand. Both Salomon and Geetruida were Jewish. They had met and married in Batavia on Nov. 25, 1850.

Dr and Mrs van Kleef had four children. The first child, Maria Elizabeth, was born in 1851. Karel was the second child. The third child, Wilhem Samuel, was born in 1856 and died a year later and was buried in a cemetery in Jakarta. The fourth child, Herman, was born in 1863 in Amsterdam.

We know nothing about Karel's childhood and education. All that I have been able to find in the Dutch National Archives and Dutch National Genealogical Centre is a certificate (undated), certifying that he was an expert in drilling in the mining industry.

Karel had worked in the mining industry in Indonesia. At some point in his adult life, Karel left Indonesia and relocated to Singapore. We are not sure what he did for a living in Singapore, but we know that he was successful and became prosperous. He left Singapore and retired in Haarlem, the Netherlands, where he died.

How much money did Karel van Kleef leave to Singapore? He left the sum of $160,000, which, in today's dollars, would be equivalent to $8.985 million.

Why did Karel van Kleef leave his entire estate to Singapore? We do not know why he chose to do so. He could have bequeathed his estate to his older sister, Maria, or her children. He could have chosen to benefit the land of his origin, the Netherlands, or the land of his birth, Indonesia. Instead, he chose to bequeath his entire fortune to Singapore. This is why I call him "the man who loved Singapore". I know of no other person, Singaporean or non-Singaporean, who has bequeathed his entire fortune to Singapore.

What did Singapore do with the money? In 1931, the municipal government set up a committee to make recommendations on the best way to use the money. The committee considered three options: a landscaped garden, an aquarium and a zoological garden. In 1933, it was decided to build an aquarium and to name it the Van Kleef Aquarium. However, the construction was delayed by the difficult situation in Europe and the outbreak of World War II.

The Van Kleef Aquarium was finally opened in 1955, 25 years after the benefactor's death. The aquarium was a great success and attracted 166,000 visitors in its first four months of operation. The annual visitorship climbed steadily from about 200,000 to a peak of 400,000.

The aquarium was closed in 1991 because it was unable to compete with the new Underwater World in Sentosa. It was privatised and re-opened as the World of Aquarium. It failed after two years. It changed hands again and re-opened as the Fort Canning Aquarium in 1993. In December 1996, the aquarium was closed for the final time. Two years later, in 1998, the building was demolished and, with it, the name of our benefactor, Karel van Kleef.

Singapore should not allow the name of the only person who loved us so much that he bequeathed his entire estate to our country to disappear from our collective memory. I cannot help comparing him with an Englishman, James Smithson, who made a similar bequest to

America. The US Congress accepted the bequest with gratitude and established the Smithsonian Institution in his memory. The Smithsonian Institution is today one of the great cultural institutions of America and of the world. Let us think of an appropriate way to perpetuate the memory of Karel van Kleef.

Note added: On 25 January 2013, the Aquatic Science Centre (an innovative cutting edge research facility along the banks of Sungei Ulu Pandan) was named after van Kleef. It is now called the Van Cleef Centre.

[Originally published in *The Straits Times*, 9 January 2012.]

Tributes to José Rizal and Emilio Aguinaldo

I congratulate Ambassador Jesus I. Yabes, Minister Minda C. Cruz, and their colleagues at the Embassy of the Philippines for their initiative and diligence in putting together this coffee table book, *A Journey of Friendship: The Philippines–Singapore Relations*. I thank the Embassy for inviting me to write this foreword. I wish to make three points.

First, contacts between our two countries go back many years and predate their independence. It will come as a surprise to many readers to learn that the national hero of the Philippines, José Rizal, had stopped in Singapore on five occasions. Rizal was born in 1861 and executed by Spain in 1896. He was a doctor, writer and patriot. He inspired the Philippine Revolution (1896–1898) through his political novels: *Noli Me Tángere* (1887) and *El Filibusterismo* (1891).

Rizal stopped in Singapore in May 1882 for two days on his way to Spain to study medicine. He stayed at the Hotel de la Paix, on Coleman Street, where the Peninsula Plaza now stands. The second time he stopped in Singapore was in July 1887 when he was on his way back to the Philippines, as a newly qualified doctor and author *of Noli Me Tángere*. After only a year back home, Rizal returned to Europe in 1888 by way of Japan and America. On his way back to the Philippines in 1891, his ship stopped in Singapore on the 10th of November for about 12 hours.

In 1892, Rizal was arrested and exiled to Dapitan, a Jesuit mission town in Mindanao. In 1896, after four years in internal exile, Rizal volunteered to serve with Spain as an army surgeon in Cuba in order to win his freedom. On his way to Spain, his ship, the Isla de Panay, stopped in Singapore on the 8th of September 1896. This was his fourth visit to Singapore. Rizal never made it to Cuba. Before he arrived in Europe, Spain changed its mind. He was again arrested and put on another ship to return to Manila. When his ship stopped in Singapore for a few hours he was in handcuffs and not allowed to leave the ship. This was his fifth and final contact with Singapore. On the 30th of December 1896, Spain executed Rizal by firing squad.

Another national hero of the Philippines who had contact with Singapore was General Emilio Aguinaldo. When the revolution against Spain started in 1896, Aguinaldo led a successful assault on the Spanish garrison in Cavite. He became a national hero overnight. He was elected President of the revolutionary government by the Tejeros Convention in March 1897. Following a military stalemate, followed by a truce, Aguinaldo and his men were exiled to Hong Kong.

From Hong Kong, Aguinaldo came to Singapore on 21st April 1898 by the S.S. Eridan. He stayed with his friend, Dr Marcelino Santos. The Americans made contact with Aguinaldo and arranged a meeting between him and the US Consul, Spencer Pratt. They met at a place called "The Mansion" on River Valley Road on the 24th of April. The meeting ended at midnight and resumed the next day at the Raffles Hotel. The US promised to support independence for the Philippines. Aguinaldo returned to Hong Kong and, from Hong Kong, returned to the Philippines on 19th May 1898 on board the US ship McCulloch. On the 12th of June 1898, Aguinaldo proclaimed the independence of the Philippines from Spain. The date, 12th of June, is celebrated by the Philippines as its Independence Day.

Meanwhile, the US did a U-turn. Instead of supporting the revolutionaries, as promised, President McKinley decided to annex the Philippines, a decision formalised by the Spanish-American Treaty of Paris of 1898. The US paid Spain $20 million for the Philippines. The Filipinos rejected the US claim of sovereignty and the Philippine–American war started in 1898. Aguinaldo led the Filipino forces against the Americans until 1901 when he was captured. On the 1st of April 1901, he swore allegiance to the US. Thereafter, the resistance to the US fizzled out and the Philippines became an American colony. Aguinaldo returned to Cavite and lived a quiet life except for 1935, when he ran unsuccessfully for the presidency of the Commonwealth Government. He died in 1964 at the age of 95.

It would be good if the National Heritage Board could consider installing two markers, at appropriate places, to record the visits of Jose Rizal and Emilio Aguinaldo to Singapore. It would strengthen the bonds of friendship between our two countries. It would also make Singaporeans aware of the role it has played in the history of the Philippines.

Second, the Philippines and Singapore are fundamentally complementary economies. Singapore is one of the biggest investors in the Philippines. Singapore is also one of the Philippines' largest trading partners. Apart from economics, the two countries also cooperate in areas such as education, culture, defence and people-to-people exchanges. Singapore offers the Philippines a number of scholarships and training courses. We cooperate closely in regional organizations, such as ASEAN, as well as, international organisations such as the UN. In recent years, cultural exchanges between our countries have nourished. The Singapore Lyric Opera and the Singapore Repertory Theatre have undertaken joint productions with their Filipino counterparts. Our poets have also started joint publications and have exchanged a number of visits.

Third, the future of Philippines–Singapore relations is bright. There are no fundamental conflicts of interest between us. On the contrary, there are many areas in which our interests are either complementary or congruent. Therefore, I foresee both the broadening and deepening of relations between the Philippines and Singapore, both bilaterally and through ASEAN.

Mabuhay!

Note added: A marker to honour José Rizal was built in front of the Singapore River near the Asian Civilisations Museum. The marker was unveiled by President S. R. Nathan and Jesli Lapus, the Education Secretary of the Philippines, on 19 June 2008.

[Originally published as a Foreword in *A Journey of Friendship: The Philippines–Singapore Relations*, Philippine Embassy, Singapore, 2002.]

Honouring Deng Xiaoping*

Vice-President Xi Jinping, Minister Mentor Lee Kuan Yew, Minister Lui Tuck Yew, Ambassador Wei, distinguished members of the Chinese delegation, ladies and gentlemen

Twenty years ago, I had the privilege of leading the Singapore delegation which negotiated successfully with a Chinese delegation led by Vice-Minister Xu Dunxin, to pave the way for the establishment of full diplomatic relations between our two countries. During the past twenty years, our bilateral relations have flourished in many spheres.

I am the Chairman of the National Heritage Board. The Board has a project to build markers to honour a highly selected number of visitors to Singapore. They must be persons who are revered by their people, have made major contributions to their countries and have links with Singapore. The first three markers were built to honour the great Polish–British writer, Joseph Conrad; the national hero of the Philippines, José Rizal; and the national hero of Vietnam, Ho Chi Minh.

The National Heritage Board had proposed the building of a marker to honour the Chinese leader, Deng Xiaoping, as part of our celebrations of the 20th anniversary of the establishment of diplomatic relations between our two countries. Deng had visited Singapore in 1920, when he was on his way to study in France, and again, in November 1978 as the Vice-Premier of the People's Republic of China. He was the architect of China's policies of economic reform and openness to the world. The

---

*Opening remarks at the Unveiling Ceremony of the Deng Xiaoping marker on 14 November 2010 at the Asian Civilisations Museum Green, Singapore.

spectacular success that China has enjoyed in the past thirty years can be said to be Deng's legacy. We must, of course, also give credit to Deng's successors for realising his vision. He had also made critical contributions to the close relations which we enjoy between our two countries.

The marker contains a bronze bust, sculpted by a leading Chinese artist Li Xiangqun, and a panel. The text inscribed on the panel has been approved by our governments. The signature of Deng appears below his bust. On the back of the marker, we have inscribed a famous quote by him: "Development is of overriding importance."

Thank you very much.

The Artist, the State and the Market

As the son of a book-loving father and an art-loving mother, I sometimes think that I was fated to play a role in our country's cultural development in the past two decades.

From 1991 to 1996, I served as the founding chairman of the National Arts Council (NAC). In 1992, I was appointed to chair the Censorship Review Committee.

I was a member of the steering committee which conceptualised and oversaw the building of the Esplanade theatres and served, subsequently, on its board from 2000 to 2007. I was the chairman of the National Heritage Board (NHB) from 2002 to 2011.

Culturally, Singapore has gone through a paradigm change since 1990. The change is both quantitative and qualitative. Today, Singapore has a rich, year-round, calendar of cultural activities. They span the whole spectrum — exhibitions, art fairs, auctions, recitals, concerts, plays, musicals, dance, theatre, film and writers festivals, book launches, lectures, workshops, conferences, etc. The quality has also risen and, in many cases, meet international standards.

World Class

We have some world class arts infrastructure such as the Esplanade theatres and the soon to be completed National Art Gallery. We have unique museums such as the Asian Civilisations Museum and the Peranakan Museum. Our two arts colleges, NAFA and Lasalle, and the Yong Siew Toh Conservatory of Music, have become internationally respected. We have the world's best collection of South-east Asian art.

We have a vibrant and growing community of writers, composers, choreographers, actors, dancers, singers, musicians, artists, curators, conservators, designers, arts administrators and gallery owners. Artistic freedom, a culture of tolerance and the acceptance of diversity, have grown stronger although they are still not optimal. The social status and incomes of our cultural workers have risen, but could go higher.

Most important of all, we have nurtured a new generation of culture-loving and heritage-loving Singaporeans. Our investments in arts education and in the successful School of the Arts have yielded rich dividends.

Although we have made tremendous progress in the past two decades, many challenges remain. Let me briefly discuss three of these challenges.

The Artist and the State

First, we should try to reduce the deficit of trust between the artistic community and the Government. The problem is partly a legacy of the past, when the Government practised heavy censorship. Some artists, such as the late theatre pioneer Kuo Pao Kun, were detained. It is also partly the result of more recent actions, such as reducing the funding of an arts group or a festival, because the Government did not like a certain play or plays.

We need better communication between the artistic community and the Government. The communication should be two-way and based on mutual respect. We also need policymakers and administrators who have domain knowledge and have an affection for culture and the arts.

When I was the chairman of NAC, I hosted a different group of artists to tea each month. My purpose was to befriend them, to earn their trust and to convince them that my agenda was to help them to succeed. Problems were often sorted out over a cup of tea.

When an attempt was made to stigmatise forum theatre and The Necessary Stage, I wrote to this newspaper to defend them. If I had not done so, my narrative that the chairman of NAC is a patron and champion of our artists would have been shown to be just empty talk. I failed, however, to protect performance artist Josef Ng from the wrath of law enforcement agencies.

The Artist and the Market

Second, many of our artists find themselves caught in a moral dilemma. They need money to survive. They need to sell their works to collectors and the art market. At the same time, they fear that by seeking to cater to the needs and preferences of the collectors and the market, they will be seduced by money and lose their integrity.

On balance, however, the market serves the interest of the artist and should not be demonised. The public sector plays a balancing role. When we acquire the works of artists for our museums, we do so based on artistic merit and not market value. We confer awards on our artists based solely on their artistic achievements and not their commercial success.

The state has an important role to play as a patron of the arts and as a balance to the power of the market. For example, theatre and dance companies are finding it increasingly hard to stage performances because of rising rentals. The state should step in to help and do so more generously. Ideally, we should try to create a virtuous triangle, consisting of the artist, the state and the market.

High Art or Popular Art

Third, one of the ongoing debates in Singapore is over whether our cultural policy should be populist or elitist. I think this is a false choice. I believe that there is no contradiction between supporting high art and popular art. Indeed, we should do both. In music, for example, we should support classical music as well as other genres such as popular (pop) and jazz. I was, therefore, very pleased when the NAC conferred the Cultural Medallion on popular performer Dick Lee and jazz pianist Jeremy Monteiro.

What we need is balance. In recent years, we may have lost that balance and veered too much towards what I would not call elitist, but the cutting edge or experimental. For example, in recent editions of the Festival of the Arts, there were too few mainstream items and too many from the sidestream.

I also think that the Singapore Biennale should refocus on South-east Asia because we cannot possibly compete with the older and well-established biennales of Venice, Sao Paolo, etc., which have a global focus.

Our comparative advantage is in presenting South-east Asian art to the world. I also think that the curators should include more works which are accessible and fewer works which are comprehensible only to experts in contemporary art.

The pendulum should come back to the centre and not swing to the other extreme. We should not dumb down the activities of NAC and NHB. We should not underestimate our citizens. We should continue to push forward and build up our intellectual and cultural capital. We should commission new works and support our talented young artists even when we find their works to be unfamiliar or uncomfortable.

When confronted by a work which provokes puzzlement or negative reactions, I always remind myself that when the Impressionist painters made their debut, they were denounced by the French artistic establishment. The lesson learnt is that we should always have an open mind.

Culturally, Singapore has passed the tipping point. The cultural renaissance of Singapore has taken off. Going forward, the Government should concentrate less on building hardware and more on building software.

This means investing more money in acquisitions, in training and human capital and in the development of our intellectual and cultural capital. The vision of remaking Singapore into the cultural capital of South-east Asia is within reach.

To reach this goal, the artist, the Government and the community will have to work even more closely and harmoniously.

[Originally published in *The Straits Times*, 6 February 2013.]

The Joy of Collecting

Literature, music and painting are the three art forms which are my daily companions. They bring me much happiness.

I collect paintings by Singapore artists. I made my first acquisition in 1962, the year I started teaching law at NUS. A young artist, Wee Beng Chong, held an exhibition to raise funds for his further study in Paris. I attended the exhibition and bought a small oil painting of two fishermen standing waist deep in water. This painting has accompanied me from Singapore to the United States and back. Wee Beng Chong is now an eminent artist and teaches at the Nanyang Academy of Fine Arts.

One of the joys of collecting is meeting our artists. Over the years I have befriended many of our artists. I got to know our pioneer artist, Cheong Soo Pieng, and used to visit him at his home on River Valley Road. I introduced his beautiful paintings to UNICEF. Soo Pieng was very happy when UNICEF used one of his paintings as a first day cover. When I got married in 1967, my students at Raffles Hall, bought a painting from Mr Cheong for me as my wedding present. In 1982 the artist gave me a painting of a dayak woman and child. These 2 paintings watch over me, from the right wall, as I work at my study table.

On the wall in front of me are six small paintings of gibbons, ducks and sparrows by Chen Wen Hsi. I used to visit Wen Hsi at his studio on Tanglin Road. Once I brought the wife of the UN Secretary-General, Mrs Kurt Waldheim, to visit his studio and to watch him demonstrate brush painting and finger painting. Most of my paintings by Wen Hsi were acquired before he became famous. They were therefore very affordable. My advice to beginning collectors is to collect paintings by artists before they become famous.

Another artist I got to know was Georgette Chen. She used to live in a small bungalow in Siglap. On a few occasions she had invited my wife and me home for dinner. After dinner she would bring out some of her paintings to show us. She regarded her paintings as her children and would not sell them. It took me several years to persuade her to sell me a painting for our mission in New York and one for our embassy in Washington. Some years later, the National Museum Art Gallery mounted a retrospective of her paintings. I was overjoyed when my wife bought me a painting of coconuts, chillis, onions and garlic. This painting, together with those by Huang Pao Fang and Quek Wee Chew, are in my dining room.

During the 1960s I became acquainted with three of our second generation artists, Tay Bak Koi, Tay Chee Toh and Quek Wee Chew. Once, when I was at the UN, I managed to persuade an art gallery owned by a friend of mine in Greenwich, Connecticut, to hold an exhibition of paintings by them. Today, Bak Koi and Chee Toh have become famous artists. Wee Chew has stopped painting in order to concentrate on his work at one of our historic temples on Philip Street. I have kept up my friendship with these three artists.

One day in 1983, when I was working in New York, I read an article in *The Straits Times* that a Singapore artist, Ong Kim Seng, had won an award from the American Watercolor Society. I arranged for Singapore Airlines to fly Kim Seng and another artist, Lee Hock Moh, to New York. I also organised an exhibition of their paintings at the Asia Society in New York. The two artists have since won the Cultural Medallion and their paintings are prized by collectors.

One of my happiest experiences of collecting was helping one of our art curators, Constance Sheares, to acquire art for our new embassy in Washington. Visitors to our embassy are impressed by the elegance of the building. They are also impressed by the lovely works of art which enhance the beauty of the building.

[Originally published as "From Collecting Paintings to Befriending Artists", *Lianhe Zaobao*, 25 November 1998.]

A Tribute to Ong Kim Seng

Ong Kim Seng is probably Singapore's best-known watercolourist. Through his art, he has done Singapore proud. He has put Singapore on the world map of watercolour painting. We may be a small county with a relatively short art history, but Kim Seng has, nevertheless, shown that it is possible to do great things beyond our limitations.

Born in humble circumstances, Kim Seng's interest in art started very early. In his kampong, people thought him a little strange. In order to win his playmates' acceptance, an eight-year-old Kim Seng hit upon the idea of drawing pictures on tracing paper and projecting the images on the wall with a torchlight for their entertainment.

Kim Seng is essentially a self-taught artist. Apart from studying books and looking at art, he would spend his weekends observing and learning from our early watercolour artists such as Lim Cheng Hoe and Gog Sing Hooi who frequently painted by the Singapore River on Sundays. So, little by little, through practice, perseverance and diligence, Kim Seng was able to hone his talent in an informal environment, amongst like-minded individuals who encouraged sharing and interaction.

For many years, Kim Seng could only dabble in art whenever he had some spare time as he was busy working to earn a living. He has been a welder, a naval policeman, a technician and lastly a graphic designer. It was only in 1985 that he finally decided to follow his passion and became a full-time artist.

By then, he had already made a great breakthrough with his first solo exhibition in Singapore in 1979. The show featured works based on his trek to the Himalayas in 1978. It earned him his first award from the American Watercolour Society in 1983. Since then, he has gone on to win five more awards from the same society. This culminated in the Dolphin Fellowship in 2000, an honour conferred on just 57 individuals in the society's 134-year history, and Ong is the only one who lives in Asia. In 1991, Kim Seng was also awarded the Cultural Medallion by the Singapore government.

Kim Seng enjoys painting on-site, in order to capture the fleeting and subtle effects of light and atmosphere. In his many painting trips, he has covered the length and breadth of Singapore, and also traveled to Europe, China, India and other countries in Southeast Asia. Through his art, we become vicarious travelers, enjoying the sights with his unique vision and expression.

I look forward to seeing Kim Seng's latest solo show "Reflections in Watercolour". I am certain that he will take us on a new journey, one which will be filled with joy and fresh vistas. I congratulate Kim Seng for this new exhibition and wish him even greater success in the years ahead.

7 September 2006

A Tribute to Lee Hock Moh

It gives me great pleasure to write this foreword.

I would like to use this opportunity to tell the story of my friendship with Mr Lee Hock Moh.

In 1983, I was Singapore's Ambassador to the United Nations in New York. One day, I read a story in *The Straits Times* about a young Singapore watercolour painter, Ong Kim Seng, who had won a prize from the American Watercolour Society. Although I did not know Mr Ong, I wrote to congratulate him and to ask whether he would like to go personally to New York to receive his prize. Mr Ong said he would and asked whether he could bring a good friend, Lee Hock Moh. I managed to get two complimentary air tickets from Singapore Airlines for Ong Kim Seng and Lee Hock Moh.

I asked the two artists to bring some of their paintings with them. I arranged two exhibitions for them, at the famous Asia Society and at the UN Plaza Hotel. The exhibitions were very successful and all their paintings were sold.

Lee Hock Moh's paintings of orchids are technically superb and stylistically unique. I could tell from his paintings that he has mastered his craft. I could also tell that he has a genuine love for orchids. His love for the flower is transmitted to his paintings. He also loves to paint orchids in their natural settings. I also like the manner in which he has introduced insects, birds and animals into his orchid paintings.

My wife and I own a painting by Hock Moh of orchids with a spider. We derive great pleasure in viewing it in our home.

Since Lee Hock Moh's retirement from *Lianhe Zaobao*, he has devoted all his time to his art. He has also travelled abroad and has executed some very beautiful landscape paintings.

I congratulate Hock Moh on this long overdue solo exhibition. I wish him success in his artistic ascent to even high peaks.

23 June 2000

A Tribute to Kuo Pao Kun

Late in the evening of 10 September 2002, after my wife had gone to bed, I received a telephone call from a journalist from *Lianhe Zaobao*, informing me that one of Singapore's cultural icons, Kuo Pao Kun, had passed away. I slept very little that night as I mourned the passing of a dear friend and beloved brother and reflected on the significance of his life.

Pao Kun had made a monumental contribution to Singapore's literature and theatre. He had written twenty-four plays, some of which, such as *The Coffin's Too big for the Hole, No Parking On Odd Days, The Silly Little Girl and the Funny Old Tree, Mama Looking for Her Cat, Lao Jiu*, and *Descendants of the Eunuch Admiral*, have become classics. Pao Kun had also translated six plays, including Athol Fugard's *The Island* into Chinese. He had directed twenty-eight plays.

Pao Kun had also left us with a number of institutions. In 1965, he co-founded the Practice Performing Arts School (PPAS) with his wife, Goh Lay Kuan. One of the most famous students of PPAS is our local hero, Sim Wong Hoo. In 1986, Pao Kun was the founding Artistic Director of the Practice Theatre Ensemble, now called The Theatre Practice. In 1990, he was the founding Artistic Director of The Substation — A Home for the Arts. In 2000, he was the founding co-director of the Theatre Training and Research Programme of PPAS, together with T. Sasitharan.

Pao Kun's achievements as an artist have been recognised both at home and abroad. In 1989, he received the Cultural Medallion. In 1993, he recevied the ASEAN Cultural Award. In 1996, the Government of France conferred on him the prestigious Chevalier de l'Ordre des Arts et des Lettres. In 2002, Pao Kun received the Excellence for Singapore Award.

Pao Kun's plays have been translated into all of our official languages and Hindi, Japanese and German. They have been performed in many Asian countries as well as in Australia, US, Europe, Africa and the Middle East. In 2000, the Tokyo Asian Art Festival paid a tribute to Pao Kun by staging three of his plays. As a reflection of Pao Kun's influence throughout Asia, the play *The Coffin's Too Big for the Hole* was directed by Putu Wijaya and performed by Teater Mandiri of Indonesia; *Lao Jiu* was directed by Anuradha Kapur and performed by Dishantar of India; and *The Silly Little Girl and the Funny Old Tree* was directed by Makoto Sato and performed by the Black Tent Theatre of Japan.

Pao Kun had a special gift, the gift of cultural versatility. He was at home in many worlds. He bridged many divides, including the divide between the Chinese-speaking and the English-speaking worlds; the divide between writing and directing; the divide between the contemporary and the traditional; and the divide between the local and the global.

Pao Kun often lamented that, as a Singaporean, he was a cultural orphan. He was, as usual, being modest. His knowledge of Chinese history and culture was actually very deep. He understood the Confucianist tradition but was closer to being a May 4th modernist. He was a descendant of Chinese civilisation but he transcended it. Because of his mastery of the English language and his education in Australia, he was just as knowledgeable about the history and culture of the West. At the same time, he was open to and respectful of the civilisations of India and of the Malay world. It is significant that Pao Kun passed away on the eve of the first anniversary of the terrorist attack on America. Perhaps Providence was telling us that in the post-911 world, we need more Kuo Pao Kuns, individuals who embody the humanistic values which are universal and which form the basis of any dialogue among civilisations.

When I was the Chairman of the National Arts Council, I had many dialogues with Pao Kun. My colleagues and I had great respect for him and for his views. He spoke for and to the arts community with clarity and courage.

Pao Kun was a great human being. He was honest and sincere. He could be very uncomprising in protecting artistic integrity and artistic freedom. He was, however, a warm, kind and generous person. He had charisma and eloquence. Whenever he spoke, I always listened and learned something new and often something profound. Pao Kun has touched our lives and made us a better people. I shall always carry a warm spot in my heart for him.

20 September 2002

A Tribute to Tan Swie Hian*

President and Mrs Nathan, Mr Edmund Cheng and Ms Carol Tan of the National Arts Council, Dr Earl Lu, Honorary Chairman, and Mr Kwee Liong Keng, Chairman of the Singapore Art Museum, Mrs Lim Siok Peng, CEO of NHB, Mr Tan Swie Hian, Ladies and Gentlemen

A very warm welcome to the opening of this joyful and important exhibition. In accordance with my wife's standing instruction, I wish to make three points.

Thank the President

First, I wish to thank the President and Mrs Nathan. The National Arts Council and the National Heritage Board wish to thank you for accepting our joint invitation to grace this occasion as our guests-of-honour. I am sure I speak for Tan Swie Hian when I say that your presence here means a lot to him and to all our artists, writers and other cultural workers. The message which your presence sends is that we value and applaud achievements in culture and the arts as we do achievements in other fields. This is an important message because, in this phase of Singapore's development, our ambition is to develop culture and the arts to a level commensurate with our education, economy and infrastructure.

Thank Our Partners

Second, I wish to thank a number of persons and institutions, without whose support this exhibition would not have been possible. This is

---

* Remarks made at the art exhibition "Embracing Infinity: Works by Tan Swie Hian", at the Singapore Art Museum, 24 August 2004.

usually left to the end of the speech. I wanted to do it at the beginning so that it does not seem like an after-thought. I wish to thank the three members of the exhibition advisory committee: Mr Lim Jim Koon (Chairman), Dr Ho Kah Leong and Mr Choo Thiam Siew. I would like to thank Wuthelam International Investment Ltd, the Singapore Tourism Board, the Hong Leong Foundation and MediaCorp TV12, for their sponsorship. I would also like to congratulate Mr Low Sze Wee for having done an excellent job in curating this exhibition.

Praise Tan Swie Hian

Third, I wish to praise Tan Swie Hian. Since we are all watching or following the Olympic Games, I wish to use an analogy from the world of sports to describe Swie Hian. Swie Hian is an Olympian. The event in which he has won a gold medal is the decathlon, the most difficult in track and field. It consists of 10 different competitions. You have to be very versatile in order to compete in the decathlon. Swie Hian is both versatile and very accomplished. He has achieved gold-medal standard in oil, acrylic and ink painting, calligraphy, illustration, sculpture, seal carving, print-making, translation, performance art, philosophy and literature. To change the analogy, I would describe Tan Swie Hian as a rare Renaissance man in a world of increasing specialisation.

Last year, 2003, was a very important year for Swie Hian. He turned 60. He was given the prestigious Crystal Award by the World Economic Forum. President Nathan conferred on him the Meritorious Service Medal for his distinguished contributions to Singapore's culture. And, his alma mater, NTU, conferred on him the honorary degree of Doctor of Letters. So, let me conclude by saying to Dr Tan Swie Hian: Congratulations for your many achievements which have put you and our country on the world's cultural and artistic map. We are very proud of you.

A Tribute to Earl Lu*

Mr Yatiman Yusof, Senior Parliamentary Secretary, MICA, Your Excellencies, members of the Lu family, friends and fellow admirers of Earl Lu

I wish to thank the Lu family for giving me the privilege of delivering an eulogy on behalf of the Earl Lu fan club. It is easy to praise Earl because he was such an accomplished and lovable man. He had made many important contributions to Singapore. Let me briefly mention seven of them.

"One of Singapore's Best Surgeons"

First, Earl Lu was considered by his peers as one of Singapore's best surgeons. Professor Tow Siang Hwa, the much respected former professor of obstetrics and gynaecology, said he used to refer complicated cases to Dr Lu. Prof Tow recalled that Dr Lu was always able to help his patients and was calm, reassuring and unflappable. Dr Richard Yung, another one of our famous obstetricians and gynaecologists, said he always looked up to Earl as a mentor. Earl loved surgery and continued to operate until 2003.

Contributions to Medical Education

Second, in spite of his busy practice, Earl found the time to teach at our Medical Faculty. He taught and examined students in anatomy, physiology

---

*Speech delivered on the occasion of "A Celebration of the Life of Dr Earl Lu", 15 September 2005 at the Singapore Art Museum.

and surgery. According to my wife, who was one of his students, Earl was a gifted teacher. He was knowledgeable, eloquent and charismatic. His charm and sense of humour helped him to connect with his students and to gain and retain their attention.

Lieutenant-Colonel Dr Earl Lu

Third, Earl loved Singapore. One of the ways in which he showed his love for Singapore was to volunteer to serve as a National Serviceman. He served in the SAF Field Hospital for quite a number of years, guiding the younger surgeons. According to my research, Lt Col Dr Earl Lu was the first surgeon to have operated on a young soldier for acute appendicitis in the field in 1974. Earl's love for Singapore was fully repaid. He was made a Justice of the Peace in 1990 and was conferred the Public Service Star in 1995.

Earl the Artist and Art Collector

Fourth, Earl loved art as much as he loved surgery. Unlike most of us, I suspect that his left brain and right brain were equally well developed. He learned to paint under our great pioneer artist, Chen Wen Hsi. Earl would master the brush as he did the scalpel. In order not to copy his mentor and to carve an artistic niche of his own, he decided to specialise in painting roses. He also painted the human figure and landscape, but his artistic moniker is roses. One of his favourite weekly activities was to go to LASALLE-SIA College on Saturday afternoons, with his second son, Paul, to join a group of fellow artists to paint nudes. After he retired from surgery in 2003, Earl rented a studio in Clemenceau Avenue and would go there each day to paint. He was also a collector and a generous patron of other artists. He collected the works of Chen Wen Hsi, David Kwo, Lim Nan Seng, Tung Ying Yung and many others.

Founding Chairman of Singapore Art Museum

Fifth, in 1992, Earl was appointed the founding chairman of the Singapore Art Museum, a position he held until 2000. Under Earl's leadership, SAM has acquired probably the most comprehensive collection of 20th century Southeast Asian art in the world, as well as works by the contemporary artists of India and China. Earl had been a student in India during the Second World War. Because of this unique experience, he was as knowledgeable about India as he was about China and Southeast Asia. Earl also guided the museum to grow into one with a comprehensive array of local and international programmes. After he stepped down as Chairman, he continued to serve on the museum's advisory committee. He had also chaired the Istana's Art Collection Advisory Committee since 2000. The Singapore Art Museum will always remember the pivotal role played by its founding chairman.

Philanthropist and Benefactor

Sixth, Earl Lu was a very generous philanthropist and benefactor. Let me cite a few examples. He gave his entire collection of Southeast Asian ceramics to the Asian Civilisations Museum. He gave his collection of Chen Wen Hsi's works to the Singapore Art Museum. He was also a benefactor of the LASALLE-SIA College. He had a special bond with Brother Joe McNally. Earl shared Brother Joe's vision and helped him to turn it into reality. He served on its board from its inception until 2003. He donated part of his art collection as well as funds to the College. In return, the College named its art gallery the Earl Lu Gallery. I had the honour of officiating at its opening in 1986. Apart from ACM, SAM, LASALLE-SIA, Earl also sold his paintings to raise funds for the Saint Andrew's Mission Hospital, the Mount Alvernia Hospital and for many other charities. As Esther, Earl's sister, has told me, "Earl's outstanding gift was his great generosity."

A Great Human Being

Seventh, we celebrate Earl's life because he was a great human being. He was always cheerful, charming, kind, witty, gracious and approachable. Professor V. K. Pillay has described him as a "perfect gentleman who could get along with anyone". Professor C. N. Lee has described him as a "classy gentleman". Esther has told me that Earl was the "best brother in the world". Earl, dear friend, we thank you for having been a blessing to all of us. We thank you for having brought sunshine, beauty, roses, optimism, humour and joy into our lives. We shall miss you very much. Today is Earl's 80th birthday. I will, therefore conclude by saying, "Happy Birthday, Earl".

A Tribute to Anthony Poon*

Family members of the late Anthony Poon, Ladies and Gentlemen

Thank you for joining us today.

It is estimated that all over the world, the contents of museums are two-thirds donated and one-third purchased. In the case of SAM, close to half of the Museum's permanent collection is built from donations from generous patrons over the years. Today we are pleased to be part of such a significant donation — gift to the nation. We understand that it was the late artist's wish for his best works to be part of the Singapore Art Museum collection. We would like to thank the Poon family for their generosity as art patrons, and to thank them for supporting SAM's vision. SAM has been actively collecting important works by Singapore artists, Anthony Poon is a key second generation artist who was in the forefront of abstract art.

A prolific and successful artist, with numerous local and international public commissions, Anthony Poon had many large-scale, site-specific sculptures, reliefs and painting on display in outdoor public spaces and corporate interiors. His meticulously executed pieces are keenly sought by collectors, and represented in public and private collections around the world, such as the Embassy of Singapore in Washington, DC, Fukuoka Art Museum, National Library Board, United Overseas Bank Art Collection, and private collectors from the People's Republic of China, Hong Kong, Malaysia and UK. He was recently commissioned to create a sculpture for the Beijing 2008 Olympics. Within Singapore, his works

---

*Speech delivered at the donation ceremony of 23 works of art to the Singapore Art Museum by the late Anthony Poon, 25 January 2007.

gracing many public spaces such as International Plaza, the Tanjong Pagar MRT Station, the MICA Atrium, and the Turf Club. A frequent participant in local and international group shows, he had also held many solo exhibitions. His accolades include winning the first prize of UOB Painting of the Year (1983) and 1991 Cultural Medallion Award, all of which testify to the significance of his contribution to the art history of Singapore, both as a painter and a sculptor.

Anthony Poon belonged to the "second-generation" group of artists, a term that broadly refers to artists who were active in the Singapore art scenes of the 1950s, 1960s and early 1970s, and who have been instrumental in shaping the development of art in Singapore. Artists of that generation explored medium and thought in innovative and meaningful ways. Inspired and encouraged by pioneer artists such as Georgette Chen, Cheong Soo Pieng and Chen Wen Hsi, who were excellent artists and passionate educators, many of our second generation artists went abroad to further their studies, returning to Singapore in the late 1960s. Filled with new ideas and fired by enthusiasm, they ushered in the 1970s — an era that can be considered the most vibrant decade for visual art in Singapore, marked by experimentation in which new styles are developed and old aesthetics are reinterpreted, as can be seen in the works by Anthony Poon.

Born in 1945, Anthony Poon began formal training at the Nanyang Academy of Fine Arts, before heading for the Byam Shaw School of Art and the Regional College of Art in the United Kingdom. He returned to Singapore after his studies in 1971, with his wife Lee Lee, and daughter, Siew Win. We are fortunate to have them with us this morning. He believed that those who had the opportunity to go overseas should return to share what they had learnt abroad. By this time, he had already formulated his personal artistic vision consisting of colour, line and balance. This was first expressed in his Kite series of shaped canvases. He never deviated from this artistic vision in his artistic practice during the rest of his life.

To date, the Singapore Art Museum has 16 artworks by Anthony Poon. some of which are his earliest paintings prior to his sojourn overseas. This morning, the Singapore Art Museum is the fortunate recipient of a donation of another 23 paintings and sculptures, a gift made by his family, Mrs Poon Lee Lee and Madam Poon Siew Win. These 23 works are representative of Anthony Poon's different phases: from the formative years in London to his subsequent venture into large-scale sculptures which reflect the extension of his interest in rhythm through colour and line into the interaction of material with space. This donation includes early pieces like *Squa-Forma* from 1975, initial attempts at the curved line like *Red Frequency Waves* from 1985, a good number of subsequent relief paintings of the Wave series, three sculptures, as well as *Cal-Ori,* an example of Anthony Poon's interest in experimentation. We are privileged to have one of Anthony Poon's last works, completed just before his passing. It is a wall relief reflecting Anthony Poon's latest interest in texture on the surfaces of what he referred to as "ribbons" in movement.

This donation of Anthony Poon's signature pieces spanning his entire career is a key event in the Museum's collection history. It is a significant contribution to the Museum's mission of preserving and presenting the art histories and practices of Singapore and the Southeast Asian region, so as to facilitate visual arts education, exchange, research and development.

With this expanded collection of Anthony Poon's works, there are plans for the Museum to publish an extensive monograph as well as stage a comprehensive retrospective of Anthony Poon's work — the first of its kind, in 2009, The retrospective will recognise his notable contributions to Singapore visual art development and in remembrance of his passing. The exhibition will display his finished artworks but more importantly, it will take visitors on a journey of discovery of Anthony Poon's creative process: from the idea to sketches, to maquettes, and the final painting, relief or sculpture. We look forward to working closely with the family of Anthony Poon in preparation for the monograph and retrospective exhibition.

To mark the donation ceremony today, the Museum has displayed a small selection of the donated works. Alongside the four artworks from the 23 donated pieces on display today, the Museum has additionally featured six maquettes that have been created for the commission of monumental sculptures, both in Singapore and abroad. This brief exhibition of Anthony Poon's works not only shows the breadth of his art practice but also provides a foretaste of his forthcoming retrospective exhibition in 2009 to mark the 3rd anniversary of his passing.

On behalf of the Singapore Art Museum, I am pleased to accept the donation and once again, my gratitude to the generosity of the Poon family.

Thank you.

A Tribute to Goh Choo San

I am so glad that the Singapore Dance Theatre is staging this special performance to pay tribute to the legacy of Goh Choo San.

In 1984, I left my post at the United Nations in New York to take up my new post as Singapore's Ambassador to the United States in Washington, DC. One of my good friends in Washington was Goh Choo San. I had known him in Singapore, through his two talented sisters, Soo Nee and Soo Khim.

Choo San was the resident choreographer of the Washington Ballet. He was a celebrity in the world of dance. Audiences and critics alike looked forward, with great anticipation, to each new ballet that he choreographed. My wife and I made it a point to attend all the performances of the Washington Ballet which premiered his works. We were so proud of him and proud of the fact that a fellow Singaporean had put Singapore on the map of ballet and dance choreography.

I will always remember the evening in 1986, when the Washington Ballet staged a tribute to Choo San, at the Kennedy Center, to celebrate his 10th anniversary as its resident choreographer. It was a glittering affair and all of America's great dancers, such as Mikhail Baryshnikov, dance critics, choreographers and artistic directors were there to pay tributes to Choo San. I had the honour to say a few words on behalf of Singapore.

Goh Choo San has left us but his legacy will live on and has become part of the world's treasury of ballets and modern dances. It is fitting that the Singapore Dance Theatre, which has danced the greatest number of Choo San's works, should have organised this concert. It will remind us of the genius of Goh Choo San.

7 September 2007

A Tribute to Pak Neka

It is one thing to have a vision; it is quite another thing to bring the vision into reality. In July 2007, the Neka Art Museum celebrates the twenty-fifth anniversary of its official opening. It was founded by Pande Wayan Suteja Neka and his wife Gusti Made Srimin, who in 1966 opened the Neka Gallery in Ubud. As business improved, Suteja Neka gave up his job as a school teacher to fully devote himself to his art gallery.

In 1975 the Dutch artist Rudolf Bonnet, who was a friend of Suteja Neka, accompanied him to visit art museums in Europe. At the British Museum in London, Neka saw fine examples of Balinese art which were rare at home. He decided that such works should remain in Bali so that Balinese and visitors could study and enjoy them. His vision was to build a museum to exhibit the works of Balinese as well as other Indonesian artists. It would also show paintings by artists from all over the world who were inspired by Bali.

Suteja Neka and Gusti Made Srimin worked very hard towards achieving this goal and opened the Neka Art Museum in 1976. The Indonesian Minister of Education and Culture, Daoed Joesoef, and his avid art collector friend, Jusuf Wanandi, visited the museum in 1981. They were impressed and proposed that the government should give it some form of recognition; the Neka Art Museum was officially opened on 7 July 1982. Both Daoed Joesoef and Jusuf Wanandi have continued to play a significant role in its development. It was through Jusuf that I made my first visit there.

The Neka Art Museum has a significant collection of Balinese paintings in various styles and from different periods. It also has works by the leading post-independence artists of Indonesia. The museum has collected paintings of the expatriate artists who have contributed so much to the evolution of modern Balinese art. Finally, the Neka Art Museum also contains works by contemporary artists from other countries who have been inspired by Bali.

Bali is a magical island; it casts a spell on those who have the good fortune to visit it. In 1952, four of Singapore's pioneer artists went on a historic field trip to Bali in search of a Southeast Asian visual experience. Bali, therefore, played a seminal role in the evolution of the Nanyang School of Art. Since then, many of Singapore's artists have continued to visit Bali in search of beauty, peace and inspiration. I am very glad that several eminent Singapore artists are represented at the Neka Art Museum.

Many exhibitions of Balinese art and culture have happened in Singapore. The Singapore Art Museum and the Asian Civilisations Museum have hosted Balinese art exhibitions, cultural performances and book launches. The Singapore Art Museum appointed Suteja Neka to its board of directors in May 2006.

The significance of the Neka Art Museum goes beyond the strength of its permanent collection; it is also a centre of research, scholarship and intercultural dialogue. The appointment of Garrett Kam as its curator in 1997 brought additional intellectual power as well as his extensive global network. The Neka Art Museum has actively promoted Balinese art abroad by holding many exhibitions from its collection in museums around the world. It has also held exhibitions of non-Balinese artists at its facilities. In these ways, the Neka Art Museum is outward looking and a centre for intercultural dialogue.

The Neka Art Museum is, in my view, the best in Bali and one of the best in Indonesia. It stands on a beautiful site, away from the hustle and bustle of Ubud, overlooking scenic countryside. Each of the museum's Balinese style buildings is devoted to a period, genre of paintings or group of artists. The grounds are beautifully landscaped; the atmosphere is welcoming and tranquil.

I salute the founding father and mother of the Neka Art Museum, Suteja Neka and Gusti Made Srimin, for their vision, passion and determination. They have built a world class institution, and I wish them peace, good health and continued success. I congratulate Garrett Kam for writing this commemorative book for the museum's silver anniversary, and I wish the Neka Art Museum even greater achievements in the years ahead.

[Originally published as a Foreword in *Neka Art Museum in Modern Balinese History: Art and the Passage of Time,* by Garrett Kam, Yayasan Dharma Semi, Ubud, Ganyar, Bali, 2007.]

A Tribute to Iskandar Jalil

This publication, *Images of My Pottery Travels,* brings into focus an important aspect in the artistic life of Singapore's master potter, Iskandar Jalil. I had written the foreword for an earlier book in 2007, *Material, Message and Metaphor* — also published by Art-2 Gallery, that featured Iskandar's biography, art philosophy and cultural legacy.

The earlier book set the stage for the more intimate approach adopted for *Images of a Potter's Travels*. Here, we are offered a fascinating visual diary of Iskandar's life in his workshop and his travels. We are shown the potter's handwritten notes, paired with the remarkably expressive photographs by Iskandar's former student, Ernest Goh — a professional photographer in his own right.

This new book is a tribute to Iskandar's role as an educator and mentor — bringing together the creative energies and skills of individuals who have been mentored by him. Iskandar's unique "tough love" method of teaching, particularly for lazy or errant students, included breaking poorly attempted vessels or tossing them out of the window. It earned him the nickname of "the Flying Missile" but also the loyalty and love of students who imbibed the master's strong sense of discipline and respect for artistic craft and process. Former students, such as Ernest and filmmaker, Royston Tan, openly testify to how Iskandar's work ethics and sensibilities have shaped their own artistic development.

Other former students attest to Iskandar's generosity and belief in exposing them to creative environments through travel and immersion programmes. Iskandar remains typically reticent about his contributions, rarely referring to or naming his protégés. He is not a name dropper. It is his former students who rally to pay tribute to their beloved "cik gu" — attesting to the private scholarships and funding he had provided them and to the overseas cultural programmes he had personally designed and underwritten over the years.

These initiatives, privately and discreetly funded by Iskandar, have furnished wonderful opportunities for his students to experience, first-hand, the pottery villages and ceramics culture of Japan as well as other parts of the world. Behind his painstakingly designed art programmes lies the conviction that exposure to a nurturing environment stimulates the imagination and releases the creative energy to flourish.

Iskandar himself is continually energised by his travels, finding in them a sense of adventure and source of inspiration. He conscientiously records his journeys in countless journals — all in his own beautiful calligraphy. He includes "souvenir" tickets and memorabilia of trips alongside his observations of the cultures he encounters.

This book also marks a new phase in Iskandar's practice, wherein his workshop and kilns have moved from the Malay Heritage Centre to Temasek Polytechnic in 2010. Iskandar had taught at Temasek Polytechnic at its inception in 1990 until his retirement in 1999. I am pleased to have played a small part in facilitating his return to his beloved second home.

Iskandar had shared with me his desperate search for new premises — a home for his ceramics — when the Malay Heritage Centre announced its temporary closure for renovations. I contacted the Principal of Temasek Polytechnic, Mr Boo Kheng Hua, who enthusiastically agreed to provide an expanded studio and ceramics centre for Iskandar. This warm reception opens another adventure and journey for this respected and much loved cik gu, captured memorably in this publication, *Images of a Potter's Travels*.

[Originally published as a Foreword in *Iskandar Jalil: Images of My Pottery Travels*, by Iskandar Jalil and Linda Chee, 2011.]

A Tribute to Joanna Wong

Ten years ago, I had the pleasure of writing the foreword to a book commemorating Joanna Wong's 50th anniversary as a Chinese opera performer. I am honoured to contribute the foreword to this book honoring her extraordinary life and achievements.

Joanna's career in Chinese opera began when she was only 12 years old. She started performing in her hometown of Penang, Malaysia, in shows put on by local clan associations. Since that youthful start, she has continued to perform and teach Chinese opera, with passion and exquisite skill. She has been a missionary of Chinese opera to the world. She has performed in many locations, including Australia, Brazil, Canada, China, Egypt, Germany and the United States.

To further increase appreciation and new audiences for Chinese opera, Joanna and her husband, Leslie, co-founded the Chinese Theatre Circle, Singapore's first professional Cantonese opera company, in 1981. The company pioneered the use of English sub-titles during its performances. It also championed the integration of Western-style instruments into the traditional Chinese orchestra and other innovations. The Chinese Theatre Circle, under Joanna and Leslie's indefatigable leadership, has established itself as one of the leading Chinese opera troupes in Singapore. It continues to perform abroad.

In recognition of her dedication to preserving and passing on to a new generation, the art of Chinese opera, the Singapore government has conferred on Joanna the Public Service Star and the Cultural Medallion. These honours are well deserved. Artistic pioneers like Joanna, who have done so much to preserve our cultural heritage and art forms, for little material reward are our national treasures.

A tribute to Joanna would be incomplete if it does not also celebrate her achievements as a career woman, wife and mother. While building a successful career as a leading Chinese opera actress, Joanna has also maintained, until recently, a full-time job as the Registrar of both the National University of Singapore and the former Nanyang University. Together with her devoted husband, Leslie, she has also raised two successful daughters, Mary — now a tenured law professor in the United States and Audrey — who has served as a Nominated Member of Parliament for the arts. Audrey is currently the Programme Leader for the MA Arts & Cultural Management programme at LaSalle College of the Arts in Singapore. I know that Leslie, Mary and Audrey are very proud of Joanna and her achievements. Mary and Audrey will tell you that they have modeled their careers and aspirations on their mother's life and achievements. It is a privilege for me to have gotten to know this close-knit, loving and successful Singapore family through my friendship with Joanna and Leslie.

In conclusion, I note that while Joanna might have announced that her recent January 2013 performance in the revival of *Wu Ze Tian: The First Woman Emperor of China* — a role written especially for her in 2001 — would be her last leading role, it is fortunate for us that she has no plans to retire from the Chinese opera stage. I am glad that she will continue to devote much of her time to teaching and mentoring young Chinese opera performers and students. I join her family, friends and supporters in wishing Joanna every success in the next phase of her life, and look forward to her continuing leadership of the performing arts community in Singapore.

[Originally published as a Foreword in *Joanna Wong: An Indomitable Life, An Operatic Legacy*, by Au Yee Pak and Huang Wenying, Chinese Theatre Circle and The Youth Book Co., 2013.]

7

NATURE AND THE ENVIRONMENT

The Earth Summit's Negotiating Process
Some Reflections on the Art and Science of Negotiation*

Mr Chairman, distinguished guests, ladies and gentlemen, I must begin by thanking the editors of the *Singapore Law Review* for inviting me to deliver this prestigious lecture. The six lecturers who preceded me are good friends, all of whom I have enormous respect for. They have set a high standard. I hope I will not let them and you down by my lecture today.

Next, I want to use this occasion to thank the members of the Singapore delegation to the Earth Summit and its Preparatory Committee. Without their help and support, I could not have succeeded in carrying out my duties as Chairman of the Main Committee at the Earth Summit and as Chairman of the Preparatory Committee.

Finally, I want to acknowledge my intellectual debt to the following friends who have made seminal contributions to the fields of conference diplomacy and negotiations:

(a) Dutch Ambassador Johan Kaufmann's 1968 book entitled *Conference Diplomacy*;
(b) Johns Hopkins University Professor, William Zartnam's 1982 book, *The Practical Negotiator*;

---

*The Seventh Singapore Law Review Lecture, delivered to the Faculty of Law, National University of Singapore, 15 December 1992.

(c) Harvard Business School Professor, Howard Raiffa's 1982 book entitled *The Art and Science of Negotiation;*
(d) Harvard Law School Professor, Roger Fisher's two books entitled *International Conflict for Beginners* and *Getting to Yes;* and
(e) Harvard Kennedy School Professor, James Sebenius' two books entitled *Negotiating the Law of the Sea* (1984) and *The Manager as Negotiator* (1986).

A Brief Background

Let me now provide you with a few salient facts about the UN Conference on Environment and Development (hereinafter referred to as the Earth Summit.) and its preparatory process. In 1989, the UN General Assembly decided to convene the Earth Summit in 1992, 20 years after the Stockholm Conference on the Human Environment. I have said, only half in jest, to the *New York Times* that the UN should learn not to hold a major international conference during a US Presidential Election year. There is no doubt in my mind that his preoccupation with winning the election was a factor which caused President Bush to adopt a defensive rather than a pro-active role. The decision to convene the Earth Summit was contained in Resolution 44/228. Some Arab colleagues referred to it as our Koran. The text contained in that resolution soon came to be regarded as sacred.

The Size of the Preparatory Committee

In order to prepare for the Earth Summit, the UN decided to set up a Preparatory Committee. Because of the great interest in the Conference, the committee was enormous in size. It consisted of all the member states of the UN as well as non-member states such as Switzerland. The size of the Committee made negotiation difficult. One of my challenges was how to gradually reduce the size of negotiating groups. I will return to this later.

The PrepCom, as it came to be known, was mandated by our Koran to hold an organisational session in New York, from 5 to 16 March 1990, and four substantive sessions in Nairobi, Geneva, Geneva and New York respectively, in 1991 and 1992. You may wonder why the four substantive sessions were held in three different cities on three continents. Was this an example of the UN diplomats awarding themselves junkets at the expense of their tax payers? It wasn't. It was an example of the kind of compromises that had to be struck in order to achieve consensus. The New York-based diplomats, who were the most politicised, wanted all the sessions to be held in New York. The Geneva-based diplomats argued that they should be held, in Geneva, the home of the UNCED Secretariat. The supporters of UNEP, which is based in Nairobi, argued that they should be held in Nairobi.

The Organisational Session

The organisational session of the PrepCom was two weeks long. It was held in New York from 5 to 16 March 1990. What were the objectives of the organisational session? It had five objectives. First, to elect its Chairman. Second, to decide on the size of the Bureau and the distribution of the number agreed upon among the five regional groups. Third, to decide how many working groups to establish and which regional groups would provide candidates for their Chairs. Fourth, to adopt a provisional agenda for the Earth Summit. Fifth, to adopt its rules of procedure.

Any reasonable person would think that you would need only one of two days, not two weeks, to agree on five such seemingly simple tasks. This was not the case and the two weeks were barely enough to complete our tasks. Of the five tasks, the only simple one was electing me. All the other candidates wisely withdrew when they realised the pain and suffering which the Chairman would have to endure for the next two years and three months! The first thing I did on assuming the Chair was to propose that we should refrain from polluting the air in our meeting rooms by prohibiting smoking at all our meetings. Before the nicotine addicts could rally their forces, I asked if there was any objection. Seeing none, I banged the gavel and pronounced that there was a consensus in favour of my proposal. The former Secretary-General of the UN, Javier Perez de Cuellar, watched, in surprise because no UN Chairman had succeeded in defeating the tobacco lobby at the UN before.

Any Objections?

The speed with which I used my gavel would later give rise to some unhappiness. As a result, I would count to five before banging my gavel. On one occasion, the Chairman of the Group of 77, a wonderful man from Pakistan, Ambassador Jamshid Marker, remarked that my counting of 1, 2, 3, 4, 5 became faster and faster the longer the meeting lasted.

The Size of the Bureau

I failed, however, to persuade my colleagues to accept a relatively small Bureau. For a Bureau to be efficient, it has to be representative but small. Many delegations wanted to be in the Bureau because they thought that it might become a negotiating forum. In the end, I had to accept a Bureau of 42 members. A Bureau of 42 is too big to be useful. I will tell you later of the steps I took to invent a smaller but more efficient group to help me manage the negotiating process.

The Politics of Drafting the Agenda

The PrepCom agreed to establish two working groups which would be chaired respectively by a West European and an African. There was, however, no agreement to establish a third working group to deal with questions relating to law and institutions. The third working group was established at the beginning of the second substantive session in Geneva. The most difficult task was in drafting the agenda. Why? Because delegations feared that the wording of an agenda item could tilt the balance in favour of their adversaries.

To return to my story. On the last day of the organisational session, 16 March 1990, there was still no agreement on the agenda. I was determined to get one. I instructed the Secretariat to arrange for interpreters to be available so that I could go through the night until 6.00am the next morning. The Secretariat did not believe me and I had no interpreters after midnight. I had to persuade the non-Anglophones to work in English. This was by no means an easy task, especially with the Francophone group.

Maintain the Pressure

My strategy was to maintain the pressure on the delegates until they agreed to compromise. By 4.30am, the delegates were so exhausted that they asked me to draft a compromise. I called for a short recess, and with the help of about a dozen colleagues representing the various interest groups, succeeded in crafting a compromise. I got my agenda. The meeting adjourned at 6.00am on Saint Patrick's Day. I felt exhausted but vindicated in my determination not to adjourn the meeting until I had secured an agreement. If I had adjourned the meeting, the pressure would have eased and delegations would again dig in their heels. I also wanted to make the point to delegates and the Secretariat that when I set a deadline, I meant to keep it. The Secretariat never doubted my resolve again. At all subsequent sessions of the PrepCom and the Main Committee, I had teams of interpreters ready to serve the meeting through the night and into the morning of the next day on the final day of each session. On two subsequent occasions, I went through the night — until 4.30am on the last day of the fourth substantive session in New York, and 6.00am on the last day of the Main Committee at the Earth Summit in Rio.

Managing the Negotiating Process

Managing a complex negotiating process requires both leadership and team work. I worked closely with the Secretary-General of the Conference, Maurice Strong, and the various members of the Secretariat. Twenty years earlier, he was the Secretary-General of the Stockholm Conference on the Human Environment. I had worked closely with him in preparing for the Stockholm Conference. The fact that our friendship went back 20 years helped us to forge a good working partnership. I kept no secrets from him and his deputy, Nitin Desai.

The Collegium

I expanded the collective leadership or Collegium to include the Chairman of Working Group I, Ambassador Bo Kjellen of Sweden; the Chairman of Working Group II, Bukar Shaib of Nigeria; the Chairman of Working Group III, Bedrich Moldan of Czechoslovakia; and the Rapporteur, Ahmad Djoghlaf of Algeria. I institutionalized the collective management of the negotiating process by holding meetings every morning at 9.00am with this group and the senior members of the UNCED Secretariat. This would be followed by a daily meeting at 9.30am with the representatives of all the UN agencies. The purpose of the second meeting was to bring all the members of the UN family together and to prevent turf fights and misunderstandings. It was also to tap the expertise and inputs of the various agencies.

The Delegation of Power

The work of the PrepCom was carried out in four principal forums: the plenary of the PrepCom and the three working groups. The agenda of the plenary was long and complex. It included the difficult questions of financing sustainable development and the transfer of technology from developed to developing countries. It also included such questions as the relationship between the environment, on the one hand, and poverty, population, the international economic order and human settlements, on the other.

A good Chairman must avoid the temptation of keeping everything under his wings. He must learn to delegate. He must choose able men and women to delegate responsibility to. When it becomes clear that a delegatee is unable to deliver, a chairman must do the very unpleasant job of replacing him with someone else.

Open-Ended Negotiating Groups

At the second substantive session held in Geneva in the spring of 1991, I established a number of open-ended negotiating groups in the plenary. I appointed Ambassador Bjorner Utheim of Norway to chair the one on technology; Deputy Foreign Minister John Muliro of Kenya to chair the one on the poverty-population-health cluster; Ambassador Enrique Penalosa of Colombia to chair the one on human settlements and Ahmad Djoghlaf of Algeria to chair the one on the international economic order. I co-opted the chairmen of the negotiating groups into the Collegium.

A Painful Duty

At the fourth substantive session, I replaced Ambassador John Bell with Deputy Foreign Minister Andres Rozental of Mexico. At the Summit, I replaced Rozental with Ambassador Ricupero of Brazil. Also, at the Summit, I replaced Utheim with the Dutch Minister of the Environment, J.G.M. Alders. As one who attaches great value to loyalty and friendship, I have always found it very difficult to abandon a colleague. However, I felt duty-bound to put the best interests of the Conference before friendship and loyalty. The fact that both Ricupero and Alders succeeded in their work showed that I was right to make the personnel changes.

The Elephantine Bureau

The Bureau of a committee or conference is supposed to act as its steering committee. The Bureau of the PrepCom and the Earth Summit was unable to play this role effectively because of its size: 42 members. It was almost as difficult to reach a consensus among the 42 members of the Bureau as among the 150-plus members of the PrepCom and the 170-plus members of the Summit. I had to invent another body to act as the steering committee.

De Facto Steering Committee

I convened twice weekly meetings of a group consisting of the Chairmen of the five groups; the Chairman of the Group of 77 (representing the developing countries); the chairman of the EC; the Chairman of the Nordic Group; the Chairman of CANZ (representing Canada, Australia and New Zealand) and the three countries which do not belong to any interest group: China, Japan and the US. This group of 12 countries and the Collegium functioned as the steering committee of the PrepCom and Summit. It proved to be a very effective body. During critical periods of the PrepCom and Summit, I would convene daily meetings of this group. In order to pacify the members of the Bureau, who quite rightly felt bypassed, I would convene meetings of the Bureau from time to time.

The Importance of Timing

In negotiation, timing is very important. A chairman who acts prematurely risks being rebuffed. A chairman who acts too slowly loses the opportunity to clinch a deal. I have observed that multilateral negotiations often pass through three phases: confrontation, crisis and resolution. A good chairman must not be unnerved by the phase of confrontation. He must wait for the period of crisis which often follows confrontation.

It is at this maximum hour of danger and opportunity that he must strike and bring about a resolution.

Let me illustrate these general observations with the following concrete example. Working Group III, on law and institutions, was established at the beginning of the second substantive session in Geneva. It elected Bedrich Moldan of Czechoslovakia as its Chairman. One of the items on its agenda was the drafting of the Rio Declaration on the Environment and Development, popularly referred to as the Earth Charter. At the beginning of the fourth substantive session, Moldan offered a compromise draft consisting of ten principles and three prerequisites. He moved too soon. Also, his draft was viewed, rightly or wrongly, by the developing countries as favouring the viewpoint of the developed countries. Because of this, the developing countries refused to continue to negotiate under his chairmanship. Instead, an informal contact group was established under the co-chairmanship of Mukul Sanwal of India and Ole Holthe of Norway.

Going from 150 to 16

On the morning of 31 March 1992, three days before the end of that session, Sanwal and Holthe asked for permission to speak to our daily meeting at 9.00am. They reported that they had gone as far as they could and were unable to make any further progress. They requested me to take over the negotiations. The meeting supported their request. I then convened a meeting of the *de facto* steering committee. I said I would be prepared to chair the negotiation provided they agreed to establish a small, closed, representative group of 16, eight to represent the North and eight to represent the South. The meeting agreed. The North was represented, by the US; Portugal Netherlands and Germany (EC); Australia (CANZ); Norway (alternating with Sweden); Japan and Russia. The South was represented by Pakistan, India, Iran, Brazil, Mexico, Nigeria, Tanzania and China.

Preparing a Negotiating Text

I made another request. I requested Sanwal and Holthe to produce a negotiating text by 6.30pm on 1 April 1992. They did so and the group of 16 began its work at 8.00pm of the same evening. It adjourned before midnight and continued the next morning. A clean text, containing 27 principles was agreed upon, *ad referendum,* at 6.15pm on 2 April 1992 (A/CONF.151/PC/WGIII/L33/Rev.). This text would eventually be adopted by the Earth Summit as the Rio Declaration on Environment and Development.

The Negotiating Process in Rio

Apart from the clean text of the Rio Declaration, the other documents submitted to Rio contained 350 bracketed, or disputed language. We had only one week in the Main Committee to remove these brackets and to find acceptable language. I was not at all sure that the job could be done.

Procedural Decisions

I persuaded the Committee to adopt a number of procedural decisions. First, that the negotiation would focus entirely on the bracketed language. I ruled out of order any delegate who tried, to re-open discussion on unbracketed language (i.e. language which had been agreed upon). I also rebuffed the attempts by several delegations to insert new brackets on the ground that they had been inadvertently omitted by the Secretariat. Fortunately, we had brought along the authoritative documents of the PrepCom. Upon verification, we found no merit in any of the requests. Second, I refused to allow any delegation to make a new proposal if it met with a single objection. The reason is that any new proposal must advance the prospect of achieving consensus. Third, I asked the Committee to allow me to establish nine open-ended negotiating groups on the understanding that not more than three would meet concurrently. Fourth, I persuaded the Committee to work from Monday to Saturday and to meet morning, afternoon and evening. Fifth, I imposed a strict time-limit on the length of statements. Sixth, whenever the negotiation got stuck on a point, I would set up an *ad hoc* open-ended negotiating group to deal with it and appoint an able colleague to chair the group. In this way, I was able to keep the negotiation moving at a steady pace.

A Long Day's Night

The final meeting of the Main Committee began at 8.00pm on 10 June 1992. It continued through the night and ended at 6.00am the next morning. I did take one short break. At 4.00am, after eight hours in the chair, I was desperate to go to the toilet. I also sensed that there was a lot of tension in the room. I announced that we would recess the meeting for five minutes in order to enable me to make a discharge of non-toxic waste. I promised to do it in an environmentally safe and sound manner. The delegates broke into laughter and the meeting resumed in a better mood. All bracketed language, excepting those relating to finance and forest, was resolved. Those two issues were referred to ministerial-level negotiations chaired by Brazil and Germany respectively. The Brazilians had consulted me on who to appoint to chair the difficult negotiation on forest. I recommended the German Minister for the Environment, Klaus Toepfer. Consensus was achieved on those two issues on 12 June. The Summit was therefore able to adopt, on 14 June, the Rio Declaration, Agenda 21 and the Statement of Principles on Forests by consensus. Thus ended the largest conference the UN had ever held. It was attended by 116 Heads of State or Government, 172 states, 8,000 delegates, 9,000 members of the press and 3,000 accredited representatives of non-governmental organisations.

The Trees of Singapore

A foreign friend, from another Asian country, had spent several days in Singapore recently. At the end of her visit, I asked her what she liked most about Singapore. I was expecting her to refer to our food, our multiculturalism, our cleanliness, our Orchard Road or The Esplanade, but she said, "your trees".

This set me thinking. It is true that the other leading cities of Asia: Tokyo, Seoul, Beijing, Shanghai, Hong Kong, Bangkok, Kuala Lumpur, Mumbai, New Delhi, have relatively few trees. Singapore stands out as a city of trees, parks and gardens. It wears a very green visage. It reminds me of another city in which I had lived for six years, Washington, DC. I also remember once asking Mrs Piroska Rajaratnam, the wife of our first Foreign Minister, what she liked most about Washington, DC. She said, "the trees".

Most Singaporeans take our trees for granted. They are not knowledgeable about our trees. I once asked an artist friend, who often included trees in his paintings, what trees they were. He confessed that he did not know. On another occasion, I was asked to sum up a conference on civil society in Singapore. A sudden inspiration led me to pick three trees to represent the colonial era, the Lee Kuan Yew era and the Goh Chok Tong era, respectively. I said that the colonial era was like a royal palm tree, tall, aloof, with a small canopy. Civil society thrived during the colonial era because the colonial government did not provide for many of the needs of the communities. The Lee Kuan Yew era was like a banyan tree, a strong and much revered tree with a huge canopy. During the Lee Kuan Yew era, civil society shrank because the government took over many of the services which used to be provided by the civil society. The Goh Chok

Tong era was like a tembusu tree, a magnificent tree with a canopy smaller than that of the banyan tree. SM Goh had wanted to expand the space for the civil society. The story I heard from an editor at *The Straits Times* was that the reporter covering the conference had no idea what the three trees looked like and had to go to the Singapore Botanic Gardens to find out.

Trees and human beings have a symbiotic relationship. Trees breathe in carbon and exhale oxygen. Humans breathe in oxygen and exhale carbon. Our trees help to keep our air quality good and keep us healthy. It is sad, but unfortunately true, that most of the major cities of Asia suffer from air pollution which affects the health of their citizens. The incidence of asthma, especially among children, increases with air pollution. Planting trees is one of the best practices of Singapore which other cities in Asia should emulate.

Trees also produce fruits for human consumption. Our doctors and the Health Ministry urge us to eat more fruits because they are good for our health. My wife and I love fruits and therefore do not need any persuasion to eat fruits. We do not understand why some of our friends, including one of our children, do not like fruits. I like all kinds of fruits. Of the local fruits, I am particularly fond of papaya, banana, mango, chiku, custard apple, rose apple, mangosteen and, of course, the king of fruits, the incomparable durian. The durian deserves an essay by itself.

Trees are beautiful. I agree with the poet, Joyce Kilmer, who wrote:

> I think I shall never see
> A poem lovely as a tree

Singapore has a wonderful variety of indigenous and imported trees. Many of our roads and highways are lined with rain trees, which grow rapidly and give good shade. There are many species of palm trees which often frame the approach to an entrance or an important building. The red flame of the forest and the yellow flame tree dress our city with their vibrant colours. The rose of India, with its rose or mauve flowers; the trumpet tree with its pink flowers; the hibiscus tree with its red or yellow flowers; the frangipani tree with its fragrant flowers; the jacaranda tree with its lilac flowers; the bougainvillea tree with its many splendid colours; the weeping fig tree aka Indian banyan tree; and the bodhi tree which is sacred to both Hindus and Buddhists, are some of my favourite trees.

My wife and I love the Singapore Botanic Gardens. We go there several mornings a week, between 6.30am and 7.30am, when the air is still cool. We would join a group of people doing an exercise called "liu tong quan". We would stand on the ring road surrounding the band stand. The road is lined with a cluster of very lovely yellow rain trees.

My favourite tree in the whole of Singapore is a tembusu tree in the Singapore Botanic Gardens. It stands on a grassy field, near the revolving globe and overlooking the Swan Lake. It must be over one hundred years old because I have been a friend of this tree since I was a child. What is unique about this tree is that it has an artistic branch, which is about waist high and which grows parallel to the ground. Children love to climb on the branch and sit on it. This tree has been featured on one of our postage stamps. It is one of our "heritage trees". I love this tree and have a photograph of it in my bedroom. Do you have a favourite tree?

[Originally published in *Chicken Soup for the Singapore Soul*, eds. J Canfield, M. V. Hansen, and C. Leong, Marshall Cavendish Editions, 2007.]

Biodiversity and Cities*

Dr Ahmed Djoghlaf, Executive Secretary of the Convention on Biological Diversity (CBD); Mr Peter Egardt, the County Governor of Uppsala, Sweden; and Friends of the Earth and of Biological Diversity

I would like to begin by thanking my good friend, Dr Ahmed Djoghlaf, for inviting me to deliver the Third Linnaeus Lecture. Ahmed Djoghlaf and I were part of the leadership team at the Earth Summit. It is hard to believe that 18 years have passed since that historic conference in Rio de Janeiro.

Homage to Linnaeus

The Swedish genius and father of modern taxonomy, Carl Linnaeus, was born on 23 May 1707. On the occasion of his 300th birthday, in 2007, I participated in a conference and exhibition to honour him, which was held at the Singapore Botanic Gardens. At the other end of the world, in the Canadian city of Montreal, the Secretariat of the CBD, with the strong support of the Kingdom of Sweden, decided to launch the inaugural Linnaeus Lecture. The lecture was delivered by Mr Yvo de Boer, the then Executive Secretary of the UN Framework Convention on Climate Change (UNFCCC) on the topic, "Climate Change Challenges". Climate change is, of course, a principal threat to biodiversity. The Second Linnaeus Lecture was delivered by Professor Jeffrey Sachs of Columbia University and Special Adviser to the UN Secretary-General, Mr Ban Ki-moon, on 23 May 2008, in Bonn, on the sideline of COP-9.

---

*The Third Linnaeus Lecture delivered on 22 October 2010, Nagoya, Japan.

Three Environmental Challenges

In my view, the three most important environmental challenges of our time are: climate change, the loss of biological diversity and desertification. All three are interrelated and it is a pity that the world has taken a rather unbalanced view of the three challenges: too much attention on climate change and too little on biodiversity and desertification. For this reason, I support Japan's proposal to designate the decade, 2010 to 2020, as the UN Biodiversity Decade. I also support the idea that the UN General Assembly consider holding a special summit, during its 70th session, in 2015, to do a mid-term review of the new 2020 Strategic Plan.

Loss of Biodiversity

At COP-6 in 2002, the world's leaders agreed to achieve a significant reduction in the rate of biodiversity loss by 2010. According to the Global Biodiversity Outlook 3 (2010), co-authored by UNEP and the Secretariat of CBD, that target has not been met. On the contrary, the evidence suggests that the rate of biodiversity loss is increasing. This trend seems to find confirmation in the first report of the IUCN Sampled Red List Index for Plants (2010), prepared by the Royal Botanic Gardens at Kew, the Natural History Museum (London) and IUCN. The key findings include the following: (i) more than 20 percent of plants are threatened with extinction; (ii) the most threatened habitat is the tropical rainforest; and (iii) the greatest threat to habitat loss is caused by human activities, such as, the conversion of natural habitats for agriculture, including palm oil and soybean plantations or to livestock farming.

Biodiversity and Human Health

Sceptics have asked, why should we care if certain species of plants and animals become extinct each year? We are all familiar with the economic and medicinal benefits of biodiversity. I think the most compelling case for why we should care, has been made by Dr Eric Chivian and Dr Aaron Bernstein, in their monumental book (2008), entitled, *Sustaining Life: How Human Health Depends on Biodiversity*. In his eloquent prologue, Mr Kofi Annan wrote:

> One of the main reasons the world faces a global environmental crisis is the belief that we human beings are somehow separate from the natural world in which we live, and that we can alter its physical, chemical and biological systems without these alterations having any effect on humanity. Sustaining life challenges this widely held misconception by demonstrating definitively, with the best and most current scientific information available, that human health depends, to a larger extent than we might imagine, on the health of other species and on the healthy functioning of other ecosystems.

In their preface, Dr Chivian and Dr Bernstein wrote:

> During the past fifty years...our actions have resulted in the loss of roughly one-fifth of Earth's topsoil, one-fifth of its land suitable for agriculture, almost 90 percent of its large commercial fisheries, and one-third of its forests, while we need these resources more than ever, as our population has almost tripled during this period of time, increasing from 2.5 to more than 6.5 billion.

They also wrote:

> We are so damaging the habitats in which other species live that we are driving them to extinction, ... at a rate that is hundreds to even thousands of times greater than natural background levels. ... as a result of all these actions taken together, we are disturbing what are called "ecosystem services", that is, the various ways that organisms, and the sum total of their interactions with each other and with the environments in which they live, function to keep all life on this planet, including human life, alive.

Urbanising Asia

For the first time in human history, the majority of human beings lives in urban settlements rather than rural areas. This process of rapid urbanisation is changing Asia dramatically. Let us take China and India as examples. In 1987, only 25 percent of China's population lived in cities. By 2007, the percentage had gone up to 42 percent. The number is expected to rise to 60 percent in 2030 and 70 percent in 2050. In the case of India, by 2050, 55 percent of its population or 900 million Indians are expected to live in cities. Of the world's 100 fastest growing cities, with a population of over 1 million, 66 are in Asia. The urbanisation of Asia will transform the world economically and environmentally.

Urbanisation and Biodiversity

Urbanisation is generally viewed as a threat to biodiversity. However, we cannot stop the process of urbanisation. We already live in an urban world and the future will be an even more urban one. This is not necessarily a bad thing because high density living, with proper planning and implementation, can improve efficiencies in transport and the use of resource. It can also free up land, which would otherwise be consumed by suburban sprawl, for green areas and biodiversity. Instead of viewing cities as the enemies of biodiversity, let us change the paradigm and focus on how cities can contribute positively to conserve biodiversity. Let me discuss Singapore's experience, as an example. Singapore is, however, not alone in this movement. Other cities, such as Nagoya in Japan, Curitiba in Brazil, Montreal in Canada, Brussels in Belgium, Montpellier in France, Bangkok in Thailand, Bandung in Indonesia, Iloilo City in the Philippines, Kuantan in Malaysia, Frankfurt in Germany, Hamilton in New Zealand, Joondalup in Australia, London in the UK, and Stockholm in Sweden, are part of the movement. The role which cities can play in the conservation of biodiversity was discussed both at the 2008 and 2010 World Cities Summits, held in Singapore. It is also significant that the theme of the highly successful 2010 Shanghai Expo is: "Better City, Better Life".

The Singapore Story

The Singapore story is important to the world because it shows that a city need not be an enemy of nature and biodiversity. On the contrary, it demonstrates three propositions: (i) that achieving economic prosperity need not be at the expense of care for the environment; (ii) that a small, densely populated city can still be clean, green and nature-loving; and (iii) that a city can play a positive role in the conservation of biodiversity and in our campaign to reduce the loss of biodiversity.

Singapore is a small island, strategically located at the junction between the Strait of Malacca and the South China Sea. It is a port of call for ships plying the East-West trade route, from ancient sailing ships to modern super tankers and container ships. It is a very small island, with a total area of 710 square kilometres. It is smaller than the city of Tokyo. Our population has exceeded 5 million, making us one of the most densely populated cities in the world.

Although the island had been inhabited since the 14th century, it had become depopulated by 1819, the year in which the British acquired it. It was a British colony from 1819 until 1963, when it became a State within the Federation of Malaysia. It became an independent State in 1965.

From 1819 until the 1970s, the imperative was to clear the original forest cover, mangrove forests and to level the hills, for development. As a result, Singapore has lost more than 95 percent of its original forest cover, about 50 percent of its animal species and 25 percent of its vascular plants. Yet, when we look at a Google Earth satellite photograph of Singapore, we are surprised to see that half the island is green. When we look closer, we will notice that forests cover 9.2 percent and dense vegetation cover 14 per cent of Singapore.

From Garden City to City in a Garden

How did Singapore, which is so densely populated, become so clean, green and nature-loving? I think the secret is that we have one of the world's first green political leaders, Mr Lee Kuan Yew. From the beginning of our journey from the Third World to the First, Mr Lee insisted that Singapore would accept no investment proposal if it did not have the support of the anti-pollution unit. The unit was located in the Prime Minister's Office and was empowered to overrule the economic agencies. Mr Lee believed that nature has economic value and that our clean and green environment would give us a comparative advantage in attracting foreign investment to Singapore. It was he who envisioned Singapore as a Garden City. We often refer to him as Singapore's Chief Gardener! Mr Lee's successors have taken the vision to another level. Our new ambition is to be a City in a Garden. Our ambition is to make Singapore one of the world's most liveable cities, not just for the rich and the elite, but for all our citizens, residents and visitors.

Singapore's Biodiversity

Singapore is fortunate to be located within the world's richest biodiversity region. For this reason, although we have lost a significant percentage of our biodiversity, what remains is not insignificant. We have more than 2,000 species of plants, 360 species of birds, 270 species of butterflies, 120 species of reptiles, 75 species of mammals, 25 species of amphibians, 256 species of hard corals, covering 55 genera and 111 species of reef fish belonging to 30 families. You will be surprised to learn that one of our four nature reserves, the Bukit Timah Nature Reserve, only 163 hectares in size, is home to more species of trees than the whole of North America. You will also be surprised to learn that there are 3 species of crabs in Singapore which do not exist anywhere else on this planet. At the suggestion of the Nature Society of Singapore, the Government has created a wetlands nature reserve at Sungei Buloh, which welcomes each year thousands of migratory birds in their annual pilgrimage to escape the northern winter. The Government also took up a proposal by the people of Singapore to conserve an inter-tidal area that comprised 7 different ecosystems at Chek Jawa. The Government had originally intended to reclaim land which would have destroyed these ecosystems.

Efforts to Conserve Biodiversity

Let me now share with you a few of the best practices which Singapore has undertaken to protect and enhance our biodiversity.

First, the government's lead agency on biodiversity, the National Parks Board (NParks) has been proactive in leading the way. In 2009, it launched the National Biodiversity Strategy and Action Plan. Apart from championing a wide range of conservation projects, the Plan also aims to give voice to biodiversity issues in policy and decision-making. NParks also has an admirable attitude of seeking to work closely with the civil society, the corporate sector, students and volunteers. Our national water agency, PUB, has turned our concrete canals and drains into landscaped rivers with plants and mangroves. As a result, we are seeing the return of birds like the magpie robin, fishes and insects such as butterflies and dragonflies, to our heartlands, thus bringing biodiversity closer to our people.

Second, I must praise the contributions of our universities, research institutions and scientists. At the Raffles Museum of Biodiversity Research of the National University of Singapore, visitors can learn about the region's plants and animals, through an extremely comprehensive collection of preserved specimens. It is also training the next generation of the region's scientists. They are also planning to build a new museum of natural history which will showcase the natural heritage of Southeast Asia. Individual scientists have been extremely active in their research, teaching and publications, on Singapore's biodiversity. One of my favourite publications is a book by four of our scientists (Hugh Tan, Chou Loke Ming, Darren Yeo and Peter Ng), on *The Natural Heritage of Singapore*. Two of our leading scholars, Professor Leo Tan and Professor Peter Ng, with the support of two dozen passionate graduate students, are co-editing an encyclopedia of Singapore's biodiversity. In 2011, the National University of Singapore will launch a new multi-disciplinary bacherlor's degree in environmental studies. We already have a master's degree on environmental management, which is co-taught by professors from seven different faculties.

Third, we have an active and responsible civil society. The Nature Society (Singapore), for example, is a blue-chip NGO. Its members conduct guided nature walks, bird and butterfly watching, talks as well as undertake conservation projects and surveys. Working closely with the Singapore Environment Council, the Nature Society (Singapore) works with schools and community organisations to promote the appreciation of nature and biodiversity. The marine volunteers are also very active in monitoring sea-grasses and hard corals in our waters. Our amateur naturalists are just as diverse as our biodiversity. For example, our High Commissioner to Brunei, Joseph Koh, is an expert on spiders, a professor of obstetrics and gynaecology, Ng Soon Chye, not only delivers human babies but is also encouraging Oriental pied hornbills to breed in Singapore, a specialist in gastroenterology, Francis Seow, is an expert on stick insects, one of our butterfly experts, Khew Sin Khoon is an architect, and one of our best natural photographers, Chua Ee Khiam, is a dentist by day. The green citizen movement is, indeed, blooming in Singapore.

Fourth, one of Singapore's best practices is our ability to bring government, academia, civil society, and the corporate sector to work together. The business community in Singapore is increasingly supportive of the environment and biodiversity. Let me give you two examples in which I was involved. A leading MNC partnered NParks to plant trees, which would attract singing birds, in one of our parks. When the trees mature and the singing birds come, the forest will resonate with the songs of birds. In another project, the Nature Society (Singapore), NParks and the private sector decided to do something which has never been done elsewhere in the world. Singapore's main shopping street, the Orchard Road, is like the Champs-Elysees in Paris. In a four-kilometre stretch linking the Singapore Botanic Gardens, on the one end, and the Fort Canning, on the other, we have planted trees and shrubs by volunteers along Orchard Road which are either host plants for butterflies or plants which provide them with nectar. Soon, when the plants mature and the butterflies arrive, the shoppers and pedestrians along Orchard Road will have the unique experience of being accompanied by butterflies. I hope that the shoppers on Orchard Road be so inspired by the experience that they will develop a love of nature and a sense of stewardship towards biodiversity and the ecosystems which sustain them.

Conclusion

Let me conclude by recapitulating my three propositions.

First, I agree with Dr Chivian and Dr Bernstein that the historically unprecedented loss of biodiversity is a threat to the ecosystems which sustain human life and welfare. *Second*, the process of urbanisation is irreversible. Therefore, instead of seeking to oppose the inevitable, we should make the cities of the world our allies and even the drivers, in our endeavour to protect our biodiversity. *Third*, Nagoya, Curitiba, Montreal, Bonn, Singapore and other like-minded cities are the thought leaders of a new movement to make our cities liveable, safe, green and rich in biodiversity. I therefore strongly support the Singapore Index on Cities' Biodiversity and hope that it will inspire cities around the world to join the movement.

We know so much more about the wonders of nature than Linnaeus did when he proposed to describe all known plant and animal species over 200 years ago. However, if we do not stop the continued loss of biodiversity, many of these species will only be found as preserved specimens in our museums and herbaria. Let us mobilise the cities of the world and the knowledge, talent, creativity, energy of their citizens, to preserve the natural heritage which Linnaeus loved and strove to document.

Thank you. *Arigato*.

Green Thoughts Inspired by Stockholm and Rio

In 1972, the UN convened the historic Conference on the Human Environment in Stockholm, Sweden. Twenty years later, the UN Conference on Environment and Development, aka the Earth Summit, was held in Rio de Janeiro, Brazil. From 20 to 22 June 2012, the UN will hold its third conference on the environment, the UN Conference on Sustainable Development, aka Rio+20, again in the Brazilian city of Rio de Janeiro. It seems like a pattern has emerged: once every 20 years, the UN will convene a major conference on the environment.

I played a small part in the preparations for the Stockholm conference. I helped to prevent the radicals in the Group of 77 (the trade union of the developing countries) from hijacking the group with their narrative that the conference was a plot by the developed countries to prevent the developing countries from their economic advancement. My counter-narrative was that developing countries, such as Singapore, were seeking to make economic progress in harmony with our environment.

In March 1990, the UN elected me to chair the preparatory committee for the Earth Summit. The committee met over a period of two years, on five occasions: three times in New York and once each, in Nairobi and Geneva. At the Summit, the conference elected me to chair the Main Committee, its principal negotiating forum.

The following were the Summit's achievements:

- Rio Declaration on Environment and Development;
- Agenda 21, containing an ambitious 470-page long programmes of action for sustainable development in the 21st century;

- Non-legally binding authoritative statement of Principles on Forests;
- Agreement to negotiate a new treaty to combat desertification;
- The opening for signature of the UN Framework Convention on Climate Change (UNFCCC), which had been negotiated on a separate track;
- The opening for signature of the UN Convention on Biological Diversity (CBD), which had also been negotiated on a separate track.

Twenty years have passed since the Earth Summit. Has the world made progress or regress during this period? On the positive side, we can point to the fact that all 193 Member States of the UN have either a ministry for the environment or an environmental protection agency. In addition, many countries have established national commissions on sustainable development and have adopted their own Agenda 21. We can also take satisfaction from the fact that there is no longer a constituency in the developing world for the view that we should develop first and clean up the environment later. The environment movement has grown stronger. It has influenced, in positive ways, the behaviour of individuals, communities, civil society, business, municipal, provincial and federal governments.

However, the positives are outweighed by the negatives. The following are the principal problem areas:

- The emission of greenhouses gases has continued to increase and we are no longer sure whether the goal to cap the rise of global temperature to 2°C is doable.
- The Kyoto Protocol will expire at the end of 2012 and it is uncertain whether the developed countries would be willing to agree to a second commitment period (Australia and Japan have said that they would not, Canada has withdrawn from the Protocol, and the US is not a party to it).
- It is also not clear whether the agreement in Durban to negotiate a post-2020 agreement, applicable to all countries, will succeed.

- The world's rainforests, including those in Indonesia and East Malaysia, are rapidly disappearing, due to illegal logging and unsustainable forestry management.
- The world is losing its biological diversity at a rate which is 1,000 times faster than the natural rate of extinction.
- In the past 50 years, we have lost 20 percent of the land suitable for agriculture, 90 percent of our large commercial fisheries, and 33 percent of our forests, leading to the loss of eco-systems.
- The oceans, which absorb 30 percent of the carbon dioxide from the atmosphere and provide the largest source of protein to human beings, are threatened by acidification, rising temperature and over-exploitation.

Singapore's Achievements

Unlike the dismal global picture, the last 20 years has been a period of progress for Singapore. I count the following as some of Singapore's most important achievements:

- 47 percent of Singapore's total land area is covered by greenery.
- The gazetting of two new nature reserves at Sungei Buloh and Labrador.
- Saving the tidal flat at Chek Jawa from reclamation.
- Saving the trees of the Lower Peirce Reservoir from being cut down to make way for a golf course.
- The building of new parks and an island-wide park connector.
- The building of the Marina Barrage and turning Marina Bay and the Kallang Basin into a reservoir.
- Opening our reservoirs for recreational use and bringing nature back to our rivers, streams and canals.
- Highlighting the role of cities in the conservation of biodiversity, culminating in the adoption of the Singapore Cities Biodiversity Index by the Nagoya Conference in 2011.
- Fostering the growth of a water industry and being a global thought leader of water policy and governance.

- Championing the movement of liveable cities and being a global thought leader on good urban planning, policies and solutions.
- Encouraging the trend to build green buildings and to retrofit old buildings to become green buildings.
- Launching multi-disciplinary environmental education, both at the undergraduate and post-graduate levels and at the Asia-Pacific Centre for Environmental Law of NUS.
- Saving endangered species of animals such as the banded-leaf monkey, welcoming the return of the hornbill and rediscovering other species that were thought to have disappeared from Singapore.
- Fostering a cooperative partnership between government, business and civil society.
- Building a new museum of natural history.

My Wish List

Singapore has done well, but we should not rest on our laurels. We should continue to forge ahead, to innovate and to learn from others. The following is my wish list.

First, I think the time has come for Singapore to enact a law on environmental impact assessment (EIA). Principle No. 17 of the Rio Declaration states: "Environmental impact assessment, as a national instrument, shall be undertaken for proposed activities that are likely to have a significant adverse impact on the environment and are subject to a decision of a competent national authority." Having been intimately involved in a legal dispute involving our land reclamation activities in the Straits of Johor, I know that we do, in fact, carry out such an assessment. The result is, however, not made public and there is no consultation with interested stakeholders. Our neighbour, Malaysia, has shown that having an EIA law need not result in inordinate delay. The two benefits are that the government could benefit from the feedback and the process is transparent and inclusive. At its best, the EIA will lead to a better decision, and the people will feel that their views have been taken into consideration in arriving at that decision.

Second, I would urge the authorities to consider designating our first marine nature reserve. We need such a reserve, with adequate protection measures for marine life in order to ensure the conservation of genetic diversity. Although Singapore has one of the world's biggest and busiest ports, it is not sufficiently known that, at the same time, we have 270 species of hard corals and 111 species of reef fishes, in our seas. A marine nature reserve will ensure the survival of this natural heritage. It will also be a great selling point and indicate our serious commitment to protect the marine environment to the world. The two potential areas are Pulau Hantu and Pulau Semakau.

Third, I would request our authorities to consider raising the bar on the recycling of waste. Singapore used to be the thought leader on the environment in Asia. In important respects, such as the recycling of waste, we have fallen behind Japan, South Korea and Taiwan. We should, where feasible, encourage the recycling of waste, such as paper, plastic, aluminium cans and glass bottles. The situation at present is not satisfactory. For example, the building in which I live and three of the clubs I belong to, do not have such facilities. We should also consider the feasibility of emulating Japan, South Korea and Taiwan by enacting a law, and to start by requiring industrial and commercial establishments, as well as hotels and food courts, to separate food waste from other kinds of waste at source. The food waste, when treated by anaerobic digestion, will produce biogas which can, in turn, be used to generate renewable electricity. We had such a plant in Singapore which, unfortunately, failed because, in the absence of a law requiring the segregation of waste, it could not get enough uncontaminated food waste for treatment. This is a pity because if it had succeeded, it was scaleable and had tremendous potential in Asia as food waste is a major source of leachate contamination of ground water and a contributor to greenhouse gas emissions.

Fourth, I would request NUS to consider starting a new School of Environmental Studies. The bachelor's degree on environmental studies and the master's degree on environmental management could be brought together in the new School. The Institute of Water Policy, currently housed in the Lee Kuan Yew School of Public Policy, and the Centre of Sustainable

Asian Cities, currently located in the School of Design and Environment, could migrate to the new School. Bringing them together would enable us to harness the synergy between them and to develop it as one of our centres of excellence. The current links between the master's degree programme and the universities of Yale and Duke should be strengthened. NUS has a strategic opportunity to become a leading centre of environmental education in Asia. Indeed, Singapore has many leading thinkers on the environment, leading environmental economists, environmentally friendly bankers, fund managers, stock exchange and a vast pool of capital in search of investment. Singapore has an opportunity to bring them and a growing family of international green groups together to make Singapore into one of the world's leading innovators in using markets and investments to encourage and reinforce best practices in sustainable development.

Fifth, Singapore's air quality is good, but it could be better. My wife and I live in a building without a covered garage. After the rain has stopped, we often dry our car with paper towels. Each time, we have observed that the paper towels are stained black by the impurities in the air, which are contained in the rain water. A major source of air pollution is the emission of our vehicles. We should redouble our efforts to promote the electric vehicle and hybrid vehicle. The government is spending $1.1 billion to buy 550 new buses. Is it possible for the government to consider buying electric or hybrid buses? We should also promote cycling and, wherever possible, to designate special lanes on our roads for cyclists. I spent 13 years living in one of the most congested cities in the world, New York City. If New York can do it, I would like to believe that so can Singapore.

Sixth, in our quest to reduce our carbon footprint, energy efficiency is a low hanging fruit. The efficient use and the conservation of energy are, however, achievable only with the cooperation and help of business and the people. Let me cite one example. Singapore has become notorious for its abuse of air-conditioning. I remember the former Dean of INSEAD, Antonio Borges, telling me, during his first visit to Singapore, that he had discovered that Singapore actually had two seasons: summer outdoors and winter indoors. I also remember, an occasion when the Mongolian trade minister said to us, at a welcome dinner for trade ministers, held in the freezing ballroom of a leading hotel in Singapore, that he did not know that Singapore was colder than Mongolia. The gentle and humourous ads on television by NEA, exhorting Singaporeans to use air-conditioning more responsibly, have not worked. I would urge the NEA and SEC to wage a more energetic campaign targeting our educational institutions, hospitals, movie theatres, hotels, restaurants, clubs, etc.

Seventh, my final wish has to do with our beloved Orchard Road. My wish is inspired by Copenhagen and New York. In Copenhagen, the main shopping street is a pedestrian mall. One of the reasons for the jury's decision to award the 2012 Lee Kuan Yew City Prize to New York is that it has turned Times Square into a pedestrian mall and, thereby, rejuvenated the whole area around it. Would it not be wonderful if we could turn the stretch of Orchard Road, between Tangs and Centrepoint, into a pedestrian mall? If the experience of New York is portable to Singapore, this will increase, not decrease, the property value and business along Orchard Road.

[Originally published in *The Straits Times*, 16 June 2012.]

The Future of Water Today*

Water is more precious than gold. Without water, there would be no life on earth. The irony is that we take water for granted. In some countries, water is treated as a public good and given away for free. This invariably leads to over-consumption and wastage.

At the first Asia-Pacific Water Summit, held in Beppu, Japan, in 2007, the leaders agreed to recognise the people's right to safe drinking water as a basic human right and a fundamental aspect of human security. The leaders also agreed to reduce by half, the number of people who do not have access to safe drinking water by 2015 and to reduce that number to zero by 2025. The situation today is that about 700 million Asians and about 20 percent of the world's population do not have access to safe drinking water.

The global demand for water is rising, but the supply has become more uncertain. According to the UN, by 2025, half the countries of the world will face water stress or shortage. By 2050, as many as three-quarters of the world's population could be affected by water scarcity. The problem could become particularly acute in Asia because of high population growth, rapid urbanisation and poor water endowment.

Water will become a security issue in this century. In 2009, the Asia Society published a seminal report on Water Security in Asia. The report drew attention to some of the most significant water-related challenges, such as, water disputes between unfriendly neighbours; water conflicts resulting from agricultural and industrial pollution; and the alarming increase in waterborne diseases due to inadequate waste water facilities.

---

*Tommy Koh is the Chairman of the Water Leaders Summit at the SIWW. He is also the Chairman of the Governing Council of the Asia Pacific Water Forum.

Five years ago, Singapore hosted the first Singapore International Water Week (SIWW). The event was highly successful because it brought together all the stakeholders on water. With each passing year, the SIWW has grown bigger and better and has become an important event on the world's water calendar. The fifth edition of SIWW will take place from the 1st to the 5th of July. Having chaired the Water Leaders Summit for the past four years, I will try to crystallise the most important lessons I have learned.

Lesson No. 1 : Treasuring Water

The first lesson I have learned is the need to change the people's mindset about water. In many countries, especially where water is given away for free or heavily subsidised, the people's attitude towards water is a wasteful one. Water should, therefore, be priced for the full recovery of the costs involved in producing it. We should also promote a culture of conserving water and of using water efficiently. In Singapore, as Prime Minister Lee has said, "conserving water is like a religion".

Lesson No. 2 : Right to Safe Drinking Water as a Human Right

The second lesson is that the time has come for the people of Asia to demand that their access to safe drinking water be regarded by their governments as a human right and a fundamental aspect of human security. The fact that 700 million Asians do not have access to safe drinking water while their governments are spending billions of dollars on wasteful and ego-boosting projects is unacceptable. The fact that in some Asian cities, the poor have to buy water from private water vendors at several times the price which the rich pay for their water is reprehensible. There is no country in Asia which is too poor to provide a few litres a day of safe drinking water to all its citizens, if there is a political will to do so.

Lesson No. 3 : The Key is Good Water Governance

The third lesson is that, in most Asian countries and cities, the problem is not the scarcity of water, but poor water governance. What are the examples of poor water governance? They include: antiquated water infrastructure, high leakage, theft, corruption and incompetence. The solution is good water governance. In the water sector, as in other sectors, what we need is good policy and competent management. Transparency, integrity and accountability are the three core values of good governance.

Lesson No. 4 : Public Sector and Private Sector

The fourth lesson is that we should be agnostic about the choice between using the public or the private sector in delivering the water service to the consumers. In the case of Cambodia, the Phnom Penh Water Supply Authority, a public sector entity, solved the city's water problem and is recognised as one of the best water authorities in the world. In the case of the Philippines, the water authority of Manila was privatised. The Manila Water Company has also solved the city's water problem and is often cited as a role model. The wisdom is that, in some situations, where the government is incompetent or corrupt, we may have to rely on the market to solve the water problem. Water is a viable business. The World Bank and the Asian Development Bank have recommended corporatising entities responsible for water services into autonomous bodies.

Lesson No. 5 : Need for a Water Minister

In many countries, water is an issue which cuts across the work of several ministries. The ideal situation is to have a minister in charge of water. If this is not possible, there should be a high-level coordinating mechanism, at the cabinet level, to deal with water, sanitation and waste water. Water should be treated in a holistic manner and not with a silo approach.

Lesson No. 6 : Harnessing Science and Technology

We should harness the power of science and technology. Four of the winners of the Lee Kuan Yew Water Prize, Dr Andrew Benedek (2008), Prof Gatze Lettinga (2009), Dr James Barnard (2011) and Prof Mark van Loosdrecht (2012), are scientists and inventors who have made enormous contributions to the recycling and treatment of waste water. The SIWW is a platform which enables scientists and inventors to meet and interact with the leaders of cities, countries and industries. With the support of international organisations, such as the World Bank and the Asian Development Bank, we are developing sustainable solutions to some of the world's water challenges.

[Originally published in *The Straits Times*, 30 June 2012.]

Timeline — Professor Tommy Koh

12/11/1937	Born in Singapore
1945–1952	Attended Kong Shang Primary School, St Joseph's Institution and Outram Primary School
1952–1957	Attended Raffles Institution. Received an Entrance Scholarship to study law at the University of Malaya, in Singapore.
1961	Received a LL.B. (First Class Honours) degree from the University of Malaya, now known as National University of Singapore
	Awards
	Sir Adrian Clarke Memorial Medal, University of Malaya (Singapore)
	Leow Chia Heng Prize, University of Malaya (Singapore)
1961–1962	Served Law Pupillage with David Marshall
	Admitted to the Singapore Bar as an Advocate and Solicitor
1962–1964	Assistant Lecturer, Faculty of Law, University of Singapore
1964	Received LL.M. from Harvard University. Was awarded a Fulbright Fellowship and a Harvard Law School Fellowship.
1964–1971	Lecturer, Faculty of Law, University of Singapore
1965	Received post-graduate Diploma in Criminology from Cambridge University

1967	Visiting Lecturer, School of Law, State University of New York at Buffalo (Spring semester)
1968–1971	Singapore's Permanent Representative to the United Nations, New York (concurrently accredited as High Commissioner to Canada)
1971	Awarded the Public Service Star
1971–1974	Associate Professor and Dean, Faculty of Law, University of Singapore
1974–1984	Singapore's Permanent Representative to the United Nations, New York (concurrently accredited as High Commissioner to Canada and Ambassador to Mexico)
1974–1982	Leader of the Singapore delegation to the Third UN Conference on the Law of the Sea
1977	Conferred a full professorship
1979	Awarded Meritorious Service Medal (Pingat Jasa Gemilang), Singapore
1981–1982	President of the Third UN Conference on the Law of the Sea
1984	Awarded an honorary degree of Doctor of Laws by Yale University Awarded Wolfgang Friedman Prize by Columbia Law School, New York
1984–1990	Ambassador to the United States of America
1985	Awarded Jackson H. Ralston Prize, Stanford Law School, California Received Annual Award from the Asia Society, New York
1987	Received Jit Trainor Award for Distinction in Diplomacy, Georgetown University, USA Received the International Service Award, Fletcher School of Law and Diplomacy, Tufts University, USA
1990	Awarded Distinguished Service Order Award (Darjah Utama Bakti Cemerlang), Singapore

	Served as Singapore's Chief Negotiator in negotiating the agreement to establish formal diplomatic relations between China and Singapore
1990–1992	Chairman of the Preparatory Committee for and the Main Committee of the UN Conference on Environment and Development
1990–1997	Director of the Institute of Policy Studies
1991–1996	Founding Chairman of the National Arts Council
1991–1992	Chairman, Censorship Review Committee
1993 & 1994	Chairman, International Jury of the Commonwealth Literature Prize in Singapore
1993	Appointed Commander of the Order of the Golden Ark by HRH Prince Bernhard of the Netherlands Appointed by the United Nations Secretary-General as his Special Envoy to lead a mission to the Russian Federation, Latvia, Lithuania and Estonia Received the Japanese Chamber of Commerce & Industry (JCCI) Singapore Foundation Arts Award and Culture Award
1993–1995	Chairman, Empress Place Museum
1993–1996	Member of the Earth Council, Costa Rica
1994–1995	Served as the Executive Secretary of the APEC Business Leaders' Forum (Pacific Business Forum)
1994–2003	Director, Development Bank of Singapore
1995–2007	President, Society of International Law (Singapore)
1995	2nd Arthur and Frank Payne Visiting Lecturer, Institute of International Studies, Stanford University, USA Co-Chair of the 1st Japan–Singapore Symposium Published book, *The United States and East Asia: Conflict and Cooperation*

1995–2008	Singapore's Agent in the dispute with Malaysia over Pedra Branca, Middle Rocks and South Ledge, including arguing Singapore's case before the International Court of Justice at The Hague, Netherlands
1996	Member, Selection Committee for the 1996 Rolex Awards for Enterprise Co-Chair of the 2nd Japan–Singapore Symposium Received Elizabeth Haub Prize from the University of Brussels and the International Council of Environmental Law (ICEL)
1996–2001	Member, International Advisory Board of Toyota
1997–2000	Chairman, International Advisory Group of the Maritime and Port Authority of Singapore Served as the founding Executive Director of the Asia–Europe Foundation
1997	Awarded the Grand Cross of the Order of Bernardo O'Higgins from the Government of Chile Member of a WTO Dispute Panel constituted by WTO Director-General, Dr Renato Ruggiero, to consider a dispute between the European Commission and the United States
1998	Awarded the 1998 Fok Ying Tung Southeast Asia Prize by the Fok Ying Tung Foundation in Hong Kong Appointed Chairman of a WTO Dispute Panel to consider a dispute brought by New Zealand and the United States against Canada Book entitled *The Quest for World Order: Perspectives of a Pragmatic Idealist*, edited by Amitav Archarya was published
2000	Appointed Chairman of a WTO Dispute Panel to consider a dispute brought by Australia and New Zealand against the United States

Awards

Commander, First Class, of the Order of the Lion of Finland, by the President of Finland

Grand Officer of the Order of Merit of the Grand Duchy of Luxembourg, by the Prime Minister of Luxembourg

LASALLE-SIA Medallion for Distinguished Service to Arts Education, by LASALLE College of the Arts, Singapore

John Curtin Medal, by Curtin University of Technology, Western Australia

Book entitled *Asia and Europe*, edited by Yeo Lay Hwee and Asad Latif, was published

2000–2007	Director, The Esplanade Co. Ltd
2000–2006	Chairman, Chinese Heritage Centre
2000–2004	Director of the Institute of Policy Studies
2000–2003	Singapore's Chief Negotiator for the US–Singapore Free Trade Agreement
2001	Conferred the rank of Officer in the Order of the Legion of Honour by the President of the French Republic
2001–2007	Founding Chairman, Animal Welfare and Ethics Committee, Wildlife Reserves Singapore
2002–2011	Chairman, National Heritage Board
2002	Conferred an honorary degree of Doctor of Laws by Monash University
2003	Presented with the Peace and Commerce Award by the US Secretary of Commerce, Donald Evans, in Washington, DC
2003–2005	Singapore's agent in the dispute with Malaysia over Singapore's land reclamation activities, including arguing Singapore's case at the International Tribunal for the Law of the Sea in Hamburg, Germany
2003–2008	Director, SingTel

2003–2006	Chairman, Steering Committee, Faculty of Law, National University of Singapore
2004	Outstanding Service Award, National University of Singapore
	Conferred Encomienda de Isabel la Católica award by His Majesty King Juan Carlos of Spain
2004–2009	Chairman, Institute of Policy Studies
2005	Eminent Person of Singapore in the China–ASEAN Eminent Persons Group
	Appointed Co-Chair of the China–Singapore Forum
	Book entitled *The Little Red Dot*, co-edited with Chang Li Lin, was published
2006	Member, Selection Committee for the 2006 Rolex Awards for Enterprise
	Co-organised the Programme of Seminars with the World Bank and IMF for their annual meetings in Singapore
	Editor-in-Chief, *Singapore: The Encyclopedia*
	Awards
	Champion of the Earth Award, by the United Nations Environment Programme
	Inaugural President's Award for the Environment from President S. R. Nathan
	"Building a Better World" Award, by CH2M Hill
2007–2011	Chairman, Advisory Board, Faculty of Law, National University of Singapore
2007	Member and Chairman of the High-Level Task Force to draft the ASEAN Charter
	Awards
	Conferred the Watermark Honorary Award by the Public Utilities Board
	Tatler Leadership Award for Lifetime Achievement by *Singapore Tatler* magazine

2008	Appointed Co-Chair of the India–Singapore Strategic Dialogue
	Awards
	Conferred the Order of Sang Nila Utama (First Class) by the Singapore government, for his outstanding contributions as a member of the team representing Singapore, in the Pedra Branca dispute with the Malaysian government
	Co-recipient of the Onassis Distinguished Scholar Award from the Rhodes Academy of Oceans Law and Policy in Rhodes, Greece
2009	Co-Chair of the 7th Japan–Singapore Symposium
	Volume II of *The Little Red Dot* was published
	Conferred the Order of the Rising Sun, Gold and Silver Star by the Japanese government
	Book entitled *Pedra Branca: The Road to the World Court*, co-written with S. Jayakumar, was published
2009–Present	Co-Chair of the Jury for the Bernard Schwartz Book Prize awarded annually by the Asia Society in New York
2010	Appointed a Judge of the annual Singapore Hawker Food Master Chef's competition
2011	Co-Chair of the 8th Japan–Singapore Symposium
	Patron, The Elephant Parade, Singapore
2012	Delivered ADB's Eminent Person Lecture
	Delivered address to ESCAP's Ministerial Meeting
	Delivered keynote address at the inaugural National Conference on Kindness
	Spoke to UNGA on the occasion of the 30th anniversary of the opening for signature of the UN Convention on the Law of the Sea
2013	Co-chair of the 6th India–Singapore Strategic Dialogue, New Delhi, February

	Co-chaired the 9th Japan–Singapore Symposium, Tokyo, March
	Co-chaired the 8th China–Singapore Forum, Beijing, October
	Leader of the Singapore delegation to the 19th Session of the International Seabed Authority, Kingston, July
	Received the Great Negotiator Award by Harvard University, 2013–2014 academic year
Present	Ambassador-at-Large, Ministry of Foreign Affairs (from 1990)
	Special Advisor, Institute of Policy Studies (from 2010)
	Professor of Law, National University of Singapore (NUS)
	Chairman, Centre for International Law, NUS (from 2009)
	Rector, Tembusu College, NUS (from 2010)
	Chairman, Advisory Committee, Master's degree in Environmental Management, NUS (from 2003)
	Chairman, International Advisory Board, Asia Research Institute (from 2002)
	Chairman, SymAsia Foundation, Credit Suisse (from 2010)
	Member, Governing Board, Lee Kuan Yew School of Public Policy (from 2005)
	Co-Chair of the China–Singapore Forum (from 2005)
	Co-Chair of the Japan–Singapore Symposium
	Co-Chair of the India–Singapore Strategic Dialogue (from 2008)
	Chairman, Governing Council, Asia–Pacific Water Forum (from 2007)
	Chairman, Singapore International Water Leaders' Summit and Chairman, Joint Plenary of the Water Summit and World City Summit (from 2008)
	Trustee of the APB Foundation
	Trustee of the Lee Wee Kheng Education Trust
	Trustee of the Tan Chay Bing Education Trust

[as at 20 November 2013]

Annex I: Books Published

1. *The United States and East Asia: Conflict and Cooperation*, 1995, Institute of Policy Studies and Times Academic Press
2. *The Quest for World Order: Perspectives of a Pragmatic Idealist,* edited by Amitav Acharya, 1998, Institute of Policy Studies and Times Academic Press
3. *Asia and Europe: Essays and Speeches by Tommy Koh*, edited by Yeo Lay Hwee and Asad Latif, 2000, Asia–Europe Foundation and World Scientific
4. *The United States–Singapore Free Trade Agreement: Highlights and Insights*, edited by Tommy Koh and Chang Li Lin, 2004, World Scientific and Institute of Policy Studies
5. *The Little Red Dot: Reflections by Singapore's Diplomats,* edited by Tommy Koh and Chang Li Lin, 2005, World Scientific and Institute of Policy Studies
6. *Singapore: The Encyclopedia,* Editor-in-Chief: Tommy Koh, 2006, Editions Didier Millet
7. *The Little Red Dot II: Reflections by Singapore's Diplomats,* 2009
8. *Pedra Branca: The Road to the World Court,* by S. Jayakumar and Tommy Koh, 2009, NUS Press
9. *The Making of the ASEAN Charter*, edited by Tommy Koh, Rosario G. Manalo and Water Woon, 2009, World Scientific, Lee Kuan Yew School of Public Policy and Institute of Policy Studies
10. *Malaysia & Singapore — The Land Reclamation Case: From Dispute to Settlement,* by Cheong Koon Hean, Tommy Koh and Lionel Yee, 2013, Straits Times Press, Centre for International Law and Institute of Policy Studies

Annex II: Awards by Singapore Government and Agencies

Public Service Star, 1971

Meritorious Service Medal, 1979

Distinguished Service Order, 1990

President's Award for the Environment, 2006

Watermark Honorary Award by the Public Utilities Board, 2007

Order of Sang Nila Utama, First Class, 2008

Annex III: Awards by Foreign Governments and Institutions

Commander of the Order of the Golden Ark, by HRH Prince Bernhard of the Netherlands, 1993

Grand Cross of the Order of Bernardo O'Higgins, by the Government of Chile, 1997

Commander, First Class, of the Order of the Lion of Finland, by the President of Finland, 2000

Grand Officer of the Order of Merit of the Grand Duchy of Luxembourg, by the Prime Minister of Luxembourg, 2000

Officer in the Order of the Legion of Honour, by the President of the French Republic, 2001

Peace and Commerce Award, by the Secretary of Commerce, USA, 2003

Encomienda de Isabel la Católica, by H. M. the King of Spain, 2004

Champion of the Earth, by the United Nations Environment Programme, 2006

Order of the Rising Sun, Gold and Silver Star, by the Japanese government, 2009

Annex IV: Awards by Academic Institutions

Entrance Scholarship awarded by the University of Malaya (in Singapore), 1957

Sir Adrian Clark Memorial Medal, by the University of Malaya (in Singapore), 1961

Leow Chia Heng Prize, by the University of Malaya (in Singapore), 1961

Fulbright Fellowship, USA, 1964

Harvard Law School Fellowship, USA, 1964

Honorary degree of Doctor of Laws, by Yale University, USA, 1984

Wolfgang Friedman Prize, by Columbia Law School, USA, 1984

Jackson H. Ralston Prize, by Stanford Law School, USA, 1985

Jit Trainor Award for Distinction in Diplomacy, by Georgetown University, USA, 1987

International Service Award, by the Fletcher School of Law and Diplomacy, Tufts University, 1987

2nd Arthur and Frank Payne Visiting Lectureship, by the Institute of International Studies, Stanford University, 1995

Elizabeth Haub Prize, by the University of Brussels and the International Council of Environmental Law (ICEL), 1996

Fok Ying Tung Southeast Asia Prize, by the Fok Ying Tung Foundation, Hong Kong, 1998

The Distinguished Service to Arts Education Medallion, by LASALLE College of the Arts, 2000

John Curtin Medal, by Curtin University of Technology, Australia, 2000

Honorary degree of Doctor of Laws, by Monash University, Australia, 2002

Onassis Distinguished Scholar Award, by the Rhodes Academy of Oceans Law and Policy, Greece, 2008

Great Negotiator Award, by Harvard University, 2013–2014 academic year

www.ingramcontent.com/pod-product-compliance
Lightning Source LLC
Chambersburg PA
CBHW071352300426
44114CB00016B/2036